The Political Role of Religion
in the United States

About the Book and Editors

The political importance of Christian churches in the 1980s is the focus of this wide-ranging book of readings. Contributors begin by placing the current involvement of religious groups in politics in historical perspective and then analyze the politics and ideologies of both the religious right and religious left. They also explore specific issues, including the separation of church and state, the impact of religious interest groups on public policy, religion and abortion, and feminist theological views.

Stephen D. Johnson and Joseph B. Tamney are professors in the Department of Sociology at Ball State University.

The Political Role of Religion in the United States

edited by Stephen D. Johnson
and Joseph B. Tamney

Westview Press / Boulder and London

A Westview Special Study

Copyright © 1986 by Westview Press, Inc.

Published in 1986 in the United States of America by Westview Press, Inc.;
Frederick A. Praeger, Publisher; 5500 Central Avenue, Boulder, Colorado 80301

Library of Congress Cataloging-in-Publication Data
Main entry under title:
The Political role of religion in the United States.
   Includes index.
   1. Religion and state--United States--History--20th
century--Addresses, essays, lectures. 2. United States
--Religion--1960-   --Addresses, essays, lectures.
3. United States--Politics and government--1981-   --
Addresses, essays, lectures. I. Johnson, Stephen D.
II. Tamney, Joseph B.
BL2525.P65 1986   322'.1'0973   85-31584
ISBN 0-8133-7030-2 (alk. paper)

Composition for this book was provided by the editors.

Printed and bound in the United States of America

The paper used in this publication meets the minimum
requirements of the American National Standard for
Permanence of Paper for Printed Library Materials
Z39.48-1984.

6   5   4   3   2   1

Contents

Acknowledgments

The authors wish to acknowledge the cooperation and word-processing services provided by the Department of Sociology at Ball State University. Special thanks go to Nancy Koons, departmental secretary, and Kathy Vogel, student secretary.

We, of course, thank all those who contributed essays to this volume. Four chapters in this book have appeared previously. They are Michael Johnston's "The 'New Christian Right' in American Politics" (The Political Quarterly 53:181-199, 1982), Ronald T. Libby's "Listen to the Bishops" (Foreign Policy, Fall 1983:78-95), "The Princeton Declaration " (Homer A. Jack, ed., Religion in the Struggle for World Community, New York: World Conference on Religion and Peace, 1980), and L. Bruce van Voorst's "The Churches and Nuclear Deterrence" (Foreign Affairs 61:827-852, 1983). Besides the editors, seven people have made original contributions to this book. They are John D. Cranor, Department of Political Science, Ball State University; James D. Davidson, Department of Sociology and Anthropology, Purdue University; Julia Benton Mitchell, Department of Philosophy, Ball State University; Richard V. Pierard, Department of History, Indiana State University; Merle D. Strege, School of Theology, Anderson College; Donald Tomaskovic-Devey, Department of Sociology, North Carolina State University; and Paul J. Weber, Department of Political Science, University of Louisville.

Stephen D. Johnson

Joseph B. Tamney

General Introduction

SECULARIZATION

To many social scientists the current burst of political activity by religious leaders that we have witnessed in the later 1970s and early 1980s has come as a surprise. A dominant scholarly thesis had been that modern-day societal trends, such as the cultural diversity of the American people and the increased use of science to solve today's problems, had brought greater seculari- zation in all of our lives. Secularization is a system of ideas and practices that disregards or rejects any form of religious faith or worship.

But despite these long-term secular trends, we have recently seen in the United States, and indeed around the world, the resurgence of religion into the secular sphere of the political arena. During the seventies, Liberation Theology, which attempts to place the church in the service of the poor and urges widespread economic reforms, became a political factor in Central and South America and it influenced the writing and thinking of many Catholic and Protestant liberals as well. In the late seventies, the Islamic revolution in Iran caught the world's attention. For some, the Iranian situation became the classic extreme example of what can happen when religion dominates politics. For others, Iran was an example of how religious leaders can gain significant power. In 1980, the Polish Catholic church joined forces with the workers in the Solidarity Movement, and, in the United States, Jerry Falwell tried to control presidential politics with his Moral Majority organization. Since then, the Roman Catholic church has issued pastoral letters challenging government policies on nuclear disarmament and social welfare. The last ten years have witnessed an apparent religious revival as religious leaders engage in political activity.

The essays presented in this book examine many of the important aspects of this political/religious revival and do so from the point of view of the concerns and activities of both conservative and liberal political/religious organizations. Let us first, however, look at the historical foundation for the secularizing trends in our society and how the recent political/religious revival fits into this historical context.

The first of what we consider to be four secular trends is the rapid development of technology and science. During the last few centuries, science has lessened our need for religious explanations for natural phenomena. When life is threatened or when forces beyond people's control reign, humans tend to feel insecure and helpless, and religion is a means of coping with such feelings. However, technology has made our lives easier and has, in turn, given human beings an increased sense of collective and individual control over their destiny. Just as technology has given people control, science is an ever-increasing source of understanding. Empirical methods have become an alternative to religious writings as a way of realizing truth.

A second secular trend contributing to a decline in religious commitment is the changes that have occurred purely within the realm of ideas. Over the centuries, philosophy and ethics have become differentiated from religious beliefs. "Humanist" is a label that has been created to identify a person who espouses a nonreligious, universalistic morality. Ethical actions are, today, being justified simply in terms of human dignity and the preservation of life. Not only ethics but also political ideology has become differentiated from specific religions. For instance, it can be argued that the major political ideologies of the modern West--the justifications for the U.S., French, and Russian revolutions--are not based on Christianity. Intellectual commitment to a religion is further weakened by the growing awareness of all the world's religions. Any one religion in the modern world context, then, competes for attention and influence with purely secular ethical systems, with secular political ideologies, and with other religions.

A third factor limiting the relevance of all religions is the importance and nature of contemporary economic systems. Especially with the spread of capitalist ideas, economic decisions, whether by individuals, businesses, or states, have become determined primarily by one motive, the desire for wealth. Moreover, because governments judge success in terms of economic growth, the pursuit of profit shapes not only economic actions but also political decisions. Supporting capitalism is the ideology of utilitarian individualism (Bellah, 1976), which establishes as ideal the pursuit of self-interest as the means to maximize private and public prosperity. Given that an important emphasis of religion is the desirability of concern and sacrifice for others, religious values often do not support actions guided by the self-interested pursuit of profit. But given the importance of this motive in many modern economic systems, the result is the seeming irrelevance of religion for economic behavior.

Because of the social changes just enumerated, social scientists have presented a fourth secularizing factor--the privatization thesis (Luckmann, 1967; Berger, 1969). This thesis states that on the one hand there are the supposedly dominant institutions of a modern society, the economy and the state. On the other hand, there is the private realm; in part, simply a residual category referring to all the institutions other than the public economic and political ones; in part, also, a haven from the evils of the corrupt public world and centering on the family where traditional morality can be preserved and is practical. In regard to religion, the privatization argument concludes that religious values in modern society influence private institutions, such as the family, but not the public institutions (i.e., the economic and political realms). Examples of religious influence on a private institution are the biblical dictates concerning sexual behavior and child disciplining in families.

This analysis of secular trends would seem to justify the conclusions that religious influence in modern life is weak and that those who attempt to change this condition will find it to be no easy task. The remarkable feature of the eighties, however, is that churches have increasingly taken up the challenge presented by secularization.

The response of the religious institution is twofold. On the one hand, there are those leaders who resist the changes associated with modernity or modern secular trends. These are mainly the Christian Rightists. On the other hand, there are those leaders and institutions that more or less accept modernity and try to adjust, not necessarily accommodate, to the new situation. These are the liberal Catholics, Protestants, and Jews.

4

THE CHRISTIAN RIGHT

The branch of Christianity called the Christian Right is a segment of fundamentalist religion, a religious movement that originated within U.S. Protestantism in the early part of this century. It was a transdenominational protest

> designed to preserve the theological essentials of historic orthodoxy against modernism. . . . Fundamentalism generally has included within its theology: (1) the infallibility and inerrancy of the Scriptures; (2) the Trinity, including the virgin birth and deity of Jesus Christ; (3) the fall of Adam and the need for personal regeneration based on the substitutionary atonement of Christ; (4) the bodily resurrection of Christ and his ascension; (5) the personal and imminent return of Christ; (6) the everlasting bliss of the righteous dead after their resurrection, and the everlasting and conscious torment of the unbelieving following the final judgment (Lindsell, 1971:221).

"Fundamentalism is basically an attitude whose major tenet is that the Bible is inerrant" (Richardson and Bowden, 1983:223). Following from this is a strong emphasis on a mythic view of current events and their causes, which are interpreted in terms of the ongoing struggle of Satan and Christ and the eventual return of Christ. Among fundamentalists, there is only sacred history, thus the importance to them of dispensationalism (religious periodization of history) and millenarianism (a belief in a future period during which Christ will reign on earth).

In 1980, a public opinion poll asked a national sample the following question: "Which of these statements comes closest to describing your feelings about the Bible?" Respondents were handed a card listing the following statements: "(a) the Bible is the actual word of God and is to be taken literally, word for word; (b) the Bible is the inspired word of God, but not everything in it should be taken literally, word for word; or (c) the Bible is an ancient book of fables, legends, history, and moral precepts recorded by men (Gallup, 1980:186)." Forty percent said the Bible is to be taken literally, 45 percent chose the second response, 9 percent the third, and 6 percent did not make a choice. A belief in Bible inerrancy was also more frequent among blacks, in the South, and among the less educated. The main point, however, is that there are many fundamentalists in the United States.

There are more fundamentalists than there are members of fundamentalist churches. In 1983, 21 percent of U.S. adults identified themselves as Baptist, and 3 percent identified with small Protestant groups or nondenominational Protestant churches (Gallup, 1984:43). Assuming that all these people belonged to fundamentalist churches, the total is only 24 percent. Fundamentalists exist not only outside churches that are considered part of the fundamentalist establishment, but are scattered among all Protestant churches.

The growth in the Christian Right corresponds to the growth in the 1970s of "televangelists" such as Jerry Falwell and James Robison. These preachers linked the technologies of direct-mail appeals and entertaining religious television to support for politically right-wing causes. The New Christian Right is epitomized by Moral Majority, Inc., the purpose of which is "mobilizing the grassroots of moral Americans into a clear, loud, and effective voice, which will be heard in the halls of Congress, in the White House, and in state legislatures across the land" (from a 1980 Moral Majority brochure, quoted in Schriver, 1981:23). This movement is rooted in fundamentalism and traditionalism and carries forward the recurring attempt of traditional Christians to resist cultural change. Historically, these people were active in the Prohibition movement. Preachers such as Billy Sunday and Billy James Hargis were precursors of this movement.

Although the specific issues commented on by Christian Right leaders are numerous, it does seem true that "concern for issues broadly defined as affecting the family is the 'glue' that holds these various groups [in the movement] together" (Schriver, 1981:30). For the Christian Right, support for the family means being against such things as the Equal Rights Amendment (ERA), pornography, abortion, homosexuality, and school busing (Kater, 1982:12-13), and being for school prayer (Jorstad, 1981:76). The Christian Right further attempts to provide a foundation for these "profamily" views in the Bible. Because a large number of issues are perceived in relation to family life, being in favor of the traditional family has served as a major rallying point for the Christian Right.

It would be a mistake to identify all fundamentalists with the Christian Right. In 1947, Carl Henry's The

Uneasy Conscience of Fundamentalism heralded a new
concern among more politically liberal fundamentalists
for social justice issues such as minority civil rights
and providing for the poor. These issues are at most of
peripheral interest to the Christian Right. Probably the
best example of liberal fundamentalism is the work and
writings of Martin Luther King, Jr.

Generally, one could consider the Christian Right
movement a broad counterresponse to three of the previously
mentioned long-term secular trends: science and technology, secular humanism, and privatization. In a more
specific sense, the movement could be considered a reaction
to the turbulence of the 1960s.

As a reaction to the new technology, such as the
computer revolution, we might surmise that the Christian
Right would be disturbed because the technology symbolizes
a rather rapid change from the more tradition-oriented
society they prefer. Natural explanations provided by
science have challenged the Christian Right's "supernatural" or religious explanations, and scientific explanations are a definite threat when they directly challenge
Christian dogma, as in the evolution versus creationism
debate.

Probably the clearest indication of the Christian
Right movement as a counterreaction to secularization is
their condemnation of secular morality. The Right sees
the teachings of "secular humanists," especially in
educational institutions, as a violation of the view that
Christian principles should direct all aspects of our
lives.

Christian Rightists have attempted to counteract
privatization ideology. They want to protect the family
from the public world of the state. Rather than keeping
the realm of the private and public worlds separated,
Rightists mobilize family-oriented people to attack the
state they see as the enemy of the traditional U.S. family.

The Christian Right has not reacted to another
secular trend, utilitarian individualism, because it is
consistent with their basic conservative political
ideology. The opposite religious ideology, a concern and
sacrifice for others, is more likely to be advocated by
liberal Christians.

Finally, it can be argued that the rise of the
Christian Right is also a belated response to events that
took place in the sixties. In the late sixties, Richard
Nixon and his advisers decided to build a new majority

based on "the traditional values of middle class Americans
--hard work, individual enterprise, orderly behavior, love
of country, moral piety, and material progress" (Hodgson,
1976:422). Many Americans perceived "hippies and black
power militants, drug addicts, Mafiosi, and 'welfare
mothers'" as trangressors of traditional morality, and
Nixon began the effort to combine people of traditional
values with the economic conservatives already associated
with the Republican party.

ROMAN CATHOLICISM

     Equally surprising as the rise of the Christian Right
has been the emergence of the Roman Catholic church as
a political force in U.S. politics. With its recent
efforts to influence public policy concerning Central
America, nuclear disarmament, and poverty, the Catholic
church is probably the most visible religious organization
attempting to bring about liberal changes in public
policy. It is not new that the Catholic church has taken
stands on public issues. What is new is the vigor with
which this church is pursuing social change and the
willingness of numerous Catholic bishops to be political
activists.
     In recent years U.S. bishops have published statements
on controversial and clearly public topics--most notably,
Latin American policies, nuclear freeze and peace, and
the economic structure of the United States. These issues
relate directly to two of the most important political
topics of our generation, anticommunism and the economy.
The U.S. Catholic church has entered the arena of U.S.
politics.
     Moreover, the church has shown a willingness to engage
in conflict. Churches in the United States in the past
have stressed their healing, comforting role. These
organizations have perceived themselves as primary sources
of solidarity and the purpose of religion as a basis for
reconciliation. This view was not prevalent among fundamentalists, whose churches often withdrew as much as
possible from the larger society to become little communities of "saints." No doubt, most Catholic leaders continue
to consider their function as mediators and comforters,
but in addition, the Catholic church has shown a greater
willingness than in the past to play a critical role in
the political process.

It is common to trace changes in Catholicism back to the Second Vatican Council of the midsixties, which introduced many changes in behavior and thinking.

Roman Catholicism has not been the same since. In the United States, nuns have traded in their religious habits for skirts, slacks, and Gucci bags. Priests appear in public dressed in shirt and tie; many of them openly differ with church authorities on such issues as birth control and divorce. Lay people occupy prominent positions in religious services. English has replaced Latin as the language of worship (Dolan, 1981:120).

But it was easy to become preoccupied with relatively superficial changes such as dress codes for the clergy. "Underlying all of this was the most fundamental change of all: As Karl Rahner has noted, since Vatican II Catholicism has become 'a world Church whose individual churches exist with a certain independence in their respective cultural spheres, inculturated, and no longer a European export'" (Dolan, 1981:132).

We live in an interdependent world. The view of the world as composed of relatively isolated nation-states is an anachronism. Of all U.S. churches, Roman Catholicism is most clearly a world church, functioning as part of a world system. Vatican II affirmed the fact and propelled the process.

Catholicism's role in the world system has had two consequences relevant to this book. First, the church has been forced to deal with communism. Indirectly, this has led to a concern with gaining a sound nuclear disarmament treaty with the Soviet Union. More directly, the Catholic church has had to deal with communist governments in Eastern Europe. In Poland the church has been politicized and has responded to current events in an activist manner that challenges existing political authorities.

A second consequence of this world role is that the Catholic church has had to confront the problem of poverty, especially in Latin America, where the church is dominant and poverty is widespread. One response has been the rise of Liberation Theology.

U.S. Catholicism has been affected by these worldwide developments. Or to put it another way, Roman Catholicism, including its U.S. branch, has become more political and more fault-finding because it has had to relate to communism and to face widespread poverty.

Beyond these rather specific consequences of its world role, Catholicism has nurtured a more general attitude that perhaps is more widespread and more deeply embedded in it than in other churches and religions. This attitude is expressed in the U.S. bishops' pastoral letter on peace. "As citizens, we wish to affirm our loyalty to our country and its ideals, yet we are also citizens of the world who must be faithful to the universal principles proclaimed by the church" (National Conference of Catholic Bishops, 1983:98). In this statement, the bishops confirm the primacy of their commitment to universal values and to their roles as citizens of the world.

Therefore, the role of U.S. Catholicism in U.S. politics needs to be understood in relation to the place of Catholicism in the modern world system.

CONCLUSION

What has happened in the eighties is that religious leaders and organizations have changed. The Christian Right and Catholicism have begun what seem to be long-term attempts to move U.S. policies in the direction of these groups' moral codes.

In his most recent book, Harvey Cox portrayed the present time as one of profound change. Supposedly, we are entering a postmodern period that will require a new form of theology.

A new age that some call the 'post-modern' has begun to appear. No one is quite sure just what the post-modern era will be like, but one thing seems clear. Rather than an age of rampant secularization and religious decline, it appears to be more of an era of religious revival and the return of the sacral. No one talks much today about the long night of religion or the zero level of its influence on politics (Cox, 1984:20).

Cox may be right. Certainly religion is not about to disappear. Undeniably, religious institutions have captured much popular attention in the United States. It is not at all clear, however, that current church activism will significantly change the events and policies of the United States. In this book, we present fifteen essays that we hope will lead to an understanding of the nature and extent of the political role of religion in this country.

10

REFERENCES

Bellah, Robert N. "New Religious Consciousness and the
    Crisis of Modernity." Pp. 333-352 in Charles Y. Glock
    and Robert N. Bellah, eds., The New Religious
    Consciousness. Berkeley: University of California
    Press, 1976.
Berger, Peter L. The Sacred Canopy. Garden City, N.Y.:
    Doubleday & Co., 1967.
Cox, Harvey. Religion in the Secular City. New York:
    Simon and Schuster, 1984.
Dolan, Jay P. "A Catholic Romance with Modernity." The
    Wilson Quarterly 5 (Autumn): 120-133, 1981.
Gallup, George H. The Gallup Poll: Public Opinion:
    1980. Wilmington, Del.: Scholarly Resources, 1980.
    _____. Religion in America. The Gallup Report
    #222, 1984.
Hodgson, Godfrey. America in Our Time. New York:
    Vintage, 1976.
Jorstad, Eiling. The Politics of Moralism. Minneapolis,
    Minn.: Augsburg, 1981.
Kater, John L., Jr. Christians on the Right. New York:
    Seabury, 1982.
Lindsell, Harold. "Fundamentalism." P. 221 in Stephen
    Neill, Gerald H. Anderson, John Goodwin, eds.,
    Concise Dictionary of the Christian World Mission.
    Nashville: Abingdon, 1971.
Luckmann, Thomas. The Invisible Religion. New York:
    Macmillan, 1967.
National Conference of Catholic Bishops. The Challenge
    of Peace: God's Promise and Our Response.
    Washington, D.C.: United States Catholic Conference,
    1983.
Richardson, Allan, and John Bowden, eds. The Westminster
    Dictionary of Christian Theology. Philadelphia:
    Westminster, 1983.
Schriver, Peggy L. The Bible Vote. New York: Pilgrim,
    1981.

PART 1

Background

Introduction

In an editorial on 15 September 1984, the New York Times was quite critical of religious leaders becoming involved in presidential politics; in fact, Americans in general seem uneasy about the mixing of religion and politics. Paul J. Weber, in Chapter 1 ("Religious Interest Groups, Policymaking, and the Constitution"), discusses the constitutional issue of the relation between church and state. He examines the different interpretations of this relationship in the U.S. context and concludes that there is a constitutional basis for and benefits to be derived from allowing religious interest groups to compete for influence on the formation of public policies.

It is customary to divide such interest groups into liberal and conservative branches and to assume that each has its own social program. Is this a valid analysis of U.S. religion? Exactly how do these types differ in terms of social policies? These questions are addressed in Chapter 2 ("The Clergy and Public Issues in Middletown," by Stephen D. Johnson and Joseph B. Tamney). In addition, the authors present the reasons conservative and liberal clergy have given for their positions. Religious beliefs and values seem to play a minor role in the ministers' justifications of their positions on social issues. The implications of this finding are discussed in the chapter.

Evangelical Christians were once considered part of the conservative branch of Christianity. But Chapter 3 (Cacophony on Capitol Hill: Evangelical Voices in Politics" by Richard V. Pierard) presents a brief history of evangelical political officeholders and makes clear that the identification of evangelical Christianity with conservative Christianity has become invalid. During the twenties and thirties, evangelicals were politically conservative, but they played a minor role in U.S. politics. The situation began to change after World War II; about the same time that liberal clergy were active in the civil rights movement, evangelicals began to be a political force in Congress. By the sixties, evangelicalism no longer was synonymous with political conservatism. For at least the last twenty years, a wide range of political viewpoints has existed among the politically active evangelicals. As Pierard concludes, "Evangelicalism, for all its conservatism, can no longer be regarded as a monolith. Its voices on Capitol Hill are a cacophony of contrasting claims and political ideologies."

1

Religious Interest Groups, Policymaking, and the Constitution

Paul J. Weber

The highly publicized 1984 lectures at the University of Notre Dame by Governor Mario Cuomo of New York and Congressman Henry Hyde of Illinois, as well as the recent pronouncements of the Catholic bishops on nuclear war and economic policy, have rekindled an old argument about attempts of religious leaders and groups to influence the policymaking process. In the minds of many people such efforts are highly suspect, if not actually unconstitutional. An article last year in a student newspaper is fairly typical:

> In an unprecedented speech Pope John Paul II asked that the United States and the Soviet Union disarm simultaneously, that they withdraw their troops from Central America and Afghanistan, that all the violence and terrorism be stopped in the Middle East, and that all the countries of the world pardon their prisoners sentenced to death.
> Aside from being a clear case of overstepping boundaries, the pontiff has entirely oversimplified matters of grave importance and extreme complexity. . . . The pope, however, has stepped into a realm in which he does not belong and for which he is not qualified to propose solutions.
> I hope that in the future, John Paul II will continue to provide spiritual strength to the peoples of the world while realizing that politics are matters that would be better left to the politicians (Stanley, 1983:5).

Such views are not confined to the relative obscurity of campus weeklies. A New York Times editorial (April

15

23, 1960) once made the rather startling claim that "we start with the premise shared by every American who believes in the constitutional principles on which our country is founded that religion has no proper place in American politics." More recently, syndicated conservative columnist William Safire attacking both the Catholic bishops' pastoral letter on nuclear deterrence and President Reagan's speech to evangelical ministers, expressed the views of many:

> Most people who take churchgoing seriously want moral guidance, not political presumption, from their clergy. Most voters who take their participation seriously want political philosophy in action, not spiritual instructions from the president. But assume that the president is 100 percent right about morality or that the clergy is 100 percent right about foreign policy. The fact that each is playing in the other's ballpark is what is wrong (Safire, 1983:A-11).

Safire's views were echoed by Philip Lawler in a Wall Street Journal editorial. "It is individuals--not economic systems--that face heaven or hell; so it is the business of the church to save individual souls. Bishops once focused on that" (Lawler, 1984:36).

If such opposition to religious involvement went no further than occasional newspaper columns and editorials it would probably not merit further comment. Unfortunately there have been numerous attempts to turn such opposition into laws prohibiting or at least emasculating religious influence. As the Harris v. McRae controversy over the Hyde amendment (prohibiting federal funding for abortion) worked its way through the courts, plaintiffs argued that the law violated the First Amendment partially because the Hyde amendment was passed as a result of "excessive" religious influence on the legislative process. The Supreme Court's acceptance of this argument (if it had occured) could have had monumental impact on religious advocacy (Harris v. McRae, 448 U.S. 297, 1980).

Why is there such widespread opposition to religious involvement in the political process? Aside from the fact that it is a handy emotional argument to hurl whenever one opposes a policy advocated by one or another religious group, there seem to be four major reasons: (1) a vague, hazy and, I would argue, erroneous understanding of the meaning of separation of church and state in the United

States, (2) a fear of the political power of the churches, (3) the Supreme Court's administrative involvement standard, and (4) a fear of political divisiveness along religious lines. The combination of these leads to opposition to religious involvement in the political process.

In this chapter I will propose not only that there is a firm constitutional basis for religious involvement in politics but also that encouraging such involvement is a sound and healthy component of the political process and does not lead to excessive entanglement.

THE MEANING OF SEPARATION

The most secure foundation for religious activism lies in the First Amendment guarantees of freedom of speech and assembly: "Congress shall make no law . . . abridging the freedom of speech, or of the press; or the right of the people peaceably to assemble, and to petition the Government for a redress of grievances." Although freedom of association is not a very well developed right in U.S. constitutional law, even in its primitive form it protects "a right to join with others to pursue goals independently protected by the First Amendment--such as political advocacy, litigation (regarded as a form of advocacy), or religious worship" (Tribe, 1978:702).

It has been argued that the freedom of speech and assembly clauses do not apply to religious groups or religiously motivated individuals because they are protected and limited by the religion clauses in the First Amendment./1/ The religion clauses of the First Amendment declare that "Congress shall make no law respecting an establishment of religion, or prohibiting the free exercise thereof".

It should to be noted first that there is nothing in the free speech, press, and assembly clauses that warrants "excluding" religiously motivated individuals or groups. In fact, not only was there no indication of such an intent in the First Congress, which debated and passed the amendment, but the primary architect of the First Amendment, James Madison, was clearly opposed to singling out religious persons or interests for special treatment. Some years earlier, when proposing a constitution for Virginia, Thomas Jefferson had suggested excluding clergymen from election to the legislature. Madison dissuaded him from pressing the point in a letter that clearly expresses his view: "Does not the exclusion of Ministers of the Gospel as such violate a fundamental principle of liberty by punishing a religious profession with the privation of a civil right?" (Boyd, 1950:311) There is no indication that he had changed his mind by the time he steered the Bill of Rights through Congress./2/

The second point to note is that the religion clauses of the First Amendment do not include any phrase remotely resembling "the separation of church and state" concept that purportedly explains the meaning of the religion clauses and that is the source of an enormous amount of confusion over what the Constitution does or does not allow. For the popularization of the separation concept we are indebted to Thomas Jefferson's letter to the Danbury Baptists, in which he wrote:

> Believing with you that religion is a matter which lies solely between man and his God, that he owes account to none other for his faith or his worship, that the legitimate powers of government reach actions only, and not opinions, I contemplate with sovereign reverence that act of the whole American people which declared that their legislature should 'make no laws respecting an establishment of religion, or prohibiting the free excercise thereof' thus building a wall of separation between church and state [emphasis added] (Padover, 1943: 518-519).

The difficulty with the "separation" interpretation of the religion clauses is not that it is wrong, but that it is inadequate. Separation is a generic term with several specific meanings, not all of which are equally valid interpretations of the amendment. A vague understanding of the type of separation required by the First Amendment leads to some opposition to participation of religious groups in the political process. An exploration of the specific types of separation may be valuable as a means of clarification. The typology begins from a public policy perspective, which, I believe, was the perspective of James Madison (Weber, 1982:166)./3/

Structural separation involves severing formal legal and systemic ties between religion and the polity. This is a fundamental type of separation; its opposite is an organic type of social organization that does not differentiate between church and state, such as the Islamic republic recently established in Iran. The characteristics

of structural separation are independent clerical and civil
offices, separate organizations, different personnel
performing different functions, separate systems of law,
and independent ownership of property. It does not exclude
the special protections, privileges, and economic supports
commonly included in the term "established church." In
the West, with few exceptions, nations have had a structural separation of church and state since the third
century. Jefferson and Madison accepted the need for it,
and where they found vestiges of organic relationships,
as in the religious elements of the common law, they
vigorously sought structural separation. At the same time
they found the separation an inadequate safeguard for
governmental independence and religious liberty (Padover,
1943:304).

Absolute separation is a term susceptible to several
interpretations. Professor Leo Pfeffer in his still
influential book Church, State and Freedom, for example,
defined absolute separation by quoting nineteenth century
jurist Jeremiah S. Black:

> The manifest object of the men who framed the institu-
> tions of this country was to have a State without
> religion and a Church without politics--that is to
> say, they meant that one should never be used as an
> engine for the purposes of the other. . . . For that
> reason they built up a wall of complete and perfect
> partition between the two (Pfeffer, 1967:179).

A more radical view of separation has been proposed
by the American Humanist Association. The policy statement
of this group reads:

> To promote the "general welfare," a particular measure
> may be favored by church interests, and consequently
> pressure and influence are brought to bear on the
> state's political machinery to assure its passage.
> Or a measure may be viewed with disfavor by the church
> with a resultant pressure on the state's political
> machinery to assure its defeat. This type of activity
> by the church harks back to pre-Revolutionary days
> both here and in Europe, where there was "cooperation"
> between government and church. But it was just that
> sort of religious-political interplay that the
> founding fathers tried desperately to prevent on
> American soil by adopting the First Amendment and

the corresponding state laws (American Humanist Association, 1964:309)./4/

Probably the most well-known statement of an absolute separationist view is that of Justice Hugo L. Black when he defined the Establishment Clause in Everson v. Board of Education of Ewing Township (330 U.S.1.):

> The "establishment of religion" means at least this: Neither a state nor the Federal Government can set up a church. Neither can pass laws which aid one religion, aid all religions, or prefer one religion over another. . . . Neither a state nor the Federal Government can, openly or secretly, participate in the affairs of any religious organizations or groups and vice versa. . . . [emphasis added] (330 U.S. 182).

Transvaluing separation is that type in which it is the objective of government to secularize the political culture of the nation, that is, to reject as politically illegitimate the use of all religious symbols or the appeal to religious values and motivations in the political arena. It would deny all aid to religious organizations under any circumstances. The basic rationale of transvaluing separation is that religion is a private matter, not only in the sense of being nongovernmental, but in the sense of being something intensely, even exclusively personal. It would emphatically reject any conception of religion as a mediating structure./5/ In its extreme form this type of separation denies to church organizations the right to legal existence, to form corporations, to hold property, to operate schools, businesses, or charitable institutions, or to publish religious tracts. It denies to individuals the right to meet for religious discussion, to proselytize, or to make a public display of their faith./6/

Supportive separation acknowledges the need for structural separation but within that framework takes as normative Justice William O. Douglas's dictum that:

> We are a religious people whose intuitions presuppose a Supreme Being. We guarantee the freedom to worship as one chooses. We make room for as wide a variety of beliefs and creeds as the spiritual needs of man deem necessary. We sponsor an attitude on the part

of government that shows no partiality to any one group and that lets each flourish according to the zeal of its adherents and the appeals of its dogma. When the state encourages religious instruction or cooperates with religious authorities by adjusting the schedule of public events to sectarian needs, it follows the best of our traditions. For it then respects the religious nature of our people and accommodates the public service to their spiritual needs (Zorach v. Clausen, 343 U.S. 306 at 310, 1952).

Supportive separation is a more accurate name for what has traditionally been called "accommodation" of church and state. The linchpin of this type of separation is that it would allow aids and privileges to all religions so long as there was no discrimination among religions.

Equal Separation rejects all political or legal privilege, coercion, or disability based on religious affiliation, belief, or practice, or lack thereof, but guarantees to religiously motivated or affiliated individuals and organizations the same rights and privileges extended equally to other similarly situated individuals and groups. It is consciously based on an equal protection interpretation of the First Amendment and requires government neutrality both among religions and between religion and nonreligious or even antireligious beliefs, values, and practices. It provides protection without privilege./7/

Unfortunately, the equal separation concept is not palatable either to those who would put religion on a pedestal or to those who would relegate it to the dungeon, the former because religious institutions and groups could lose their privileges, the latter because religion would retain its protections.

THE FOUNDERS' VIEW OF SEPARATION

It is one thesis of this chapter that the founders (in this case, that means primarily the members of the First Congress who voted for the First Amendment and the members of the state legislatures who ratified it) intended to form a nation based on the principles of structural and equal separation, and that interpretations of the First Amendment that rely on absolute, transvaluing, or supportive separation lead to erroneous views of what

religious groups and individuals may or may not do within
the confines of the Constitution. What the original
founders intended is not the last word on the meaning of
the religion clauses, but their intent is certainly a major
component in determining the meaning of that clause./8/
It is especially important when an interpretation, such
as that of the American Humanist Association or Justice
Black, purports to explain what the founders intended.

Although a complete development of this point would
go beyond the scope of this chapter, it will be helpful
to look at one document often quoted by those who hold
the absolute separationist view, Madison's "Memorial and
Remonstrance" of 1785.

Although meant for popular consumption and the
accumulation of signatures, the "Memorial" contains a
tightly argued thesis against a bill proposing assessments
for religious purposes, pending in the Virginia
legislature. Some have seen the "Memorial" as an attack
on religion. Rather it was an attack on privilege,
coercion, and disability--the elements of establishment,
and a defense of equal treatment of religion. In assessing
this document, commentators have focused on the defense
of religious liberty, neglecting the balance Madison struck
between freedom and equality. Two quotations from the
document should suffice to make the point:

> The bill violates that equality which ought to be
> the basis of every law. . . . Above all, all men are
> to be considered as retaining an equal right to the
> free exercise of religion, according to the dictates
> of conscience. While we assert for ourselves a
> freedom to embrace, to profess, and to observe, the
> religion which we believe to be of divine origin,
> we cannot deny an equal freedom to those whose minds
> have not yet yielded to the evidence which has
> convinced us.
> . . . As the bill violates equality by subjecting
> some to peculiar burdens, so it violates the same
> principle by granting to others peculiar exemptions
> (Meyers, 1973:9).

Toward the end of the essay Madison focuses not on
the equality between religions, but on the equality between
religious rights and other rights. "The equal right of
every citizen to the free exercise of his religion,
according to the dictates of conscience, is held by the

same tenure with all our other rights. . . . Either [the
Legislature] . . . may sweep away all our fundamental
rights or they are bound to leave this particular right
untouched" (Meyers, 1973:11).

Madison was committed to separation, to be sure, but
the modality of this separation was one of equality. It
was not Madison's objective to limit the influence of
religion or religious groups, much less to suppress them
as a political force. As we shall see in the next section,
he sought both to direct religious motivations and
objectives into normal political channels where they could
be treated equally with other motivations and objectives,
and to protect and promote religious liberty equally with
other natural rights. One can, without exploring the
intentions of the other founders, state that Madison sought
to establish an equal separation.

THE POWER OF THE CHURCHES IN POLITICS

To those familiar with the normal operations of
churches and church bureaucrats, fear of their political
power may seem more like an amusing fantasy than a realistic evaluation. Nevertheless, like the writer in the
student newspaper, many express a fear of church power
and consequently oppose the political activism of religious
interest groups. Partially the fear has been fanned by
the rash ebullience of preachers like Pat Robertson, who
is reported to have boasted, "We have enough votes to run
the country. And when the people say 'we've had enough,'
we are going to take over" (Courier-Journal Louisville,
Kentucky , p. D-1, June 29, 1980), and Robert Grant,
cofounder of Christian Voice (a conservative political
activist group), who stated "If Christians unite, we can
do anything. We can pass any law or amendment. And that
is exactly what we intend to do" (U.S. News and World
Report, December 7, 1981, p. 37). Even such a thoughtful
moderate as Dean M. Kelley of the National Council of
Churches has made the unsettling observation that "when
a handful of wholly committed human beings give themselves
fully to a great cause or faith, they are virtually
irresistible" (quoted in U.S. News and World Report,
April 4, 1983, p. 36).

The potential for impressive church power has a
certain plausibility. Far more citizens belong to "faith
groups" and are active in church and synagogues than in

any other type of organization. As of 1982, roughly 131 million people, about 60 percent of the total population, held formal membership in a church or a synagogue (U.S. News and World Report, April 4, 1983, p. 35)./9/

If that portion of the population were to be politically motivated to act in one direction, it would, of course, be an overwhelming political force. But such calculations ignore the obvious facts of religious and political divisions. Of those holding membership, 73.4 million are Protestant, 51.2 million are Catholic and 5.9 million are Jewish. Even more significant are the divisions within the traditions. By one count, there are some 200 Christian and Jewish and 1,300 "unconventional" denominations (U.S. News and World Report, April 4, 1983, p. 42)./10/ One must recall that there are so many denominations precisely because groups have different, often conflicting, beliefs, values, opinions, traditions, and objectives. It would be an extraordinary issue indeed that would bring all such groups to work together politically.

A more sophisticated fear is that if a significant number of adherents of certain traditions were to become politically active, they would have overwhelming power. The plausibility of this argument is weakened by an examination of the membership of even the largest groups as a percentage of the total population (see Table 1.1)./11/

Of the groups listed, only the Roman Catholic and the evangelical Christians could conceivably muster enough votes to constitute a "threat" at the polls. But again, these figures are deceptive. Since the administration of John F. Kennedy in the early 1960s destroyed the myth of a monolithic Catholic Church bent on acquiring political power, that issue need not be addressed specifically here. Of more recent concern has been the discovery of the evangelical vote. Although 30 million evangelicals represent a significant segment of the population, not all are religiously active. Evangelicals display the same range of fervor as other religious affiliates. A Washington Post poll in 1980 revealed that only 23.5 percent identified themselves as "very religious" (reported in the Courier-Journal [Louisville, Kentucky] June 29, 1980, p. D-1). The rest range from moderately to nominally religious./12/ This is true on a more general level as well. Although 60 percent of the population hold formal church membership, only 41 percent attend a religious

TABLE 1.1
Religious Membership as Share of Population

Denomination	Adherents	Share of Population (Percent)
Roman Catholic	47,502,152	21.0
*Evangelical Christians	30,000,000	13.2
Southern Baptist	16,281,692	7.2
United Methodist	11,552,111	5.1
Jewish	5,921,205	2.6
United Presbyterian	2,974,186	1.3
Lutheran Church in America	2,911,817	1.3
Episcopal	2,823,399	1.2
Mormon	2,684,744	1.2
Lutheran Church, Missouri Synod	2,622,847	1.2
American Lutheran Church	2,361,845	1.0
United Church of Christ	2,096,014	0.9
American Baptist	1,922,467	0.8
Assemblies of God	1,612,655	0.7
Churches of Christ	1,600,177	0.7
Disciples of Christ	1,212,977	0.5
Christian Churches and Churches of Christ	1,127,925	0.5

*Overlaps other Christian denominational membership

Sources: Parts comes from U.S. News and World Report, January 3, 1983, p. 58 and are based on data from the Glenmary Research Center, Atlanta, Georgia. For that reason total numbers differ from figures presented above. Figures on Evangelical Christians are taken from a Gallup Poll reported in U.S. News and World Report, September 15, 1980, and overlap the other Christian affiliations. Jewish Membership is taken from the New York Times, June 26, 1983, p. 18.

service on a weekly basis (U.S. News and World Report, p. 35, April 4, 1983)./13/
Moreover, not all religiously active people are politically active. Evangelicals in particular have been traditionally nonpolitical. This is changing; however, as of 1980 only 70 percent of those professing to be

Evangelicals were even registered to vote (U.S. News and World Report, p. 25, September 15, 1980).

Finally, those who fear the "sleeping giant" must recognize that political divisions, although not touching every policy area, do exist within religious traditions. A breakdown of the presidential votes in 1980 and 1984 shows the splits within each tradition (see Table 1.2).

The white born-again Christian vote was more united than the other groups, but taken as a whole it constituted only 15 percent of the vote. Particularly noteworthy is the fairly equal distribution of the Catholic vote. It can be asserted that any religion that includes Paul M. Weyrich, director of the Committee for the Survival of a Free Congress, a conservative group, and the Reverend Robert Drinan, S.J., chairman of Americans for Democratic Action, as well as General Alexander Haig and former Governor Jerry Brown can hardly be seen as a monolith!

The purpose of the above discussion is not to argue that religious groups are without influence. That is simply not true (Weber and Stanley, 1984:28). The point is that myths of church power are vastly overdrawn and that religious associations are subject to gradations of associational commitment and political interest as well as to political divisions and cross pressures just as are other groups within society. Religious associations have power and influence, but it is limited and divided.

Granted this realistic view of church power, how are the political efforts of such groups to be handled in a democratic society? We can do no better than return again to James Madison's vision of a democratic republic, specifically as expressed in The Federalist Papers (Madison, Hamilton, and Jay, 1961).

"The Federalists No. 10" is particularly appropriate because it deals not only with factions in general but also with factions based on religious differences. It might be assumed that Madison argued for absolute, total, or complete separation of church and state here. What he urged instead was a limited, equal separation, placing religious factions into the same political position as any other faction, neither granting them greater privileges nor imposing on them special restrictions. Madison trusted in the large size of the country and the proper republican structure of the government to protect against tyranny. As he wrote in the penultimate paragraph:

The influence of factious leaders may kindle a flame within their particular States but will be unable

TABLE 1.2
Vote Distribution by Religious Affiliation: 1980 and 1984
Presidential Elections (in Percentages)

	1980 Vote			1984 Vote		All 1984 Voters
	Reagan	Carter	Anderson	Reagan	Mondale	
TOTAL	51	41	7	59	41	
White						
Protestant	63	31	6	73	28	51
Catholic	49	42	7	55	44	26
Jewish	39	46	15	32	66	3
White Born-again Christians	63	33	3	80	20	15

Source: New York Times/CBS News poll, published in New York Times, November 8, 1984.

Note: The 1984 data are based on voter exit interviews of 8,696 voters, November 6, 1984. The 1980 data are based on voter exit interviews of 15,201 voters in the 1980 presidential election.

to spread a general conflagration through the other States. A religious sect may degenerate into a political faction in a part of the Confederacy; but the variety of sects dispersed over the entire face of it must secure the national councils against any danger from that source (Madison, Hamilton, and Jay, 1961:84).

Traditionally this text has been read as expressing Madison's opposition to, or at least great suspicion of, religion and his intent to limit the influence of sects. I consider this an erroneous reading. What is critical to a proper understanding of the text, in my view, is the context within which it is written and the means by which religion is to be limited. The latter must occur not by limiting the access of religious leaders to the political process or building a "wall of separation" between religion and politics. On the contrary, the limitation comes precisely from eliminating all special privileges or disabilities and forcing religious groups

into the political mainstream where the number of sects
and size of the country will provide safeguards, both for
the religious groups and against factious spirits. This
vision of protection without privilege appears again in
"The Federalist No. 51" where Madison observes:

> In a free government the security for civil rights
> must be the same as that for religious rights. It
> consists in the one case in the multiplicity of
> interests, and in the other in the multiplicity of
> sects. The degree of security in both cases will
> depend on the number of interests and sects; and this
> may be presumed to depend on the extent of the country
> and number of people comprehended under the same
> government (Madison, Hamilton, and Jay, 1961:324).

Madison's statement in "The Federalist, No. 10," that
a religious sect may degenerate into a political faction
must again be seen in context. First, by faction Madison
does not mean simply an interest group, but something by
definition much more sinister, namely, "a number of
citizens, whether amounting to a majority or minority of
the whole, who are united and actuated by some common
impulse of passion or of interest adverse to the rights
of other citizens, or to the permanent and aggregate
interests of the community" [emphasis added] (Madison,
Hamilton, and Jay, 1961:78).

The distinction, as applied to religion, is not
between some groups that are politically active and others,
inactive, but between groups seeking to further private
rights and/or public goods and those seeking objectives
adverse to the rights of other citizens or public
interests. Only the latter may be considered to have
degenerated into political factions. Madison was not
opposed to political activity by those with religious
motivations; to the contrary, he thought that by participating in the political process religionists would learn
to curb excessive zeal and to live harmoniously in civil
society.

A second contextual point is somewhat related.
Madison considered property to be the primary cause of
factions. Yet the protection of the rights of property
has been one of the primary reasons why governments have
been formed. Religion he considered to be a similar if
less-potent cause of faction, yet the right to practice
one's religion he held to be as fundamental as the right

to own property and equally to be protected. The brilliance of Madison's "republican solution" is that the rights of property and religion could be vigorously protected, and the effects of the factions that would inevitably follow could be controlled without impinging on economic, political, or religious liberties.

Although Madison's solution to religious group activism may be disconcerting to those who wish to exclude such groups from the political process and is certainly incompatible with either the absolute or the supportive separation positions, the continued proliferation and competition among groups throughout U.S. history has proven the wisdom of Madison's vision.

Finally, Madison's view assures that there will be continuous interaction between religion and government. Whatever excessive entanglement might mean, it cannot be understood as stifling normal political advocacy and interaction, even of religious groups. That, at least, is the heritage Madison left us.

EXCESSIVE ENTANGLEMENT

A third reason given for opposition to religious interest groups (RIGs) in politics is that such efforts create excessive entanglement--part of the three-prong test developed by the Supreme Court as a basis for deciding establishment clause issues (those that may be covered by the First Amendment prohibition of the establishment of religion). The test is whether the challenged legislative enactment (1) has a secular purpose, (2) either advances or inhibits religion, and (3) leads to an excessive entanglement of government and religion (Lemon v. Kurtzman, 403 U.S. 602, 612-614, 1971.).

As developed by the Court, excessive entanglement has two components that we shall analyze separately: administrative involvement and potential for political divisiveness./14/

Administrative Involvement

With respect to administrative involvement, perhaps the first thing that should be pointed out is that the religion clauses of the First Amendment limit Congress, and, as extended through the Fourteenth Amendment in a series of court cases, the states; they do not limit

religious groups or individuals. It follows that one
should distinguish between government involvement in
religious affairs and religious involvement in government
affairs./15/ In light of the First Amendment strictures,
the excessive entanglement test should touch religious
groups only when they are seeking some aid from government,
and then it is not the seeking but the aiding that raises
an entanglement problem. Nevertheless, since at least
one noted church-state scholar has raised the point and
a Supreme Court justice implied it, excessive entanglement
must be analyzed as it applies to religious group participation in the political process. In Harris v. McRae
(a suit challenging limitations on Medicaid-funded
abortions) (448 U.S. 297, 1980), the plaintiffs, represented by Leo Pfeffer, argued that the Hyde amendment had
been sponsored as a result of religious pressure on
Representative Henry Hyde: "Exhaustive testimony was heard
during the trial on the views of religious leaders
regarding the morality of abortion, and on the participation by opposing religiously motivated groups in the
lobbying process surrounding the Hyde Amendment" (Gaffney,
1980:208).

The plaintiff's contention was rejected by Justice
Dooling at the District Court level,/16/ but the issue
of religious involvement in policymaking was brought up
again by Justice William Brennan in his Marsh v. Chambers
dissent:

> With regard to most issues, the Government may be
> influenced by partisan argument and may act as a
> partisan itself. In each case, there will be winners
> and losers in the political battle, and the losers'
> most common recourse is the right to dissent and the
> right to fight the battle again another day. With
> regard to matters that are essentially religious,
> however, the Establishment Clause seeks that there
> should be no political battles./17/

I would respectfully object that Justice Brennan's
reading of the establishment clause is certainly not
consistent with the intent of James Madison and if
Brennan's reading means religious influence must be
limited, is simply dangerous. As mentioned above, Madison
would allow all groups, including religious groups, to
contend in the political arena and let the losers take
their lumps./18/ Moreover, any attempt to define what

is "essentially religious" is fraught with difficulties.
Some contemporary groups consider opposing the arms race,
fighting world hunger, or ending abortions as essentially
religious. For others, aid to Israel or freedom of choice
in abortion is essentially religious./19/ An essentially
religious test is no more workable than an excessive
entanglement test as now used by the Court. The major
difficulty with Justice Brennan's position, however, is
that it would potentially limit RIG involvement in politics
on the basis of excessive entanglement. Not only would
this deny RIGs equal treatment with other interest groups,
but it would also lead policymakers into the very swamp
the Court wishes to avoid.

A recent case shows why: In Widmar v. Vincent the
Court, speaking through Justice Lewis Powell, held that
a regulation at the University of Missouri-Kansas City
denying religious groups equal access to the use of
university facilities violated a fundamental principle
that a state's regulation of speech must be content-neutral
(454 U.S. 264, 1981). In a footnote Justice Powell wrote:

> The University would risk greater "entanglement" by
> attempting to enforce its exclusion of "religious
> worship" and "religious speech" . . . Initially, the
> University would need to determine which words and
> activities fall within "religious worship and reli-
> gious teaching." This alone could prove an impossible
> task in an age where many and various beliefs meet
> the constitutional definition of religion (Citations
> omitted, 454 U.S. 272, 1981).

Larkin v. Grendel's Den (456 U.S. 913, 1982),
decided in 1982, provides the most significant advance
in the administrative component of the excessive establishment test since Lemon v. Kurtzman. For the first time
the Court had occasion to consider a statute vesting
government authority in churches: The court ruled that
a Massachusetts statute that gave churches and schools
an absolute veto over the issuance of liquor licenses for
premises within a 500-foot radius of their buildings
enmeshed churches in the "exercise of substantial governmental powers" (456 U.S. 913, 1982). Although few would
argue that the Court's ruling was unsound, the rationale
for the decision is uncomfortably broad. The court quoted
dicta from Lemon that "under our system the choice has
been made that government's are to be entirely excluded

from the area of religious instructions and churches
excluded from the affairs of government" (Lemon v.
Kurtzman, 1971, 403 U.S. 625), and from Watson v. Jones
that "the structure of our government has, for the preservation of religious liberty, rescued the temporal institutions from religious interference. On the other hand,
it has secured religious liberty from the invasion of the
civil authority" (Watson v. Jones, 80 U.S. 679 at 730,
1871).

One might wish that the Court had clarified the
distinction between the process of policy formation in
which the advocacy of all groups, including religious ones,
is an appropriate form of political participation and the
process of policy implementation that is clearly a
governmental function. As it applies to the latter,
Grendel's Den is a solid precedent.

What conclusions can be drawn from this survey of
the Court's use of the administrative oversight component
of the excessive entanglement test? First, the test is
still a vague, amorphous, and developing principle. It
allows, indeed requires, a great deal of subjective
judgment on the part of justices./20/

Second, there is a seed of hope that the test can
be made useful and safe for RIGs. The core of the
administrative involvement component is the potential for
"comprehensive, discriminating, and continuing state
surveillance" of religious institutions (403 U.S. 619,
1971). Unfortunately the Court has not been willing to
accept the proposition that the actions of religious
institutions could, and I would urge, should be measured
by standards applicable to all similar voluntary, nonprofit
institutions interacting with government. If taken in
this sense, excessive entanglement would mean deviation
from the norm--either providing religious institutions
unique privileges and special exceptions from standard
reporting and auditing procedures or subjecting them to
more stringent standards of accountability.

Political Divisiveness

The second part of the excessive entanglement test
is political divisiveness. For the most part there has
simply been restatement rather than development since
political divisiveness was first enunciated, so it may
be useful to criticize the concept as developed by its
strongest proponent, chief justice Warren Burger. "A

broader base of entanglement of yet a different character
is presented by the divisive political potential of these
state programs" (403 U.S. 602, 622, 1971), wrote the Chief
Justice in Lemon. After sketching a scenario of rising
political activism in a community where people "will find
their votes aligned with their faith," he continued:

> Ordinarily political debate and division, however
> vigorous or even partisan, are normal and healthy
> manifestations of our democratic system of government,
> but political division along religious lines was one
> of the principle evils against which the First
> Amendment was intended to protect. . . . The potential
> divisiveness of such conflict is a threat to the
> normal political process (403 U.S. 602, 622, 1971).

Chief Justice Burger's reasoning is troubling in
several regards. By writing that "ordinary . . . debate
and division, however vigorous or even partisan, are normal
and healthy manifestations," he implies that religious
debate is abnormal and unhealthy. The chief justice seems
to take a narrow, negative view of religious conflict as
evil, without acknowledging that conflicting religious
viewpoints, properly channeled, can be a major asset
in a society. "Individuals and groups of persons can
differ in their ways of thinking, feeling and behaving
without negative consequences for themselves or for
society. In fact, such differences can be enriching and
beneficial" (Nye, 1973:xii).
Chief Justice Burger, of course, distinguishes
religious conflict from other divisions, but even here
his argument rests on weak grounds. In speaking precisely
to the question of religious conflict, it has been
suggested that:

> conflict is a form of social interaction. It relieves
> tensions. It forces contending groups to modify their
> claims. It is often the only way that groups may
> express opposition to ideas and practices they abhor.
> Uncontrolled conflict (and violence) can be
> destructive, but the important task of creating and
> maintaining a productive social system is subverted
> by denying the efficacy of conflict in stabilizing
> the social order and advancing the commonwealth.
> [Emphasis added] The important task is not,
> therefore, the indiscriminate and undisciplined

elimination of conflict, but rather the creation and preservation of devices whereby conflict can be socially productive (Hager, 1956:7).

Religious group conflict and interplay conducted in a peaceful manner "are of the very essence of our kind of democratic society, which abhors in its ideals every form of uniformitarianism and totalitarianism" (Herberg, 1964:157). In fact, properly channeled religious conflict has been defended precisely because of its value in the political arena (Marty, 1964: 174). Without conflict over society's basic values, there will be no reform or revolution of ideas, "no self-purification and examination of motives, no progress or setting of new goals; there will be only a shallow tolerance which holds everything to be true because nothing is true" (Marty, 1964:174).

Not only does the chief justice ignore the good consequences that may result from well-channeled religious conflict, but he also seemingly misunderstands the nature of such conflict by assuming that religion can be separated from other issues. This might theoretically be possible if policy battles were limited to noncontroversial economic details, but it is contrary to the facts of U.S. history. The political process in its most significant moments has concerned itself with the great human issues, which, not surprisingly, have been entwined with great religious issues: religious freedom, freedom from England, abolition of slavery, freedom of the press, civil rights for blacks, Indians, women, homosexuals, and so on, the moral rightness or wrongness of U.S. wars, birth control, abortion, and euthanasia, and of course aid to private schools./21/ Any attempt to eliminate religious views from public debates on issues having religious ramifications is not only impossible but could itself constitute a form of religious discrimination. Indeed, attempting to separate religious conflict from other conflict and to remove it from the political process might well have the opposite effect, i.e., to deepen social cleavages by reducing the cross pressures that come from individuals having varieties of interests and the need to compromise, persuade and combine forces, a need inherent in the political process (Coleman, 1956).

Finally, the chief justice wishes to separate ordinary political debate and division from religious debate and division on the principle that political divisions along religious lines was "one of the principle evils against which the First Amendment was intended to protect" (Lemon v. Kurtzman, 403 U.S. 602, 622, 1971). This recent, often-repeated Court interpretationmay be traced to an unsubstantiated one-sentence statement of Professor Paul A. Freund. Freund stated that "while political debate and division is normally a wholesome process for reaching viable accommodations, political division on religious lines is one of the principal culls that the first amendment sought to forestall" (Freund, 1969, 1680). This assertion does the founding fathers an injustice. Neither Madison nor Jefferson was ever under the illusion that he could forestall political divisions along religious lines; the historical record indicates that they were quite willing to use the existing divisions for their own purposes. Their attitudes toward religious divisions were far more sophisticated than Professor Freund's statement would indicate.

At the risk of being repetitive, if one may take the "Federalist No. 10 and No. 51" as indicating the mind of Madison (and there is no indication that Jefferson disagreed with Madison on this point): "As long as the reason of man continues fallible, and he is at liberty to exercise it, different opinions will be formed" (The Federalist, No. 10). Religion, along with economics and government, is one of the areas in which different opinions will always be found and around which factions will form. There are two ways to control the effects of such factions: Control their causes, or control their effects. In order to control the causes of faction, one must either destroy the liberty that is essential for differences of opinion to flourish, or "give every citizen the same opinions, the same passions and the same interests" (The Federalist, No. 10). Because Madison saw the control of the causes of faction to be worse than the factions themselves, he turned to the effects. In other words, he was not interested in protecting against potential political divisions along religious lines, but in controlling the effects of such divisions precisely by treating religious divisions on an equal basis with other cleavages.

In protecting against the effects of division, Madison took precisely the opposite tack of Chief Justice Burger; he reduced religious division to ordinary dimensions, giving religion neither special consideration nor special hindrance. Madison treated religion as an equal cause of faction with others (although he thought that property is the most potent and durable source of faction), and he proposed the same republican remedy for religious divisions. As he wrote to an acquaintance after the first amendment was adopted:

> The tendency to an usurpation on one side or another, or to a corrupting coalition or alliance between them, will best be guarded against by an entire abstinence of the government from interference in any way whatever, beyond the necessity of preserving public order and protecting each sect against trespasses on its legal rights by others (quoted in Everson v. Board of Education, 330 U.S. 1, 40 n.28, 1947, Rutledge, J., dissenting).

Chief Justice Burger writes impatiently, "[It] conflicts with our whole history and tradition to permit questions of the Religion Clauses to assume such importance in our legislatures and in our elections that they could divert attention from the myriad issues and problems that confront every level of government" (Lemon v. Kurtzman, 403 U.S. 602, 623, 1971). One may respectfully disregard the historical inaccuracy of this assertion and rely on Madison's answer that it is the size of the country and the structure of the government that must secure the national councils from that danger, and that it is precisely in the legislature that such conflicts must be resolved.

Logically, the chief justice's statement might be read to imply: (1) that legislatures and elections cannot properly handle conflict arising from differing religious views; or (2) that legislatures and elections might legislate an establishment of religion or something contrary to the common good; or (3) that it is up to the courts to resolve the conflicts in spite of the will of the majority. Madison's response to each of these was succinctly stated:

> In the extended republic of the United States, and among the great variety of interests, parties and sects which it embraces, a coalition of a majority of the whole society could seldom take place on any other principles than those of justice and the general good: whilst there being thus less danger to a minor from the will of a major party, there must be less pretext, also, to provide for the security of the

former, by introducing into the government a will
not dependent on the latter, or in other words, a
will independent of the society itself (The
Federalist, No. 51).

Madison was aware that conflict over issues as deeply
emotional as religion might well tie up a legislature for
a time, but he was also aware that political realism would
eventually form moderation and compromise that in the long
run would be far more healthy than fiats imposed on
contending parties by a will independent of the society
itself. In declaring legislation unconstitutional on the
basis of potential political divisiveness, the Court
encourages something akin to the heckler's veto. If
potential conflict is sufficient to tip the balance
against a particular legislative policy touching on
religion, a group opposed to the policy will be tempted
to initiate or escalate conflict rather than work for an
acceptable compromise. Indeed, anyone familiar with recent
church-state litigations must have strong suspicions that
this is exactly what happens.
    To his credit, Chief Justice Burger confronted that
issue in his opinion for the majority in Lynch v.
Donnelly upholding the constitutionality of a nativity
scene erected by the city of Pawtucket, Rhode Island./22/
Observed the chief justice:

> In any event, apart from this litigation there is
> no evidence of political friction or divisiveness
> over the creche in the 40-year history of Pawtucket's
> Christmas celebration . . . A litigant cannot by the
> very act of commencing a lawsuit, however, create
> the appearance of divisiveness and then exploit it
> as evidence of entanglement./23/

At least three of the members of the Supreme Court
seem well on the way toward abandoning the divisiveness
component altogether. The Court's most influential swing
vote, Justice Powell, observed in Wolman v. Walter that
"the risk of significant religious or denominational
control over our democratic processes--or even of deep
political divisions along religious lines--is remote . . .
and such risk seems entirely tolerable in light of the
continuing oversight of this Court" (433 U.S. 229 at
263)./24/ Writing for a 5-4 majority in Mueller v.
Allen, a tuition tax credit case, Justice William
Rehnquist seemed to go out of his way to strike a blow

at the test. He noted that although the litigants hadn't raised the political divisiveness argument, one of the amicus briefs had, and he then proceeded to make short shrift of the argument. Given its treatment in recent cases, observed Rehnquist, political divisiveness language is confined to cases of direct financial subsidy to parochial schools or teachers (103 S.Ct. 3062, 3071, N. 11, 1983). Because such subsidies are already unconstitutional, there is not much left to the test.

Even more critical is Justice Sandra Day O'Connor. Concurring in Lynch v. Donnelly, she may well have sounded the death knell for the test: "Guessing the potential for political divisiveness inherent in a government practice is simply too speculative an enterprise, in part because the existence of the litigation, as this case illustrates, itself may affect the political response to the government practice."/25/

If Justice O'Connor's view is accepted by the Court, the threat posed by the political divisiveness test to religious interest group activism will have been eliminated.

To summarize, the historical and political assumptions underlying the political divisiveness test are faulty in that they fail to recognize that (1) conflict, even among competing religious viewpoints, can be healthy for society if religious groups are allowed equal access to normal political channels; (2) conflict over religious views and values cannot be separated from other political views and values because they involve many of the same issues; (3) excluding religious conflict from normal political process is precisely the opposite of what the founders intended; and (4) utilization of a political divisiveness test is more likely to lead to the initiation of conflict rather than its resolution, especially when the concept is broadened to include "potential" divisiveness.

SUMMARY AND CONCLUSION

I began this chapter examining the reasons for widespread opposition to religious involvement in politics. There are four basic reasons: an erroneous understanding of the meaning of separation of church and state, fear of church power, fear of excessive administrative entanglement, and fear of potential political divisiveness along political lines. Concerning the first, I have argued that the founders intended to provide equal separation, not absolutist or supportive, and that under the equal separation concept, religious interest groups have the same right to participate in the political process as other similar groups--with no further privileges or disabilities.

Concerning church power I have argued that religious groups are like other organizations in society-- experiencing varied levels of commitment and divisions both within and among various groups, and having members subject to numerous cross pressures for their allegiance. As a result, fears of church power are vastly overdrawn and the Madisonian solution that takes into account the size of the country and the number of sects is the most effective control on such groups.

Excessive entanglement through administrative involvement is a more difficult problem. A basically sound concept, the principle at its current stage of development is still vague, requiring too much subjective judgment by the courts. Since there will be continuing interaction between religious organizations and government, it would be helpful if the Supreme Court would distinguish between policy formation, in which religious group participation is appropriate, and policy implementation, when it is not. Moreover, the court should define excessive entanglement as a failure to apply standard investigating, reporting, and auditing procedures to religious groups in the same manner as they are applied to other nonprofit, charitable groups.

The "potential political divisiveness" test was shown to be a judicial construct that ignores the solution intended by the founders for the "problem" of religion in the political arena, the values of well-channeled religious conflict and the futility of trying to remove such conflict from politics. Even the Court now seems inclined to limit the reach of this test.

We may conclude then, that there are both a firm constitutional basis and sound policy reasons for allowing religious groups and individuals to compete equally with other groups and individuals in attempting to influence the formation of public policy.

NOTES
1. A more subtle version of this argument was proposed by the American Civil Liberties Union in Harris v. McRae, namely that religious interests do have the right to

advocate public policies, but if they are too successful, the resulting legislation must be declared unconstitutional! (See Will, 1978.)

2. For an extensive review of Madison's thought on the relations of religion and law, see Weber, 1982:163.

3. The present typology is somewhat different from the one previously developed. It is, I hope, a somewhat more accurate reflection of the various kinds of separation.

4. This, as I understand it, is also the current position of the American Civil Liberties Union.

5. For developments of this intriguing concept, see Peter Berger and Richard Neuhaus, 1977 and Novak, 1980.

6. For a discussion of the development of one form of transvaluing separation, see Paul D. Steeves, 1977:37.

7. Probably the best, although by no means perfect, example of equal separation is found in the treatment of religious groups on a par with other not-for-profit groups such as literary, scientific, fraternal and charitable ones in section 501 (c) 3 of the Internal Revenue Code.

8. They did not, for example, envision the incorporation of the clauses through the due process clause of the Fourteenth Amendment and the consequent extension of the Bill of Rights to each state. They intended the prohibition to limit only the federal government; hence the phrase "Congress shall make no law . . . ;" nor did they foresee the development of the most difficult of church-state areas--compulsory education.

9. Basic data is from a Gallup Poll and reported in the Yearbook of American and Canadian Churches, 1983. Other sources report somewhat higher figures. The New York Times reports 1981 church and synagogue membership of 138 million (June 26, 1983, p. 18).

10. By unconventional is meant non-Christian, non-Jewish groups.

11. Please note that the data from this table are assembled from several sources.

12. It has long been an axiom of political analysts that intensity of religious belief correlates heavily with the extent to which religion influences one's political behavior.

13. A Gallup study of people who are unaffiliated with a church or synagogue shows that 26 percent of all baptized Catholics are not practicing.

14. I am indebted to two authors for their discussion of this issue: Kenneth F. Ripple, 1980 and Gaffney, 1980. (See, also, Weber, 1979.)

15. Although the general conclusions I will draw apply equally to both involvements, my primary concern in this chapter is religious involvement in government affairs. For an excellent discussion of the other issue, see Braiterman and Kelley, 1982. Although I do not agree with all the authors' conclusions, it is the best current discussion of the topic.

16. No. 76-C-1804, slip op. at 326-27 (E.D.N.Y. decided January 15, 1980).

17. No. 82-83 slip op., Justice Brennan dissenting at 11. (Decided July 5, 1983). The case involved the constitutionality of prayer by a paid chaplain in the Nebraska legislature. The majority upheld the practice.

18. Clearly this does not imply that any bill that survived the legislative battles would ipso facto be constitutional. For example, a bill allowing coerced confessions might pass a legislature, but it would (and should) be struck down as violation of the Fifth Amendment.

19. In all fairness to Justice Brennan, one should note that he was dealing with prayers. No matter where one draws the line, it is hard to conceive of anything more essentially religious than prayer.

20. This is the major criticism of Ripple, 1980, 1216ff.

21. For an excellent discussion of the interrelations of religion and politics throughout U.S. history, including an analysis of voting behavior, see Lipset, 1964.

22. Slip op. 82-1256 (decided 5 March, 1984).

23. Ibid., pp. 14-15

24. Justice Powell concurring in part and dissenting in part.

25. Slip op. 82-1256 Justice O'Connor concurring, p. 3 (5 March, 1984).

REFERENCES

American Humanist Association. "In Defense of Separation of Church and State." In Joseph L. Blau, ed., Cornerstones of Religious Freedom in America. New York: Harper and Row, 1964.

Berger, Peter and Richard Neuhaus. To Empower People: The Role of Mediating Structures in Public Policy. Washington, D.C.: American Enterprise Institute, 1977.

Boyd, Julian P., ed. The Papers of Thomas Jefferson, Vol. 6 (Princeton: Princeton University, 1950), p. 311.

42

Braiterman, Marvin and Dean M. Kelly, "When is Government Intervention Legitimate?", in Dean M. Kelly, ed. Government Intervention in Religious Affairs. New York: The Pilgrim Press, 1982, pp. 170-193.

Coleman, James S. "Social Cleavage and Religious Conflict," Journal of Social Issues 12:44-56, 1956.

Freund, Paul A. "Public Aid to Parochial Schools," Harvard Law Review 82:1680-1692, 1969.

Gaffney, Edward McGlynn Jr. "Political Divisiveness Along Religious Lines: The Entanglement of the Court in Sloppy History and Bad Public Policy." Saint Louis Univerity Law Journal 24 (Spring):205-236, 1980.

Hager, Don J. "Religious Conflict in the United States." Journal of Social Issues 12(7):3-11, 1956.

Herberg, Will. "Religious Group Conflict in America". In Lee, Robert and Marty Martin, eds., Religion and Social Conflict. New York: Duell, Sloan and Pearce, 143-158, 1964.

Jefferson, Thomas. "Notes on Virginia." In Saul Padover, The Complete Jefferson. New York: Duell, Sloan and Pearce, 1943.

Lawler, Philip F. "At Issue Is the Prophet Motive." Wall Street Journal, (13 November):36, 1984.

Lipset, Seymour Martin. "Religion and Politics in American History." In Earl Raab, ed., Religious Conflict in America. New York: Doubleday & Company, Inc., 60-89, 1964.

Madison, James, Alexander Hamilton, and John Jay. The Federalist Papers. New York: New American Library, 1961.

Marty, Martin E. "Epilogue: The Nature and Consequences of Social Conflict for Religious Groups." In Lee Robert and Marty, Martin, eds., Religion and Social Conflict. Oxford University Press, 173-193, 1964.

Meyers, Marvin, ed. Mind of the Founder: Sources of the Political Thought of James Madison. Indianapolis, Indiana: Bobbs-Merrill, Inc., 1973.

Novak, Michael, ed. Democracy and Mediating Structures. Washington, D.C.: American Enterprise Institute, 1980.

Nye, R. Conflict Among Humans. New York: Springer Publishing Co., 1973.

Padover, Saul K. The Complete Jefferson. New York: Duell, Sloan and Pearce, 1943.

Pfeffer, Leo. Church, State and Freedom. Boston: The Beacon Press, 1967.

Ripple, Kenneth F. "The Entanglement Test of the Religious Clauses - A Ten Year Assessment." UCLA Law Review 27 (August):1195-1239, 1980.

Safire, William. "He and the Clerics have Abused Their Authority." Courier-Journal (Louisville, Ky), 16 March, 1983, A-11.

Stanley, T. L. The Louisville Cardinal. January 20, p. 5, 1983.

Steeves, Paul D. "Amendment of Soviet Law Concerning Religious Groups." Journal of Church and State 19:37-52, 1977.

Tribe, Lawrence H. American Constitutional Law. Mineola, N.Y., The Foundation Press, 1978.

Weber, Paul J. "Building on Sand: Supreme Court Construction and Educational Tax Credits." Creighton Law Review 12 (Winter):531-565, 1979.

Weber, Paul J. "James Madison and Religious Equality: The Perfect Separation." Review of Politics 44(2), 1982.

Weber, Paul J. and T. L. Stanley. "The Power and Performance of Religious Interest Groups," Quarterly Review 4 (No. 2), Summer, 1984.

Will, George. "Involvement of Religious Groups in Public Affairs is Threatened," Courier-Journal (Louisville, Ky.), September 25, 1978.

2

The Clergy and Public Issues in Middletown

Stephen D. Johnson
and Joseph B. Tamney

Nineteen eighty-four surely proved George Orwell to be a poor prophet. Religious leaders have become important political activists, and they appear along the entire political spectrum. Most well known are the efforts of the Roman Catholic bishops through their pastoral letters and the Moral Majority preachers through the electronic media. Jesse Jackson has furthered the political grassroots role of black churches. Future analyses of 1984 may mark that year as a milestone in the politicization of religion, or perhaps the moralization of politics.

This paper reports a study of the clergy in "Middletown" in 1984. "Middletown" is Muncie, Indiana. It was studied in the 1920s by Robert and Helen Lynd (1929) and their analysis of Muncie has come to be considered a classic in the study of community structure and processes. Today, Muncie is a community of 80,000 residents. Some of the questions investigated in this study were: (1) what are the positions of the clergy on key political issues, (2) why do they hold these positions, and (3) what are Middletown churchgoers hearing their clergy say in sermons about these issues?

CLERGY AND THE ISSUES

U.S. religion is organized along denominational lines, although the nondenominational, or independent, churches are a significant group. For the most part, however, individual churches are part of complex organizations with several levels of authority and multiple staff components. This study is concerned only with the grass-roots level, i.e., with church pastors.

A consistent finding is that clergy are more critical
of existing social policies than laity (see the review
of literature in Woodrum, 1978). Woodrum (1978:221)
explained this fact in terms of isolation; because clergy
are less involved in the economic and political institutions, they are less committed to the secular goals of
these institutions. However, clergy have not been equally
involved in all types of issues; moreover, clergy with
different theological positions are not similarly critical
of social policies.

Religious Types and Public Issues

As Johnson (1967:433) has noted, during this century
theologically liberal Protestants have tended to be to
the political left on social and economic issues, while
fundamentalists have tended to support the political
right. However, Johnson found that "the associations
between theological and political liberalism seems to be
much greater than the association between theological and
political conservatism. The conservatives do not approach
the degree of consensus that the liberals have attained."
Moreover, the degree of consensus among conservatives
varied widely from issue to issue. On some issues "the
likelihood of a conservative pastor's taking a conservative
political position appears to vary directly with the
proportion of his colleagues who share his theological
views" (Johnson, 1967:436). That is to say, theologically
conservative pastors in conservative churches have
politically conservative issue positions more often than
such pastors in liberal churches. But the greater
consensus among liberals, Johnson (1967:440) argued,
occurred because social issues are religiously more
important to liberals.

> Liberalism and the social gospel broke with tradition
> by virtually abandoning the historic Christian
> preoccupation with preparing the individual soul for
> the next world. For the hope of glory in the beyond,
> liberalism substituted the hope of the good society
> in the present world. Moreover, it defined the duty
> of the Christian as helping to build the good society.

Sermons on Public Issues

Liberal clergy have been more likely than conservative
clergy to speak out on a variety of public issues (Hadden,

1970:126). Stark et al. (1973:172) studied the frequency
of sermons given on fifteen issues, and on all but four
topics, the liberal (as compared to conservative) clergy
more often spoke out from their pulpits. The four
exceptions were: crime and juvenile delinquency, drugs,
alcoholism, and sexual conduct--issues that can be
considered traditional concerns relating to private
morality. Only with regard to such issues did conservative
ministers speak out about as frequently as liberal
ministers. Similarly, Nelson and Maguire (1980:78) found
that clergy belonging to sectlike denominations were more
likely to give sermons concerning personal morality than
were church-affiliated clergy. Such sermons were also
given frequently by clergy belonging to church-affiliated
denominations who served conservative congregations and
who had a farm background.

The distinction, however, between private and public
morality is becoming outdated. Issues such as family life
and homosexuality, which were considered private in nature,
have become politicized and thus have entered the public
domain. Rather than to contrast private and public
moralities, it is preferable to discuss traditional and
modern ethical concerns (as did Quinley, 1974:127). It
is expected, then, that on modern ethical issues, liberal
clergy will more often speak out in sermons but that
regarding traditional issues liberal and conservative
clergy will speak out equally.

Justification of Views

Johnson concluded that liberal and conservative
Protestantism are two subcultures, but theology may not
be the major influence on these cultural constructs.
Rather,

> the major source of the political views of liberal
> religious leaders is simply their common commitment
> to humanistic social values. . . . The source of the
> political norms of Protestant conservatives is
> probably a common interest in safeguarding traditional
> beliefs, values, and policy positions within an
> environment that is perceived to be actively hostile.
> Conservatives appear most interested in preserving
> their theologies against modern heresies, but many
> of these are also interested in preserving other
> traditional commitments of their religious subculture
> (Johnson, 1967:441).

Johnson's analysis suggests that conservative clergy are more likely than their liberal counterparts to justify their positions on public issues in religious terms or simply as a defense of tradition. But Nelson (1975:71) found that political ideology was more important than theology in predicting the preaching of sermons on traditional moral topics, suggesting that religious ideas themselves are not the important motivating forces even for conservative clergy. It is a question, therefore, to what extent attitudes on, and action on behalf of, public issues is religiously motivated among either liberal or conservative clergy./1/

Previous research suggests, therefore, that: (1) theologically liberal clergy will be politically liberal, and theologically conservative clergy will be politically conservative; (2) liberal clergy will have attitudes different from conservative clergy on social issues, and there will be greater consistency of opinion among liberal clergy on social issues; (3) liberal clergy will more often give sermons on issues concerning modern morality, but liberal and conservative clergy will speak out equally often on issues relating to traditional morality; (4) political ideology will be more important than religious ideology in influencing opinions and sermons on social issues; and (5) liberal clergy will justify their opinions in humanistic terms, while conservative clergy will tend to use religious justifications. These hypotheses will be tested; however, it is also expected that the current study will show that conservative clergy have been speaking out more frequently on social issues than liberal clergy; at least more so relative to liberal clergy than was the case in the past.

Methodology for this Study

Ninety-one ministers from "Middletown" (Lynd and Lynd, 1929) were selected by a modified-random stratified sampling technique. In August 1983, the Christian Ministries of Delaware County compiled The Church and Clergy Directory of Delaware County ("Middletown" is located in this county). The Religious Programs Office of Ball State University, located in Delaware County, kept the directory up to date, and the sample is based on this office's copy of the church directory.

The total number of churches in "Middletown" (Muncie, Indiana) was 210. They were first stratified into four groups: Catholic churches, black churches, white liberal churches, and white conservative churches. This stratification was imposed because these strata tend to differ significantly in political and religious ideology, an important concern in this study; it was therefore important to ensure proportional representation for all these strata./2/ The population size for each stratum was as follows: Catholic churches: 3/3/, black churches: 25, white liberal churches: 53, and white conservative churches: 129. Because the first two categories were small, all cases in each category were included in the sample. Within each of the white Protestant categories, churches were selected so as to ensure representation for all denominations and of all large, individual churches./4/ The sample used in this study includes 2 Catholic churches, 16 black churches, 25 white liberal churches, and 48 white conservative churches. Only one minister from each of these churches was interviewed.

Each minister responded to a brief phone interview that included the following questions: (1) the respondent's position, for, against, or not sure, and the reasons behind his or her position on eight important, present-day issues (a mutual nuclear freeze by the U.S. and the USSR, laws controlling industrial plant closings, a constitutional amendment allowing prayer in public schools, U.S. policies in Central America, affirmative action programs, laws protecting homosexuals, the Equal Rights Amendment (ERA), and the federal government's requirement of medical treatment for all severely handicapped infants--the media-dubbed Baby Doe or Baby Jane Doe issue); (2) the respondent's self-perceived overall political ideology (from very liberal to very conservative); (3) his or her self-perceived overall religious ideology (the categories were fundamentalist, conservative, neo-orthodox, and liberal); (4) the respondent's assessment of whether or not politicians use religion to support the politician's political causes, and, if so, the respondent was asked to give examples; (5) the size of the respondent's congregation; (6) the size of the community in which the minister had grown up; (7) whether or not the minister had ministerial education, and if so, what type; (8) the minister's age; and (9) for each of the eight issues mentioned in number 1 above, whether or not the respondent had spoken out in a sermon on the issue within the last year.

Results

The basic nature of the sample of ninety-one ministers was as follows: (1) only two ministers were women; (2) ages ranged from 24 to 81, with 30 percent under 40; 70 percent, 40 or older; (3) 30 percent had lived on farms when they grew up, 48 percent had lived in communities with populations between 1,000 and 50,000, and 22 percent in cities of more than 50,000; (4) 18 percent had no ministerial education, and of those who had, 30 percent had a mainline church education, and 64 percent had either a conservative or a fundamentalist education; and (5) 36 percent serviced congregations of 100 people or less; 40 percent serviced between 101 and 300, and 23 percent serviced between 301 and 1,560 (one minister, or 1 percent, had a congregation of 4,000).

Table 2.1 shows the clergy's attitudes on the issues studied. By far the greatest uncertainty concerned Central American foreign policies. We believe this reflects a general ignorance in Middletown about foreign policies that do not directly involve the Soviet Union. A great deal of uncertainty also existed regarding plant-closing laws, the Equal Rights Amendment, and Baby Doe regulations. In each case, about one-fourth of the clergy had no firm opinion.

As can be seen in Table 2.1, the clergy in this study strongly favored a nuclear freeze, the prayer-in-school amendment, and affirmative action programs, although they rejected laws protecting homosexuals against job discrimination.

Liberal and Conservative Religious Subcultures

Table 2.2 shows the religious and political views for ministers in each of the four church types. As can be seen, black ministers are quite diverse. In contrast, the ministers at white conservative churches tend to be homogeneous, being both religiously and politically conservative. Ministers at white liberal churches show yet another pattern: They tend to be religiously liberal but politically moderate. If we consider each group of churches to be a potential organizational network, then it seems clear that because of their greater theological and political homogeneity, the white conservative churches is the group that could be most effectively organized into a coalition.

TABLE 2.1
Middletown Clergy's Positions on Social Issues

Issues	N	Clergy Attitude		
		For	Not Sure (Percent)	Against
A freeze on development of nuclear weapons by the U.S. and the USSR	88	75	3	22
Laws controlling how quickly industrial plants can be closed	89	37	28	35
A constitutional amendment allowing vocal or silent prayer in public schools	90	63	7	30
U.S. policies in Central America	90	23	48	29
Affirmative action programs to assist minorities	90	74	7	19
A law protecting homosexuals from being fired as teachers in public schools	90	26	7	68
The Equal Rights Amendment	89	36	21	43
The federal government's requirement that severely handicapped infants with little chance of normal lives receive aggressive medical treatment (regardless of parents' wishes)	90	46	21	33

It had been expected that theologically liberal clergy would be politically liberal and that theologically conservative clergy would be politically conservative. As can be seen in Table 2.3, this prediction is confirmed by the data. Because of their similarity on issues, we combined the liberal and neoorthodox theological adherents in one group and the fundamentalists and conservatives

TABLE 2.2
Church Type and Clergy's Religious and Political Views
(in Percentages)

	Church Type			
	Roman Catholic (N=2)	Black Churches (N=16)	White Liberal (N=25)	White Conservative (N=45)
Religious Views				
Fundamentalist		19		48
Conservative		31	36	42
Neo-Orthodox			32	
Liberal	50	38	28	6
Other	50	12	4	4
Political Views				
Very Liberal		7		
Liberal	100	33	32	
Moderate		26	40	20
Conservative		27	28	69
Very Conservative		7		11

TABLE 2.3
Theological and Political Views of Clergy

		Political Ideology		
Theological Ideology	N	Liberal	Moderate (Percent)	Conservative
Liberal	24	50	42	8
Conservative	62	5	21	74

in the other, as had Johnson in his study in the sixties
(Johnson, 1967:435). For Table 2.3, three categories for
the analysis of political ideology were used because such
distinctions were meaningful in the analysis of issue
positions. Theologically conservative people are more
politically consistent than theologically liberal people,
who divided between political liberalism and moderation.

To what extent did liberal and conservative clergy
differ on the social issues discussed in this paper? The

relevant information is in Table 2.4. With regard to plant-closing laws, affirmative action, and Baby Doe regulations, there are no significant differences between liberal and conservative clergy. However, the liberal clergy more often support a nuclear freeze, the Equal Rights Amendment, and a law protecting homosexuals against discrimination (although only a bare majority of the liberal clergy supported the last-mentioned law). Conservative clergy gave greater support to a school prayer amendment and were undecided about and more in favor of the U.S. policies toward Central America. The strongest differences between liberal and conservative clergy concerned a school prayer amendment and the Equal Rights Amendment; on these issues the battle lines are well drawn./5/

The black clergy tended to be religiously conservative, but about forty percent were politically liberal (see Table 2.2). It would be expected, therefore, that the black clergy would fall between the white liberal and white conservative subsamples. This was true for some issues. However, the black clergy supported the nuclear freeze and affirmative action programs about as often as the liberal white clergy. Moreover, among all the subsamples, the black clergy gave the highest support to plant-closing laws and Baby Doe regulations. The racial comparisons are not presented in detail because of the small number of black clergy in the study. However, the results suggest that black Christianity is a distinctive subculture--although tending to theological conservatism, it is liberal on peace and prejudice issues and sympathetic to the less privileged (the unemployed and handicapped children).

How effective a subcultural group can be is affected by the degree of agreement among members of the subgroup. Is there more consistency among the liberal or the conservative clergy? If we consider only the issues regarding which there are significant religious differences in Table 2.4, we see that the liberal clergy are strikingly more consistent than the conservative clergy concerning a nuclear freeze and slightly more consistent in relation to the Equal Rights Amendment and Central American policies. Regarding the school prayer amendment, both camps are about equally homogeneous. Only with regard to laws protecting homosexuals are the conservatives clearly more consistent. All in all, then, the liberals are more homogeneous than the conservatives.

54

TABLE 2.4
Religious Ideology and Issue Positions (in Percentages)

| Issue and Position | Religious Ideology | |
	Liberal (N=24)	Conservative (N=64)
Nuclear freeze(a)		
Against	0	30
Not sure	4	3
For	96	67
Plant-closing law		
Against	33	37
Not sure	33	24
For	33	40
School prayer amendment(a)		
Against	75	14
Not sure	8	6
For	17	80
Central American policies(a)		
Against	63	14
Not sure	29	56
For	8	30
Affirmative Action		
Against	13	22
Not sure	0	9
For	87	69
Homosexual antidiscrimination law(a)		
Against	38	80
Not sure	8	6
For	54	14
Equal Rights Amendment(a)		
Against	21	52
Not sure	17	22
For	62	25
Baby Doe regulations		
Against	38	30
Not sure	21	22
For	42	48

(a) Chi Square significant at .05 level.

Johnson (1967:436) had found that conservative consistency was greater when conservative clergy worked for a conservative church. We compared liberal clergy with conservative clergy working for liberal churches and conservative clergy working for conservative churches. Table 2.5 shows the results; only white clergy are included in the table; there were only two liberal ministers working in conservative churches, and they are not presented in the table. Table 2.5 presents only information in relation to issues on which liberals and conservatives differed. As can be seen in the table, conservatives working in liberal churches are distinctive. On the nuclear freeze issue, they are similar to liberal clergy. On all the other issues, the conservatives in liberal churches are closer in outlook to the conservatives in conservative churches.

It does seem useful to divide Protestant Christianity into liberal and conservative subcultures. The clergy working at white liberal churches are more theologically and politically diverse than the clergy at white conservative churches; the difference suggests that the latter could more easily be mobilized into a political coalition than the former. It is also true that with respect to the social issues studied, the theologically liberal clergy are more homogeneous than the conservative clergy; in part, this difference occurs because conservative clergy in liberal churches are inbetween their liberal colleagues and the conservative clergy in conservative churches.

The issues studied fall into several categories: (1) religiously ambiguous issues, i.e., a plant-closing law and Baby Doe regulations; the clergy are divided on these issues; (2) issues receiving widespread support from both liberal and conservative clergy: only the affirmative action issue fits this type; (3) liberal issues, i.e., nuclear freeze (however, this almost fell into the second category), criticism of Central American policies, and the Equal Rights Amendment; and (4) conservative issues, i.e., school prayer and homosexuality.

Sermons on Social Issues

Respondents were asked if they had presented their views on each of the issues discussed in the interview in a sermon during the last year. It was expected that theologically liberal clergy would more often give sermons on modern issues but that liberals and conservatives would

TABLE 2.5
Issue Positions by the Religious Ideology of Clergy
and Church Type (in Percentages)

Issue and Position	Liberal Clergy (N=14)	Conservative Clergy in Liberal Churches (N=10)	Conservative Clergy in Conservative Churches (N=45)
Nuclear freeze			
Against		10	38
Not sure			4
For	100	90	58
School prayer amendment			
Against	93	20	11
Not sure	7	10	7
For		70	82
Central American policies			
Against	80	20	16
Not sure	20	60	47
For		20	38
Homosexual antidiscrimination law			
Against	27	60	87
Not sure	7	10	7
For	67	30	7
Equal Rights Amendment			
Against	7	44	60
Not sure	13		27
For	80	56	13

not differ in the frequency they spoke out on traditional
issues.

The relevant information is in Table 2.6. Concerning
the nuclear freeze, Central American policies, and to some
extent affirmative action, the more liberal clergy had
spoken out. In almost all cases, their sermons espoused
the politically liberal position on these issues. In
contrast, the more conservative clergy had delivered

sermons on the school prayer amendment and the law to protect homosexuals./6/ On the other issues, the differences between liberal and conservative clergy were quite small.

Because all the clergy came from the Middletown area, the survey allowed us to estimate crudely what the church-going Middletown population was hearing about the issues studied. Respondents had been asked, "About how many adult members are there presently in your congregation?" We determined the total church memberships of all clergy who had given a sermon in favor of an issue, of all clergy who had given a sermon against an issue, of all clergy who had given a sermon about a topic he or she had not been sure about, and of all clergy who had not given a sermon on an issue. We then estimated the percentages of all church members who had heard a pro, anti, not sure, or no sermon on each issue by dividing these four totals by the total church membership of all clergy studied. For instance, we added up the total church membership of all clergy who had spoken out for a nuclear freeze and divided this by the total church membership of all the ministers in the study. This resulted in the estimate that 51 percent of the membership of the churches studied could have heard a pro-nuclear freeze sermon. All the results of these calculations are seen in Table 2.7. This information must be seen only as suggestive because not all churches were studied, the sample was not a strict random one, we do not know whether the churches are equal in the proportion of members likely to attend church regularly. However, the sample did include most large churches and did represent a cross section of Middletown clergy.

As can be seen in the table, almost no one heard sermons on the plant-closing law issue, and very few heard discussions about Baby Doe regulations. It is probable that large numbers of people heard sermons in which the nuclear freeze, the Equal Rights Amendment, and affirmative action were supported. Somewhat fewer people heard sermons against Central American policies and a law to protect homosexuals against discrimination. There was little difference in the percentage of church members hearing opinions for and against the school prayer amendment. These results reflect the small size of many congregations led by conservative clergy. About the same percentage of liberal and conservative clergy spoke out on the Equal Rights Amendment (Table 2.6), but many more churchgoers

TABLE 2.6
Theologically Liberal and Conservative Clergy's Sermons on Social Issues (In One Year)

Issue	Liberals	Conservatives
	(Percent)	
Nuclear freeze(a)	63	20
Plant-closing law	21	16
School prayer amendment	42	64
Central American policies(a)	50	23
Affirmative Action	42	23
Homosexual antidiscrimination law	25	47
Equal Rights Amendment	58	55
Baby Doe regulations	29	36

(a) Chi square significant at the .05 level.

Table 2.7
Adult Church Members Hearing Sermons on Various Issue Positions (in Percentages)

	Issue Position			
Issue	No Sermon	Against	Not Sure	For
Nuclear freeze	46	2	0	51
Plant-closing law	90	2	1	7
School prayer amendment	57	16	1	25
Central American policies	55	30	8	7
Affirmative Action	62	3	0	35
Homosexual anti-discrimination law	69	25	1	5
Equal Rights Amendment	39	14	4	43
Baby Doe regulations	78	5	4	13

heard opinions favoring rather than opposing this amendment.

In sum, there are issues--a plant-closing law, Baby Doe regulations--on which liberals and conservatives do not differ and about which few Middletown people heard their pastors' ideas. The affirmative action issue is supported by liberals and conservatives but is addressed in sermons more often by liberal clergy; few churchgoers

in Middletown heard sermons critical of affirmative action,
and many heard supportive sermons. On the liberal issues,
churchgoers were much more likely to hear liberal viewpoints; this was especially true regarding the nuclear
freeze and the Equal Rights Amendment. Regarding homosexual antidiscrimination very few people heard ministers
defend a law to protect homosexuals, and many heard sermons
critical of laws to protect homosexuals. However, although
conservative ministers have strongly rallied behind the
school prayer amendment, it would appear that only about
one-fourth of the churchgoers heard sermons in which this
amendment was supported, and about half as many heard the
amendment criticized.

Religious Justification

Are the differences between the liberal and conservative religious subcultures due to theological differences
themselves? Previous research had suggested that issue
differences between religious groups seem explained by
political differences rather than by differing theological
orientations. This interpretation is partially supported
by the present study. As can be seen in Table 2.8, neither
religious nor political ideology is related to clergy
attitudes concerning plant closing laws, affirmative
action, or Baby Doe regulations. On the other issues,
the zero-order relations between each issue and the two
ideologies are quite similar in magnitude. The table also
shows the correlation between each issue and each ideology,
holding constant the other ideology. The partial correlations for religious ideology are significant for the
school prayer and Equal Rights Amendment. Controlling
for religious orientation showed that political ideology
remained significant in regard to the school prayer
amendment, the nuclear freeze, Central American policies,
and the protection of homosexuals against discrimination;
for the last three issues, only political ideology was
important./7/ Overall, political ideology seems more
important in this study; however, religious ideology itself
does appear to explain, in part, clerical attitudes toward
the two proposed constitutional amendments./8/
Another way to study the importance of religion in
shaping clergy attitudes is to examine how they justify
their opinions. If a respondent was either for or against
a topic, the interviewer asked, "Why do you feel this way?"
Then, if only one reason was given, the interviewer asked,
"Any other reason for your attitude?" The reasons given

TABLE 2.8
Zero-Order and Partial Correlations of Religious Ideology
and Political Ideology with Issue Positions

| Issue | Correlation with | | Partial Correlation with | |
	Religious Ideology*	Political Ideology*	Religious Ideology	Political Ideology
Nuclear freeze	-.31**	-.37**	-.10	-.23**
Plant-closing laws	.02	-.02	.04	-.04
School prayer amendment	.61**	.55**	.39**	.26**
Central American policies	.44**	.52**	.15	.34**
Affirmative Action	-.16	-.10	-.12	.01
Homosexual anti-discrimination law	-.42**	-.49**	-.16	-.31**
Equal Rights Amendment	-.35**	-.32**	-.19**	-.13
Baby Doe regulations	.07	.09	.02	.06

*A high score means conservatism.
**Chi square significant at the .05 level.

were considered religious if the respondent made explicit reference to God, the Bible, or Christianity. Table 2.9 shows for each issue the percent of reasons that were religious.

Generally, only a minority of justifications used by the clergy were religious. But the use of religious reasons varies by issue and by issue position. The clergy made almost no use of religion in explaining their attitudes toward plant-closing laws or Central American policies, and religion played only a minor role in justifying attitudes toward the nuclear freeze. For the other issues religious reasons were of some importance.

Regarding the school prayer amendment, religion was used only in defense of the amendment. The clergy argued that God and prayer are sources of the nation's greatness, that we must bring religion back into the schools, and that prayer is good for people. In short, religion is good; therefore, religion in the schools is desirable.

Religion was used only to justify affirmative action, not to attack it. Clergy defended this program because God has created us all equal.

TABLE 2.9
Religious Reasoning Given for Positions on Social Issues

| | Religious Reasons | | | |
| | For | | Against | |
Issue	%	N	%	N
Nuclear freeze	9	79	4	23
Plant-closing law	0	46	0	37
School prayer amendment	46	69	0	54
Central American policies	0	23	3	38
Affirmative Action	21	87	0	20
Homosexual antidiscrimination law	6	33	30	91
Equal Rights Amendment	18	33	12	60
Baby Doe regulations	14	59	12	43

In contrast, religion was used to criticize a law to protect homosexuals against job discrimination in the schools. Twenty-seven clergy said that God or the Bible said homosexuality is immoral and used this reason to justify their rejection of the law to protect homosexuals.

It is interesting that religion was used both to justify and to reject the Equal Rights Amendment. Clergy defended support for this amendment by saying that all men and women are equal in God's eyes. Some clergy, however, criticized the amendment because they believed that God has ordained that males should head the family.

Religion was also used to defend both responses to the Baby Doe issue. In defense of the regulations, clergy argued that God gives life and only he can take it. In opposition to the regulations, it was said that the government should not play God or interfere with God's will.

It was expected that conservatives would use religious reasons more often than liberals. Given the high percentages of reasons in defense of the school prayer amendment and against the law protecting homosexuals against discrimination that are religious, it would appear that conservatives did make greater use of religious justifications. We attempted a more systematic test of this conclusion.

To analyze which ministers are the most likely to give religious reasons to justify their positions on all the political issues, we computed the total number of nonreligious, political issue positions. Thus we excluded the school prayer amendment issue, for which the minister gave a religious reason. (In this particular analysis only the first mentioned reason for each position was used.) All variables that might logically be considered antecedent to or at least reciprocally related to the tendency to give religious reasons for issue positions were then correlated with this measure of "religious reasoning." Two of these variables had significant zero-order correlations with "religious reasoning." They were whether one had religious education or not ($r=-.18$, $p < .05$), and overall self-perceived political views ($r=.34$, $p < .01$), i.e., those with no religious education and who considered themselves politically conservatives were more likely to give a religious rationale for their political positions.

To assess further the relative importance of these two possible independent variables in predicting and/or possibly determining "religious reasoning," we placed both variables into a multiple regression equation as predictor variables, along with "religious reasoning" as the dependent variable. Although religious or ministerial education continued to have a moderate negative impact on religious reasoning ($beta=-.18$, $p < .08$), one's self-perceived political ideology had a greater impact on this tendency among these ministers ($beta=.32$, $p < .01$).

That is, religious ideology was unimportant in explaining the use of religion as justification for issue positions. It is unlikely that political conservatism itself motivates adherents to use religious reasons. Rather, it seems that political conservatives have positions on issues that allow for the direct use of religion as justification. Political conservatives are defending issues long upheld by conservative Christianity. Thus, politically conservative ministers find it easy to use religious justification for their political positions./9/

Nonreligious Justifications

A majority of the clergy, on all the issues, did not justify their attitudes on clearly religious grounds. How did these clergy justify their convictions?

Table 2.10 shows the most frequent nonreligious reasons used by the clergy. Most of the arguments for and against the nuclear freeze are quite practical, although some clergy defend the freeze because they reject war as a way of settling differences. With regard to a

TABLE 2.10
Nonreligious Justifications by Issue Positions
===

| | Dominant Non-religious Reasons |
| Issue and Position | (Number of Responses in Parentheses) |

Nuclear freeze

For — Fear destruction, disappearance of life (19)
Have enough nuclear weapons, arms race ridiculous
(10)
Against war, pacifist (9)

Against — Cannot trust Soviet Union (8)
Must be strong militarily (6)

Plant-closing law

For — Companies have responsibility to warn employees (10)
Avoid employee hardship (9)

Against — Government should not interfere with private economy (17)

School prayer amendment

For — People have basic right to pray (17)

Against — Already have freedom to pray (6)
Need to separate church and state (5)

Central American policies

For — Need to fight communism (8)

Against — Interfering with other's self- determination (7)
Supporting immoral governments (7)

Affirmative Action

For — Believe in equality, justice (22)

Against — Is reverse discrimination (7)

Homosexual antidiscrimination law

For — For protection of human rights and equality (10)

Against — Homosexuality is a perversion (7)
Can influence children to accept beliefs (5)
Don't want them in contact with children (5)

Equal Rights Amendment

For — Needed to provide equality, equal opportunity (16)

Against — Women already have protection, equal rights (6)

Baby Doe regulations

For — Believe in all attempts to save life, sanctity of life,
right to life (18)

Against — Against government invasion of privacy (6)
Parents, doctors, and pastors can make best decision (5)
Parents, not government, have to take care of children
(5)
All need dignity to die if life is hopeless (5)

plant-closing law, opponents espouse a laissez-faire philosophy; supporters refer both to the practical matter of employee hardship and to the principle of the moral responsibility of business. In relation to other issues, the clergy mention human rights and the rights of national self-determination, of equality and justice, of equal opportunity, of life, and of a dignified death, and they also mention the preference for a minimal government.

It is apparent from the justifications in Table 2.10 that on some issues clergy are not debating each other but talking past each other. Concerning school prayer, supporters argue that people have a right to pray, and opponents claim that people now have the freedom to pray. Proponents of the Equal Rights Amendment claim that the amendment is necessary to achieve equality, and opponents say woman are already equal or at least already have the legal tools to achieve equality.

As can be seen in Table 2.8, three issues were unrelated to religious or political ideology--plant-closing laws, affirmative action, and Baby Doe regulations. The lack of relation between ideological categories and position on affirmative action can be explained in part because of widespread acceptance of affirmative action and in part because black conservatives accept this government program. During the 1984 presidential campaign, Walter Mondale favored plant-closing laws, which makes the absence of relation between attitude on this issue and political ideology surprising. As can be seen in Table 2.10, reasons for and against such laws are ideological: those favoring plant-closing laws arguing about social responsibilities of business, those against, espousing a laissez-faire philosophy. Similarly, attitudes on Baby Doe regulations show sharp ideological differences. Those favoring such regulations defended their attitude in the name of the sacredness of life; those opposing these regulations argued against government involvement and for protection of the private realm. That positions on the issues of plant-closing laws and Baby Doe regulations are ideological, yet not related to political or religious self-identification, attests to the existence of important meaning systems not equated with current political or theological labels.

Three issues were related only to political ideology--nuclear freeze, Central American policies, and homosexual discrimination (Table 2.8). The arguments for and against the first two (Table 2.10), reveal that political conservatives apparently give especial importance to the perceived danger of communism. Liberal and conservative political labels are related to whether or not one evaluates situations primarily in terms of attitudes toward communism.

The issue of homosexual discrimination is unusual. It is more strongly related to political than religious ideology (Table 2.8), and yet those against the law to protect homosexuals frequently used religious reasons. Those favoring such a law tend to see the issue in terms of equal rights (Table 2.10). The interesting question is what is motivating the politically conservative clergy who use religion to justify their opposition to the antidiscrimination law.

As can be seen in Table 2.8, religious ideology is related to attitudes on the school prayer and Equal Rights Amendment, even after controlling for political ideology. The data in Table 2.9 show that religious reasons are frequently given for favoring the school prayer amendment but are less often used regarding the ERA, although such reasons are used by clergy both for and against the Equal Rights Amendment. It can be seen from Table 2.10 that a significant number of those favoring this amendment justified their opinion in the name of equality and equal opportunity. Considering all the information, we see that only the issue of the school prayer amendment seems to be specifically a religious issue and then only for those favoring the amendment.

All in all, the data in Tables 2.8, 2.9, and 2.10 suggest that in itself religion has played a minor role in shaping the attitudes of clergy on the issues studied. Instead, practical considerations, especially regarding the nuclear issue, are quite important in shaping attitudes. In addition, humanistic and laissez-faire ideologies, as well as attitudes toward communism, are significant in shaping clerical opinions.

DISCUSSION AND CONCLUSION

In the 1980s, it is meaningful to view Christianity as divided into liberal and conservative factions. At least in Middletown, but we believe nationally, the liberal churches are less homogeneous than the conservative ones; there are more theologically conservative ministers in liberal churches than vice versa. However, theologically

66

liberal ministers are more homogeneous on the issues
studied than conservative ministers. It would seem easier
to organize conservative churches than liberal churches
and liberal ministers rather than conservative ministers.

An obviously important question is how significant
are the attitudes of clergy in affecting public policy.
Two criteria seem useful: (1) the number of people hearing
the clergy's opinions and (2) the perceived expertise of
the clergy on an issue. We believe that the clergy are
perceived as being appropriate experts on a subject only
to the extent that an argument is justified in religious
terms. That is to say, clergy are likely to be effective
advocates only when they justify their issue position in
religious terms.

Which issue positions, then, are heard discussed by
many churchgoers in sermons and are justified in religious
terms? Fitting these criteria best are the conservative
positions in favor of the school prayer amendment and
against a law protecting homosexuals against discrimination
(Tables 2.7 and 2.9); next are the liberal positions in
support of affirmative action and the Equal Rights
Amendment. The high degree of public support given the
nuclear freeze in sermons is weakened, in our opinion,
by the lack of religious justification for this position.

We anticipate that conservative clergy will become
more effective political advocates. This is based on the
tendency of liberal clergy to use nonreligious justifications and the countertendency of theologically conservative leaders to cloak all issues in religious garb.

The editors of the Catholic publication Commonweal
recently discussed the Catholic church's teaching on
abortion.

The briefest investigation into Catholic teaching
would show that the church's case against abortion
is utterly unlike, say, its belief in the Real
Presence, i.e., of Christ in the Eucharist, known
with the eyes of faith alone, or its insistence on
a Sunday obligation applicable only to the faithful.
The church's moral teaching on abortion, as it
happens, is for the most part like its teaching on
racism, warfare, and capital punishment, based on
ordinary forms of moral reasoning common to believers
and nonbelievers (Editorial, 1984).

In this case, a somewhat liberal church justified a
conservative position, using a moral code no longer the

province of the Christian churches. Thus, ministers may not be perceived as the only interpreters of this code; in fact, the clergy may not even be accepted as the most authoritative source for learning about the application of this humanistic morality.

Characteristic of theological conservatives is the linking of major social issues with biblical arguments. President Ronald Reagan illustrated this approach when speaking before the conservative National Association of Evangelicals (Associated Press, 1983). The president urged the evangelists to use their pulpits to argue against the nuclear freeze. They should do this, he argued, because the struggle between the United States and the Soviet Union is a contest between good and evil. The president labeled the Soviet Union an evil empire. Obviously, this was an attempt to link the Soviets and Satan and thus justify opposition to the nuclear freeze.

Similarly, the Christian Right has set up an Institute for Christian Economics. A critic summarized the orientation of those at the institute as follows:

> The proper economic function of the state is to maintain conditions conducive to a free-market economy, i.e., to enact and to enforce rules supportive of private property, freedom of enterprise, freedom of contract, and the profit motive . . . , the Bible clearly and explicitly teaches that not only is the free-market economy totally compatible with God's will, but it is the only economic system acceptable to God (Van Dahm, 1984:29).

As an example of institute policy, the income tax is condemned because it is stealing. Thus, among the conservative leaders social issues are perceived directly in relation to biblical ideas and themes.

It may happen, therefore, that conservative clergy become more effective advocates of their conservative attitudes because of linking their positions on numerous issues to religion and thus to the source of their legitimacy and power. Whereas liberal churches such as the Catholic church are trying to gain confederates by using universalistic moral arguments, conservative preachers defend their arguments in quite particularistic terms. It may be that the liberal clergy, according to the general public, are going beyond their expertise, and are thereby less effective with their political voices than the conservative clergy.

NOTES

1. It seems that actions beyond preaching, such as civil disobedience, are related more to political than theological ideology (Nelson, Yokley, and Madron, 1973:384).

2. The classification was done by Professor George Jones, director of religious programs at Ball State University. All churches serving predominantly black congregations were placed in one category both because of the small number of such churches and because it was difficult to classify black churches using the liberal-conservative dichotomy. The categories contained independent churches and denominations, i.e., all churches of a denomination were classified as either liberal or conservative. White liberal denominations included the mainline Protestant churches and the Baptist Church of U.S.A.-American Convention, the Disciples of Christ church, Church of the Brethren, Friends church, Lutheran church (L.C.A. or A.L.C.), Unitarian-Universalist church, and the United Church of Christ.

3. Although there are only three Catholic churches in Middletown, all three are quite large (500 or more).

4. However, quite small white conservative denominations in Middletown were grouped together with independent churches for sampling purposes. Because of budget considerations, we tried to attain one hundred cases; the final number of completed cases was ninety-one. To attain this sample, we tried to interview 124 clergy (3 Catholic priests, 25 black ministers, 30 white liberal ministers, and 66 white conservative ministers). Only 7 persons refused to be interviewed (2 from white liberal churches, and 5 from white conservative churches). One problem encountered was simply reaching ministers of small churches either on the phone or in person at the churches.

Our primary goal in selecting the sample was to ensure diversity of religious orientations; the secondary goal was to include numerically important churches in the study. With respect to the black churches, all large congregations are represented in the study, except one church with a congregation of about a hundred persons; the other eight black churches not contacted each had thirty or fewer people as members. Among the white churches only one big church (a conservative church with perhaps six hundred participants) was not included in the study.

5. The data, of course, refer to Protestantism. There are only two Catholic clergy in the study. They agreed on only one issue; both favored a nuclear freeze.

6. For these issues, although chi square was not significant at the .05 level, the tau b statistic was significant.

7. Political liberals and moderates tended to be against the school prayer amendment and to favor the freeze. Only liberals were against Central American policies and for a law protecting homosexuals against discrimination.

8. As would be expected, political ideology was related to giving sermons on social issues. With regard to what we have labeled the liberal minister's issues--the nuclear freeze and Central American policies--it was only the political liberals who frequently gave sermons on these subjects; there was relatively little difference between the moderates and the conservatives. Concerning the conservative issues--the school prayer amendment and homosexuality--it was the political conservatives who spoke out. Being a political moderate meant being less outspoken on social issues.

9. A final religious and political topic dealt with in our analysis was the ministers' perception of how politicians use religion to support their political causes. Of the sixty-seven ministers who presented a clear example of this use when they were asked to give such, 47 percent referred to the attempt on the part of politicians, especially Ronald Reagan, to gain the votes of Christian fundamentalists by supporting their causes, such as school prayer.

To analyze which ministers were most likely to have this perception, all variables that might be considered antecedent to, or at least reciprocally related to, the perception that politicians use religion to seek the Christian fundamentalist vote were correlated with this judgment. Those variables that were significantly related were self-perceived political ideology, ($r=.33$, $p < .01$), self-perceived religious ideology, ($r=.29$, $p < .02$), and whether or not one had ministerial education ($r=.28$, $p < .02$); i.e., religious and political liberals with ministerial education were the most likely to see politicians employing religion to gain the support of Christian fundamentalists. This perception of the situation is consistent with our general analysis. It is the conservatives who use religion overtly and directly in regard to political issues.

REFERENCES

Associated Press. "Preach Against Weapons Freeze: Reagan." Ball State Daily News (9 March):1, 1983.

Editorial. "Religion and Politics: Clearing the Air." Commonweal, 7 September 1984.

Hadden, Jeffrey K. The Gathering Storm in the Churches. Garden City, N. Y.: Doubleday Anchor, 1970.

Johnson, Benton. "Theology and the Position of Pastors on Public Issues." American Sociological Review 32 (June):433-442, 1967.

Lynd, Robert S., and Helen M. Lynd. Middletown. New York: Harcourt, Brace, and World, 1929.

Nelson, Hart M. "Why Do Pastors Preach on Social Issues?" Theology Today 32 (April):56-73, 1975.

Nelson, Hart M., and Mary Ann Maguire. "The Two Worlds of Clergy and Congregation: Dilemma for Mainline Denominations." Sociological Analysis 41 (Spring):74-80, 1980.

Nelson, Hart M., Raytha Yokley, and Thomas Madron. "Ministerial Roles and Social Actionist Stance: Protestant Clergy and Protest in the Sixties." American Sociological Review 38 (June):375-386, 1973.

Quinley, Harold E. The Prophetic Clergy. New York: Wiley, 1974.

Stark, Rodney, et al. "Ministers as Moral Guides: The Sounds of Silence." Pp. 163-186 in Charles Y. Glock, ed., Religion in Sociological Perspective. Belmont, Calif.: Wadsworth, 1973.

Van Dahm, Thomas E. "The Christian Far Right and Economic Policy Issues." Journal of the American Scientific Affiliation (March):28-35, 1984.

Wood, James R. "Authority and Controversial Policy: The Churches and Civil Rights." American Sociological Review 35 (December):1057-1069, 1970.

Woodrum, Eric. "Toward a Theory of Tension in American Protestantism." Sociological Analysis 39(3):219-227, 1978.

3

Cacophony on Capitol Hill: Evangelical Voices in Politics

Richard V. Pierard

The picture of evangelical involvement in U.S. political life is confusing and complicated. In the two decades after the death in 1925 of fundamentalism's most prominent public figure, William Jennings Bryan, conservative Protestants lacked a personage in high office with whom they could identify and who seemed to speak for their interests. But in the 1940s a few voices began to be heard on Capitol Hill and in various statehouses that bore witness to a vital evangelical faith, and their numbers and influences increased during the 1950s, an era of genteel civil religiosity that was presided over by Dwight D. Eisenhower. By and large these evangelicals reflected a conservative political philosophy; however, emerging from the turmoil of the 1960s was a new breed of evangelical politician that was not prepared to bless every manifestation of the political and social status quo. In the 1970s, it became almost fashionable to claim a born-again experience, but the cleavages in political philosophy among evangelical public servants were so pronounced that it was virtually impossible for them to speak with unanimity on any political issue whatsoever. The clarion voice of conservatism that marked evangelical politics in the 1940s and 1950s had turned into a cacophony, a situation that was best exemplified in the campaign of 1980 when three avowedly born-again, presidential candidates with widely differing political programs presented themselves to the electorate.

The factor that considerably complicates any discussion of the role of evangelicals in politics is that of definition. Politicians are notorious for saying what their constituency wants to hear, and if they hail from a region characterized by a high level of religiosity,

their public statements and behavior tend to manifest a
certain measure of piety. Church membership or at least
identification with a specific denominational background
is obviously politically expedient, and few members of
Congress allow themselves to be placed in the category
of "none" in the tabulation of their religious affiliations
published biennially in Christianity Today. In fact,
a recent study by Peter L. Benson and Dorothy L. Williams
reveals that 90 percent of the members of Congress belong
to a church or synagogue, 71 percent affirm the divinity
of Jesus, and 46 percent regard Jesus as their personal
savior (Benson and Williams, 1982:41-42, 61). Few are
naive enough to believe that our elected officials are
appreciably more godly than the public at large, but this
study does reflect the current trend of politicians to
appropriate the trappings of evangelicalism.

It is patently clear that the evangelical world is
quite diverse, encompassing a spectrum of beliefs ranging
from strict Calvinism through confessional Lutheranism,
Wesleyan Arminianism to Anabaptist radicalism, and
including a variety of orientations on liturgy and church
polity, but nevertheless I will argue that two things can
be regarded as common denominators. The first is the
experience of regeneration, a spiritual renewal or rebirth
brought about by faith in the atoning death of Jesus Christ
and through the power of the Holy Spirit. The commitment
to Christ results in a personality reorientation as one
experiences divine forgiveness, and he or she is empowered
for a new life of worship, fellowship, and service. The
second is an unswerving belief in the divine inspiration
and authority of the Scriptures. The doctrinal structure
contained in the Bible implements and safeguards the
experience with Christ, prepares one for service in this
world, and ensures the hope of eternal life and joy in
the world to come.

I do not find it profitable to follow Gallup and
others like him who count anyone as an evangelical who
assents to a few selected religious propositions contained
in a survey (Gallup and Poling, 1980)./1/ This leads
to the grossly inflated estimates found in the media about
the numbers of evangelicals in the United States, estimates
that in turn feed an evangelical triumphalism. Also,
evangelicalism has evolved historically in different
directions from the nineteenth-century consensus that
existed. Southern denominationalism more or less preserved
the essential expression of the nineteenth-century
evangelicalism; in the North it took on a strongly

interdenominational character. Most of the leadership as well as the laity in the southern denominations continue to reflect a kind of conservative evangelicalism in the context of their institutional life rather than in the cooperative sense that typifies modern-day northern evangelicalism. This, however, has been breaking down in recent years as a result of the impact that interdenominational enterprises like the Billy Graham Crusades, Inter-Varsity Christian Fellowship, and Campus Crusade for Christ have had in the South and the internal dissension produced in such denominations as the Presbyterian church in the United States and the Southern Baptist Convention by doctrinal controversies, most notably biblical inerrancy./2/ When one thinks of fundamentalist-modernist controversies, one usually thinks of those in some mainline Protestant denominations that carried over into the twentieth century, but two important components of modern evangelicalism that should not be overlooked are the black church and Pentecostalism.

THE RELIGIOUS DEPRESSION

In his presidential address to the American Society of Church History in 1959, Robert T. Handy called attention to the "religious depression" that began settling in within U.S. Protestantism in the mid-1920s. The large denominations lost members, and income declined dramatically; foreign missionary interest and activity rapidly dwindled as well. The so-called sects prospered somewhat more during this era among the economically disinherited, and a strong interest in meeting social needs persisted within the churches, even among those on the theological right. It became apparent to many Protestants that the U.S. culture in which they had flourished and with which they so closely identified was on the way out, and conservatives and liberals divided in their response to the newly emerging situation. The conservatives withdrew from involvement in the larger culture and concentrated on the internal development of their institutions. Liberals came to accept almost without question the new order in which the idea of a national Protestant church was passe. They accepted their status as just one of the three religious communities into which the United States was divided (Judaism and Catholicism were the other two--see Handy, 1960).

It is safe to say that with the passing of William Jennings Bryan from the scene, conservative evangelicals

were left without an effective voice in national politics.
To be sure, there were some political figures from the
South who participated in antievolution and fundamentalist
endeavors at the state level, and in 1925, George F.
Washburn was able to recruit a few nationally known
personalities to serve on the "International Advisory
Council" of his Bible Crusaders of America. Among these
were Florida Governor John A. Martin, U.S. Senator Park
Trammell (Florida), and Representatives T. W. Wilson
(Mississippi) and H. E. Rowbottom (Indiana). The group
wanted to bring the country "back to Christ, the Bible,
and the Constitution," and ultimately they hoped to secure
an amendment making the United States a Christian nation,
but the venture fizzled out within a year (Furniss,
1954:58-62). Actually, as Robert Miller suggested, there
was no real consensus on opposition to the teaching of
evolution, even among Southern Baptists, and the crusade
was doomed to defeat (Miller, 1958:159-166)
     After the antievolution, fundamentalist forces failed
to secure legislative victories, they redirected their
efforts into the campaign against Alfred E. Smith's bid
for the presidency. This was clearly the case in North
Carolina in 1927, as Willard Gatewood showed in his study
of the controversy there (Gatewood, Jr., 1966). Conservative Protestants in general were leery of the Catholic
New Yorker's candidacy, and no major fundamentalist figure
was probably more active in working for his defeat than
John Roach Straton, pastor of Calvary Baptist Church in
New York City, who denounced Smith as "the deadliest foe
in America today of the forces of moral progress and true
political wisdom." Straton's fight to keep Smith out of
the White House was part of his old struggle with the
evolutionists. In his view, the teaching of evolution
and materialism was responsible for the effort to "nullify"
Prohibition legislation and for what he felt was Smith's
laxity toward its enforcement (Moore, 1956:188-189).
     Conservative Protestants freely engaged in anti-
Catholic bigotry against Smith, especially those in the
Deep South, where they linked Catholicism, Tammany Hall,
repeal of Prohibition, and antisegregation into a package
of hate directed at the Democratic standard- bearer. Some
even insisted that if Smith were to win, Anglo-Saxon,
Protestant civilization would be in jeopardy. Methodist
Bishop James M. Cannon, Jr., of Virginia, was the principal
figure in mobilizing southern Protestant feeling, but
Edmund Moore's study of the 1928 campaign identified a

number of other Methodists, Baptists, Presbyterians, and Lutherans who were equally as bigoted. Cannon, who headed the Southern Methodist Board of Temperance, Prohibition, and Public Morals, gained so much public attention in 1928 that he considered the possibility of running for the U.S. Senate seat of Carter Glass.

In a dramatic speech before an audience of hostile clergy in Oklahoma City on September 20, 1928, Governor Smith tried vainly to disarm the ecclesiastical opposition, much as John F. Kennedy was to do in Houston thirty-two years later. The next day Straton, who had come to Oklahoma City for the occasion, launched the counter-attack. With him on the platform was Mordecai Fowler Ham, a fiery southern evangelist (Only six years later he would bring a young North Carolina boy named Billy Graham to Christ), who thundered forth, "If you vote for Al Smith, you're voting against Christ and you'll all be damned" (Moore, 1956:188-189).

How much of a role anti-Catholic bigotry actually played in the evangelical campaign against Smith is a matter of debate. Robert Miller (1958:51-58) thought that the principal factor in Protestant opposition both in the North and the South was Smith's anti-Prohibition stance./3/ Whatever the case, the evangelicals had won only a skirmish in 1928. The repeal of the Eighteenth Amendment in 1933 constituted an even greater defeat than the one they suffered on the evolution issue.

It was clear by the mid-1920s that widespread public dissatisfaction with National Prohibition existed, while the effectiveness of the most important lobby against the liquor traffic, the Anti-Saloon League, steadily waned. Moreover, the evangelicals' most ardent spokesman, Bishop Cannon, was discredited in 1930 by revelations that he had engaged in stock speculation, in profiteering on hoarded flour in World War I, and in some irregular financial dealings as a lobbyist in 1920 and had carried on an affair with his secretary (whom he eventually married) even before his first wife's death (Kyvig, 1979:135-136). With the onset of the depression, the unpopularity and unworkability of National Prohibition became more and more obvious, and the evangelical drys were in such a state of disarray that they could no longer hold back the tide of sentiment for repeal. With the demise of Prohibition and the coming of the New Deal, the conservative Protestants seemed politically paralyzed.

THE EVANGELICALS REENTER POLITICS

The later 1930s were a period of political reaction
for the fundamentalists. Some, like Gerald B. Winrod and
Gerald L. K. Smith, drifted into the fascist camp, but
most fundamentalists contented themselves with denouncing
communism, the New Deal, and the social gospel from their
pulpits and publications. Winrod himself ran
unsuccessfully for the Republican nomination for U.S.
Senator in Kansas in 1938.

A few people began to appear on the congressional
scene who openly identified themselves as Christians of
the evangelical variety. One of these was Frank Carlson,
a teetotaling Baptist farmer from Kansas who entered the
House of Representatives as a Republican in 1935 and served
six terms. From 1947 to 1950 he was governor of his state
and after that was elected to the U.S. Senate where he
remained until his retirement in 1968 at the age of
seventy-five. A regular advocate of Christian causes,
Carlson was a prime mover behind the presidential prayer
breakfast idea (Current Biography, 1949, pp. 93-94;
Biographical Dictionary of the American Congress
1774-1971, p. 706).

A second prominent evangelical in Congress was Dr.
Walter H. Judd. A Congregationalist, Judd had been a
leader in the Student Volunteer Movement and had gone out
under the American Board of Commissioners for Foreign
Missions as a medical missionary to China in the periods
1925-1931 and 1934-1938. Forced out by the Japanese
occupation of his area, he returned home and opened a
medical practice in Minneapolis. He spent considerable
time on the lecture circuit discussing U.S. foreign policy
interests in the Pacific. This experience led to his
decision to run for the House of Representatives in 1942.
He served ten terms as a Republican until liberals in his
state finally succeeded in ousting him from office in 1962.

Judd was an unwavering critic of communism and Red
China, and in the 1950s he was a principal figure in the
so-called China lobby. His outspoken conservatism made
him a popular figure in conservative circles, and he was
a frequent recipient of the George Washington Medal from
the Freedoms Foundation, a leading right-wing
organization. His outlook is typified by the following
quotations from a 1968 interview:

Neither China nor Vietnam was just a civil war. Both
of them were armed Communist rebellions to overthrow

a legitimate government as part of the Communist drive
for world dominance. By calling it "civil war" it
made it easier to demand our withdrawal. The
Communists are masters of propaganda, and when they
start a line, the first thing you know you have
professors and clergymen and businessmen reciting
as by rote, the Communist slogans, the phrases which
slant people's thinking. . . .

[Richard] Nixon's bad image has been skillfully
created, like the image of Chiang Kai-shek. The
Communists and those "liberals" who insisted on
trusting Russia never forgave Nixon for one reason--he
was an effective anti-Communist. The two men the
Communists have hated worst of anybody in the world
are Chiang Kai-shek and Franco. I would say the third
one is Nixon. He exposed their darling, Alger Hiss.

With some, his name has been mud ever since.
So where do his enemies attack him? They attack him
where he's really strongest, his integrity. I have
not known one man in political life who's straighter
than Richard Nixon (Rozek, 1980:16, 25-26).

Another outstanding Christian to enter national public
life in this period was Democrat Brooks Hays of Arkansas
(Hays, 1959; Hays, 1981). After failing in earlier
attempts to win the governorship and a seat in Congress,
in 1942 Hays was elected to the House of Representatives
where he quickly established a reputation as a moderate
on the race question and worked for the passage of civil
rights measures. He supported bills to abolish segregation
in interstate travel, eliminate poll taxes, combat
lynching, and implement fair employment practices. His
unwillingness to back Govenor Orval Faubus in the Little
Rock school crisis led to his defeat in 1958 by a
segregationist candidate in a write-in campaign engineered
by the governor's office. He accepted a post at Wake
Forest College in North Carolina, and some years later,
in 1972, friends persuaded Hays to try to unseat the local
Republican congressman, Wilmer D. "Vinegar Bend" Mizell.
Mizell was a staunch conservative (Americans for Democratic
Action rating of 0 for his total lack of support for any
liberal legislation) who himself publicly expressed his
Christian commitment and belonged to a Christian and
Missionary Alliance church. However, the Nixon-Helms
landslide of that year doomed this to failure (Hays,
1981:262-269; Pippert, 1973:141-151).

An active Baptist layman, Hays served as president
of the Southern Baptist Convention from 1957 to 1959 and
in Washington was a member of the dually-aligned Calvary
Baptist Church. He often expressed his Christian
convictions on the race issue and even helped to secure
passage of the landmark Christian Life Commission report
"Call for Racial Reconciliation" by the convention in
1958. Also, in 1953 Hays sponsored the House resolution
for the establishment of a prayer room in the Capitol.
He declared that the action was quite consistent with his
devotion to the doctrine of separation of church and state
because the impregnable wall must not be impenetrable.
He said there must be communication between religion and
politics, even though church people and politicians must
not dictate to each other. He confessed that on several
occasions when he was faced with problems, he used the
prayer room to meditate on the resources available to him,
and thus it was valuable not only "as a symbol of our moral
foundations, but more importantly as a practical facility
for individual use" (Hays, 1981:174-176).

Among the more noteworthy politicians at the state
level during this period who openly confessed their
Christian faith were Governor Arthur B. Langlie of
Washington (1941-1945; 1949-1957) and especially Governor
Luther W. Youngdahl of Minnesota (1947-1951). While in
office the latter spoke of combatting social problems that
threaten the survival of freedom--slums, overcrowded
schools, neglect of the mentally retarded and handicapped,
and racial discrimination--and he utilized the assistance
of church people to secure passage of a bill banning slot
machines in his state. At the same time, he declared that
the nation's "freedom comes from God and it will be under
God that we will continue to be free." The most important
prerequisite for a strong and free nation is "a worn and
beaten way to where the people go to pray" (Youngdahl,
1961:45-48).

Two noteworthy developments in this period that helped
mobilize the reawakening political consciousness of
evangelicals were the creation of International Christian
Leadership (ICL) and the National Association of
Evangelicals (NAE). ICL was the vision of Abram Vereide,
a Norwegian immigrant who became a Methodist preacher in
Washington state and did fruitful work among new arrivals
from Scandinavia. He fell in love with his adopted country
and worked to make the immigrants into industrious and
patriotic citizens. The depression brought him more into

social ministries, especially Goodwill Industries, and he became convinced that it would take changed men to change society. In 1935, he initiated the practice of meeting with civic and business leaders in Seattle for breakfast to study the Bible and pray together. One of the people who came was a city councilman and later mayor, Arthur B. Langlie, and after Langlie became governor, he asked Vereide to help plan a prayer breakfast. The idea soon caught on around the country.

Then Vereide went to Washington, began calling on people in Congress and other notable figures, and in January 1942, organized the first prayer breakfast at the Willard Hotel. About the same time, prayer groups formed independently in both the House and Senate. Vereide moved to the capital in 1943 and formed an organization that eventually settled on the name International Christian Leadership. The group secured a building that it named "Fellowship House" to be a center for its ministry of reaching and nurturing for Christ the nation's leaders. Although a firmly committed evangelical, Vereide possessed a loving and ecumenical spirit that contributed immeasurably to his ability to communicate to people in public life. As the years went by, ICL sponsored prayer breakfasts in Washington and around the country, but at the same time, it continued to work quietly in ministering on a small-group or even an one-on-one basis with people in places of leadership. In order to keep the operation as low key as possible, ICL was formally disbanded in 1971, and the group is now simply called "the Fellowship" (Grubb, 1961; Hefley and Plowman, 1975:81-100).

The creation of the National Association of Evangelicals in 1942 provided conservative Protestants with a cooperative voice that quickly took on a political dimension. In the following year, space was secured for a Washington office and a "director of public affairs" appointed to provide services for missionary agencies affiliated with the NAE, certify chaplains for the military, and counter the machinations of Catholics who might undermine church-state separation. A former missionary, Dr. Clyde W. Taylor, took charge of the NAE Office of Public Affairs in 1944 and served in the post until named general director of the NAE in 1963. Then retired naval officer Floyd Robertson, Taylor's assistant, ran the office and after his retirement from the NAE position in 1977 was succeeded by Robert P. Dugan, a Baptist pastor and unsuccessful Republican candidate in Colorado for Congress.

As James L. Adams points out, the NAE OFfice of Public Affairs was the nearest thing to a conservative church lobby in Washington until the 1970s, but it did not see itself as such and its staff members did not register as lobbyists. Its function was to inform the NAE constituency about legislation and to intercede with the government in missionary and chaplaincy matters. This was done through informational letters, organizing seminars in Washington, and establishing personal contact with government officials and lawmakers (Adams, 1970:264-266).

However, the NAE was particularly interested in things relating to separation of church and state, and one spokesman in the 1950s called it a "watchman" in the nation's capitol. The NAE appointed a special committee in 1948 to look after religious liberty concerns and sent Stephen W. Paine as its representative to the National Conference on Human Rights in 1949 in order to present the "evangelical Christian" viewpoint on civil rights. It is interesting that Paine, in his speech, criticized the United Nations Declaration of Human Rights for being based on false (i.e., humanistic) assumptions and leading in the direction of statism and socialism. The NAE also campaigned to have the U.S. representation at the Vatican discontinued, a matter that had upset many of them since December 1939 when Franklin Roosevelt, as a war measure, had named Myron C. Taylor as the president's special envoy to the Vatican. When Harry S. Truman reappointed him as envoy, the NAE kept up the attack, and Taylor resigned in January 1950. The following year Truman announced the appointment of a regular ambassador to the Vatican, and the NAE Washington office in cooperation with Protestants and Other Americans United engaged in a vigorous propaganda effort to arouse public opinion. As a result, the effort to send an ambassador was dropped (Murch, 1956:135-150).

A 1956 listing of the Office of Public Affairs interests reveals the basic conservatism of the NAE's political endeavor. These include religious liberty (from Catholic encroachment), civil rights (for the individual citizen), no federal aid for or control of public schools as well as rights for Bible reading and distribution in public schools, reasonable limitations on immigration, legislation to restrict the advertising, sale, and manufacture of liquor, outlawing the sale and distribution of pornographic literature, encouraging the investigation of subversive activities and enactment of laws protecting the nation from the menace of communism, and opposition to statism and fascism (government regimentation and bureaucratic controls) (Murch, 1956: 151-152).

THE EVANGELICALS ARRIVE--THE EISENHOWER YEARS

Evangelicals greeted the election of Dwight D. Eisenhower with the highest level of enthusiasm in decades. The time had finally arrived when the nation would return to godliness, because Eisenhower had "brought in a new moral tone and spiritual vitality into American life" and was "the focal point of a moral resurgence and spiritual awakening of national proportion," as his pastor Edward L. R. Elson put it (Pierard, 1979). On inauguration day the president-elect, cabinet members, and their families attended a special worship service at Elson's National Presbyterian Church to secure strength from "prayer and the Word of God for his overwhelming new responsibilities." After taking the oath of office Eisenhower recited a "little private prayer" that he had composed in his hotel room that morning; in his inaugural address he called for spiritual rededication and moral renewal on the part of the people of the United States. A few days later, Eisenhower was baptized and received into the membership of National Presbyterian Church, an event unique in presidential history. He appointed a staff assistant, Congregationalist minister Frederic E. Fox, to coordinate the president's religious activities and serve as a liaison with the public and religious interest groups on such matters. He annually declared a National Day of Prayer (as required by a law passed in 1952) and lent his prestige to a Pray for Peace movement that authorized postage stamps to be cancelled with this motto.

On February 5, 1953, at the Mayflower Hotel, Senator Carlson presided over the first Presidential Prayer Breakfast. Now known as the National Prayer Breakfast, this has become an annual event in the capital (Pierard, 1982). Eisenhower expressed his feelings about prayer in terms that must have made every evangelical heart in the room throb with joy:

When we came to that turning point in history, when we intended to establish a government for freemen and a Declaration and Constitution to make it last, in order to explain such a system we had to say, "We hold that all men are endowed by their creator."

82

> In one sentence, we established that every free
> government is imbedded soundly in a deeply felt
> religious faith or it makes no sense. . . .
>   I think that prayer is just simply a necessity,
> because by prayer I believe we mean an effort to get
> in touch with the Infinite. Our prayers are imperfect
> but if we make the effort, then there is something
> that ties us all together and we have begun in our
> grasp of that basis of understanding which is that
> all free government is firmly founded in a deeply
> felt religious faith (Congressional Record 99,
> February 10, 1953:A573).

Although attempts continued during the 1950s to secure
passage of a "Christian Amendment" acknowledging the
country's allegiance to Jesus Christ, they came to naught,
but two highly significant acts of official religiosity
did gain congressional approval, the addition of the words
"under God" to the Pledge of Allegiance in 1954 and the
adoption of "In God We Trust" as the national motto in
1956. One of the principal stimuli for the former was
a sermon by a distinguished evangelical preacher, the
Reverend George M. Docherty, and a groundswell of opinion
expressed by people in conservative churches helped to
secure its passage. The proposal to put on paper money
the four words that had been on coins since the early 1900s
was defended by Representative Charles E. Bennett of
Florida in words that almost any conservative evangelical
preacher in the decade might have used:

> In these days when imperialistic and materialistic
> communism seeks to attack and to destroy freedom,
> it is proper for us to seek continuously for ways
> to strengthen the foundations of our freedom. At
> the base of our freedom is our faith in God and the
> desire of Americans to live by His will and by His
> guidance. As long as this country trusts in God,
> it will prevail. To remind all of us of this
> self-evident truth, it is proper that our currency
> should carry these inspiring words (Congressional
> Record 101, April 13, 1955:4384).

During this era, Billy Graham established a working
relationship with the White House that was to become the
hallmark of his career as a preacher. It was one of the
best examples of how evangelicals were then finding

acceptance and exercising influence in high places. The
youthful evangelist had learned from his disastrous visit
with President Truman in 1950 the necessity to be
circumspect in his dealings with the chief executive;
moreover, Graham, a boundless admirer of Eisenhower, was
essentially mesmerized by him. The president utilized
his assistance in helping to relax tensions generated by
civil rights and desegregation measures, and in turn Graham
offered Eisenhower gratuitous advice on spiritual and
political matters./4/

Especially interesting is the relationship that
developed between Graham and Nixon. Graham, during his
1952 crusade in Washington, had become acquainted with
Senator Nixon, and their friendship blossomed in the en-
suing years. As vice president, Nixon even addressed the
huge crowd that assembled in Yankee Stadium at one of the
principal rallies of Graham's New York campaign in 1957.
The Graham-Nixon correspondence during Nixon's vice
presidential years has recently become available, and it
reveals just how close the two were in the 1950s./5/

Beginning in August 1956, Graham usually addressed
him as "Dear Dick," and the level of effusive praise was
even greater than that which he showered upon Eisenhower.
Graham wrote, "you are the greatest Vice President in
history" (January 7, 1956). "I want to commend you for
adhering to the highest moral and spiritual principles"
in the 1956 campaign (November 10, 1956). In your trip
to Africa, "you have done the greatest job of goodwill
building in modern times. Your own personal stature has
grown considerably. I am convinced you are well on the
road to being the next president of the United States"
(March 28, 1957). "I have been reading your speeches word
for word. They are excellent!" (December 2, 1957). "I
am gratified that your prestige continues to rise
throughout the country" (August 27, 1958).   As for
criticisms of you, they "do not bother me in the
slightest. . . . I believe with God's help you are going
to be the next president" (November 17, 1959).

In 1960, Graham actually functioned as an unofficial
adviser to the Nixon campaign. In letter after letter,
he passed on information he had heard and suggested how
Nixon might use the religious issue to his advantage.
For example, in a letter on June 21, Graham told Nixon
that Kennedy would capture almost 100 percent of the
Catholic vote, and no matter how much "you play up to
them--even if you had a Catholic running mate, you would

not even crack five or ten percent of the Catholic vote."
Thus, since Protestant voters outnumber the Catholics three
to one, "you must concentrate on solidifying the Protestant
vote." The way to do this is choose as your running mate
the "one man in the Republican Party that has the support
of both liberals and conservatives within the Protestant
church, and that is Dr. Walter Judd. . . . It is my opinion
he would be almost a must." Graham went on to give what
must have been some of the most amazing advice in the
campaign:

> Though, as I have said before, Dr. Judd ought to be
> Secretary of State, yet if Kennedy is nominated you
> must seriously consider him as your running mate.
> I am desperately afraid that there is a possibility
> of your not only losing all of the Catholic votes
> but much of the tolerant Protestant vote. With Dr.
> Judd, I believe the two of you could present a picture
> to America that would put much of the South and border
> states in the Republican column and bring about a
> dedicated Protestant vote to counteract the Catholic
> vote.

Graham concluded by saying he would "appreciate your
considering this letter in utter confidence--you would
do me a favor by destroying it after reading it."
Unfortunately for Graham, Nixon neglected to destroy it,
as he failed to do with some tape recordings a dozen years
later.

In September, a number of evangelical clergy took
part in a one-day meeting of Citizens for Religious
Freedom, which Donald Gill of the NAE Office of Public
Affairs convened in Washington. Graham encouraged Peale
to attend, but he left after the morning session when he

Although he spent the summer in Switzerland, Graham
followed things from afar and kept sending letters advising
Nixon on the religious angle of the campaign. In fact,
he had a conference there with twenty-five clergy from
the United States, including Norman Vincent Peale, and
he and Peale were commissioned to urge Nixon to say more
about his religious convictions in his speeches (August
22, 1960). Graham wavered about whether he should come
out publicly for Nixon, said in several letters that he
was about to do so, and actually wrote an article for
Life magazine testifying to Nixon's merits, but it was
withdrawn at the last minute (Pierard, 1980)./6/

saw the direction in which the conference was going. It discussed the possible impact of the election of a Catholic president on religious liberty and was heavily criticized in the press (Pierard, 1980:120). This flurry of activity in the 1960 election campaign symbolized just how far evangelicals had come in the 1950s in making their presence felt in public life, but the activity was essentially conservative in orientation. The evangelicals had nothing to offer toward solving the pressing problems of the time except to sweep them under the rug of piety and patriotism.

AT HOME IN CAESAR'S PALACE

In the 1960s, evangelicals had arrived politically. Several of their number were elected to the Congress in the 1950s and early or mid-1960s, and identification with a denominational body was the accepted thing to do. Representatives James C. Wright, Jr., (Texas), Elford A. Cedarberg (Michigan), Albert H. Quie (Minnesota), Charles E. Bennett (Florida), John Duncan (Tennessee), and John Dellenback (Oregon) all were known as active Christians. At the beginning of the 1970s, they were joined by two dynamic black clergymen, Walter Fauntroy (Washington, D.C.), and Andrew Young (Georgia). In the Senate were people like John Stennis (Mississippi), John McClellan (Arkansas), Carl T. Curtis (Nebraska), Jennings Randolph (West Virginia), and Harold E. Hughes (Iowa) who began to articulate Christian convictions publicly. Active prayer groups existed in both houses of Congress and in various governmental units around the capital city. Although John Kennedy tended to keep Billy Graham at arm's length, presidents Lyndon Johnson and Richard Nixon welcomed him into the circle of their advisers./7/
By far the two best known evangelical lawmakers who entered Congress in this period were Representative John B. Anderson of Illinois and Senator Mark O. Hatfield of Oregon. They were distinguished by a sense of courage and forthrightness that set them apart as leaders among the evangelical grouping in Congress. Anderson, an Evangelical Free Church layman, was elected to the House in 1960 and was a moderately conservative Republican. The NAE even named him Layman of the Year in 1974. His moment of truth came in 1968 when in the aftermath of the assassination of Martin Luther King, Jr., the capital city was racked by fires and rioting. He was in a position

to cast the swing vote in the House Rules Committee on the open housing bill that would become the Civil Rights Act of 1968. Anderson decided on the basis of his Christian conviction about the need for justice to vote in favor of the bill even though this action went against his conservative upbringing. From this point on, he became known as a man of conscience (Anderson, 1970; Anderson, 1975).

Mark Hatfield, a Conservative Baptist layman and like Anderson, a Republican, first was governor of Oregon and in 1966 was elected to the Senate. One of the bright young men of his party, he was selected to give the keynote address at the 1964 Republican National Convention and was widely considered to be a likely candidate for vice president within a few years. In fact, in 1968 Billy Graham urged Nixon to name Hatfield as his running mate, but Nixon opted instead for Spiro Agnew. Hatfield, meanwhile, had strayed from the party line for conscience's sake and had come out firmly against the war in Vietnam. At both the 1965 and 1966 national governor's conferences, he cast the lone dissenting vote on a resolution supporting the U.S. Vietnam policy (Eells and Nyberg, 1979; Hatfield, 1968; Hatfield, 1971; and Hatfield, 1976).

The fact that two evangelical Republicans could break with their traditional conservative outlooks to vote their conscience on distinctively moral issues indicated that a cleavage was developing in the solidly conservative political outlook that had characterized evangelicalism since Bryan's death. Two recent studies of evangelical political involvement, by Erling Jorstad and by Robert Booth Fowler, demonstrate that conservatism had reigned virtually supreme in the evangelical camp until into the mid-1960s (Jorstad, 1981:20-27; Fowler, 1983)./8/ Lyndon Johnson had won over many erstwhile conservatives for his civil rights program and War on Poverty, and even Billy Graham came out in favor of the president's domestic policy. Graham's old conservatism was beginning to erode as well. Although many evangelicals had backed the Barry Goldwater candidacy in 1964, Johnson succeeded in keeping Graham loyal to him. The Far Right, which had made so many inroads into evangelicalism in the 1950s and early 1960s, was also losing its appeal (Roy, 1953; Jorstad, 1970; and Pierard, 1970).

Richard Nixon, however, was proving to be seductive to evangelicals, and Graham naturally became his principal religious adviser. Graham offered a prayer at the inauguration in 1969, preached at more of Nixon's White House religious services than any other minister and was frequently called on the telephone for spiritual counsel or a friendly chat. The president spoke at Graham's East Tennessee crusade in Knoxville in 1970 and at the Billy Graham Day celebration in Charlotte, North Carolina, on October 15, 1971. Critics began labeling him as the "White House chaplain" and "court preacher." Reinhold Niebuhr suggested in the August 4, 1969, issue of Christianity and Crisis that there was a "Nixon-Graham" doctrine that all religion is virtuous in guaranteeing public justice and that a religious change of heart, such as that occurring in an individual conversion, would cure the problem of sin.

But a solid front on political questions no longer existed in evangelicalism. Those clustered around the radical publications The Other Side (founded 1965) and Sojourners (begun as The Post-American in 1971) challenged the social and economic status quo and had little patience with the conservatism of evangelical establishment organs like the NAE and Christianity Today. More and more ministers were speaking out against the Vietnam conflict, and Graham in particular came under increasing pressure to condemn the war. When most of the established evangelicals openly supported Nixon's reelection in 1972, a group of dissenters (not all of whom were young) formed an "Evangelicals for McGovern" committee to raise the moral issues that were being ignored in the campaign--social and racial justice, Vietnam, idolatry of the nation, and something new, Watergate (Fowler, 1983).

THE ERA OF BORN-AGAIN POLITICS

Mark Hatfield became increasingly concerned about the malaise that was settling over the country because of Vietnam and the Watergate cover-up, and he used the occasion of the 1973 National Prayer Breakfast to call attention to the

danger of misplaced allegiance, if not outright idolatry of failing to distinguish between the god of an American civil religion and the God who reveals Himself in the Holy Scriptures and in Jesus Christ. . . . If we as leaders appeal to the god of civil religion, our faith is in a small and exclusive deity,

a loyal spiritual advisor to power and prestige, a
defender of only the American nation, and the object
of a national folk religion devoid of moral content.
But if we pray to the Biblical God of justice and
righteousness, we fall under God's judgment for
calling upon His name, but failing to obey His
commands.

He went on to tell "the wealthy and the powerful" who were
sitting there that those "who follow Christ will more often
find themselves not with comfortable majorities, but with
miserable minorities," and that individually and as a
nation we must repent. Lives lived in obedience to Christ
"may well put us at odds with values of our society, abuses
of political power, and cultural conformity of our church."
We need to take seriously the necessity to be transformed
by Christ and be His messengers of reconciliation and peace
so that "we can soothe the wounds of war and renew the
face of the earth and all mankind" (Hatfield, 1976:94-95).
    This ringing attack on civil religion, an attack that
brought down the wrath of the Nixon administration upon
Hatfield and even a mild rebuke from Billy Graham, showed
that the evangelical support for the status quo was
eroding. Evangelicals had finally become entrenched in
the "corridors of power," but there were some who felt
uneasy about it. The Watergate revelations and the
resignation of Richard Nixon proved just how fragile the
evangelicals' newly found political power base was. Even
the embarrassed Graham had to admit he had been deceived
by his longtime friend (Fowler, 1983:227-232; Pierard,
1980:8-9). He would no longer be the spiritual adviser
and intimate of presidents, although he continued on
friendly terms with the next three occupants of the White
House.
    It is interesting that some of the Watergate
principals, most notably Charles Colson, James McCord,
and Jeb Magruder, found Christ in the wake of the
experience that shattered their lives. Douglas Coe, who
had succeeded Vereide at the Fellowship, and Harold Hughes,
who had retired from the Senate, along with others,
witnessed to them and showed them the way of Christianity
(Hefley and Plowman, 1975; Hughes, 1976; and Magruder,
1974)./10/
    The Bicentennial observance gave the nation an
opportunity to relax and to recover from the twin traumas
of Watergate and Vietnam. Evangelicals plunged
wholeheartedly into the national exultation, and their

expressions of civil religiosity knew virtually no bounds. A group of conservative Christians brought together by Campus Crusade leader Bill Bright and Arizona Representative John B. Conlan developed a scheme to capture more positions of power in the government and counteract the growing liberal influence among evangelicals in politics, but it misfired when Sojourners magazine exposed the venture, and Conlan was defeated in a bid for a U.S. Senate seat (Pierard, 1976; Wallis and Michaelson, 1976).

The evangelicals were now in deep disarray. The conservative camp was led by personalities like Conlan and Senator Jesse Helms of North Carolina (Helms, 1976; Conlan, 1976), while Anderson and Hatfield were looked up to by liberals. Other figures of liberal or moderate persuasion began to appear in the evangelical constellation--Representative Paul Simon (Illinois), Governor Reubin Askew (Florida), and above all the former governor of Georgia, Jimmy Carter, who was campaigning for the Democratic presidential nomination. The last had the most impeccable evangelical credentials of any other candidate since Bryan, and he fearlessly and frequently expressed his convictions as a born-again Southern Baptist. An active churchman as well, he taught Sunday School and even took part in a short-term mission among Spanish-speaking people in Massachusetts (Carter, 1975; Kucharsky, 1976; Norton and Slosser, 1976; and Baker, 1977).

With the nomination of Carter, conservatives found it would be expedient to portray the incumbent, President Gerald Ford, as being born again as well, and the story was widely disseminated that he was "an acknowledged follower of Jesus Christ." During his congressional years, Ford allegedly had come to know Billy Zeoli, an evangelical film producer from Michigan, who brought him to a knowledge of Christ and met often with him to pray and discuss Scriptures. Ford's son, Michael, who was studying for the ministry at Gordon-Conwell Theological Seminary at the time of the Watergate crisis, and Zeoli were essentially his spiritual counselors. It is odd that Ford did not mention Zeoli at all in his memoirs and his press secretary Jerald terHorst is silent on this as well (Hefley and Plowman, 1975:13-36; Ford, 1979; terHorst, 1974).

Recognizing the need to strengthen his ties with the evangelical community, Ford decided to address the joint convention of the NAE and the National Religious Broadcasters in Washington on February 22, 1976, the first

time a president had ever done so, and he was received
with "thunderous and enthusiastic applause," as one
eyewitness put it. He delighted his audience with a
description of how the United States was a "uniquely
blessed nation" and said the answer to the country's
problems today is to "believe in God" and "believe in the
faith of our fathers" (Michaelson, 1976:8-9).

As president, Jimmy Carter sought to implement the
compassion he had spoken about so much in his campaign
speeches, but the deteriorating economy and Iranian hostage
situation together with his own political inexperience
forestalled this. Still, as Wesley Pippert brought out,
he was a deeply spiritual man and one of the most
articulate spokesmen for the Christian faith ever to sit
in the Oval Office (Pippert, 1978; Maddox, 1984).

These qualities did not satisfy the evangelical
conservatives who saw his liberal views as anathema. They
began to form a new coalition with secular conservatives
called the "New Right," and in 1978 scored spectacular
victories by ousting liberal senators in New Hampshire,
Iowa, and Colorado. In 1979, three distinctly religious
organizations were formed, Moral Majority, Christian Voice,
and The [Religious] Roundtable, and the "preachers in
politics" girded up their loins to do battle for the Lord
against the "godless liberals" and "secular humanists"
who had seized the positions of power in this country.
The electronic preachers of the New Christian Right
immediately attracted the attention of the mass media,
which believed their vastly inflated claims to have a
viewing audience in the tens of millions and the power
to control the votes of these people./11/

The most anomalous situation of all came in 1980 when
the three men who vied for the presidency all professed
to be born again--Jimmy Carter, John B. Anderson, and
Ronald Reagan. Evangelicals in large numbers, urged on
by the prophets of the New Right, abandoned the two proven
advocates of a evangelical Christian presence in politics
and supported the "Johnny come lately." Reagan, the
once-divorced movie actor from California, was now
considered the upholder of the ideals of morality and
national righteousness because he opposed abortion,
homosexuality, and the teaching of evolution and favored
public school prayer, tuition tax credits for private
schools, increased defense spending, a sound dollar, and
dismantling much of the welfare state.

Reagan's victory was due to dissatisfaction over high
inflation and unemployment, not to the efforts of the New

Christian Right televangelists. Consequently, they did not gain access to the inner sanctum of political power; only a few of their people received appointments in the administration, and their primary concerns, the social issues, were not given priority. The New Right, both Christian and secular, soon found that Reagan was much more a traditional conservative politician than it had thought. He understood the need for compromise and working with people of differing beliefs to achieve his main objectives. For all practical purposes the New Christian Right found itself disregarded, the media soon began ignoring it, and the 1982 mid-term elections made it obvious that it did not possess the clout it had claimed to have.

EVANGELICALS IN POLITICS--SUCCESS OR FAILURE?

If one looks back over fifty years of evangelical's involvement in U.S. politics, how does one assess their achievement? If one means by success an increased level of political awareness and participation, then they certainly have been successful. Probably more public servants identify themselves today as believers than at any time since the early years of the century. The organizations that seek to inform Christians about political matters and to guide them in voting intelligently are legion--the Association for Public Justice, Baptist Joint Committee on Public Affairs, American Studies Program of the Christian College Coalition, Office of Public Affairs of the National Association of Evangelicals, Americans United for Separation of Church and State, Mennonite Central Committee Peace Section, Christian Life Commissions of the Southern Baptist Convention and the Baptist General Convention of Texas, Friends Committee on National Legislation, Moral Majority, and numerous others. A list of books advising Christians on how and why they should engage in the political process would fill pages, and conferences on the topic of politics are frequently advertised in the religious press.

But there is a less appealing side to the picture. On this side is the triumphalism reflected in the prayer breakfasts and the outpouring of books and articles on public personalities, as well as the shallowness and superficiality of so much of the religiosity in Washington. More serious, however, is the argument advanced by Benson and Williams that there can really be no hope for consensus on the part of Christians on vital public issues. These analysts demonstrate that believers in Congress (and by implication all Christians who are strongly committed to political action) operate not on the basis of Christian faith per se, but the type of religious faith each particular person has, that is, whether it is an "Individualism-Preserving" or a "Community-Building" religion (Benson and Williams, 1982).

In other words, the values of "Christian" legislators are not really determined by the Scriptures but by the personal philosophies and prejudices that they bring to the Word of God. And, as Fowler reminds us, "The Bible serves many purposes in the diversity of evangelical political thought, seeming to support everything from laissez-faire to communitarian socialism and much in between, and many leading evangelical thinkers unmistakably apply it with one eye on the texts and one eye on contemporary culture" (Fowler, 1983:243). Evangelicalism, for all its conservatism, can no longer be regarded as a monolith. Its voices on Capitol Hill are a cacophony of contrasting claims and political ideologies. The tragedy of this is that there can be no clarion call for national righteousness and social justice coming from our Christian legislators. And, I would say, we are much the worse for this.

NOTES

1. Helpful for defining evangelicalism are Marty, 1976:80-105, and Piepkorn, 1979:3-99.

2. I am indebted to James A. Hedstrom, "Evangelical Program in the United States, 1945-1980, "Ph.D. dissertation, Vanderbilt University, 1982, for this insight.

3. On the other hand, Allan J. Lichtman (1979) argues that religion was the decisive factor.

4. I deal with Graham's involvement in the racial issue in Pierard, 1983:425-426. His relations with the various presidents are detailed in Pierard, 1980:107-127.

5. All references are to letters contained in the Richard M. Nixon Pre-presidential Materials Project, Federal Archives and Records Center, Laguna Nigues, California, Series 320 Vice Presidential General Correspondence, Box 299, Folder: Graham, Dr. Billy.

6. The manuscript of the Life article is in the Graham file cited in note 5.

7. On Graham see Pierard, 1980:121-125, and Pierard, 1976. The Christian faith of these and other lawmakers are presented, albeit in a highly impressionistic manner, in Hefley and Plowman, 1975, 1974, and Frazier, 1974.

8. Fowler maintains that during the 1960s and early 1970s Christianity Today "became a pole around which conservatives in the fold rallied as political consensus broke apart after the mid-1960s" and it was "the most important center for the old values resisting the new tide of ideas, intellectuals, and activists" (pp. 23-24).

9. Hatfield described the controversy surrounding the brief speech in his Chapter 7. Evangelical participation in civil religion is dealt with in Linder and Pierard, 1978.

10. Wallace Henley (1976) is the autobiography of a Southern Baptist preacher who was caught in the corrupting web of the Nixon presidency but was able to break out before it was too late.

11. The reality of their audience size is documented in Haddan and Swann, 1981.

REFERENCES

Adams, James L. The Growing Church Lobby in Washington. Grand Rapids: Eerdmans, 1970.

Anderson, John B. Between Two Worlds: A Congressman's Choice. Grand Rapids: Zondervan, 1970.

Anderson, John B. Vision and Betrayal in America. Waco: Word Books, 1975.

Baker, James T. A Southern Baptist in the White House. Philadelphia: Westminster, 1977.

Benson, Peter L., and Dorothy L. Williams. Religion on Capitol Hill: Myths and Realities. New York: Harper & Row, 1982.

Carter, Jimmy. Why Not the Best? Nashville: Broadman Press, 1975.

Conlan, John B. "Politics: Tug-of-War Needing Godly Values." Good News Broadcaster, July-August, 1976:7-9.

Eells, Robert and Bartell Nyberg. Lonely Walk: The Life of Senator Mark Hatfield. Chappaqua, NY: Christian Herald Books, 1979.

Ford, Gerald R. A Time to Heal. New York: Harper & Row, 1979.

Fowler, Robert Booth. A New Engagement: Evangelical Political Thought, 1966-1976. Grand Rapids: Eerdmans, 1983.

Frazier, Claude A. ed. Politics and Religion Can Mix! Nashville: Broadman Press, 1974.

Furniss, Norman F. The Fundamentalist Controversy, 1918-1931. New Haven: Yale University Press, 1954.

Gatewood, Willard B. Jr. Preachers, Pedagogues and Politicians: The Evolution Controversy in North Carolina. Chapel Hill: University of North Carolina Press, 1966.

Grubb, Norman P. Modern Viking: The Story of Abram Vereide, Pioneer in Christian Leadership. Grand Rapids: Zondervan, 1961.

Hadden, Jeffrey, and Charles E. Swann. Prime-Time Preachers: The Rising Power of Televangelism. Reading, MA: Addison-Wesley, 1981.

Handy, Robert T. "The American Religious Depression, 1926-1935." Church History 29 (March 1960):3-14.

Hatfield, Mark O. Not Quite So Simple. New York: Harper & Row, 1968.

Hatfield, Mark O. Conflict and Conscience. Waco: Word Books, 1971.

Hatfield, Mark O. Between a Rock and a Hard Place. Waco: Word Books, 1976.

Hays, Brooks. A Southern Moderate Speaks. Chapel Hill: University of North Carolina Press, 1959.

Hays, Brooks. Politics Is My Parish. Baton Rouge: Louisiana State University Press, 1981.

Hefley, James C. and Edward G. Plowman. Washington: Christians in the Corridors of Power. Wheaton: Tyndale House, 1975.

Helms, Jesse. When Free Men Shall Stand. Grand Rapids: Zondervan, 1976.

Henley, Wallace. The White House Mystique. Old Tappan, NJ., 1976.

Hughes, Harold E. The Man from Ida Grove. Lincoln, Va.: Chosen Books, 1976.

Jorstad, Erling. The Politics of Doomsday: Fundamentalists of the Far Right. Nashville: Abingdon, 1970.

Jorstad, Erling. Evangelicals in the White House: The Cultural Maturation of Born Again Christianity 1960-1981. Lewiston, NY: Edwin Mellen Press, 1981.

Kucharsky, David. The Man from Plains: The Mind and Spirit of Jimmy Carter. New York: Harper & Row, 1976.

95

Kyvig, David E. Repealing National Prohibition. Chicago: University of Chicago Press, 1979.

Lichtman, Allan J. Prejudice and the Old Politics: The Presidential Election of 1928. Chapter Hill: University of North Carolina Press, 1979.

Linder, Robert D. and Richard V. Pierard, Twilight of the Saints. Downers Grove, IL: InterVarsity Press, 1978.

Maddox, Robert L. Preacher at the White House. Nashville: Broadman, 1984.

Magruder, Jeb Stuart. An American Life: One Man's Road to Watergate. New York: Atheneum, 1974.

Marty, Martin E. A Nation of Bahavers. Chicago: University of Chicago Press, 1976.

Michaelson, Wes. "NAE in Washington: Bicentennial Faith." Sojourners 5 (March 1976):8-9.

Miller, Robert Moats. American Protestantism and Social Issues, 1919-1939. Chapel Hill: University of North Carolina Press, 1958.

Moore, Edmund A. A Catholic Runs for President: The Campaign of 1928. New York: Ronald Press, 1956.

Murch, James DeForest. Cooperation Without Compromise. Grand Rapids: Eerdmans, 1956.

Norton, Howard and Bob Slosser. The Miracle of Jimmy Carter. Plainfield, NJ: Logos, 1976.

Piepkorn, Arthur C. Profiles in Belief: Volume IV, Evangelical, Fundamentalist, and Other Christian Bodies. San Francisco: Harper & Row, 1979.

Pierard, Richard V. The Unequal Yoke: Evangelical Christianity and Political Conservatism. Philadelphia: Lippincott, 1970.

Pierard, Richard V. "Evangelicals and the Bicentennial," Reformed Journal 26 (October 1976):19-23.

Pierard, Richard V. "One Nation Under God: Judgment or Jingoism?" Pp. 82-99 in Perry C. Cotham, ed., Christian Social Ethics. Grand Rapids: Baker, 1979.

Pierard, Richard V. "Billy Graham and the U.S. Presidency." Journal of Church and State 22 (Winter, 1980):107-127.

Pierard, Richard V. "Billy Graham: A Study in Survival." Reformed Journal 30 (April 1980):8-9.

Pierard, Richard V. "On Praying with the President." Christian Century 99 (March 10, 1982):262-264.

Pierard, Richard V. "From Evangelical Exclusivism to Ecumenical Openness: Billy Graham and Sociopolitical Issues." Journal of Ecumenical Studies 20 (Summer 1983):425-26.

96

Pippert, Wesley. Faith at the Top. Elgin, Ill.: David
    C. Cook, 1973.
Pippert, Wesley G. The Spiritual Journey of Jimmy
    Carter. New York: Macmillan, 1978.
Roy, Ralph Lord. Apostles of Discord. Boston: Beacon
    Press, 1953.
Rozek, Edward J., ed. Walter H. Judd: Chronicles of
    a Statesman. Denver: Grier, 1980.
terHorst, Jerald F. Gerald Ford and the Failure of the
    Presidency. New York: Third Press, 1974.
Wallis, Jim and Wes Michaelson, "The Plan to Save America."
    Sojourners 5 (April 1976):5-12.
Youngdahl, Luther W. The Ramparts We Watch.
    Minneapolis: T. S. Denison, 1961.

PART 2

The Christian Right

Introduction

An alliance between religion and politics has been evident during several periods of U.S. history. These alliances between the church and the state have promoted various causes. For example, in the 1800s, northern liberal ministers were the major inspiration behind the attempt to abolish slavery in the United States, and many of these ministers eventually became leaders of the abolitionist movement. In the early 1900s, conservative rural Protestants mobilized to bring about the "noble experiment" called Prohibition. By applying the necessary political pressure, these church men and women played a major role in bringing about the passage of the Eighteenth Amendment to the Constitution (forbidding the sale and distribution of alcoholic beverages). More recently, the effectiveness of a religious and political alliance was demonstrated during the civil rights movement in the 1960s, when fundamentalist preacher the Reverend Martin Luther King, Jr., successfully challenged many of the discriminatory laws that maintained the status quo of U.S. race relations.

Now in the 1980s, a new religious/political movement is proclaiming, "Our time has come." This movement is commonly referred to as the New Christian Right. During the 1984 political campaign, John Neuhaus, a leader of the Lutheran church, stated:

The religious New Right has shocked the cultural elites of America, because the elites assumed that "those people" had been thoroughly dismissed and discredited, going back as far as the Scopes trial of 1925, the so-called monkey trial. But beginning after World War II, with the emergence of the

new-evangelicals, those people have come back from
the wilderness to which they had been consigned by
the educational, media and mainline religious
leadership. (Rev. Richard John Neuhaus, Lutheran
pastor and director of the Center on Religion and
Society, Time, September 17, 1984, pp. 28.)

This movement has been organized and directed mainly
by conservative fundamentalist preachers of generally large
churches. The preachers appear regularly on religious
television. Probably the best known of them is Rev. Jerry
Falwell, who in the latter 1970s founded the most widely
publicized of the Christian Right religious/political
action groups--the Moral Majority. Through religious
television, direct-mail campaigns, and political lobbying,
Falwell and other representatives of the Christian Right
are attempting to influence judges, legislators, and
government executives to institute decisions that will
bring back more conservative Christian values and practices
in the family, educational, political, and economic lives
of all U.S. citizens. During the 1984 presidential
campaign in particular, Ronald Reagan and the Christian
Right had a well-publicized alliance: In fact, Falwell
described Reagan and Vice President George Bush as "God's
instruments in rebuilding America." In turn, Reagan accused
opponents of school prayer (an important Christian Right
issue) of being "intolerant of religion."
    The chapters that appear in this section address a
number of important questions concerning the nature of
the Christian Right and its impact on U.S. political
behavior. The first three chapters explore the religious
and political roots of the Christian Right. Merle D.
Strege (Chapter 4--"Jerry Falwell and 'The Simple Faith
on Which this Country Was Built'") proposes that Falwell's
particular mixture of religion and politics has its
foundation in the biblical theme of the jeremiad. Strege
elaborates on this spiritual idea and explains how Falwell
applies it to achieve his political goals. Michael
Johnston (Chapter 5--"The 'New Christian Right' in American
Politics") describes the entrance of the New Christian
Right into the political arena and its development as a
more effective political force. Donald Tomaskovic-Devey
(Chapter 6--"The Protestant Ethic, the Christian Right,
and the Spirit of Recapitalization") argues that much of
the Christian Right's political effectiveness is derived
from its alliance with conservative probusiness groups.

Tomaskovic-Devey explores this alliance and suggests that these politically active probusiness groups may be using the moral image of the Christian Right to advance their conservative economic goals.

One of the major issues of the Christian Right is the elimination of legal abortion. Joseph B. Tamney (Chapter 7--"Religion and the Abortion Issue") explores the religious and nonreligious reasons behind the Christian Right's antiabortion position, as well as the reasons behind the proabortion position of other activists such as feminists. Tamney, in his analysis, finds that there is a great diversity of ideologies that serve as a basis for the positions people take on the abortion issue. As a result, Tamney believes the Christian Right will have a difficult time reaching a consensus on a single public policy on abortion, even among antiabortion advocates.

The last two chapters examine the political impact of the Christian Right. Chapter 8, by Stephen D. Johnson ("The Christian Right in Middletown") details the characteristics of those individuals who support the major Christian Right political-action organization--the Moral Majority. Johnson further presents data describing the role of this organization, and the Christian Right in general, in the victories of Ronald Reagan in 1980 and 1984. Finally, John D. Cranor focuses on yet another important political/religious group--the Jews--and their recent support for the politics of the Right. In Chapter 9, "Jews, Jesse Jackson, and Democrats: 1984", Cranor suggests that public policy conflicts between blacks and Jews led many Jews to support Republican candidates and, in particular, Ronald Reagan in 1980. However, did Reagan's well-publicized association with the Christian Right in 1984 result in a return of Jewish support for the Democratic presidential candidate in the 1984 election? Cranor's chapter provides an answer.

4

Jerry Falwell and "The Simple Faith on Which This Country Was Built"

Merle D. Strege

During one of the televised debates of the 1984 campaign for the presidency of the United States, Walter Mondale raised the question of whether the Republican party platform proposed a religious test for the office of Supreme Court justice. Twice Mondale stated his objection to the possibility that the Reverend Jerry Falwell might exercise a closet veto on Supreme Court nominations. For the purposes of this study, the veracity of Mondale's charge is not nearly so interesting as the fact that the name of a Baptist minister could be inserted into a presidential debate in a manner bearing on the issues of domestic policy. Even more interesting, perhaps, is that the minister's name was used by Mondale in such a way as to indicate that he presumed everyone--or nearly everyone--in the television audience knew who he was talking about when he said "Jerry Falwell."

Whether or not his name has become a household word, Jerry Falwell is among the best-known clergy in this country. His name evokes strong emotion, whether positive or negative. Some people place great trust in him; others are deeply suspicious. He is often quoted; he is also misquoted. That a Protestant minister could be the center of such attention is an indication of Falwell's ambition, influence, and enormous energy. It also is an illustration of a distinctive style of integrating politics and religion. That style is by no means new or unique to Jerry Falwell. That style has been part of political and religious life in the United States since the time of Puritan New England. Moreover, it has persisted in various forms among religious people of considerable theological diversity. Jerry Falwell must be understood in the context of this tradition if he is to be understood correctly.

Thus the place to begin a presentation of the issues and
themes of Jerry Falwell and the Moral Majority is not
Lynchburg, Virginia, in 1980, but Massachusetts Bay Colony
in 1679.

THE PURITANS AND THEIR HEIRS

The peace and prosperity of the first forty years
of the settlement of the Massachusetts Bay Colony were
seriously disrupted after 1650. Settlers and Indians had
lived at peace in the colony's early days, but that peace
was broken by King Phillip's War of 1675–1676; more than
half the towns of Massachusetts Bay and Plymouth colonies
were damaged, and about 10 percent were utterly destroyed.
Other disasters struck the colonies. Twice in less than
four years fire ravaged large sections of Boston.
Merchants experienced unusually heavy losses through
shipwreck. Smallpox, always feared, made its way through
the colonial population in virulent epidemics. Perhaps
worst of all in the minds of the Puritan preachers whose
parents and grandparents had left England to establish
a fully reformed church free of the fetters of Anglican
bishops, agents of that church and episcopacy were now,
in 1679, seeking an Anglican beachhead in New England.
Puritans did not believe that historical events were
accidental occasions. History, rather, was guided by the
providence of God. Thus it was possible to discern in
historical events the evidence of divine goodwill or
anger; prosperity was a sign of God's favor as surely as
calamity was evidence of his wrath. Therefore, when
calamities multiplied during the 1670s, Puritan ministers
from towns throughout the colony considered the possible
sources of divine displeasure.
At the Synod of 1679 the ministers concluded that
the descendants of the founding generation had forgotten
the original purposes of their ancestors' settlement.
Upon leaving England, the minister Frances Higginson had
bade his homeland a tender farewell, announcing that he
was sailing to Massachusetts Bay as a part of a godly
community intent on "practicing the positive part of church
reformation." Higginson and his ministerial colleagues
sought in the New World no tolerant principle of religious
liberty but a place where they could practice their form
of Christianity, a form that they also believed was the
only true one. At the 1679 meeting nearly fifty years

after the first colonists arrived, the ministers decided
that contemporary colonists had lost sight of that original
purpose. As evidence of that neglect the synod cited a
mournful record of sinful departures from the holy
standards of the past: overweening pride, profanity,
Sabbath-breaking, "unordinate passions," gossip and the
inability to get along with one's neighbors, drunkenness,
"unordinate affection to the world" (seeking material
wealth before seeking God), and "as to what concerns
families and the government thereof, there is much amiss"
(Walker,1960:426-432). The ministers also informed the
colonial government, to which their findings were
respectfully addressed, that unless the settlers mended
their ways, the colony could expect more disasters as signs
of God's displeasure at their sinful behavior.

The importance of this episode in early colonial
history lies in the continuing importance to U.S. religion
and politics of the jeremiad style of sermonizing, of which
the Synod of 1679 and its results are a grand example.
"The American jeremiad was ritual designed to join social
criticism to spiritual renewal, public to private identity,
the shifting 'signs of the times' to certain traditional
metaphors, themes, and symbols" (Bercovitch, 1978:xi).
The Synod of 1679 and countless Puritan sermons on a
variety of occasions used the interpretive formula
"prosperity equals divine favor, calamity equals divine
wrath" as a vehicle of social criticism. The Puritans
did not invent this formula. It is deeply embedded in
the Old Testament, and biblical scholars are accustomed
to referring to it as the deuteronomic doctrine of reward.

Puritan ministers were disturbed about what might
be termed the "drift" of their society. The conclusions
of the 1679 synod criticized this drift. But the ministers
also hoped that their criticism would provoke repentance
and rebirth of the original spirit of the colony. Whereas
late twentieth-century readers might regard the results
of the Synod of 1679 as a sample of unwarranted meddling
in personal affairs, Puritan ministers did not separate
identity or morality into public and private spheres.
The vices of individuals might very well produce calamities
for the entire colony. In blurring the distinction between
public and private identity and morality, New England
ministers employed the basic Puritan theological metaphor
of covenant.

Puritan theology taught the idea that covenants were
the basis of all relationships, divine and human. At

creation God had instituted the covenant of works with
Adam; if Adam were to keep the commandments, he would live
in God's favor. When Adam and Eve failed to keep covenant
with God, they were promised a second covenant, Christ.
On the basis of participating in this new covenant of
grace, the redeemed then formed congregations by entering
into the church covenant. Puritan politics also made
extensive use of the covenant idea, the Mayflower Compact
being perhaps the most noteworthy example in U.S. history.
Puritans believed that God implicitly made covenants with
nation-states, and those that promoted morality and
righteousness would experience national prosperity.
Nations that permitted injustice and failed to secure
righteousness among their inhabitants could expect a
decline in their status in the community of nations, if
not ultimate dissolution (Morgan, 1958:19). In clear
language John Winthrop, governor of Massachusetts Bay
Colony for several years, laid out the terms of the
covenant between the colonists and their God in his 1630
sermon, "A Model of Christian Charitie" (Miller and
Johnson, 1963:194-199).

The Synod of 1679 needed only to allude to the
structures of this national covenant, so well known was
this symbol to the people accustomed to hearing and reading
the sermons of the synod members. And according to the
ministers, the events in the 1670s pointed to serious
breach of the covenant by the colonists. In its belief
in the deuteronomic doctrine of reward, its blurring of
distinctions between public and private morality, and its
invocations of the symbols of covenant, the Synod of 1679
clearly produced a jeremiad. But the jeremiad and some
of its underlying assumptions were not phenomena of Puritan
New England only. They are, in fact, recurring themes
of such persistance as to allow Jerry Falwell a certain
measure of confidence when he refers to "the simple faith
on which this country was built."

The themes of the jeremiad and what Edmund Morgan
has called the "Puritan ethic" played an important role
in the thought of revolutionary Americans. In 1775 the
Continental Congress called for a day of "public
humiliation, fasting, and prayer" for the government of
the colonies to coincide with divine intention and also
to acknowledge God's providential control of history, an
acknowledgment important "especially in times of impending
danger and public calamity" (Miller, 1961:322). Perry
Miller has detected in this proclamation a congressional

appeal for "first, a national confession of sin and
iniquity, then a promise of repentance, that only
thereafter may God be moved so to influence Britain as
to allow America to behold 'a gracious interposition of
Heaven for the redress of her many grievances'"
(1961:322). In the revolutionary period, then, the
jeremiad was the property of southern colonials as well
as the descendants of the New England Puritans. Miller
concluded that "the Congressional recommendations of June
12, 1775, virtually took over the New England thesis that
these Colonial peoples stood in a contractual relation
to the 'great Governor' over and above that enjoyed by
other groups; in effect, Congress added the other nine
colonies . . . to New England's covenant" (1961:326).
In a point also shared by Edmund Morgan (1967) Miller
contended that the covenantal structure basic to the
Puritan ethic and jeremiad was the cultural inheritance
of wide segments of colonial society.

> Therefore the people had little difficulty reacting
> to the Congressional appeal. They knew precisely
> what to do: they were to gather in their assemblies
> on July 20, inform themselves that the afflictions
> brought upon them in the dispute with Great Britain
> were not hardships suffered in some irrational
> political strife but intelligible ordeals divinely
> brought about because of their own abominations
> (Miller, 1961:326).

Nathan O. Hatch recently has described the manner
in which millenialism increased the fervor with which
jeremiad and covenant could be applied in revolutionary
America. Millenialism has to do with beliefs about the
coming to earth of the kingdom of God. Christian
postmillenialists believe that the peaceable kingdom of
Christ will be established prior to the last judgment and
end of history. Premillenialists reverse this order of
events. The postmillenial view predominated during the
colonial and revolutionary years and continued to be the
popular view in this country until the Civil War. Out
of this theology New England clergy insisted on the
establishment of a "republic of Christian virtue" (Hatch,
1977:97-138). Ernest Tuveson has illustrated with great
effect how these ideas passed into the broad stream of
U.S. letters and culture in the early nineteenth century
(1968). Thus the themes important to Jerry Falwell,

jeremiad, covenant, and millenial expectancy, were not unknown to revolutionary and enlightenment America.

Nineteenth century U.S. culture exhibits the continuing importance of the ideas of covenant and the deuteronomic doctrine of reward and punishment. A major goal of Protestant clergymen in the nineteenth century was the construction of a Christian civilization in the United States. They began this task under some disadvantages, so they believed, because the First Amendment to the Constitution had disestablished religion. But ministers and interested laypersons were soon industriously at work in a host of voluntary societies, the purpose of which was the reform of U.S. society and the foundation of a godly nation. Public education in "the common schools" was a major arena of this activity (Tyack, 1966:455). Here religious people "identified their common beliefs with those of the nation, their common beliefs with those of the nation, their mission with American's mission" (Smith, 1966:207).

The textbook most identified with the common school of the nineteenth century was William Holmes McGuffey's series of Eclectic Readers, "by mid-century the basic school reader in thirty-seven states," and "for seventy-five years the textbooks used by four-fifths of the nation's school children" (Westerhoff, 1982:27). We may conclude that the themes of covenant and deuteronomic reward and punishment were part of the schooling of children in the United States through McGuffey's readers. For as John Westerhoff says:

> The students using these texts were to understand themselves as among a chosen people with whom God has made a conditional covenant. If they did their part, God would reward them; if they did not, God would harshly punish them. God set firm requirements upon them and, to help them, gave them clear laws to obey. In return for obedience God promised them all good things, all they needed and craved, and most importantly--peace. He also gave them a warning; if they failed to do his will they would suffer disaster and ultimately death and eternal punishment (1982:38).

In the common schooling of the nineteenth century the familiar warnings of the jeremiad itself were also invoked. The moral crisis surrounding the issue of slavery provided northern clergymen with the opportunity to warn

---

the country of its perilous condition in the hands of an angry God. The Civil War was commonly interpreted in the North as divine punishment of the entire nation. In the memorable words of Julia Ward Howe, God was "treading out the vintage where the grapes of wrath are stored." But the jeremiad was so thoroughly a part of U.S. culture that its theme of social decline and restoration could be invoked on several occasions by a wide variety of individuals. The Congregationalist minister at Hartford, Connecticut, in the mid-nineteenth century was Horace Bushnell. Among this very moderate minister-theologian's numerous publications is an essay entitled "Barbarism: The First Danger." It is what might be called an urbane jeremiad. In this piece Bushnell expressed his alarm at the "uncivilized" conditions in the newly settled and still unsettled regions of the U.S. West. He worried that "a new settlement of the social state involves a tendency to social decline" and warned that unless extraordinary efforts were made on behalf of education and religion "nothing will suffice to prevent a fatal lapse of social order" (1847:4-5). If some of the direct references of the jeremiad have disappeared from Bushnell's discussion, its structure is still apparent in the warning that calamity would occur unless steps were immediately taken to insure the progress of moral life and true religion.

In the nineteenth century we find the ideas of covenant and jeremiad, sometimes recast but nonetheless identifiable, in the schooling of children and the interpretations of events made by laypersons and clergy alike. These themes have antecedents in Puritan New England and revolutionary America. They persist into the twentieth century, particularly among the branch of Protestants known as "fundamentalists," the last link in the chain between "the simple faith on which this country was built" and the reform program of Jerry Falwell.

Historically considered, the fundamentalism that was a feature of life in the first quarter of the twentieth century can be defined as "militantly anti-modern Protestant evangelicalism" (Marsden, 1980:4) Fundamentalists were critical of modern U.S. culture in the name of an earlier "Christian" U.S. culture. As George Marsden has observed, in fundamentalism there was a "paradoxical tendency to identify sometimes with 'establishment' and sometimes with 'outsiders'" (1980:6). The beginnings of fundamentalism lay in a time when evangelical Protestantism was the dominant religious tradition in the country. But by the 1920s fundamentalists were objects of ridicule and scorn. "Heave an egg out the window of a Pullman car," wrote H. L. Mencken in his caustic obituary of William Jennings Bryan, "and you are sure to hit a fundamentalist in the side of the head." The result of this disdain was to drive fundamentalists deeper into the separatism toward which they were already directed. Thus they came to attack the evils and moral folly they saw and to press for a restoration of a Christian civilization in the United States. If "Scottish Common Sense Realism" and the principles of Baconian science (Marsden, 1980:7) provided the intellectual unity of fundamentalism, the rhetoric of the jeremiad and symbol of the covenant provided its basic assumptions about the need for social reform.

Not all fundamentalists were millenialists, but Ernest R. Sandeen has demonstrated the importance of dispensational premillenialism to those who were. This particular form of millenialist thought divides all history into "dispensations," distinct and specific eras. The last of these dispensations, according to this view, will be the thousand-year reign of Christ after the last judgment. This strain of millenialism became increasingly popular among evangelical Protestants after the Civil War and was widely adopted within fundamentalist circles. The belief that humans were living in the last days of history lent a special urgency to fundamentalist appeals for reform and renewal. In this view the evil influences of modernism, Darwinism, and denial of the Bible's authority combined to pull down the pillars of Christian civilization--church and school. On behalf of these two institutions fundamentalists were prepared to battle. If men and women would acknowledge the folly of their modern ways, the nation might be spared the worst horrors of the final chapters of history.

Fundamentalists regarded themselves as the heirs of "the best" and "the true" in U.S. history. Certainly one can identify persistent ideas about how some people have understood themselves, and fundamentalists included those ideas within their system. Among those ideas were covenant and the rhetoric of the jeremiad. Jerry Falwell is proud to refer to himself as a fundamentalist, and he must be regarded as standing in a long tradition of preachers of jeremiads, calling the nation to return to its Christian values, the terms of its covenant with God. The pluralism of the United States notwithstanding, this jeremiad

tradition has played an important role in the formation
of the national self-understanding. When Jerry Falwell
refers to "the simple faith on which this country was
built" he stands within this tradition and points to its
values. The truth of Falwell's assertion is not at issue;
I have tried to show, rather, that his ideas and especially
his manner of presentation have a long history in the U.S.
experience. To Jerry Falwell and the program of Moral
Majority, Inc., we may now turn.

JERRY FALWELL AND THE PROMOTION OF TRADITIONAL VALUES

The Reverend Jerry Falwell is a hometown boy who made
good. He was born August 11, 1933 in one of the tougher
sections of the same town where he now is a pastor:
Lynchburg, Virginia; his congregation, Thomas Road Baptist
Church, is the largest in town. Falwell was a bright
teenager, graduating as valedictorian of his class at
Brookville High School. However he did not attend
commencement ceremonies due to a disciplinary suspension
for a prank. He was converted or "born again," as he would
say, at Park Avenue Baptist Church in Lynchburg. Other
than his mother, Falwell's family was not particularly
religious. In fact he and his friends allegedly attended
Park Avenue Baptist because they had heard that several
pretty girls were members there. Once converted, Falwell
felt himself under a divine call to the ministry.
Therefore, he dropped his plans for an engineering career
and enrolled at a Baptist Bible College in Springfield,
Missouri, an institution operated by a small association
of fundamentalist Baptist churches known as the Baptist
Bible Fellowship. After graduation from college in 1952,
Falwell returned to Lynchburg, where he began a new church
on Thomas Road. He has never been a person limited by
a narrow vision. Within five years of the founding of
Thomas Road Baptist Church, Falwell had begun work as a
radio and television preacher (in 1979 his program,
Old-Time Gospel Hour, by Falwell's estimate had an audience
of twenty million) and also had founded Liberty Baptist
College.
Falwell and other preachers on the "television church"
such as James Robison and Jim Bakker began attracting
attention outside the orbit of religious broadcasting after
the 1976 presidential election. New Right political
strategists had urged conservative Protestants and

112

Catholics to become more politically active (Viguerie, 1981:126). Falwell responded to the growing interest in the political muscle of evangelicals by organizing his 1979 Clean Up America campaign, which began with a rally of 12,000 persons on the capitol steps in Washington. In May 1979 direct-mail supporters of Falwell's programs received the following message, quoted here from Falwell's authorized biography:

> My heart is burning within me today. It is about time the Christians here in America stand up and be counted for Jesus Christ. We are the "moral majority," and we have been silent long enough!
>
> I realize that it is "popular" to be a born-again Christian. But for some strange reason it is "unpopular" to stand up and fight against the sins of our nation. Will you take a stand and help me Clean Up America? How would you answer these questions: Do you approve of pornographic and obscene classroom textbooks being used under the guise of sex education? Do you approve of the present laws legalizing abortion-on-demand that resulted in the murder of more than one million babies last year? Do you approve of the growing trend towards sex and violence replacing family-oriented programs on television?
>
> If you are against these sins, then you are exactly the person I want on my team. I have put together a Clean Up America! campaign that is going to shake this nation like it has never been shaken before. I cannot do it alone. Together we must awaken the moral conscience of our nation. The battle has just begun.
>
> I am going to send ballots with the three questions I asked you in this letter to two million friends like you. Then special ballot ads will be run in the major magazines across America. The results from these ballots will be tabulated and sent to each and every lawmaker, state legislature, governor, U.S. senator and representative, judge, school board, P.T.A. president, TV network, the fifty major advertisers in the country, and to President Carter himself. I am devoting the entire month of May to Clean Up America. Every week, on television and radio, I will preach on a different sin our nation is committing. On May 27 we will televise on the

Old-Time Gospel Hour the Clean Up America Rally
we held on the steps of our nations's Capitol on April
27. And finally, throughout the coming year, I will
appear on talk shows and campaign across the country
supporting programs to Clean Up America.

It will cost us hundreds of dollars to accomplish
these ends, but we must do it. If we do not
accomplish the task, I am afraid that America will
face the judgment of God. Proverbs 14:34 says,
"Righteousness exalteth a nation: but sin is a
reproach to any people." There is no way to escape
this biblical fact. We do not have a moment to lose!

This year's campaign goals are to reverse the
current trend towards uncensored sex and violence
on television which are replacing family-oriented
programs, to remove pornographic and obscene classroom
textbooks (placed in the hand of minors under the
guise of sex education) from the classrooms of
America, and to stop the wholesale slaughter of unborn
babies caused by legalized abortion. It is vital
that you cast your vote to "Clean Up America" today!
If several million concerned individuals will start
praying and working to Clean Up America, and if
hundreds of groups and churches work together, we
will be able to bring this nation back to her moral
senses. Only then can God once more bless our
republic (Strober and Tomczak, 1979:174-176).

Moral Majority, Inc., is the outgrowth of this effort,
and Falwell describes it as a political, rather than a
religious, organization. As he himself put the matter,
"You're not going to hear doctrine here in Moral Majority,
Inc. " (Falwell, 1981b:23). But religious values do lie
behind the goals for Moral Majority stated by Falwell in
a recent magazine interview:

I would like to see Moral Majority become a very
powerful and positive movement for morality in this
country. And I would hope that in this decade we
will be able to bring the nation back to an
appreciation of the traditional values and moral
principles that really have been the American way
for two hundred years. I would like to see the family
become prominent in our society again. I would like
to see television featuring united families rather
than broken or distorted families. I would like to

see language on the television screen again assume
some dignity and gravity, and not be seasoned with
profanity. I would like to see the country become
more sensitive. I can see Moral Majority creating
a sensitivity among the American people for the needs
of the unfortunate, the poor, and the disenfranchised
that will come from the private sector, particularly
the churches, to fill the vacuum that is going to
be created by the government's necessary withdrawal
from that sphere. I would like to see us remaining
non-partisan within the two-party system (Falwell,
1981b:22).

Falwell preaches a message that calls for the nation
to return to its past. For three hundred years this has
been a theme of jeremiad preachers. The covenant theme
of the jeremaid lies behind Falwell's goal of restoring
the nation "to the traditional values and moral principles
that really have been the American way for two hundred
years." Falwell implicitly invoked this covenant theme
when he said, "America has become the greatest nation on
earth because of what Solomon said in Proverbs 14: Living
by God's principles promotes a nation to greatness;
violating God's principles brings a nation to shame."
If a nation or a society lives by divine principles, even
though the people personally don't know the One who taught
and lived those principles, that society will be blessed
(Falwell, 1981b:24). By the same token, the nation that
ignores those divine principles, wrote Falwell in the
time-honored jeremiad structure, can anticipate calamity
and ruin.

That religious ideas permeate the thought of the Moral
Majority is further illustrated by the manner in which
Falwell's dispensationalist premillenialism undergirds
his ideas about the place of the United States in the
divine determination of history:

I am fully expecting between now and the coming of
the Lord that this world is going to experience a
spiritual awakening unlike anything in the past.
There is going to be an invasion of God on this
planet, and changing of lives: real biblical
evangelism. There is going to be a terrific harvest
of souls somewhere between here and the Rapture.
[Used by dispensational premillenialists to refer
to Jesus' return to earth for his faithful followers

near the end of history.] I believe that God's role
for America is as catalyst, that he wants to set the
spiritual time bomb off right here. If that is the
case, America must stay free. And for America to
stay free we must come back to the only principles
that God can honor: the dignity of life, the
traditional family, decency, morality, and so on.
I just see myself as one to stand in the gap and,
under God, with the help of millions of others, to
bring the nation back to a moral standard so we can
stay free in order that we can evangelize the world.
And protect the Jews (Falwell, 1981b:27).

"America," said Falwell, "is great, but not because it
is a Christian nation: it has never been a Christian
nation, it is never going to be a Christian nation. It
is a nation under God" chosen for a divine mission
(1981b:24).

THE MORAL MAJORITY PROGRAM

The Moral Majority's program for the restoration of
the United States to its former position of strength and
morality rests on the assertion that biblical values were
once at the very center of the nation's character. Falwell
often quotes references linking God and the affairs of
nations from a list of persons including Benjamin Franklin,
William Bradford, John Adams, and George Washington. He
also cites inscriptions on federal buildings referring
to or quoting from the Bible as well as depictions of
biblical characters (Falwell, 1980:25-43). The nation's
faithfulness to the values of the Bible is the source of
its greatness, concludes Falwell, on the basis of the
oft-quoted verse from Proverbs 14:35, "Righteousness
exalteth a nation; but sin is a reproach to any people."
The decade of the eighties is the crisis point in U.S.
history (Falwell, 1980:7-8). Thus the Moral Majority puts
forth its appeal for the restoration of the nation: A
return to the "seven principles that made America great"
will bring with it the return of U.S. superiority in the
world (Falwell, 1980:239-241).

The Principle of the Dignity of Human Life. The
first concern of Jerry Falwell and the Moral Majority in
this area is the matter of abortion. As he states his

116

position, "Life is a miracle. Only God can create life,
and He said, 'Thou shalt not kill.' Nothing can change
the fact that abortion is the murder of human life"
(1981a:195). Human life begins at the moment of
fertilization and "any further formulation of the
individual is merely a matter of time, growth, and
maturation" (1981a:196). In Roe v. Wade, the Supreme
Court, according to Falwell, opened the possibility of
a national rejection of the first biblical principle of
U.S. greatness. Now the country has on its hands the blood
of millions of babies (Falwell, 1980:147).

Falwell's book, Listen, America!, opens with a
moving description of some of his encounters with the
victims of the war in Cambodia between Vietnamese and Khmer
Rouge forces. This led Falwell to a discussion of world
hunger and the U.S. responsibility for its alleviation.
He claimed that while "liberals" have debated and theorized
about the problem, the Moral Majority has raised "millions
of dollars to feed starving people" (1981a:208). The
elimination of hunger is a responsibility that must fall
increasingly to the private sector and particularly the
churches. U.S. citizens should take the lead because,
until Roe v. Wade, the United States has always defended
the weak and homeless.

His militant stand against abortion led Falwell to
serious reservations concerning the practice of
euthanasia. Whether Falwell meant to include passive as
well as active forms of euthanasia is unclear when he said,
"Even in the cases of those massively defective, miserably
infirm, or terminally ill, I find no biblical justification
or encouragement for euthanasia" (1981a:212). But he
warned that an epidemic of euthanasia in the 1980s will
follow the abortions of the 1970s unless the nation returns
to the first biblical principle of the sanctity of human
life.

The Principle of the Traditional, Monogamous
Family. "The Christian family is the basic unit in
society so far as God is concerned. . . . When the family
begins to falter, when that basic Christian unit is slowly
destroyed as is happening in our country today, we are
on the precipice of real peril" (quoted in Strober and
Tomczak, 1979:116-117). Based on this conviction, Falwell
and the Moral Majority are decidedly "profamily," as they
put their stance. People are guilty of demeaning the
importance of the family through a host of means:

television programs that "honor divorce [and] glorify broken homes," "permissive" theories of child rearing that undermine parental authority and encourage rebellious children, and the absence of God-fearing, authoritative men in the roles of husband and fathers. "If America is going to stand, she must get back to the Word of God and back to holy living in her homes" (quoted in Strober and Tomczak, 1979:117).

When Falwell used the word "traditional" in descriptions of the family, he meant to exclude the possibility of homosexual marriages in particular, for homosexuality is regarded as an abomination by the Moral Majority. "What was once considered a deviant lifestyle is now considered by many Americans as an alternative lifestyle. . . . Today thousands of men and women in America flaunt their sin openly. The entire homosexual movement is an indictment against America and is contributing to its ultimate downfall" (Falwell, 1981a:203). Falwell maintained that he was genuinely concerned about the needs of homosexuals, but he regarded homosexuality as sinful or abnormal and warned that the continued tolerance toward it "will bring down the wrath of God on America" (1981a:205).

Another outgrowth of Moral Majority's profamily position is its reservation concerning such practices as artificial insemination and selective breeding. Technology has raised moral questions that many people are, as yet, unprepared to answer. These questions include the rights of embryos and surrogate mothers as well as broader questions about the ethics of practices considered by the Moral Majority to be experimental. On the basis of the Old Testament injunction against the wasting of semen (see the story of Onan in Genesis 38:1-11), the Moral Majority condemns artificial insemination because the only means of collecting semen for this purpose is through the prohibited practice of masturbation. For the same reason, and also because it will "foster an attitude that technical intelligence is a quality to be preferred over moral sensitivity" (1981a:209-210), Falwell opposes the idea and practice of "selective breeding" through artificial insemination.

The Principle of Common Decency. "Common decency in a race that is fallen begins with the covering of the human body" (Falwell, 1980:250). Ever since the discovery of their nakedness in the Garden of Eden men and women

have modestly clothed their bodies, at least until
contemporary society's preoccupation with nudity,
particularly as mediated through the television and motion
picture industry, often termed the "Hollywood culture,"
and, worst of all, in pornography. In Falwell's mind,
"TV is the greatest vehicle being used to indoctrinate
us slowly to accept a pornographic view of life.
Pornography is more than a nudey magazine, it is a
prevailing atmosphere of sexual license" (1980:174).
    Moral Majority's objections to pornography include
its distorted view of women, the separation of love from
sexual intercourse and the destruction of "the privacy
of sex" (Falwell, 1980:173). Even though the majority
of U.S. citizens oppose pornography, its proliferation
"into our society is striking evidence of our decadence.
The moral fiber of our nation is so deteriorated that we
cannot possibly survive unless there is a complete and
drastic turnabout soon" (Falwell, 1980:176).

    The Principle of the Work Ethic. According to
Falwell the welfare system has stripped from millions of
people the dignity that accompanies honest labor. He is
an unabashed champion of the free enterprise economic
system and for that reason believes the number of welfare
recipients should be severely curtailed. He also believes
that "there are generally enough jobs to go around" and
that "too many people who could work, do not" (1980:66).
The growth in the number of welfare recipients Falwell
interprets as evidence of political and economic decline.
"Belief in individual responsibility, laissez-faire, and
a decentralized and limited government changed to belief
in social responsibility and a centralized and powerful
government" (1980:61). This change is responsible for
the instability in the U.S. economy, and such problems
are inevitable whenever people ignore biblical principles.
"God said in the first book of the Bible, Genesis, that
we are to earn our bread by the sweat of our brow. He
was giving us the principles of reward for work" (1980:63).
    If people will encourage the government to allow the
independent development of a free market economy, job
opportunities will be created for those who want to work.
More than any other measures this will "free minority
groups from the virtual 'prison' of the welfare system"
(Falwell, 1981a:207) and thereby end racial injustice.
Christianity knows no racial boundaries and "we must help
our racial minorities to genuinely feel that they are fully
accepted, first-class citizens in our society"

(1981a:207). It should be noted that Falwell has acknowledged an absence of fundamentalists in the quest for racial justice and exhorts his followers to take up the cause.

The Principle of the Abrahamic Covenant. This segment of the Moral Majority's reform program deals with the political and military support of Israel by the United States. Falwell believes that God's covenant with Abraham, promising to make him the patriarch of a great nation, is everlasting. Moreover, he argues that the modern nation-state of Israel is the fulfillment of that promise. But what has this biblical tradition to do with the United States? Falwell answers by saying that since the descendants of Abraham are God's chosen people, he will look favorably on those nations who defend them (1980:98). Falwell's dispensational premillenialism is a major source of his stress on U.S. support for Israel. The restoration of Jews to their ancient homeland is an important step in God's plan to drive the Jews from their rejection of Jesus as the Messiah back to full fellowship with God. The restoration, in turn, is an important link in the chain of the final events of history that dispensationalists believe are predicted in the apocalyptic books of the Bible. All this does not mean Falwell endorses every action of the Israeli government, but he does believe that (1) the modern state of Israel is a fulfillment of biblical prophecy; (2) the Jews have been divinely elected; (3) the Jews have a privileged position in the kingdom of God; and (4) Israel has a "God-given right to the land" (Falwell, 1982:50). From this decidedly pro-Israel position Falwell looks disfavorably upon recent U.S. State Department efforts in the Middle East that he believes signify an eroding American-Israeli relationship. Warmer relations with Arab oil suppliers and with Egypt as well as the U.S. willingness to confer with the Palestine Liberation Organization are distressing developments to Falwell. "If this nation wants her fields to remain white with grain, her scientific achievements to remain notable, and her freedom to remain intact, America must continue to stand with Israel" (Falwell, 1980:98).

The Principle of God-centered Education. In the view of the Moral Majority, recent court decisions against the practices of prayer and Bible reading in the public schools have led to the schools' deterioration and decadence (Falwell, 1980:251). The substitution of the theory of evolution for the biblical doctrine of creation, "moral permissiveness," and "the drug culture" are the results of the sinister influence of "secular humanism." Citing an interview with Mel Gable of Educational Research Analysis that appeared in a "Moral Majority Report," Falwell listed the areas where humanism has influenced the writing of school textbooks: "situation ethics, self-centeredness, evolution, the neglect or negation of Christianity, sexual freedom, death education, and internationalism" (1981a:199). Since humanism is, for Falwell, the arrogant attempt by humans to place their own wisdom above divine revelation, it must be opposed.

Falwell's objection to humanism in the public schools leads to his concern about sex education. Humanist textbooks "belittle the concept of sexual virginity and sexual abstinence and teach the legitimacy of abortion, premarital sex, homosexuality, lesbianism and incest" (Falwell, 1981a:199). Moreover, the materials used in public school sex education programs constitute what Falwell calls "academic pornography" in their "wholesale endorsements of masturbation, premarital sex, extramarital sex, and homosexuality" (1981a:200). He finds a humanist orientation in the work of the Sex Information and Education Council of the United States and on the basis condemns its work.

In addition to encouraging parents to examine carefully the contents of textbooks, to become involved in the public school systems, and to support the return of the Bible and voluntary prayer to U.S. schoolrooms, Falwell believes that "Christian schools" provide an alternative to the dismaying conditions present in public education. He takes hope in his knowledge that "there are 14,000 conservative Christian schools in America and they are increasing at the rate of three a day" (1980:190). Falwell views these schools as the training grounds that will provide the nation with future generations of patriotic leadership of a high character.

The Principle of Divinely Ordained Establishments. The last of the seven principles that made the United States great deals with the institutions of home, church, and government. Since Martin Luther and the Reformation, segments of Protestantism have taught that human society is organized by these three orders of creation. Falwell's emphasis on the family and home already has been

summarized. He has curiously little to say about the
church as a social institution and a marked preference
for addressing "Christians." From this we might infer
that he thinks of church as a collection of individuals
rather than as a cohesive entity such as St. Paul had in
mind when he referred to the church as the "body of Christ"
in I Corinthians 12. About government, however, Jerry
Falwell has a great deal to say.

National self-defense is a matter of great importance
to the Moral Majority. In this connection Jerry Falwell's
views on communism must be stated. He regards communism
as an immoral, godless international conspiracy against
freedom and Christianity. The tactics of communist
takeover include closing churches, suppressing Bible
reading, and executing ministers. This destruction of
religious institutions weakens the cause of liberty. As
Falwell said, "When God is taken out of a society, all
freedom is lost" (Falwell, 1980:78). Since communists
intend the destruction of the idea of God, Falwell
concluded that their influence lay behind efforts to remove
prayer and Bible reading from public schools and the slogan
In God We Trust from U.S. currency. Thus he sounded the
alarm that "America is in trouble" (1981a:213).

The nation's security from communism is also
threatened by a weakened defense capability. Not only
must the United States have the will to fight; it must
also possess the capacity. But "by militarily disarming
our country, we have actually been surrendering our rights
and our sovereignty and, as the Soviets would soon like
to see--our freedoms and our liberties" (Falwell,
1980:84). The nation's faltering defenses are the evidence
of growing moral and spiritual corruption in the nation.
Therefore, Falwell's solution for this crisis is spiritual
renewal accompanied by an aggressive rebuilding of the
nation's defense structure.

Falwell's militant and muscular patriotism rises out
of his interpretation of St. Paul's instruction to Roman
Christians about their attitudes toward government. In
principle, those who govern deserve loyalty and respect
because government is a divinely appointed institution.
Based partly on his devotion to this principle, Jerry
Falwell's patriotism also stems from his belief that the
nation has a divine mission: "God has raised up America
in these last days for the cause of world evangelization
and the protection of his people, the Jews. I don't think
America has any other right or reason for existence other
than these two purposes" (Falwell, 1981b:25).

SUMMARY

The Reverend Jerry Falwell preaches the American Jeremiad. He is a harsh social critic who merges public and private identity and morality. He interprets the "signs of the times" according to the traditional metaphors and symbols of an important current in the broad stream of U.S. culture. His call to repentance and renewal so that the nation might avert disaster has forerunners in U.S. history. The structure that makes possible his Agenda for the Eighties is remarkably akin to the structure that enabled the Puritan Synod of 1679 to formulate an agenda for the 1680s.

Like past jeremiad preachers, Falwell interprets the nation's precarious situation as the result of a crisis of the spirit. Thus the first method for renewal is religious revival. God's hand of judgment may yet be stayed, "but that hope rests in the sincerity of national repentance led by the people of God" (Falwell, 1980:219). This repentance must include: (1) an acknowledgement that we are dependent on God for deliverance from the sins that beset America (abortion, homosexuality, pornography, humanism, and the "fractured family"), (2) prayer for God's mercy upon us, (3) forsaking "ourselves as the measure of all things, and acknowledging that God alone is the measure of truth," and (4) the U.S. populace, including "God's people, must turn from their wicked ways" (Falwell, 1980:219-221).

Falwell complements his call to repentance with a call to action. "Moral Americans" must take those steps that will lead to a national recovery of "the simple faith on which this country was built." Thus political involvement is an important dimension of Moral Majority's program. The implementation of Moral Majority's goals assumes a variety of political forms. The distribution of information about matters of concern to Moral Majority is accomplished through seminars, training programs, syndicated radio commentary, and a newsletter, "Moral Majority Report." Part of this information process also includes the distribution of voting records of senators and representatives. Voter registration among "morally conservative Americans" is another goal. Since the Carter-Ford presidential campaign of 1976 there have been varying estimates of the electoral impact of evangelicals in the United States. Moral Majority believes this impact to be significant and uses that belief to energize intense lobbying efforts in Congress. Moral Majority seeks to inform and influence through the electoral process; it also seeks to mobilize. The nation can be brought back to "moral sanity" through the organization, training, and political activism of millions of the heretofore "silent majority" of moral citizens (Falwell, 1981a:193). To this end a loose confederation of state and local chapters of Moral Majority, Inc., has come into being.

When we hear the Reverend Jerry Falwell preaching his version of the jeremiad and when we see the Moral Majority pursuing its political program of national renewal, we may be justified in asking whether the goals they pursue with such passion and certainty are achievable, indeed, whether their claim about the earlier character of the nation ever was true, and whether the idea of a godly nation was ever more than a vision rather than a reality. (However, that is the subject that deserves a longer answer than can be given here). We should note Alasdair MacIntyre's haunting observation that to invoke shared moral first principles in the United States is futile, "for our society as a whole has none" (1984:253). If that is the case, then the political process cannot achieve the moral consensus so earnestly sought by the Moral Majority, and Jerry Falwell preaches a jeremiad for which the country as a whole has no ear.

REFERENCES

Bercovitch, Sacvan. The American Jeremiad. Madison: University of Wisconsin Press, 1978.

Bushnell, Horace. "Barbarism, The First Danger." New York: American Home Missionary Society, 1847.

Day-Lower, Donna. "Who is the Moral Majority? A Composite Profile." Union Seminary Quarterly Review 37: 4:335-349, 1983.

Falwell, Jerry. Listen America! New York: Bantam Books, 1980.

_____. "Agenda for the Eighties," in The Fundamentalist Phenomenon. Garden City: Doubleday, 1981a.

_____. "An Interview with the Lone Ranger of Fundamentalism." Christianity Today (September 4):22-27, 1981b.

_____. "Jerry Falwell Objects." Christianity Today (January 22):50-51, 1982.

Fitzgerald, Frances. "Reporter at Large: The Reverend Jerry Falwell." New Yorker (May 18):53-141, 1981.

Handy, Robert T. A Christian America: Protestant Hopes and Historical Realities. New York: Oxford University Press, 1971.

Hatch, Nathan O. The Sacred Cause of Liberty. New Haven: Yale University Press, 1977.

MacIntyre, Alasdair. After Virtue, rev. ed. Notre Dame: University of Notre Dame Press, 1984.

Marsden, George M. Fundamentalism and American Culture. New York: Oxford University Press, 1980.

Miller, Perry. "From the Covenant to the Revival." The Shaping of American Religion, ed. by James W. Smith and A. Leland Jamison. Princeton: Princeton University Press, 1961.

Miller, Perry, and Johnson, Thomas H., eds. The Puritans: A Sourcebook of Their Writings. Vol. 1. New York: Harper and Row, 1963.

Morgan, Edmund S. The Puritan Dilemma: The Story of John Winthrop. Boston: Little, Brown, 1958.

_____. "The Puritan Ethic and the American Revolution." William and Mary Quarterly, 3d ser., 24 (January):3-43, 1967.

Sandeen, Ernest R. The Roots of Fundamentalism. Chicago: University of Chicago Press, 1970.

Smith, Timothy L. "Protestant Schooling and American Nationality." Journal of American History 53 (June):207-26, 1966.

Strober, Gerald S., and Tomczak, Ruth. Jerry Falwell: Aflame for God. Nashville and New York: Thomas Nelson, 1979.

Tuveson, Ernest Lee. Redeemer Nation: The Idea of America's Millenial Role. Chicago: University of Chicago Press, 1968.

Tyack, David. "The Kingdom of God and the Common School." Harvard Educational Review 36:447-69, 1966.

Viguerie, Richard A. The New Right: We're Ready to Lead. Falls Church, Va.: Viguerie, 1981.

Walker, Williston. The Creeds and Platforms of Congregationalism. Philadelphia and Boston: Pilgrim Press, 1960.

Westerhoff, John. "The Struggle for a Common Culture: Biblical Images in Nineteenth Century Schoolbooks." The Bible in American Education. Philadelphia: Fortress Press, 1982.

5

The "New Christian Right" in American Politics

Michael Johnston

Politics and religion have played a loud and at times discordant counterpoint in the United States for many generations. A general linkage between fundamentalist religion and conservative politics is an enduring theme in American history. During the 1960s and early 1970s, clerics and laity of a more liberal bent were actively involved in civil rights and antiwar movements. The Reverend Billy Graham was a frequent guest at the White House during Richard Nixon's presidency. The elections of 1980, however, brought forth a more unusual phenomenon: aggressive political activity in the name of fundamentalist Christianity. "Video ministers" such as the Reverends Jerry Falwell, Pat Robertson, and James Robison enter the homes of millions of viewers each week. Their broadcasts are slick and sophisticated productions which frequently emphasize political and policy issues. Reverend Falwell's national organization, known as "Moral Majority Incorporated," is especially active, not only at the national level but also in states, cities, and school districts across the nation. The thrust of this "born-again" political action was overwhelmingly conservative, and in the eyes of many it played a key role in electing Ronald Reagan to the presidency.

This "New Christian Right" (or "NCR") is a movement remarkable for its size, media visibility, and rapid development. It is also of interest because fundamentalist ministers and their followers have historically been decidedly reluctant to venture into the political arena

Reprinted with permission from author, Michael Johnston. This chapter first appeared in The Political Quarterly, Vol. 53, pp. 181-199, 1982.

under an explicitly religious banner. Salvation took
precedence over worldly politics. Thus, it is important
to ask where the New Christian Right came from: Who are
its members, and what is its organizational base? Further,
the movement raises serious questions about rights and
values. Is the NCR a threat to democracy, civil liberties,
and separation of church and state? Or is it merely an
unusually well-organized political interest group?
Finally, what might be the future of the NCR in the era
of Reagan?

WHO ARE THE NEW CHRISTIAN RIGHT?

In this article, I will offer tentative answers to
such questions about the NCR. By "New Christian Right"
I refer to a loose and at times uneasy alliance of
religious political action groups, "media ministers," and
their evangelical Christian following, which has in recent
years been the source of much conservative political
action. "Born-again" Americans, as we shall see, are
surprisingly diverse in background, political sentiments,
and even religious outlook; yet NCR groups pursue a
specific and coherent political agenda and are able to
frame seemingly nonreligious issues, such as foreign
policy, in religious terms for many of their followers.
The movement's political language will be the specific
focus of analysis. The idea that there is a "politics
of language" is hardly a new one. More than thirty-five
years ago George Orwell emphasized this interplay between
politics and language, contending not only that the English
language "becomes ugly and inaccurate because our thoughts
are foolish, but [that] the slovenliness of our language
makes it easier for us to have foolish thoughts (Orwell,
1968, p. 128)." This problem is of more than theoretical
consequence, he reminded us, because political writing
is "largely the defense of the indefensible." In our
lifetime, the "indefensible" has become so horrible, in
its many varieties, that the potential cost of "slovenly
language" and "foolish thoughts" can be quite large
indeed. For examples of this we might point to what
Richard Hofstadter (1965) termed the "paranoid style" of
American politics; to the magnificent obfuscations of the
Pentagon Papers, which protected an agency's self-interest
by reducing a war to little more than a harmless parlor
game for which no one could be called to account and to

the labyrinths of self-delusion emerging from the Oval
Office on Richard Nixon's White House tapes. In none of
these cases do I suggest that tricks of the language
somehow "caused" entire outcomes. Rather the language
and the outcomes grew out of a common process; and one
way to understand the outcomes can be to look at the
language to study the underlying process. Just as we can
examine election returns in order to learn about more basic
political trends and processes, we can study the language
of politics to learn about the ways people and groups
understand the political world and their role in it. The
political language of NCR organizations and leaders are
extracted from America's national print media. Clearly,
this represents only a fraction of the political language
of the NCR, and the examples which I will present represent
only a fraction of that. I will be passing over, for now,
the language of the "video church," and of the movement's
own print media through which it appeals to followers and
sympathizers. But this approach does get at the specific
concern of this paper: The basic political strategies
that NCR leaders and organizations are pursuing as they
are presented to the rest of the political world. The
language of NCR leaders in the national media illuminates
these strategies at least to some extent, for here the
leadership is describing and justifying their movement
to others who are curious and concerned about its general
political role. I will argue that this political language
points to a significant change in NCR strategy over the
past year, from fundamentalist insurgency to a group also
practicing traditional interest-group politics.
     America's "New" Christian Right is both old and new.
It taps cultural currents which run deep in American
politics and culture. In its regional and religious base
the movement reflects fundamental divisions in American
society. Yet the NCR also manifests new strategies and
concerns, and displays a mastery of modern communications
techniques which Father Coughlin--the leading radio
minister of the 1930s--could only dimly comprehend.
     Why, if its roots run so deep, did the NCR come upon
the political stage when it did? Several factors probably
enter into this development, ranging from the destabilizing
and (to some) frightening political and economic developments of the past twenty years (such as assassinations,
cultural change, and the agony of Vietnam) to the continuing growth of the "Sunbelt" in population and affluence.
A more recent development which deserves particular

attention, however, is the strange career of Jimmy Carter. Carter's rise to national prominence in 1975 and 1976 as an avowedly "born-again" politician explicitly raised the issue of the relationship between fundamentalist religion and politics. For many who considered themselves "born again," it compelled a consideration of that relationship. The evangelical vote was important in Carter's 1976 victory: Among white Baptists nationwide, Carter defeated Gerald Ford by a 56-43 percent margin (Time, 1980). Once in office, however, the man who seemed so closely tied to fundamentalist Christianity acted in ways which disappointed many of his "born-again" backers. Political activist Mr. Colonel Donner of the NCR organization Christian Voice expressed that sort of reaction: "It was a tremendous letdown, if not a betrayal, to have Carter stumping for the [Equal Rights Amendment], for not stopping federally funded abortions, for advocating homosexual rights" (Newsweek, 1980, p. 31).

Carter's presence on the national political stage thus was a kind of catalyst in the rise of the NCR, first drawing attention to the role of born-again Christianity in politics, and then giving NCR leaders a sense of betrayal and a set of grievances around which to build a movement. Ironically, the movement Carter helped to bring into being was instrumental in his defeat: In 1980 he lost the white Baptist vote by 56-34 percent. One interpretation of poll results had it that as much as two-thirds of Reagan's margin over Carter could be explained by this shift in white fundamentalist sentiment (Time, 1980).

The New Christian Right can be looked at in two ways: at the elite level, as a group of organizations and as a highly visible presence in the media; and at the mass level, as a very large "born-again" Christian constituency. A brief examination reveals a tightly organized presence at the elite level, but surprising diversity in the ranks of the mass following.

ORGANIZING THE NEW CHRISTIAN RIGHT

Most visible and widespread of the NCR's activities are the broadcasts of such "media ministers" as the Reverends Jerry Falwell, Pat Robertson, and James Robison. These media efforts win for the NCR a presence and income which would make any political organizer envious.

Falwell's "Old-Time Gospel Hour," for example, appears
on 681 television and radio stations each week, drawing
an audience estimated at over 21 million persons. These
programs generate approximately $1 million in contributions
each week. The New York Times reports survey data
indicating that 30 percent of the American public and 46
percent of those Protestants who regard themselves as
evangelicals watch or listen to religious broadcasts
"frequently" (New York Times, 1980c). The political
content of these broadcasts is at times quite clear: Jerry
Falwell held a 1980 broadcast on the steps of the United
States Capitol. James Robison has hosted such guests as
Governor John Connally and Congressman Philip Crane and
has also invited viewers to send in for political pins
and bumper stickers. Yet these programs are usually
regarded as religious broadcasts by the Federal
Communications Commission and by the stations which
transmit them and are thus free from "fairness"
requirements and other policies generally applying to
political programming.

What are the effects of the video ministry on the
political attitudes and behavior of the audience? The
viewers' survey cited above showed that those who
frequently watch or listen to religious programs are, as
a group, "far more conservative than other groups on a
wide array of issues." Audiences are self-selected, so
it is unlikely that the broadcasts have created a
conservative constituency by sheer force of persuasion.
But these broadcasts may well reinforce and add political
saliency to viewers' existing sentiments and also serve
to provide a religious interpretation for newly emerging
political issues and personalities.

Beyond the NCR's media image lie a number of important
organizations which work to organize evangelical Christians
for political action. Three of the most important groups
are Christian Voice, Religious Round Table, and Moral
Majority Incorporated (New York Times, 1980a). Christian
Voice, with offices in Pacific Grove, California, and
Washington, D.C., is a policy-oriented lobby group made
up of clergy. It claims a membership of 2,000 ministers
and a yearly budget of $3 million. The group was formed
initially to win passage of school prayer legislation but
has since moved into a number of other policy areas.
Religious Round Table is a group of about fifty-six conservative clergy, including some Catholics and Jews. From
its headquarters in Rosslyn, Virginia, the organization

sponsors "educational seminars" on religious and political matters. It is supported not only by contributions from sympathetic church congregations, but by funds from some businesses as well. Of all New Christian Right groups, Religious Round Table has the closest ties to the other political action arms of the New Right. The Reverend Jerry Falwell's Moral Majority, Incorporated, is probably the best known NCR organization because of his extensive use of the mass media. Indeed, "moral majority" has become a shorthand term for the whole New Christian Right. Moral Majority claims to have over 72,000 clergy on its mailing list and a mass following as large as 4 million. Its national office in Forest, Virginia, is home to four main branches, devoted to education, lobbying, endorsement of candidates, and legal aid in court cases involving religious issues. The first three of these suborganizations enjoy tax-exempt status.

These organizations do not necessarily speak for all who consider themselves "born again." Indeed, the considerable diversity of born-again America will be the focus of the next section. They do, however, formulate and pursue basic political strategies--and they are the sources of much of the political language which will be employed to study those political approaches.

EVANGELICAL CHRISTIANS: SURPRISING DIVERSITY

Evangelical or born-again Christians are the basic mass constituency of the NCR. The extensive attention focused upon their religion and politics, the fact that many evangelicals insist upon a strictly literal interpretation of Scripture, and the overwhelmingly conservative flavor of NCR broadcasts and statements make it tempting to conclude that evangelicals constitute a large, disciplined political army ready and willing to back a single line of policy. But in truth, born-again Christians are diverse in background, in political preferences, and even in religious outlook. They differ among themselves as to what role, if any, religion should play in politics. And while they are generally of one mind on some issues, such as prayer in public schools, on many others they are no less divided than the population as a whole.

As we might expect, the size and characteristics of the born-again movement depend upon how we define being born again. When survey researchers have simply asked people whether or not they consider themselves born-again Christians, responses have been sizable. In March 1980, a Washington Post (1980) poll reported that 44 percent of the Christians surveyed called themselves "born again." The New York Times (1980c) in June of 1980 noted that various surveys have found that as many as 29 percent of the Catholics and "over half" of Protestants contacted claim to be born again. The New York Times (1980c) added that one of its own surveys had found that born-again respondents made up 42 percent of a national sample. This sort of self-labeling, though, hides much diversity. For some respondents, being born again may correspond to an intense personal religious experience, while for others it may simply mean adherence to a particular style of religion. And, as we shall see in a moment, there are many styles of born-again religion.

A 1980 Gallup survey (New York Times, 1980d) used a more restrictive definition of what it means to be born again, and yielded an interesting picture of the backgrounds of fundamentalist Christians. Respondents were asked three questions: whether or not they would describe themselves as being "born again" or as having had a "born-again experience"; whether or not they actively encouraged others to believe in Jesus; and whether or not they believed in a strictly literal reading of the Bible. Only those who answered "yes" to all three questions--19 percent of the national sample--were regarded as "born-again" Christians. Survey data on the number of "born-again" respondents in various social categories are presented in Table 5.1.

The major tendencies revealed in the data in Table 5.1 are not surprising: The born-again movement is strongest, it seems, among Baptists, in the South, in small towns, and among people with only modest educational and occupational status. But the poll data also suggest that many who meet this rather restrictive definition of being "born again" do not fall into those dominant categories. Many would seem to be from outside the South, from larger communities, to be members of other religious denominations than the Baptist (a term which embraces considerable diversity in its own right), and to be young and somewhat more educated. Particularly striking is the fact that, while the born-again movement as a whole is predominantly white, a nonwhite person seems proportionally twice as likely to be "born again" than a white. Clearly, behind the white Southern Baptist facade there is much social diversity.

132

TABLE 5.1
Born-again Christians as Percentages of Major Social
Groupings

Category	Percent	Category	Percent
National sample:	19		
Sex:		Political affiliation:	
Female	22	Southern Democrat	39
Male	15	Republican	22
		Northern Democrat	15
Race:		Independent	14
Nonwhite	36		
White	16	Religion:	
		Baptist	42
Education:		(All Protestants)	28
Grade school	30	Methodist	18
High school	19	Presbyterian	16
College	12	Lutheran	10
		Catholic	6
Region:		Episcopalian	4
South	33		
Midwest	16	Age:	
West	13	50 or over	22
East	10	30-49	19
		25-29	15
Occupation:		18-24	13
Clerical, sales	25		
Manual labor	21		
Not working	21		
Professional	11		
Size of Community:			
2,500 or less	26		
2,500-49,999	20		
50,000-499,999	17		
500,000-999,999	14		
1,000,000 or more	14		

Source: New York Times, September 7, 1980, p. 34.
Poll data gathered by The Gallup Organization.

This diversity is reflected in religious terms as
well, particularly if we look at the larger number of
people who simply describe themselves as born again
(Washington Post, 1980). Within this group we find both
"true evangelicals" who believe in literal readings of

the Bible, and "worldly evangelicals" who see room for
interpretation. About a third of the evangelicals are
"charismatics" and Pentecostal Christians, whose practices
include glossolalia, or speaking in tongues. Catholic
evangelicals tend to be less conservative than their
Protestant counterparts, yet more conservative than other
Catholics. Some evangelicals feel it is their duty to
make their religious convictions known through active
political efforts, while others object to such practices
on principle. Still others see "worldly politics" as
futile, contending that the world is nearing its last days
and that Christians should be preparing for their final
judgment. Leaders of the New Christian Right have at times
been strongly criticized by religious figures even more
conservative than they: the Reverend Jerry Falwell has
been taken to task by the Reverends Bob Jones, Jr., and
Bob Jones III for associating with Equal Rights Amendment
opponent Phyllis Schlafly, on the grounds that Schlafly
is a Roman Catholic.

Born-again Christians are also surprisingly diverse
in their views on questions of public policy. They tend
to regard themselves as conservatives: 37 percent of the
evangelicals in a September 1980 Gallup survey described
their own "political position" as being "right-of-center,"
compared to 31 percent of all voters. And on certain
issues, evangelicals speak with near unanimity: 81 percent
favored prayer in public schools (compared to 59 percent
of all voters), and only 15 percent supported the right
of homosexuals to teach in public schools (versus 31
percent of respondents overall). But on other issues,
evangelicals' opinions are neither monolithic nor
distinctive: 51 percent of evangelicals favored the death
penalty in murder cases, compared to 52 percent of all
voters; 54 percent favored government programs "to deal
with social problems," compared to 53 percent of all
voters; and 41 percent favored banning all abortions,
compared to 31 percent of all voters (Newsweek, 1980).
Nor should we conclude that evangelicals' opinions are
rigid and unchanging: while Jimmy Carter led Ronald Reagan
among evangelicals by 52-31 percent margin in September
1980 (compared to a 39-38 percent standoff among all
voters), Reagan ended up carrying the born-again vote by
a wide margin, as noted above (New York Times, 1980e).

How, out of this diverse constituency, did the NCR
fashion a palpable presence in the 1980 campaign? While
they certainly did not enlist the backing of all evangelical Christians and did not necessarily "deliver" the votes

of those who did enlist, they still brought significant
numbers of people together in a common political strategy.
I would suggest that at the outset of the 1980 campaign
the NCR was predominantly a "fundamentalist insurgency"
emphasizing populism, redemption, and what David Apter
(1971) has called "consummatory" values--questions of
"ultimate" ends or "meaning." During this phase, the NCR
was storming a corrupted political system from without,
with the goal of totally redeeming it. As the campaign
developed, however--and particularly after the election--
important segments of the NCR added a second strategy:
that of interest-group politics. Here, the values are
"instrumental" (Apter's term again); policy concerns are
rather specific, and the movement works for rights within
the existing political order.

TWO PHASES OF THE NEW CHRISTIAN RIGHT

The Reverend Jerry Falwell has at times been regarded
as "America's Ayatollah." Like the Ayatollah and his
followers, the NCR at one point defined itself as a
redemption crusade storming the existing political order
from without. NCR leaders held out an image of a once-
moral nation gone astray. Politics and decision making,
the schools, and popular culture had become dominated by
"humanists," who allegedly acted on secular, amoral whims
and desires, rather than on biblical moral precepts. The
litany of humanist sins emphasized issues of culture and
morality--pornography, the rights and status of homosexuals, and drug use--but also included more general
policies, such as the welfare system, the proposed Equal
Rights Amendment, foreign policy, and arms-limitation
efforts. An important theme was one of disdain for
existing parties, elites, and interest groups, for
virtually the entire political process had become tainted
by humanism. The New Christian Right's "redemption" of
that process, therefore, would of necessity be redemption
from without.

The political language of the NCR in this phase
emphasized several strategic themes, in addition to the
overall issue of "morality." One was struggle. The
nation was seen as caught in the grip of strong, dangerous
forces, forces which NCR supporters were obliged to fight.
James Robison, a video minister, advertised one of his
broadcasts in the New York Times (1980c) by proclaiming,
"WAKE UP AMERICA--We're All Hostages!" and added: "America

is in Trouble! We face losing all our forefathers fought to provide as runaway government and godless forces attack our freedom and families! Find out what you can do!"

A second theme was mobilization: maximizing the strength of unified numbers. The Reverend Jerry Falwell, speaking to a Florida branch of his Moral Majority, Incorporated, argued such a theme, again in the New York Times (1980a): "What can you do from the pulpit? . . . You can register people to vote. You can explain the issues to them. And you can endorse candidates right there in church on Sunday morning." Falwell later claimed that while he did not make endorsements as such, he did discuss his views on candidates and that upon hearing such discussions 97 percent of his parishioners would vote accordingly. This theme of mobilization has significance at several levels. First, of course, it is simply an appeal for like-minded persons to join forces. But it implies two related ideas: first, that the mobilized movement will be characterized by singleness of purpose and conviction; and secondly, that it can become a dominant, even a majority, movement. These subthemes are common to many mobilization movements and are not the property of the NCR alone; still, they are the basis for much of the concern which has been voiced over the movement and its goals.

That some of this concern has a real basis can be seen in the third theme of the fundamentalist insurgency's political language: victory and redemption. Growing out of the themes of struggle and mobilization, this theme suggested that the NCR would not only "win," but that its mandate would be virtually unlimited. Rev. Jerry Falwell spoke of "making America a Christian nation." A New Christian Right political caucus in Dallas, at which then-candidate Ronald Reagan spoke, featured the opinion of one minister that "God doesn't hear the prayers of a Jew." Television evangelist Pat Robertson voiced perhaps the clearest expression of this theme when he said: "We have enough votes to run the country. . . . And when the people say, 'We've had enough,' we are going to take over" (Washington Post, 1980). It is this theme of victory and total redemption which most clearly marked the NCR as a "fundamentalist insurgency" during this phase of its existence, and which most clearly set it apart from many other mobilization movements--such as civil rights groups-- which have emphasized the struggle and mobilization themes.

In a sense, the political language of this first phase offered a complete scenario of political conflict and redemption. America is attacked, and seemingly conquered, by the sinister forces of humanism; right-thinking citizens mobilize their unified strength and win a great victory which redeems the nation, presumably once and for all. Such a scenario, it seems, would have a natural attraction for people who think of the world in millenarian terms. The redemption part of the scenario in particular presents a virtually unlimited conception of the majoritarian mandate: that a majority--especially a "moral" one--need not be reluctant to make a nation over in its own image.

The NCR's political language, in this phase, bears a superficial resemblance to that identified by Hofstadter (1965) as embodying the "paranoid style." Fundamentalist insurgents spoke heatedly of the menace of "humanism"; and for them, as for the politically paranoid, "time is forever just running out." But the language lacks the full degree of exaggeration and fantasy which marks the true paranoid style: While allegations of a "humanist threat" certainly seem exaggerated, they do not measure up to the visions of a "vast, insidious preternaturally effective international conspirational network" which Hofstadter found to be a basic paranoid theme. Further, where the truly "politically paranoid" tend to see conspiracy itself as the fundamental "moving force" of history, NCR followers, by and large, do not; indeed, those who believe in a literal interpretation of the Bible and its explanation of history probably cannot concede that much power to the humanists.

The political language of the fundamentalist insurgency phase instead resembles more closely the "pseudo- conservative" style identified by Adorno (1969) and elaborated upon by Hofstadter (1965). The NCR's symbolism is conservative--"big government," "godless forces"--and while specific policy proposals took a back seat to more sweeping cultural and "morality" issues in this phase, they too are conservative in nature. But the struggle-mobilization-redemption scenario discussed above is anything but conservative. Indeed, it is revolutionary, and envisions a virtual theocracy in which basic constitutional guarantees of privacy, separation of church and state, and traditions of cultural pluralism would be swept aside. While opponents of the NCR have indulged in their share of political exaggeration, it is little wonder that many people found the rise of the movement quite disturbing.

In sketching out these dominant themes of NCR political language in this phase, I do not mean to imply

that all public utterances followed precisely this format,
nor that all who sympathized with the NCR were of one mind
on every issue and tactic. And of course I have not
attempted to present all of the political language of this
phase. Rather, I am trying to identify dominant themes
in political strategy; and in this phase the themes are
those of fundamentalist insurgency and redemption from
without. As the 1980 campaign unfolded, however, and
particularly after it reached its conclusion, the NCR found
itself very much interested in, and constrained by, the
very political system it sought to redeem. The result
was a fundamental change in strategy--one which did not
take place overnight, and which may yet be incomplete,
but one which added a second major strategic role--that
of an interest group.

THE SECOND PHASE: NCR AS INTEREST GROUP

The NCR's interest-group strategy began to emerge
during the 1980 election campaign and has further developed
since Ronald Reagan's victory. Change has come gradually,
affecting some wings of the movement more than others,
and is not necessarily permanent. It is a significant
change nonetheless. By "interest group" I refer to groups
which work within the political order, rather than seeking
to storm it from without; to groups whose norms and goals
are predominantly specific and instrumental, rather than
diffuse and consummatory (to borrow Apter's distinction
again); and to those which are more or less ad hoc
alliances of citizens and groups which share some, but
not all, concerns, sentiments, and commitments. The League
of Women Voters and the American Farm Bureau Federation
are American interest groups, by this definition; the New
Christian Right, in its first phase, was not.

To some extent, the addition of an interest-group
strategy is hardly surprising, for the tasks of politics
between elections differ somewhat from those during
campaigns. In election years, mass mobilization efforts
and participation in the electoral arena are a major order
of business, while between elections the emphasis shifts
toward lobbying and bargaining in legislative and
bureaucratic arenas. This is not to imply that lobbyists
close up shop in election years, or that efforts at
mobilizing the public cease between elections. Rather,
I refer to changes in emphasis. Thus, the NCR placed major
emphasis on voter registration in the months leading up

to the 1980 election; but since that time, efforts have
shifted to support for important pieces of legislation,
such as the so-called Family Protection Act.

The strategic changes which are my concern in this
section, however, are more fundamental than those cyclical
changes of emphasis. What is emerging is a new track of
NCR activity in which strategies, relationships with the
rest of the political system, and even organizational
self-image resemble much more those of interest groups
than those of the old fundamentalist insurgency. These
changes can be seen in the major themes of recent NCR
language.

The first major theme is a declared intent to work
within the established political order. While the idea
of a humanist threat remains, the NCR is now less given
to depicting the political system and its major actors
as hopelessly compromised. Moral Majority, Incorporated,
published a manifesto in the New York Times (1980b) of
March 23, 1981, for example, which stated that: "We are
not a political party. We are committed to work within
the two-party system in this nation. . . . We are not
attempting to elect 'born-again' candidates. We are
committed to pluralism." Perhaps most striking in this
regard is the following statement:

> Moral Majority, Inc., is not a religious organization
> attempting to control the government. . . . We simply
> desire to influence government--not control
> government. This, of course, is the right of every
> American, and Moral Majority, Inc., would vigorously
> oppose any Ayatollah-type person rising to power in
> this country.

A major subtheme in this connection is that members
of the NCR are simply insisting on their rights within
the system--asking that their status and values be given
the same respect accorded to others. Rev. Jerry Falwell
in 1980 began to refer to his following as "the largest
minority bloc in the United States." He also stated:
"we're 40 percent of the electorate. . . . If President
Carter named good Christians to 40 percent of the good
jobs we'd think about supporting him" (New York Times,
1980a). This last sounds almost like an affirmative action
program for the righteous and resembles the arguments of
other minority- and ethnic-based interest groups much more
than those of a fundamentalist insurgency. The New York

<u>Times</u> (1980b) manifesto reinforces this subtheme by
contending at several points that all the Moral Majority
is really doing is exercising those political rights which
all citizens hold in a democracy.

One question which must be raised at this point is
whether or not these assurances can be taken at face
value. The NCR in general, and the Reverend Mr. Falwell's
Moral Majority, Incorporated, in particular, aroused
considerable opposition and concern during the 1980
campaign; perhaps the reassurances, and the <u>Times</u>
manifesto in particular, are simply intended to put a less
threatening face on the fundamentalist insurgency. Such
a question is difficult to answer absolutely. But even
if the NCR were <u>simply cleaning up its image</u>, that fact
in itself would be of interest. Presumably, fundamentalist
insurgents who wish to reshape a nation in their own image
would feel little need to brush up their image in the pages
of the most "establishment-oriented," cosmopolitan
newspaper in the nation. Further, while we need not take
every statement solely at face value, there are systemic
developments and historical precedents suggesting that
the NCR's changes are more than superficial.

Secondly, among the newly emerging themes is that
of <u>tolerance for pluralism</u>. While the NCR still sees
a threat from "pornographers, abortionists, and humanists,"
they seem more likely now to express at least a tolerance
for the fact that America is a diverse nation. This notion
is consistent with the intent to work within the existing
order and with the idea that NCR members are simply
insisting on their own democratic rights; and it is quite
a change for a movement which formerly proclaimed its
intent to "make America a Christian nation." The <u>Times</u>
manifesto of Moral Majority, Incorporated, states that:
"We are not a censorship organization. . . . Moral
Majority, Inc., is not an organization committed to
depriving homosexuals of their civil rights as Americans.
. . . No anti-semitic influence is allowed in Moral
Majority, Inc." (<u>New York Times</u>, 1980b). A final
statement on this theme is:

> We do not believe that individuals or organizations
> which disagree with Moral Majority, Inc., belong to
> an immoral minority. However, we do feel that our
> position represents a consensus of the majority of
> Americans. This belief in no way reflects on the
> morality of those who disagree with us.

A third and final theme is that of internal diversity
and ad hoc commitments. A fundamentalist insurgency
demands single-mindedness and total commitment of its
followers. But the New Christian Right as interest group
emphasizes diversity in its membership and in their
convictions. "We are Catholics, Jews, Protestants,
Mormons, Fundamentalists--blacks and whites--farmers,
housewives, and businessmen," says the Times manifesto
(New York Times, 1980b). In describing the group's stand
against abortion, it adds: "Some of us [oppose abortion]
from a theological perspective. Other Moral Majority,
Inc., members believe this from a medical perspective."
In affirming its support for Israel it states:

> Many Moral Majority, Inc., members, because of their
> theological convictions, are committed to the Jewish
> people. Others stand upon the human and civil rights
> of all persons as a premise for support of the state
> of Israel. Other support Israel because of historical
> and legal arguments.

The image sought by this "new manifestation of Moral
Majority Incorporated" is one of an organization
characterized by ad hoc commitments: one which people
join in order to voice common concerns and to support
specific initiatives. Hence:

> Moral Majority, Inc., is a political organization
> providing a platform for religious and nonreligious
> Americans, who share moral values, to address their
> concerns in these areas. Members of Moral Majority,
> Inc., have no common theological premise.

These themes of political language--the intent to
work within the established political order, the tolerance
for pluralism, and emphasis on internal diversity and ad
hoc commitments--point to a new interest-group strategy
for the NCR. While the language of the fundamentalist
insurgency implied a complete political scenario of
struggle, mobilization, and redemption, the interest-group
role proposed no such millenarian view. Rather, it
suggests a more open-ended role as one of a number of
forces within a diverse political order, and a strategy
of pushing for relatively specific goals: a Family
Protection Act, and an antiabortion constitutional
amendment. These goals are hardly modest, but they fall
well short of reshaping the entire political system.

We should remember, at the same time, that this change represents the addition of a new strategic initiative and not necessarily a complete reorientation of the entire movement. Local groups in the New Christian Right have recently indulged in book burnings, for example, which hardly display much tolerance for pluralism. Moral Majority's own manifesto speaks of the group as "united by one central concern--to serve as a special interest group providing a voice for a return to moral sanity in these United States of America" and of "organizing and training millions of Americans who can become moral activists." Much about the NCR has not changed: While it may be in the midst of a transition to new strategies, its substantive positions on cultural and ethical issues remain rather extreme. A complete understanding of the significance of the changes outlined above--indeed, a conclusive verdict on how much has changed at all--must await the passage of time and more extensive study. Still, we can speculate on reasons for the change in strategy and on possible future roles for the NCR.

WHY THE CHANGES?

To the extent that the changes in NCR strategies are real ones, they grow not merely out of the whims of the movement's leadership but out of the more basic events and aspects of American politics. NCR leaders may have originally conceived of their movement as transcending the traditional dynamics of politics, but its strategic development has been directly affected by some of those very forces. Indeed, there are even some historical precedents for the sorts of changes I have discussed.

Brokerage Politics

The predominant style of American politics at the national level is one of brokerage and compromise among a variety of interests and constituencies. This is an incremental politics characterized by instrumental goals and is clearly a style not suited to a fundamentalist insurgency. Indeed, in the Congress, this brokerage style has swallowed up many a political crusade, such as the Populist movement of the late nineteenth century. In the electoral arena, brokerage among interests is common as well and has been reinforced in recent years by campaign finance legislation, which to an extent imposes a common interest-group structure upon a wide range of institutional participants in campaigns. It is also still true that American campaigns are won and lost in the ideological middle.

These factors create strong incentives for the NCR to act as an interest group. Fundamentalist insurgencies by definition cannot bargain and compromise; and if they cannot do that, they can accomplish little in Congress or in the bureaucracy. This generalization holds true even in the Ninety-seventh Congress, for new members will still encounter the dominant brokerage style, will still have to look after their own districts if they wish to be reelected, and will also find that morality issues are but a small segment of the problems that will confront them. Campaign finance reforms treat political organizations as interest groups regardless of their agendas; if they spend money on elections, they must report expenditures and otherwise account for their activities. And winning elections "in the middle," even in years such as 1980, encourages groups not to antagonize middle-of-the-road voters. These incentives do not render all political organizations identical, but they do significantly encourage "insurgents" to behave in more traditional ways, lest they accomplish very little politically.

Diversity of Born-again America

In an earlier section, I discussed the rather surprising degree of diversity to be found in the ranks of the born again. This factor, too, probably encourages an interest-group strategy.

To win single-mindedness and total commitment from a group of people as large and differentiated as the born again would be virtually impossible. As an interest group, however, the NCR could survive with a degree of internal diversity and limited, ad hoc commitments. In this sense, the video ministers and other NCR leadership are constrained by the size and diversity of their flock. And paradoxically, it may well be that if the flock grows larger, it will become even more unruly. Pared down to a true insurgency of the totally committed, it would be so reduced in size as to be largely ineffective.

The Reagan Landslide

Ironically enough, the NCR is also constrained in its strategies by the very success it, and the Right in general, encountered at the polls in 1980. Reagan won the White House by a wide margin; the Republicans gained in the House and took control in the Senate. But these developments, far from giving the NCR total license, encourage it instead to adopt the interest-group role.

One reason for this is that the new Congress presents the NCR, and the Right in general, with its best opportunity in many years to win passage of favorable legislation. To succeed at this, the NCR will have to adopt the time-honored methods of other interest groups and will have to be prepared to hold on through a long process of political pulling and hauling in order to achieve relatively specific ends. Those followers truly interested in the millenarian politics of redemption may well find this process discouraging and move off to other pursuits; those who do not will find themselves immersed in a complex process of legislative politics which consists of much in addition to their "Christian agenda." Either way, the NCR's strategy and presence in the legislative process will be very much like that of hundreds of other groups seeking favorable action from Congress.

The Reagan landslide constrains the NCR in a more general sense as well, for it is very difficult to be insurgents when your side is in power. Daniel Bell (1963) has commented on the same phenomenon in reverse, as it related to the "Far Right" of the 1950s. However much they may have felt the urgency of their political tasks, Dwight Eisenhower's presence in the White House--as a Republican, a moderate conservative, and a military man--kept right-wing organizations from unleashing the full scope of their discontent and resentment. When John Kennedy took over the presidency in 1961, however, they were once again able to point to weakness and treachery in high places, and right-wing activity showed a substantial increase. Similarly, with Reagan in power, the NCR will find it very difficult to contend that "immorality" holds the political high ground; but should the Democrats return to power, many constraints would be removed.

THE FUTURE OF THE NCR

Predicting the future of a strategically ambivalent political movement can be a risky business. As noted above, I am discussing changes and transitions which are still in progress and whose permanence and implications can only be guessed. Much of the future of the NCR depends

144

upon the presidency--upon how long Ronald Reagan holds
power, who will succeed him when he leaves office, and
also upon the degree to which he satisfies or disappoints
the NCR.   Just as Jimmy Carter's election and subsequent
policies did much to encourage the rise of the NCR,
Reagan's administration will have much to do with its
course over the near future. Should Reagan prove
satisfactory to the NCR and should his successors be
similar in their convictions and policies, it is not
difficult to imagine the NCR evolving into an institutionalized interest group, unusual in its policy
preferences, but certainly no insurgency: something of
a "Conservative Council of Churches." But should Reagan
give way to a liberal successor or should he badly
disppoint the NCR and its leadership, the insurgency model
could surface again, and in a climate of weakened political
parties and an alienated, frustrated electorate, could
make many of its critics' fears come to pass.

REFERENCES

Adorno, T. W., et al. The Authoritarian Personality.
    New York: American Jewish Committee; W. W. Norton,
    1969.
Apter, David E. Choice and the Politics of Allocation.
    New Haven: Yale University Press, 1971.
Bell, Daniel. "The Dispossessed." In Daniel Bell (ed.),
    The Radical Right. New York: Doubleday, 1963.
Hofstadter, Richard. "The Paranoid Style in American
    Politics." In Hofstadter, The Paranoid Style in
    American Politics and Other Essays. New York:
    Alfred A. Knopf, pp. 3-40, 1965.
New York Times. "Militant Television Preachers," January
    21, 1980, p. 21, 1980a.
New York Times. "They Have Labeled Moral Majority the
    Extreme Right Because We Speak Out Against Extreme
    Wrong!", (advertisement) March 23, 1981, p. B-11,
    1980b.
New York Times. "Evangelicals' Vote is a Major Target,"
    June 29, 1980, p. 16, 1980c.
New York Times. "Poll Finds Evangelicals Aren't United
    Voting Bloc," September 7, 1980, p. 34, 1980d.
New York Times. New York Times/CBS News exit polling,
    November 9, 1980, p. 28, 1980e.

Newsweek. "A Tide of Born-Again Politics," September 15, 1980, p. 31.

Orwell, George [Eric Blair]. "Politics and the English Language" (1946), In Front of Your Nose, Vol. 4, Collected Essays, Journalism, and Letters of George Orwell, New York: Harcourt, Brace, and World, 1968.

Time. "New Resolve by the New Right." December 8, 1980, p. 24.

Washington Post. "Born-Again Politics," March 30, 1980, p. C-1.

6

The Protestant Ethic, the Christian Right, and the Spirit of Recapitalization

Donald Tomaskovic-Devey

This chapter looks at the recent political importance of the New Christian Right and asks: Why did the social movement organizations known as the New Right or the New Christian Right emerge to social prominence and political power in the late 1970s and early 1980s? I suggest that the New Christian Right provided a diffuse ideological justification for the recapitalization of U.S. capitalism. Unlike Weber's original Protestant ethic thesis, I reject any notion that the New Right or its ideas had a deterministic function for recapitalization. Rather, I argue that just as the original Protestant ethic was coopted and reformulated by capitalism, the current Christian Right's beliefs and energy have been coopted and diverted by economic elites who favor recapitalization policies. The religious and moral energy of the New Right has served to legitimate new forms of economic activity and government policy.

Weber described ascetic Calvinism and its Protestant ethic as the social psychological base that made possible the development of Western capitalist society (Weber, 1958; Tawney, 1958). The "Protestant ethic" is the idea that an individual earns his or her way to heaven by hard work and that if the person is successful, it is a sign of God's favor upon the individual. Weber argued that although the structural preconditions for capitalist development had existed at other times and in other cultures, it was only after the development of an ascetic, rational religious ethos conducive to private capitalist accumulation, like the Protestant ethic, that capitalism could displace prior class and economic systems. Similarly, the most successful capitalists and capitalist nations were those in which this rational religious ethic were strongest.

Weber expected and most social scientists assume that with the growth of rational capitalist/industrial society a corresponding decline in the social importance of religion and religious belief would occur. The Protestant ethic would have to be secularized in order to survive in rational society. And yet in the 1980 election in particular, and from recent U.S. politics in general, it is clear that the religious principle has been an important factor in political debate and motivation. Part of the explanation for this anomaly lies in the unusual resiliance of religion in U.S. society. Burnham (1981) presents cross-cultural data that portray a general decline in religiousness as national economic development rises. The data are surprising both for the strength of this expected relationship and for the exceptionalism of the United States and Canada, in both of which religiousness is high despite economic development.

The United States is a very religious country. The Christian Right is joined in the political arena by a religious Left organizing around issues of poverty and nuclear war. The expectation that religiousness would decline in the face of capitalist rationality does not seem to fit the U.S. case. In the United States the secular Protestant ethic is a part of a general value structure or ideology that remains extremely religious. Although the secularization of the Protestant ethic undoubtedly did take place, it does not follow that religiousness or specifically religious explanations and justifications for individualistic capitalism have disappeared.

The Protestant ethic can best be understood as religious orientation that legitimated the acquisitive spirit of the capitalist entrepreneur, which was previously considered immoral and illegitimate. Conversely, the religious and secular success of the Protestant ethic was precisely the result of its applicability and attractiveness for capitalism as an emerging social system. As Hughey (1982) wrote (referring to both Weber's Protestant ethic and belief systems in general): "In order to attain dominance in a society an idea or ideology must appeal to those groups who have power . . . to translate convictions into policies." It is my contention that the current religious Protestant ethic and the group that has incorporated this idea, the New Christian Right, achieved prominence and some measure of power because their beliefs and movement activity reinforced political and structural changes in U.S. capitalism being implemented by secular economic elites.

THE NEW CHRISTIAN RIGHT

The New Christian Right is a coalition of social movement organizations that includes politicized evangelical religious organizations (e.g., Moral Majority), single-issue social movement organizations (e.g., American Eagle-STOP ERA), and multi-issue conservative political organizations (e.g., National Conservative Political Action Committee and the Conservative Caucus). The single-issue social movements and evangelical organizations are the distinctly Christian or religious part of this movement. The multi-issue political organizations form a more secular leadership with distinctively economic as well as cultural movement objectives. (Lienesch (1982) points out that the New Christian Right is a counterexample to Michels's (1915) iron law of oligarchy. Here the organizational elite is more radical than the movement participants.) Although each organization has its own movement agenda, they share a general ideological consensus, and through the secular leadership network routinely coordinate activity to achieve national political goals.

There are two current explanations for New Right mobilization. The first, found in Lipset and Raab (1981), Crawford (1980), Mottle (1980), see the New Right (and most conservative movements) as examples of status politics. The concept "status politics," the attempt to defend against declining prestige, has a long history in sociological analysis of conservative U.S. social movements (Hofstadter, 1955, 1964; Bell, 1960; Lipset, 1964; and Lipset and Raab, 1970). The second explanation presented by Brienes (1981) characterizes the New Right mobilization as essentially a backlash against the cultural questions and alternatives proposed by the women's movement and the New Left. Both approaches assume that it is the mass evangelical and/or Christian base of the movement that has political impact. Although this may be true for the single-issue social movements operating largely in local politics, it does not explain the national impact of the New Christian Right.

Why doesn't the mass New Christian Right membership have an identifiable effect on national politics? The Christian Right movement activity is largely local. Book burnings, limiting abortion access through intimidation or legislation, antipornography campaigns, creationism, and antibusing activity have all made some headway on the local or state, rather than national levels. The coalition of this local movement activity with a national conservative political movement was a cooptation of that energy.

The secular, economically oriented leadership of the New Right such as Richard Viguerie and Patrick Dolan tried through the media preachers to divert this local energy to support national conservative goals (Leinsch, 1982). Hughey (1982) argued that this economic leadership emanates from the historically declining Main Street (as opposed to Wall Street) capitalist class. He viewed the political cowboys who first came to Washington with Richard Nixon and who got rich through the postwar western expansion, particularly in California, as the carrying class of the still religious and individualistic Protestant ethic. They are promoting a total ideology that links Christianity, the family, and economic freedom in a new holy trinity. The New Christian Right has played a national political function by promoting an ideology (see Leahy, 1975) that expands and thus generalizes the conservative attack on the state. The high level of religiousness in the United States, even among nonevangelical Protestants, made the religious phrasing of political messages generally appealing.

The New Right ideology is similar to older conservative traditions represented by such groups as the John Birch Society (see Westin, 1964). The New Right is concerned with protecting traditional cultural and economic forms from the onslaughts of liberalism. The New Right, however, has introduced two striking innovations in ideology that make it generally more attractive to potential supporters than previous conservative movements were. When one remembers the unusually religious orientation of people in the United States these innovations take on added significance.

The government, because of its legitimation and occasional fostering of new cultural and economic forms such as abortion or socialized medicine, is seen by the Christian Right as the primary enemy to be fought and if possible curtailed. The conservative attack on the state--traditionally criticizing the government as disruptive of otherwise free markets--has new dimensions--cultural and spiritual--because Christians have joined in the criticism.

The second ideological innovation of the Christian Right is its emphasis upon the family. In many ways the profamily campaign of the New Christian Right is a striking ideological addition to the well-entrenched (but now broadened) attack on big government. By championing an attractive and deeply emotional institution like the traditional family, the New Christian Right has provided conservatives (and potential conservatives) a more appealing focal point for political action than capitalism alone. Fairly (1980) has suggested that for the New Right, the liberal antifamily conspiracy has replaced the communist conspiracy that the "radical right" feared in the 1950s and 1960s (see Bell, 1964). It is no longer communists but secular humanists and their efforts to undermine the God-given traditional nuclear family that New Christian Right ideology sees as the single most alarming and destabilizing threat to the American way of life.

This ideological shift in problem areas is highly significant in that it opened the federal government to a new type of criticism. Although conservative ideologies have long criticized the state for interfering in economic affairs, the characterization of the state, politicians in particular, or state policies as antifamily has effectively shifted the conservative attack on the state to cultural instead of purely economic issues and so broadened its potential appeal. Voters who might have rejected Republican candidates out of hand in the past on the grounds of economic self-interest could have reevaluated their assumptions in the face of a religious-cultural criticism that was broadly aimed at big government, and that threw an especially murky shadow over Democrats in particular.

The use of family and Christianity as "positive symbols" (see Edelman, 1964) provides the New Right with an ideology that is appealing to a broad spectrum of the public, cutting across social classes, and as American and wholesome as apple pie. No U.S. politician can argue against the family or Christianity and retain political effectiveness. Thus the ideology of the New Right is in its own right a persuasive force leading to the concrete social and legislative goals of this conservative social movement and a persuasive force for any politician who identifies publicly with this profamily, antistate ideology.

Just as there are "positive symbols" for New Right ideals, there are "negative symbols" for what the New Right considers evils. Foremost among these negative symbols is secular humanism. (See Gusfield (1963) on alcohol and Zurch et al. (1971) on pornography for other negative symbols.) Secular humanists, as portrayed by prominent New Right leaders such as Jerry Falwell and Phyllis

Schlafly, reject or ignore the existence of God, have raised human beings above God, and encourage "moral relativism and amorality, [that] challenges every principle on which America was founded" (Negri, 1981). Simply put, secular humanists are anti-God, antifamily, and anti-American. Such an ideology makes secular humanists easy to hate, even for economic liberals in the United States who remain deeply religious. The New Right belief system goes further, and posits secular humanism as the ruling ideology of the state, especially the educational system. Therefore, it must be fought.

Killian (1964) describes three components that tend to be embodied in social movement ideologies: (1) A version/revision of history; (2) Two visions of the future, one glorious, the other hell; (3) Stereotypical heroes and villains. All three of these components are tied up in the opposed ideological types, the secular humanist and the Christian family. The historical version is one in which the strength of the United States can be understood as a reflection of the Christian values embodied in the traditional family. The current waning of that strength is the result of the dominance of secular humanist values, especially in the educational system and the destruction of the family by feminism. This version of U.S. history leads to two alternative fates for the nation. The first is that the moral and economic salvation of the United States will be accomplished through a return to Christian principles and traditional family patterns. The second, the fate the country is presently heading toward, or at least was before the Reagan victory in 1980, is both damnation because of godless hedonism and economic paralysis because of the leadership of an amoral government. The heroes of this historic struggle between salvation and damnation are the good Christian families of Middle America. The villains are secular humanists, including educators, social scientists, bureaucrats, and assorted liberals. Through its ideology, the New Right has established a powerful position, and an effective disincentive for opposition, especially by politicians.

RECAPITALIZING U.S. CAPITALISM

Although political activity in the name of Christianity was a relatively new development, the beliefs of the New Christian Right have existed for a long time

(Johnston, 1982; Lipset and Raab, 1981; Ribuffo, 1980; Leinsch, 1982). We can see how these beliefs were appealing for various reasons to many people, but why did these old ideas become politically prominant? Clearly, the conscious social movement activity of the more secular New Right elite has to get much of the credit. They not only packaged a total conservative ideology that combined economic and religious issues in a way which was attractive to many people, they also created a coalition of existing movements and media preachers to get the message out and add legitimacy to their economic objectives. We can in some ways think of Viguerie and company as successful "social movement entrepreneurs" who, although not creating grievances for their constituency (as McCarthy and Zald (1973) suggest in their original usage of the term), capitalize on existing social movement and religious energy. They do not build, they co-opt. They are more akin to conglomerate entrepreneurs than to creators of new businesses.

But if the New Right leadership and the media preachers are the carrying group of this New Christian conservatism, it does not follow that they alone have the power to ensure the promotion and success of the ideology. On the contrary, as Hughey (1982) explained, for an idea to have some social effect, it must appeal or at least be tolerated by those elite groups in society that have "the power to translate convictions into policies."

The political and economic milieu of the late seventies and early eighties in the United States is the ultimate determining factor in an understanding of the New Right as a social movement. The goal of New Right movement activity is to change U.S. society in a specific cultural direction. The ability of the New Right to accomplish that goal is largely limited by the availability of political space and elite receptivity for movement activity.

In the mid-seventies, it became apparent that the socially liberal, economically conservative New Deal/Great Society electoral coalition was crumbling. The activist state supported by an expanding economy and socially liberal Congress that had dominated the past thirty-five years of U.S. political history had fallen into disrepute as the economy stagnated and Congress legislated increased social programs without the revenue to cover them (see Miller and Tomaskovic-Devey, 1983). The New Right, among other political groups, is trying to fill the space left by the political fragmentation of liberalism.

The political message of the Christian Right has undoubtedly benefited the economically conservative offensive that the biggest corporations have been waging against the welfare state since the mid-seventies (Miller, 1978; Piven and Cloward, 1982; Miller and Tomaskovic-Devey, 1983).

The conservative political drift in the United States was largely economically conservative until the advent of the New Christian Right. The New Deal/Great Society era has been replaced by a conservatizing political and ideological trend which I have called the "recapitalization of U.S. capitalism" (Miller, 1978; and Miller and Tomaskovic-Devey, 1981, 1983). Recapitalization is an attempt by economic elites and their allies to deal with the declining economic and political fortunes of the United States. The recapitalization solution to this decline has three aspects. The first is to provide additional physical capital to U.S. business through an upward redistribution of income. The second is to increase the role of capitalist (private) activity in the economy by reducing the role and functions of government. And the third aspect of recapitalization is to redefine the cultural expectations of the public, assigning a diminished role and responsibility to the government in personal well-being. Recapitalization is an elite conservative economic program that expects to find the solution to current economic and political problems through the return to simpler capitalist forms. In the short run, almost all of the benefits of recapitalization will accrue to the rich and the largest corporations.

Recapitalization is an economic movement by and for major capitalists; the New Christian Right is a cultural movement by and for fundamentalist Christians. They share little more than conservatism and commitment to free enterprise economies. The shared commitment to free enterprise, however, probably has different bases. The New Right is attracted to the aura of freedom attached to the notion of laissez-faire capitalism. Big business, in contrast, is attracted to the lower cost and higher profit implied by a lessening of regulation and taxation. Although recapitalization-inspired policies were already being instituted during the Carter presidency, it was only with the Reagan election in 1980 that both recapitalization and the New Christian Right had substantial political representation.

Keller (1980) described the Christian Right as "the new troops of political conservatism." The mobilization

of U.S. voters around conservative <u>cultural</u> issues has
served to move the United States, particularly elected
officials, in a further conservative direction. The
political need of elites for electoral support for economic
policies that were clearly not beneficial to the various
working classes (at least in the short run) have added
both prominance and attention to the New Christian Right
message. Secular Wall Street and religious Main Street
have spoken with one tongue, at least on economic issues,
since the 1980 election. The cultural message of the
conservative Christian, profamily New Right helped in a
diffuse ideological sense to promote the legitimacy of
an economic ideology that was basically hostile to the
current needs of many if not most citizens. Religion and
the family helped to provide a moral base for recapitalist
activity.

The cultural issues that mobilized the supporters
and voters of the New Right will not, however, be the main
benefactors of the current conservative politics. Rather,
recapitalization policies aimed at strengthening the
economic position of big business have already been the
primary beneficiaries. All three aspects of recapitali-
zation--upward income redistribution, a more limited social
role for the federal government, and lowered expectations--
have been instituted since 1980. The New Right may have
served, and still be serving, as the moral force for
recapitalization, legitimating the upward redistribution
of national income. The first four years of the Reagan
administration, with its high tax cuts for the rich and
slashes in social programs for the poor, seems to bear
out this assertion. I would suggest that the popular
"mandate" that the Reagan administration has frequently
cited to legitimate these cuts (in taxes and programs)
was at least in part the result of the spread of the
cultural conservatism of the New Right message. In the
first three years of the Reagan government, the major
activities were recapitalization policies of class-based
redistribution, while the cultural issues of the New Right,
although occasionally publicly reaffirmed by the president,
languished.

If the cultural isues of the New Right are not
addressed, however, either the political support of the
current administration from the Christian Right or the
Christian Right movement itself will dry up. Can the New
Right carry through the legislative agenda generated by
its cultural issues? (Reagan has continually expressed
support for the New Right profamily agenda. Although this

is his personal opinion, it does not mean that the president commands sufficient congressional support for this agenda.) Do the Reagan government and future Republican candidates require the continued support of the fundamentalist Christians? If the answer is no, if the New Right is expendable or too weak to carry through its initiatives, then it is likely that the Christian Right will wither in the next political moment. Its energy and organization will be appropriated by recapitalization policies that are mainly economic and favor large corporations and their owners.

In many ways the Christian Right's ideological support for recapitalization policies may no longer be necessary. The investment-productivity-export, free-market analysis is currently shared by almost all national politicians, economists and journalists. In Gramsci's (1971) words, recapitalization has achieved ideological hegemony: It is now the accepted wisdom (Miller and Tomaskovic-Devey, 1983). The morality of recapitalization may no longer be in question. Whether or not the New Christian Right endures as a national political movement, it may have already served its purpose.

REFERENCES

Bell, Daniel. "Status Politics and New Anxieties of the Radical Right." In The End of Ideology. New York: Free Press, 1960.

Bell, Daniel (ed.). The Radical Right. Garden City, N.Y.: Anchor Press, 1964.

Brienes, W. "Backlash and the New Left" presented at the Massachusetts Sociological Association, Wellesley College, 1981.

Burnham, W. "The 1980 Earthquake: Realignment, Reaction or What?" In The Hidden Election, ed. Ferguson and Rogers. New York: Pantheon, 1981.

Crawford, A. Thunder on the Right: The New Right and the Politics of Resentment. New York: Pantheon, 1980.

Edelman, M. The Symbolic Uses of Protest. Urbana: University of Illinois Press, 1964.

Ellerin, M., and A. Kestin. "The New Right." Social Policy 11, 5:55-62, 1981.

Fairly, H. "Born Again Bland." New Republic, Aug. 2, pp. 16-20, 1980.

Gramsci, Antonio. Selections from the Prison Notebook. New York: International Publishers, 1971.

Gusfield, J. Symbolic Crusade. Urbana: University of Illinois Press, 1963.

Hofstadter, Richard. The Age of Reform. N.Y.: Knopf, 1955.

_____. "The Pseudo-Conservative Revolt." In The Radical Right. See Bell 1964.

Hughey, M. "The New Conservatism: Political Ideology and Class Structure in America." Social Research 49,3:791-829, 1982.

Johnston, M. "The New Christian Right in America Politics." Political Quarterly 53,2:181-199, 1982.

Keller, B. "Evangelical Conservatives Move from the Pewsto Polls, But Can They Sway Congress?" Congressional Quarterly, Sept. 6, pp. 2627-2634, 1980.

Killian, L. "Social Movements." In Handbook of Modern Sociology, ed. R. L. Farir. Chicago: Rand McNally, 1964.

Leahy, P. J. "The Anti-Abortion Movement: Testing a Theory of the Rise and Fall of Social Movements." Unpublished Ph.D. thesis, Dept. of Sociology, Syracuse University, New York, 1975.

Leinsch, M. "Right-Wing Religion: Christian Conservatism as a Political Movement." Political Science Quarterly 97,3:403-426, 1982.

Lipset, Seymour Martin. "The Sources of the Radical Right." In The Radical Right. See Bell 1964.

Lipset, Seymour Martin, and E. Raab. "The Politics of Unreason: Right Wing Extremism." In America, 1790-1970. New York: Harper & Row, 1970.

_____. "The Election and the Evangelicals." Commentary 71,3:25-31, 1981.

McCarthy, J. D., and M. Zald. The Trends of Social Movements in America. New York: General Learning Press, 1973.

Michels, R. Political Parties. Glencoe, Ill: Free Press, 1915.

Miller, S. M. "The Recapitalization of Capitalism." Social Policy, Vol. 9, 1978.

_____. Recapitalizing America: The Corporate Distortion of National Policy. Boston: Routledge & Kegan Paul, 1983.

Miller, S. M., and D. Tomaskovic-Devey. "A Critical Look at Reindustrialization." Social Policy 11,4:5-8, 1981.

158

_____. Recapitalizing America: The Corporate
    Distortion of National Policy. Boston: Routledge
    & Kegan Paul, 1983.
Mottle, T. L. "The Analysis of Countermovements." Social
    Problems 27,5:620-635, 1980.
Negri, M. "Humanism Under Fire." Humanist 41,2:4-7,
    1981.
Page, A., and D. A. McClelland. "The Kanawha County
    Textbook Controversy: A Study of the Politics of
    Life Style Concern." Social Forces 57:265-281,
    1978.
Piven, Fran, and Richard Cloward. The New Class War.
    New York: Basic Books, 1982.
Ribuffo, M. "Liberals and That Old-Time Religion."
    Nation. 29:570-73, 1980.
Tawney, R. H. "Forward." In Max Weber, The Protestant
    Ethic and the Spirit of Capitalism. New York:
    Scribner's, 1958.
Weber, Max. The Protestant Ethic and the Spirit of
    Capitalism. New York: Scribners, 1958.
Westin, A. "The John Birch Society". In The Radical
    Right. See Bell 1964.
Zald, M., and R. Ash. "Social Movement Organizations:
    Growth, Decay and Change." Social Forces 44:327-341,
    1966.
Zurch, L. A., et al. "The Anti-Pornography Campaign:
    A Symbolic Crusade." Social Problems 19:217-238,
    1971.

7

Religion and the Abortion Issue

Joseph B. Tamney

In the 1980s abortion is an important political topic. Politicians now debate about when life starts and about the relative rights of mothers and fetuses. Public interest in abortion was no doubt heightened by the attention given the topic in the 1984 presidential election. "The issue of abortion has become so prominent in this year's Presidential campaign that many people on both sides of the question believe that it will not go away whatever the outcome of the election and that the resulting conflict could be bitterly disruptive" (Herbers, 1984b: E3). In the 1984 election, "nine percent of Mr. Reagan's voters identified abortion as a key issue, and two-thirds wanted to prohibit abortions altogether" (Clymer, 1984:16). It would appear, then, that the Reagan victory was due in part to his opposition to abortion. The question of abortion does not, and probably will not, dominate U.S. politics. But it is not likely to go away or become insignificant either.

THE ISSUE

In this paper abortion means the intentional ending of gestation prior to the full development of the fetus. The political question is whether abortion should be legal, and if so, under what conditions. No one defends abortion as good in itself, and there are many people who support the "permanent human life amendment" to the Constitution that would prohibit all abortions. President Reagan strongly supports a constitutional amendment that would ban all abortions except to save the mother's life, but the majority of citizens do not agree with him. The National Opinion Research Center has been asking national samples of adults about abortion since 1972 (in General Social Surveys, or GSSs). The results are shown in Table 7.1. As can be seen, despite all the lobbying and agitation over the last twelve years, attitudes have remained basically the same. Most people accept legalized abortion if the woman's health is endangered, if it is likely that the baby has a serious defect, or if the pregnancy was the result of rape. The country is quite divided, however, concerning legalizing abortion for other reasons that are less objective, i.e., are more a matter of subjective judgment about what the right situation is for childbirth; these reasons, also, seem to give more importance to the woman's own personal goals. An analysis of survey results for 1980 found that only 7 percent of the respondents disapproved of legal abortion for all the reasons listed in Table 7.1 (Granberg and Granberg, 1980:250).

The purpose of this paper is to determine the reasons for public opinion concerning abortion policy, with special attention given to the role of religion in this process. The motivations that lead women to have an abortion will not be considered. Our focus is why people in the United States believe as they do about abortion laws.

DETERMINANTS OF ABORTION ATTITUDES

Among the basic social status characteristics studied by social scientists, formal education has been shown to be the best predictor of abortion attitudes (Granberg and Granberg, 1980:254)./1/ Granberg and Granberg analyzed the General Social Surveys for each of eight years between 1965 and 1978, using statistical techniques that allowed them to isolate the importance of each characteristic studied independently of the other variables in their analysis. Approval of legal abortion was more frequent among the better educated, urbanites, wealthier people, and whites. Age and sex in themselves were not related to abortion attitudes.

More important in predicting people's attitudes toward abortion than social status characteristics were attitudes on other social issues related to private life. People who rejected legal abortion also disapproved of premarital sex, preferred large families, and believed that divorce should be made more difficult. In some years studied, the rejecters also tended to be people who were against

TABLE 7.1
Public Attitudes Toward Abortion, 1972-1984
(In percent)

Agree that an abortion should be legal for a pregnant woman....	1972	1974	1976	1978	1980	1982	1984
...if there is a strong chance there is a serious defect in the baby	79	85	84	82	83	85	80
...if a woman is married and doesn't want any more children	40	47	46	40	47	48	43
...if the woman's own health is endangered by the pregnancy	87	92	91	91	90	92	90
...if the family has very low income and cannot afford any more children	49	55	53	47	52	52	46
...if a woman became pregnant as a result of a rape	79	87	84	83	83	87	80
...if a woman is not married and doesn't want to marry the father	44	50	50	41	48	49	44

Source: General Social Surveys data, National Opinion
Research Center, University of Chicago.

homosexuality and who favored making pornography illegal
(Granberg and Granberg, 1980:256).
     Abortion attitudes were related to a woman's rights
index. For instance, those who rejected abortion also

162

tended to believe that women should devote their energy
to their home and family and leave the running of the
country to men (Granberg and Granberg, 1980:259; and see
also Baker, Epstein, and Forth, 1981). There was no
relation between abortion attitude and approval of capital
punishment, but those who rejected abortion also tended
to disapprove of suicide and euthanasia (Granberg and
Granberg, 1980; and Baker, Epstein, and Forth, 1981).

Regarding religion, people claiming no religious
affiliation and Jews showed more approval of legal abortion
than did Protestants and Catholics, between whom the
differences were small. However, there were significant
differences among Protestants, with Episcopalians tending
to favor legal abortion and Baptists tending to reject
abortion. Interestingly, "the difference between Baptists
and Catholics is not statistically significant in any year"
(Granberg and Granberg, 1980:257; see also D'Antonio and
Stack, 1980). In general, degree of personal religiosity
is related to rejection of abortion; this is especially
true for Catholics; in contrast, this association is weak
or nonexistent among Presbyterians and Episcopalians (see
Baker, Epstein, and Forth, 1981).

Okraku and Halebsky (n.d.) analyzed the 1977 GSS in
a manner similar to the Granbergs'. Trying to organize
the wealth of information available, they interpreted the
disagreement over abortion as a clash between groups
espousing different lifestyles. Reviewing research on
Prohibition (Gusfield, 1963), a public school textbook
controversy (Page and Clelland, 1978), and the Moral
Majority (Tamney and Johnson, 1983), they concluded that
"cultural fundamentalism and the desire to protect
threatened traditional values and lifestyles rest at the
base of a number of highly charged social issues" (Okraku
and Halebsky, n.d.:4). According to Okraku and Halebsky,
antiabortionists are cultural fundamentalists defending
threatened traditional values; proabortionists are those
who have accepted new cultural values centered on
self-actualization. Okraku and Halebsky found abortion
attitudes to be strongly related to attitudes toward family
size and divorce, women's roles, sexual behavior, and the
right to die. They interpret these results as support
for their argument that the abortion struggle is a clash
between cultural fundamentalists and those motivated by
the modern aspiration for self-realization.

Analyzing GSS data from 1974 and 1982, Harris and
Mills (1985) offer a somewhat different interpretation

of the opposing forces on abortion. They perceive the abortion question as related to two conflicting values--responsibility for others and freedom to determine one's own life. Harris and Mills (1985:139) suggested that people tend to believe in both values, i.e., that "individuals should be loyal . . . , do what is good for those who depend upon them . . . and not insist upon their own way where that might injure others," as well as that "individuals should be free to determine their own lives." Whether a person decides in favor or against an abortion, according to Harris and Mills, depends upon the person's background and the specifics of the situation, which factors determine whether responsibility to the fetus or freedom is the dominant value followed by the decisionmaker. The researchers found evidence that was consistent with this interpretation but far from proof of the correctness of their hypothesis.

In a sense we know more about abortion than we understand. Abortion attitudes are related to a number of variables; what is not clear is the causal order among all the relationships found. Moreover, recent work suggests that reasons for abortion attitudes are different for men and women, and this means the need for analytic techniques more sophisticated than used in much of the previous research (Barnartt and Harris, 1982). All researchers, however, agree that religion is related to abortion attitudes.

IDEOLOGY AND ABORTION

Numerous commentators agree that the abortion controversy is a conflict between two opposing camps, but they do not agree on the characterization of the two sides; according to Woodward and Uehling (1985), opponents of abortion are motivated by their belief that abortion is murder, and those on the other side seek to increase women's control over the reproductive process; Harris and Mills (1985) portray the abortion controversy as a struggle between people who give primacy to social responsibility and those who give primacy to freedom of the individual; Okraku and Halebsky (n.d.) describe abortion opponents as people committed to the defense of cultural traditions, and prochoice advocates as those who value self-realization. In reality there are numerous reasons for abortion attitudes. The literature on abortion, however, suggests that a few ideologies dominate the abortion conflict. Needless to say Christianity has a prominent role, especially, but not inclusively, among antiabortionists.

The Christian Tradition and Abortion

There is only one passage in the Old Testament that explicitly refers to abortion "and this passage concerns spontaneous abortion incidental to a quarrel. . . . By implication, the unborn was not considered an individual having a life regarded as human" (Grisez, 1970:123; the biblical reference is Ex 21:22-23)./2/ There is no explicit discussion of abortion in the New Testament. In the writings of early Christians there are condemnations of abortion, i.e., of taking the life of an unborn child. For instance, in 374 St. Basil the Great wrote, "Whoever purposely destroys a fetus incurs the penalty of murder" (quoted in Grisez, 1970:142). The topic received little attention during the medieval period and among Protestant reform leaders. A papal decree in the thirteenth century considered all abortions as sins, but only the abortion of an animated or vivified fetus was considered murder. It was assumed that "a male embryo receives a soul at forty days of development [i.e., became animated], a female at eighty" (Grisez, 1970:153). But strong papal condemnations of all abortions appeared in the sixteenth century. However, even after this period some Catholic scholars allowed abortion of a nonanimated fetus to save the mother's life. As recently as the nineteenth century some Catholics argued that if the fetus threatened a mother's life, the fetus could be dealt with as any other aggressor; it was also argued that if the lives of both fetus and mother were threatened, the life of the latter should have priority. But the papal office has consistently condemned all abortions, even to save the mother's life. As Pope Pius XII wrote in 1951, "The child, formed in the womb of the mother, is a gift from God, who confides it to the care of its parents" (quoted in Grisez, 1970:182). The pope linked the embryo with God, thus minimizing the rights of parents.

Catholics have been dominant among Christian writers on abortion.

Any Protestant moralist writing about abortion is necessarily indebted to the work of his Roman Catholic colleagues. Their work on this subject shows historical learning that is often absent among Protestants; it shows philosophical acumen exercised with great finesse once their starting principles are accepted; it shows command of the medical aspects of abortion beyond what one finds in cursory Protestant discussions; and it shows extraordinary seriousness about particular moral actions (Gustafson, 1970:101).

The Christian tradition on abortion, then, has been mostly influenced by Catholic writers who have generally condemned all abortions.

But it is also true that there have been dissenting voices throughout Christian history. Moreover, there are no explicit condemnations of all abortions in the Bible. Christian policy depends on tradition rather than explicit biblical references. This tradition has been criticized as so influenced by culture as to be an inadequate guide to the present and the future. Christian discussions of abortion have occurred in the context of societies in which women were regarded as male property and have been written by men who condemned sex for pleasure. "Denunciations of abortion as homicide and murder in Christian theological writings were often rhetorical flourishes, while the moral reason for opposition was condemnation of women's sexuality, aimed at censuring wicked, 'wanton' women--that is, those who expressed their sexuality apart from procreative intent" (Harrison, 1983:128-129).

In sum, although most Christian writers on abortion have condemned all such acts, this position is not explicitly biblical and is part of a tradition that is criticized as reflecting an unchristian patriarchal bias.

ANTIABORTION FORCES

Conover and Gray (1983) studied a sample of delegates to the White House Conference on Families. Antiabortion attitudes occurred in two different groups: antifeminists, who constituted the larger group, and women opposed specifically to abortion for religious reasons. Many of the latter were Catholics (Conover and Gray, 1983: 106-107). No doubt many of the antifeminists were affiliated with or supporters of the Christian Right. The Christian Right, bolstered by sympathy from President

Reagan, and Roman Catholic bishops have increasingly made abortion a religious political issue. "In the past, the [right-to-life] movement was largely secular but with roots in the churches. Now it is directly connected with religious denominations" (Herbers, 1984b: E3).

The Moral Majority, the strongest organization within the Christian Right, is prolife and protraditional family, favors a strong military and the defense of Israel and opposes illegal drugs, pornography, and the ERA (Falwell, 1981:189-190). What seems to tie these issue positions together is an interest in defending traditional values./3/ Falwell (1981:23) said, "I would hope that in this decade we will be able to bring the nation back to an appreciation of the traditional values and moral principles that really have been the American way for 200 years." No doubt it is necessary that Falwell and others of similar mind be able to trace their beliefs and values back to the Bible, but their rhetoric routinely identifies their movement with a defense of tradition./4/ The Christian Right exemplifies a religious form of cultural fundamentalism.

Illustrative of the work of the Moral Majority are the efforts of a related state organization, Pennsylvanians for Biblical Morality (PBM), which lobbied on behalf of the Pennsylvania Abortion Control Act. Their moral concern "centered on the sanctity of the tradition of family, defined by fundamentalists as a patriarchal arrangement in which the father provides the income; the mother raises the children, does not work outside the home, and obeys her husband; and the children are obedient to authorities" (Cable, 1984:289). This concern translated into opposition not only to abortion but also to such things as sex education, pornography, homosexuality, and the ERA. In addition, the Christian Right has sought to curtail federally funded family planning services. Birth control, like abortion, supposedly contributes to sexual freedom (Schwartz, 1985). The Christian Right opposes a set of practices all in the name of tradition, invoking especially the traditional family.

There are opponents of abortion who are not part of the religious Right but accept the same issue positions and organize around being "pro-family" (Conover and Gray, 1983:76). They are secular traditionalists.

Pro-life activists agree that men and women, as a result of . . . intrinsic differences, have different roles to play: men are best suited to the public world of work, and women are best suited to rear children, manage homes, and love and care for husbands. Most pro-life activists believe that motherhood--the raising of children and families--is the most fulfilling role that women can have (Luker, 1984:160).

But members of the prolife movement do more than defend motherhood. They, also, tend to oppose contraception, sex education (Schwartz, 1985), and the ERA (Granberg, 1982). It is suggested, then, that many of those in the prolife movement whose involvement is not religiously motivated are guided by concerns similar to those of the Christian Right. Such people are secular cultural fundamentalists, committed to defending values that are important because they give significance to their lives and that are legitimate and unquestionable because these values are part of tradition.

There is, however, another aspect of the prolife movement. Luker's work contains several statements by those opposing abortion that imply a desire to have their lives shaped by nature, although for some, nature is a surrogate for God's will. "Because pro-life people believe that the purpose of sexuality is to have children, they also believe that one should not plan the exact number and timing of children too carefully, for it is both wrong and foolish to make detailed life plans that depend upon exact control of fertility" (Luker, 1984:170-171). The point is that some individuals find justification for their life in the belief it is according to nature. Like tradition, nature has the power to give meaning to our lives.

A third major force opposing abortion has been the Catholic Church./5/

The moral malice of abortion is found simply in the fact that it is a directly intended and totally indefensible destruction of innocent human life. . . .

The only consideration that could make direct abortion tenable would be the supposition that the fetus is not human until after it has been delivered and has its existence completely separate from the mother. This is unacceptable legally, physiologically, philosophically, and theologically. After a certain stage of intrauterine development it is

perfectly evident that fetal life is fully human.
Although some might speculate as to when that stage
is reached, there is no way of arriving at this
knowledge by any known criterion; and as long as it
is probable that embryonic life is human from the
first moment of its existence, the purposeful
termination of any pregnancy contains the moral malice
of the violation of man's most fundamental human
right--the right to life itself (O'Donnell, 1967:28,
29).

Of course not all Catholics accept the official position.
In 1984 more than one hundred Catholics published an ad
in the New York Times calling for discussion of the
abortion issue (Editorial, 1985). A specific alternative
proposal was presented in the Catholic lay journal
Commonweal. Peter Steinfels (1981:663-664) beginning
with the assumption that "the moral status of the fetus
in its early development is a genuinely difficult problem,"
argued on practical grounds for a law prohibiting abortion
after eight weeks of development: "At this point . . . all
organs are present that will later be developed fully . .
. the unborn individual has a distinctly human appearance
. . . and is over one inch in size." Steinfels would allow
abortions after this stage of development only for a few
most serious reasons such as danger to the mother's life.
There is, then, diversity of opinion among Catholics, but
the official representatives of Catholicism in the United
States, the bishops, have presented a united front against
all abortions./6/
    Almost ten years ago, the National Conference of
Catholic Bishops adopted the Pastoral Plan for Pro-Life
Activities. However, the issue became especially relevant
in the 1984 presidential election because the Democratic
candidate for vice president was Catholic and because some
bishops made abortion the most important campaign issue.
However, writing on behalf of the Administrative Board
of the United States Catholic Conference, Bishop James
W. Malone emphasized that the Catholic church is concerned
about many issues.

As I said on August 9, these concerns range from
protecting human life from the attack of abortion,
to safeguarding human life from the devastation of
nuclear war; they extend to the enhancement of life
through promoting human rights and satisfying human
needs like nutrition, education, housing, and health
care, especially for the poor. We emphasize that

the needs of the poor must be adequately addressed if we are to be considered a just and compassionate society (Malone, 1984a:13).

The bishop did add that two issues were being given special emphasis: "the prevention of nuclear war and the protection of unborn human life." But in his address to the recent annual meeting of the Conference of Bishops, Bishop Malone, who is president of the conference, opposed a "single-issue strategy" (Malone, 1984b:16).

There is disagreement within the Catholic church between those who make abortion the primary political issue (notably, Bishop Law of Boston and Archbishop O'Connor of New York City) and others such as Bishop Malone and Cardinal Bernardin of Chicago who has referred to the issues of abortion, nuclear warfare, and poverty as forming a "seamless garment." "'There is danger in the seamless garment,' Archbishop O'Connor explained in a recent interview. 'The danger is in losing the focus. We are all concerned about nuclear war, but it is a potential slaughter. Abortion is the slaughter that is taking place all around us'" (Goldman, 1984:38). There is significant disagreement among the bishops, therefore, but the "seamless garment" perspective seems dominant.

In a recent speech, the conservative Archbishop John O'Connor seemed to suggest that a compromise might be possible with supporters of legalized abortion.

As Father Hesburgh of Notre Dame has observed, tragically, in essence, we may never again come to an agreement in our land that all abortion should be declared illegal, and some may passionately believe that exception should be made in cases of rape, of incest, or truly grave threat to the actual physical survival of the mother. Whatever we may believe about such exceptions, however, we know that they constitute a fraction of the abortions taking place, so that at the very least we can come to grips with what is the real and the frightening issue of the day: abortion on demand (O'Connor, 1984:14).

The Archbishop seems to be willing to accept as a compromise a law that would prohibit abortions for what I have called the more subjective reasons, which the bishop (and others) referred to as abortion on demand.

There are also people who accept the primacy of a right to life, but whose reasons for doing so are not particularly related to Catholic pronouncements on abortion. For instance, some doctors and nurses, believing that medical ethics implies a primary obligation to protect life, support the prolife movement (Smith, 1985), and some lawyers aid this movement because they fear acceptance of abortion will lead to euthanasia (Chambers, 1984).

Thus, on the antiabortion side there are four distinct ideological positions: the Christian Right traditionalists, the secular traditionalists, the Catholic moralists, and others who accept the moral argument of the Catholic church but who ascribe no special authority to Catholic clergy on this issue. Specific individuals, of course, may accept more than one ideological position, and formal organizations representing these ideologies are working together to make abortion illegal.

An important question is whether the abortion issue will produce a broad political religious coalition of the Christian Right and the Catholic church. Jerry Falwell is working toward this end, yet such a coalition seems highly unlikely. Recently, the bishops made public a draft of a pastoral letter on the economy. In an article about this draft, Falwell (1984:12A) referred to "their courageous stand against abortion" but was quite critical of the draft letter. The Christian Right and the Catholic church come to the abortion issue from two different frameworks. The Right defends a tradition linked to a literal interpretation of the Bible; the bishops are developing a "seamless garment" of moral positions crafted for use in the modern world./7/ Consistent with this interpretation, an analysis of GSS data found that among Protestant fundamentalists attitude toward abortion was more strongly related to traditional sexual attitudes than to respect for life, while the reverse was true for Catholics (Jelen, 1984). No politician can simultaneously espouse both the traditional and the Catholic worldviews./8/

PROLEGALIZED ABORTION FORCES

Those supporting legalized abortion do so to varying degrees and for a variety of reasons. Religious leaders from mainline Protestant churches and Reform Jewish congregations have supported the prochoice movement (Tatalovich and Daynes, 1981:151). "The mainline Protestant churches generally oppose abortion but consider it a matter of personal choice and have preferred to pursue such social issues as poverty and nuclear arms control"

(Herbers, 1984b: E3). There are liberal Protestant scholars, however, who take a more lenient position than either the Christian Right or the Catholic church. For instance, George Williams (1970) of Harvard Divinity School, accepted abortion for a number of reasons including rape and a seriously defective fetus. There also exists among Protestant scholars an unwillingness to be dogmatic regarding abortion. Gustafson, for example, noted the difficulty of reaching moral decisions in specific cases of abortion. In general he preferred avoiding abortion but was ready to tolerate exceptions to save the mother's life, if the pregnancy resulted from sexual crimes, or if "the social and emotional conditions do not appear to be beneficial for the well-being of the mother and the child" (Gustafson, 1970:116). He presented a hypothetical case, and commented, "There can be no guarantee of an objectively right action in the situation I have discussed since there are several values which are objectively important, but which do not resolve themselves into a harmonious relation to each other. Since there is not a single overriding determination of what constitutes a right action, there can be no unambiguously right act" (Gustafson, 1970:119). Given such ambiguity, there are those who want no state regulations so that individuals can reach their own decisions about the relative importance of conflicting values.

But there are also people who go beyond opposing state regulation of abortion and affirm that a woman has a right to have an abortion if she so chooses. We will consider next the different ideological bases for a belief in such a right.

Abortion and Freedom of Choice

Support for abortion often comes from people who believe in minimizing control, especially state control, over any individual. Rather simplistically, an officer of a prochoice group remarked, "It is a question of control: who controls reproduction--the government or the individuals" (quoted in Tatalovich and Daynes, 1981:153). But prochoice advocates seek more than elimination of state control: They want individual women, free from all social pressures, to have the right to determine whether or not an abortion will occur.

Fundamental to this orientation is valuing individual freedom. John Garvey, a Catholic writer who does not support abortion rights, has acknowledged the seriousness

to freedom. "Choice is the thing that makes us human. . .
. Our freedom is terrifying, and essential. This is the
special insight of the modern West" (Garvey, 1982:10).
When the Supreme Court handed down the famous Roe v. Wade
decision on abortion in 1973 the justices tried to balance
the duty of the state to protect human life and the
mother's right to privacy. The latter, of course, reflects
the basic role of individual freedom in U.S. culture.

Many prochoice people seek a law that gives complete
control over abortion to the mothers. Such a goal is often
accompanied by a rejection of the assertion that the fetus
is a human person. In fact there is no agreement among
the public as to when a person exists. In the Roe decision
the Supreme Court decided that a state could act to protect
a fetus when it attained viability, that is, "the point
at which a fetus could live by itself outside the mother's
womb, albeit with artificial aids. . . ." (Mohr, 1978:
249). But that is simply one approach to a difficult
issue. It has been suggested that we distinguish "a form
of human life" from an "individual human being" and both
of these from a "person." Harrison (1983:216) stated the
opinion "that the most plausible early biological criteria
for justifiably imparting to a fetus the status of an
individuated human life form comes with the development
of fetal viability," and that "one criterion that must
be included as a foundational requirement of 'personhood'
is the discrete bodily existence achieved through birth"
(p. 220). In the view of another author, "an individual
becomes a person only when he or she becomes a responsible
moral agent--around age three or four." (Woodward and
Uehling, 1985:29), although these people do not support
taking a life after birth regardless of their stance as
to when a living entity becomes a "person." But when
distinctions such as the aforementioned are made, the
equation of all abortions to murder is of course rejected.
Thus, weight can be given to the mother's right to decide
her own life.

The defense of individual freedom is an important
justification for proabortion laws, especially when
abortion or some abortions are not considered destructive
of an individual human being.

Self-realization Ideology

Some prochoice supporters go beyond defending their
position in the name of freedom. They stress not the

importance of the absence of restraint by others but the desirability of having opportunities for self-fulfillment. They argue that for women to be truly human, i.e., to be able to live up to the demands of being a person, they must have control over their lives, and for women this especially means control over procreation. The goal is a society that bases its social policies on the need to maximize individual freedom, growth, and creativity. In such a society women would have the power of procreative choice (Harrison, 1983).

Among those espousing this view, abortion is understood in the context of womens' issues. "Safer contraception, greater economic and social security, stronger support for childrearing, lessening of racial brutality, reduction of violence against women (including incest, rape, and sterilization abuse) are not on the horizon. It is not a promising time for enhancing the quality of most women's lives" (Harrison, 1983:4). Harrison (p. 197) stated further that "bodily integrity, or the power of self-direction as an embodied human being, is even more substantively conditional of human worth and dignity than most of the political rights reputed to be basic in a liberal society." Legalized abortion, in this perspective, is one means for achieving the conditions conducive to women having dignity and reaching fulfillment as persons.

For some the self-realization perspective is rooted in religion. Beverly Wildung Harrison uses a feminist liberation theological orientation, but the self-realization perspective need not be specifically feminist or religious.

Compounding the problem of communication and understanding among those who disagree about abortion is the fact that the self-realization ideology is a modern phenomenon. The belief that an individual can and should shape her or his own life is the seed for the self-realization ideology. "Of course, this emphasis on human beings as shapers of history, nature, even God, is a peculiarly modern sensibility. . . . Certainly, a volitional approach characterizes much contemporary feminism, which rejects appeals to 'woman's nature' and to biological determinism" (Segers, 1983:411). Prochoice activists emphasize responsibility and planning. People should have children when they want them, can afford them, and have the emotional capability to care for and have children (Luker, 1984:181-182). In contrast, "because

most pro-life people have a deep faith in God, they also
believe in the rightness of His plan for the world" (Luker,
1984:186). Behind all the antiabortion ideologies is a
passivity before tradition or nature or God's will, and
behind the prochoice ideologies is an activist orientation
that is peculiarly modern.

OTHER REASONS FOR ABORTION ATTITUDES

There are many reasons for supporting or opposing
abortion that fall outside the ideologies just discussed.
Men may feel threatened by women in the work force, feel
a diffuse hostility toward women, and express their
feelings by refusing to give women reproductive control
(Luker, 1984:238). Some people reject the Supreme Court's
abortion decision in the name of states' rights (Mohr,
1978:260). Others condemn abortion laws because religious
leaders urge such action. On the other side, men may
support abortion leniency because they believe it results
in increased sexual activity, since people have less fear
of the consequences of pregnancy (Harrison, 1983:163).
Especially important among health professionals is the
desire to avoid the deaths and harm that result when
illegal abortions are performed. Working women may support
legal abortion as a way of ensuring they can avoid
childbearing and thus be able to continue working.
Legalized abortion is supported by some because they hold
"a subtle white supremacy doctrine and an anti-working-
class bias," and thus want to reduce births among
minorities and those not affluent (Harrison, 1983:171).

Abortion is an issue related to many important
cultural beliefs and values, and therefore those who seek
to outlaw abortions as well as those who seek its
legalization act from diverse motives. Undoubtedly,
individuals often have multiple reasons for their attitude
toward abortion and at times waver in their stance toward
abortion because of their different responses to this
issue.

Admitting all this, I have tried in the preceding
pages to highlight what seem to be the major ideologies
related to the abortion controversy. No doubt there are
specific cases in which abortions occurred that would be
offensive to people both pro- and antilegalized abortion.
"Abortions performed on women without the knowledge and
consent of their husbands, abortions performed on

'promiscuous' teenagers, abortions performed on women who
'couldn't be bothered' to use contraception--all offend,
to some degree, certain deeply held American values"
(Luker, 1984:228). Yet some people believe it necessary
for ideological reasons to have a public policy legalizing
abortion. I want to emphasize that the abortion struggle
needs to be seen as a battleground on which numerous
ideological forces contend with each other for control
of the state.

Social Class and Ideology

As discussed earlier in this chapter, research has
shown that approval of legal abortion is higher among
wealthier, more educated people. "The fight over abortion
is a battle between classes and worldviews; between a
primarily working-class group that sees its values under
attack, and a middle- and upper-class group that sees
itself fighting for freedom and enlightenment" (Dionne,
1982:78). But there is no perfect fit between class and
ideology. Many educated Catholics, for instance, oppose
legalizing abortion. Yet it is true that ideological
positions are not randomly distributed across the social
structure. The association of class and ideology adds
another dimension to the abortion issue because legalizing
abortion can be perceived as an attempt by the
establishment to impose its will on the relative powerless,
thus creating working-class resentment about the
legalization of abortion.

CONCLUSIONS

The issue is not whether abortion is or is not
desirable. None of the ideologies discussed in this paper
is a defense of abortion itself; rather, the issue is the
legalization of abortion. Those favoring legal abortion
do so because they uphold values that under certain
conditions justify, in their eyes, aborting a fetus. But
from all points of view there would be no abortions in
the best of all possible worlds.

As of 1984, public opinion remained divided on the
issue of abortion. Although religion is an important
determinant of abortion attitudes, the stability of
attitudes since 1972 implies that pronouncements by the
Christian Right and the Catholic church might not have

significantly affected public opinion. It is possible, however, that as these religious groups increase their political and propaganda campaigns, they may become more effective forces on behalf of laws to limit abortions./9/

The Christian Right and some in the Catholic church reduce a complex moral issue to a clean-cut struggle between right and wrong; thus, the disagreement over abortion is perceived as a contest between the "Army of God" and Satan (Ridgeway, 1985). But such is not the reality of the situation. The Moral Majority and the bishops are confronted by people who have chosen different ideologies that give purpose and meaning to their lives. The abortion controversy lays bare not the selfishness of the public, as the Christian Right would have us believe, but the ideological diversity within the U.S. population, which makes the search for a perfect policy on abortion a chimera.

NOTES

1.   Among Catholics, education is not related to abortion attitudes (Jones and Westoff, 1973; Granberg and Granberg, 1980). However, this result may have occurred because researchers did not divide Catholics into those who attended Catholic schools and those who did not.

2.   Jewish tradition is more flexible than Christian traditions on the subject of abortion. "Thus a Jewish thinker of our day can find in his tradition justification for an extremely elastic concept of therapeutic abortion. He can also find a basis for regarding any abortion not justified by a direct threat to the mother's life an infanticide" (Grisez, 1970:135).

3.   It should not be assumed that supporters of the Moral Majority all accept the leadership's positions. One study in Texas found that 34 percent of people who supported the Moral Majority disagreed that abortion is a sin (Shupe and Stacey, 1982:36).

4.   However, at a meeting of the Harvard Law Forum Falwell said that the battle for abortion "is a battle for the civil rights of the unborn." (Herbers, 1984b:15). It would appear that Falwell used a humanist argument rather than the argument from tradition in this talk.

5.   Other churches that have issued antiabortion statements include the Church of Jesus Christ of Latter-Day

Saints, the Church of Christ, the Southern Baptist church, and the Lutheran church (Missouri Synod) (Tatalovich and Daynes, 1981:157-158).

6. In 1980, about half of the Catholic population agreed with the church position forbidding all abortions under any circumstances (Dolan, 1981:125). In 1984, 46 percent of Catholics who attended church about weekly supported a constitutional amendment banning all abortions. The figure for other Catholics was 21 percent. Data were from a sample of probable voters (New York Times/CBS News Poll, 1984).

7. It should be noted, however, that a small number of bishops have taken stands on homosexuality that align them with the Christian Right (Goldstein, 1984). Fundamentalists and some Catholics have found common ground on opposition to abortion and homosexuality, and aid to private schools.

8. There are theologically conservative Christian groups such as Evangelicals for Social Action that are similar in perspective to the bishops. (For a brief discussion of this group consult Cox, 1984:17-18.)

9. However, technological development may make the illegalization of abortion either unenforceable or irrelevant. "It is anticipated that a low-priced suppository or pill that can induce abortion in the early weeks of pregnancy will soon be available. If such a product is marketed, it is likely to become a popular form of contraceptive--not only discouraging research on other contraceptives, but making abortion a completely privatized and commercialized act" (Kolbenschlag, 1985:182).

REFERENCES

Baker, Ross K., Laurily K. Epstein, and Rodney D. Forth. "Matters of Life and Death." American Politics Quarterly 9 (January):89-102, 1981.
Barnartt, Sharon N., and Richard J. Harris. "Recent Changes in Predictors of Abortion Attitudes." Sociology and Social Research 66 (April):320-334, 1982.
Cable, Sherry. "Professionalization in Social Movement Organization: A Case Study of Pennsylvanians for Biblical Morality." Sociological Focus 17 (October):287-304, 1984.
Chambers, Marcia. "Advocates for the Right to Life." New York Times Magazine (16 December):94-105, 1984.

178

Clymer, Adam. "Long-Range Hope for Republicans is Found
     in Polls." New York Times (11 November):1, 16,
     1984.
Conover, Pamela Johnston, and Virginia Gray. Feminism
     and the New Right. New York: Praeger, 1983.
Cox, Harvey. Religion in the Secular City. New York:
     Simon and Schuster, 1984.
D'Antonio, William V., and Steven Stack. "Religion, Ideal
     Family Size, and Abortion: Extending Renzi's
     Hypothesis." Journal for the Scientific Study of
     Religion 19 (December):397-408, 1980.
Dionne, E. J. "Liberals and the Class War on Abortion."
     Commonweal 109 (12 February):76-78, 1982.
Dolan, Jay P. "A Catholic Romance with Modernity."
     Wilson Quarterly 5 (Autumn):120-123, 1981.
Editorial. "American Nuns Face Vatican Ultimatum."
     Christian Century 102 (23 January):67-68, 1985.
Falwell, Jerry. "An Agenda for the Eighties." In The
     Fundamentatlist Phenomenon, eds. Jerry Falwell,
     Ed Dobson, and Ed Hindson, 186-223. New York:
     Doubleday, 1980.
_____. "The Lone Ranger of Fundamentalism."
     Christianity Today 25 (4 September):22-27, 1981.
_____. "Churches Should Care for Poor." USA
     Today (15 November):12A, 1984.
Garvey, John. "Choice as Absolute." Commonweal 109
     (15 January):9-10, 1982.
Goldman, Ari L. "New York's Controversial Archbishop."
     New York Times Magazine (14 October):38-42, 46-51,
     and 70, 1984.
Goldstein, Richard. "John O'Connor's Dark Victory."
     Village Voice 29 (25 September):23-24, 1984.
Granberg, Donald. "Pro-Choice, Pro-Life: More on
     Stereotypes." Commonweal 109 (12 February):78-80,
     1982.
Granberg, Donald, and Beth Wellman Granberg. "Abortion
     Attitudes, 1965-1980: Trends and Determinants."
     Family Planning Perspectives 12 (September/
     October):250-261, 1980.
Grisez, Germain G. Abortion. New York: Corpus Books,
     1970.
Gusfield, Joseph R. Symbolic Crusade: Status Politics
     and the American Temperance Movement. Urbana:
     University of Illinois Press, 1963.

Gustafson, James M. "A Protestant Ethical Approach."
   In The Morality of Abortion, ed. John T. Noonan,
   Jr., 101-122. Cambridge: Harvard University Press,
   1970.
Harris, Richard J., and Edgar W. Mills. "Religion, Values,
   and Attitudes Toward Abortion." Journal for the
   Scientific Study of Religion 24 (June):137-154,
   1985.
Harrison, Beverly Wildung. Our Right to Choose.
   Boston: Beacon, 1983.
Herbers, John. "Abortion Fight Likened to Battle on Civil
   Rights." New York Times (23 September):15, 1984a.
_____. "Abortion Issue Threatens to Become
   Profoundly Divisive." New York Times (14
   October):E3, 1984b.
Jelen, Ted G. "Respect for Life, Sexual Morality, and
   Opposition to Abortion." Review of Religious
   Research 25 (March):220-231, 1984.
Jones, Elise F., and Charles F. Westoff. "Changes in
   Attitudes Toward Abortion: With Emphasis Upon the
   National Fertility Study Data." In The Abortion
   Experience, ed. Honard J. Osofsky and Joy D.
   Osofsky, 468-481. New York: Harper and Row, 1973.
Kolbenschlag, Madonna. "Abortion and Moral Consensus:
   Beyond Solomon's Choice." Christian Century 102
   (20 February):179-183, 1985.
Luker, Kristin. Abortion and the Politics of
   Motherhood. Berkeley: University of California
   Press, 1984.
Malone, James W. "Text of Bishops' Statement on Role of
   the Church in Politics." New York Times (14
   October):13, 1984a.
_____. "Excerpts From Address to Bishops on Shaping
   Public Policies." New York Times (13 November):16,
   1984b.
Mohr, James C. Abortion in America. Oxford: Oxford
   University Press, 1978.
New York Times/CBS News Poll. "Religion and Politics:
   The 1984 Campaign." New York Times (19
   September):13, 1984.
O'Connor, John J. "Key Portions of Archbishop's Speech
   on Abortion and Politics." New York Times (16
   October):14, 1984.
O'Donnell, T. J. "Abortion, II (Moral Aspect)." In New
   Catholic Encyclopedia, Vol. 6, 28-29. New York:
   McGraw-Hill, 1967.

180

Okraku, Ishmael O., and Sandor Halebsky. "Individual
     Autonomy and Attitudes Toward Elective Abortion."
     Unpublished manuscript, n. d.
Page, Ann L., and Donald A. Clelland. "The Kanawha County
     Textbook Controversy: A Study of the Politics of
     Life Style Concern." Social Forces 57
     (September):265-81, 1978.
Pollit, Katha. "Letter to the Editor." Village Voice
     20 (16 October):8, 1984.
Ridgeway, James. "Unholy Terrorists." Village Voice
     30 (15 January):18-19, 93, 1985.
Schwartz, Amy E. "Bitter Pill." New Republic (18
     February):10-12, 1985.
Segers, Mary. "Abortion: A Feminist Perspective."
     Christianity and Crisis 43 (31 October): 410-413,
     1983.
Shupe, Anson, and William A. Stacey. Born Again Politics
     and the Moral Majority: What Social Surveys Really
     Show. New York: Edwin Mellen Press, 1982.
Smith, Harold. "An Interview with Thomas Elkins."
     Christianity Today 29 (18 January):18-25, 1985.
Steinfels, Peter. "The Search for an Alternative."
     Commonweal 108 (20 November):660-664, 1981.
Tamney, Joseph B., and Stephen D. Johnson. "The Moral
     Majority in Middletown." Journal for the Scientific
     Study of Religion 22 (June 1983):145-156, 1983.
Tatalovich, Raymond, and Byron W. Daynes. The Politics
     of Abortion. New York: Praeger, 1981.
Williams, George Huntston. "The Sacred Condominium."
     In The Morality of Abortion, ed. John T. Noonan,
     Jr. 146-171. Cambridge: Harvard University Press,
     1970.
Woodward, Kenneth L., and Mark D. Uehling. "The Hardest
     Question." Newsweek (14 January):29, 1985.

8

The Christian Right in Middletown

Stephen D. Johnson

This paper reports the results and conclusions of a series of studies conducted by the author and Joseph Tamney on the Christian Right in "Middletown." Middletown is Muncie, Indiana, which had been the subject of the Lynds' (1929 and 1937) classic study of the nature of communities. Developments in Muncie have been considered representative of what has gone on in many U.S. communities since the Lynds' work. The Johnson and Tamney studies took place in the fall of 1980, 1981, 1982, 1983, and 1984, when Muncie had become a city of some 80,000 residents. The first and last of the studies (1980 and 1984) were directed mainly toward the influence of the Christian Right on people's vote for president of the United States. The middle three studies (1981, 1982, and 1983) focused on what types of people support the most prominent organizational force behind the Christian Right movement--the Moral Majority.

THE 1980 PRESIDENTIAL STUDY

In the 1980 presidential study, Johnson and Tamney (1982) first noted that conservative evangelical Christians were being organized into a political force by national television preachers like Jerry Falwell and by secular New Right leaders such as Richard Viguerie and Paul Weyrich. The electronic ministers were preaching the importance of their "congregations'" becoming politically involved to support conservative causes, and the political Right operatives were attempting to organize both conservative religious and conservative political leaders from their base in Washington, D.C.

In this study, we defined the Christian Right as people who are

> conservative evangelicals who have abandoned the long-held belief that political activism is incompatible with their religion and assert that the church has a role, indeed a duty, to change America by becoming politically active. These are people who believe in a "civil religion" (Bellah, 1968), i.e., that America is a Christian nation, a nation "under God," existing to do God's will. However, they have what might be called a "right-wing" interpretation of what a Christian America should be like and thus feel betrayed by the Federal government and courts and other forces of "secular humanism" who have supported abortion, equal rights for women, homosexual rights, and other practices they believe are destroying the American family and handing America over to the Communists. Members of the Christian Right are also very fundamentalistic in their religious beliefs; they believe in a literal interpretation of the Bible in all respects. Finally, they believe that "secular humanists" are taking over America's schools, and school prayer needs to be restored (Johnson and Tamney, 1982).

Two hundred and sixty-two residents of Middletown who were going to vote in the 1980 presidential election participated in the study. They were randomly selected by a random-digit-dialing technique in which all residents of Muncie with phones (about 98 percent) had an equal chance of being selected. The telephone interview assessed basic demographic factors such as the respondent's sex, age, and education; political factors such as political party preference, the respondent's self-perceived political ideology (liberal to conservative), which of nine campaign issues he or she considered the most important, which candidate he or she was going to vote for, and a measure of what we called a Christian Right orientation. The latter measure consisted of four dimensions: (1) religious political involvement, measured by two Likert items (statements to which respondents are asked how much they agree or disagree) one of which, for example, was "One's Minister (Priest or Rabbi) should come out in support of a presidential candidate"; (2) right-wing civil religion, measured by two Likert items, one of which was "America

is God's chosen nation today"; (3) religious fundamentalism, measured by two Likert items, one of which was
"Every word of the Bible is true"; and (4) support for
voluntary school prayer, which was assessed by one Likert
item that stated, "Voluntary prayers should be allowed
in the classroom."

To examine the impact of the Christian Right on the
election, we tallied scores for the seven measures of
Christian rightism. Based on these total scores,
classifications of people were determined within five
categories. Table 8.1 shows the difference in these five
levels of Christian rightism with respect to vote. As
can be seen from this table, there was no relationship
between these two factors, i.e., Christian Rightists were
no more (or less) likely to vote for Reagan than
non-Christian Rightists.

Therefore, this study indicated that the Christian
Right had no effect at all on the election of Ronald Reagan
in 1980. But what did have an effect? Our data indicated
that those who thought inflation was the most important
issue (and presumably Carter's inability to keep it down)
voted overwhelmingly for Reagan (87 percent). This
economic condition was by far the most important factor
leading to Reagan's election. Also, our data indicated
that traditional Republicans, or conservatives of high
education, voted heavily for Reagan.

We explained the results of this 1980 election study
as follows:

The importance of the economic factor of inflation
in the election provides a possible explanation of
the lack of influence of the Christian Right
movement. Especially during times of economic
difficulties like those currently faced by most
Americans, economic well being is no doubt more
salient than the perceived moral decline in the more
private American institutions. It seems like
something akin to Maslow's hierarchy of needs exists
(Maslow, 1954). That is, one's basic economic needs
have to be satisfied first and then, what might be
considered higher needs, like building a more just
and moral society in which to live, can be pursued.
Thus, inflation, and Carter's seeming inability to
do anything about it, led large numbers of people
to vote for Reagan, no matter what their religious
convictions were (Johnson and Tamney, 1982).

TABLE 8.1
Vote for Reagan by Christian Right Orientation

Orientation	Percent for Reagan
High Christian Right	62
Moderate Christian Right	54
Neutral	61
Moderate Anti-Christian Right	49
High Anti-Christian Right	67

SUPPORT FOR THE MORAL MAJORITY

The author and Joseph Tamney conducted three studies on the degree of support for the Moral Majority and the types of people who support this organization (Tamney and Johnson, 1983; Johnson and Tamney, 1984; and Johnson and Tamney, 1985a). In the first study, we defined the Moral Majority as a religious/political organization that is attempting to use the political process to bring back more traditional values and practices, like school prayer and a ban on abortions, by lobbying efforts and backing political candidates who support their conservative/ traditional positions. Moreover, because of the great media attention Falwell and the Moral Majority have received, they have become the personification of the Christian Right movement. As Shupe and Stacy (1981:6) have said, "this visibility has 'literally turned the proper name, 'Moral Majority,' into the generic term 'moral majority'" and they assumed "that the term 'moral majority' is understood by the general public to represent not only Reverend Jerry Falwell's group but also the larger conservative movement seeking to infuse politics with evangelical morality."

A random sample of 281 residents of Muncie and its immediate surrounding area (Delaware County) was selected by a random-digit-dialing technique and interviewed over the phone in the fall of 1981. Face-to-face interviews were also conducted in some more economically depressed areas where people were less likely to have phones. Among other factors, the interview schedule contained questions measuring the following factors: (1) basic demographic factors such as sex, age, and education; (2) a four-item measure of cosmopolitanism (e.g., "Do you like trying new kinds of food?"); (3) a four-item measure of status quo orientation (e.g., "Do you feel a need for new experience" --"No," indicating a status quo orientation); (4) the extent to which respondents watched religious television; (5) the four-dimension measure of a Christian Right orientation explained in describing the 1980 election study; and (6) a measure of the degree of support for the Moral Majority.

Support for the Moral Majority, which was the major focus of this study, was measured by just asking the respondents if they had heard of the Moral Majority. If they answered "Yes," they were then asked, "How do you feel about the Moral Majority? Do you: (1) strongly support this group, (2) generally support this group, (3) feel somewhat against this group, or (4) feel strongly against the Moral Majority?" Only those who had heard of the Moral Majority and expressed an opinion were included in the analysis (about 135 respondents).

The results indicated that about 65 percent of the respondents had heard of the Moral Majority in the fall of 1981. Of these, 26 percent supported this group (or about 17 percent of the total sample), 47 percent were against it, and 27 percent had no opinion. Thus, our first study of support for the Moral Majority indicated that allegience to this religious/political group was not extensive.

The statistical analyses conducted on the data from this study resulted in three factors having an independent effect on support for the Moral Majority (i.e., each factor influenced Moral Majority support independent of the other). These were a Christian Right orientation, religious television viewing, and a status quo orientation. Specifically, people with a Christian Right perspective, who watched a lot of religious television, and who did not want things changed in their lives were more likely to support the Moral Majority. In this study, as in the two others reported in this chapter, age and education were indirectly related to Moral Majority support, i.e., older people tended to have more of a status quo orientation, and less-educated individuals tended to have more of a Christian Right orientation, which made these groups more susceptible to the appeals of the Moral Majority. Also in this study, cosmopolitanism was indirectly related, through status quo orientation, to Moral Majority support, i.e., less-cosmopolitan people had more of a status quo perspective, and these people were more likely to favor the Moral Majority.

The role of a Christian Right orientation was explained by pointing out that religious fundamentalists who believed that political action should be taken to "Christianize" the country would logically support a political organization, headed by a conservative religious fundamentalist, which is trying to do precisely that. The Moral Majority's pursuit to return the United States back to a traditional Christian lifestyle and the appeal this goal has for people who are somewhat upset by today's fast pace of change were presented as an explanation of the independent influence of a status quo orientation on Moral Majority support. The independent influence of religious television viewing was explained in the following way:

The third influence on Moral Majority support is religious television. The fact that both the Christian Right Index and status-quo orientation were directly and independently related to favoring the Moral Majority means that information about this movement has been successfully disseminated by means other than religious television. On the other hand, the independent significance of religious television suggests that some people support the Moral Majority simply because they have experienced effective persuasion urging such support. Similarly, Shupe and Stacey (1981) found that watching religious television affected support for the Moral Majority independent of several other religious measures. The significant, independent path between religious television and support for the Moral Majority has a further interesting implication. If those people who watch a lot of religious television come away with solid support for a right-wing political organization independent of their cultural or religious orientation, it might be concluded that an extreme conservative perspective and political issue orientation dominates religious TV programming, and other more liberal, orientations are non-existent or suppressed. Thus, unlike public and commercial television, religious television rather overtly advocates definite political positions and expects its audience to adhere to them (Tamney and Johnson, 1983).

A status quo orientation, and to a certain degree a Christian Right orientation, have been described as examples of cultural fundamentalism (Gusfield, 1966). This is a more basic ideological perspective that involves the idea that people should become politically active to defend and extend traditional lifestyles.

In the second (1982) study, we expanded our model of Moral Majority support by analyzing the role of a characteristic of the United States that could be considered a societal basis or foundation for the emergence of most political/religious groups such as the Moral Majority. That characteristic is religious conflict. Religious ideological conflicts have existed among many different religious groups throughout U.S. history (Lipset, 1964): e.g., the struggle over Prohibition that pitted fundamentalists against liberal Christians. Moral Majority supporters and other conservative Christians face a conflict between their desire for a traditional, Christian country (they are cultural fundamentalists) and the secular, change-oriented goals of a significant number of educators and political leaders today.

We went on to say in our second study of the Moral Majority (Johnson and Tamney, 1984):

> These basic conflicts have particularly intensified recently by the perception on the part of very conservative Christians that major political forces in America today are trying to destroy their traditional ideals. Recent Congressional and Supreme Court decisions legalizing abortion and providing increased rights for women and homosexuals are seen as a threat to traditional American families (Viguerie, 1981). The Supreme Court ban on school prayer and the increase in scientific, versus religious, interpretations of all subject matter taught in America's classrooms are also seen as threats to the Moral Majority's belief in a "Christian" education (Newsweek, 1982, and Viguerie, 1981).

Due to these and other perceived threats, we hypothesized in our second study that those who support the Moral Majority were cultural ethnocentrics; in other words, there would be a direct effect of cultural ethnocentrism on Moral Majority support. We defined a cultural ethnocentric as "a person who has very little tolerance for and does not trust people who do not hold the same family, religious, and other social beliefs that he does. Further, these other people are considered a threat to one's own traditional family and religious lifestyle" (Johnson and Tamney, 1984, p. 186).

We also proposed that a major cause of cultural ethnocentrism, as with racial and ethnic ethnocentrism, is authoritarianism (Adorno et al., 1950). Authoritarians are rather rigid, dogmatic people who are quick to condemn other people who deviate from conventional norms and values. We surmised that this type of person would be the most likely to perceive changes in the traditional family structure and the "invasion of secular humanists" in the classroom as a threat and be the most disturbed by these events (a cultural ethnocentric viewpoint) and thus would be more likely to support the Moral Majority.

In this second study, a random sample of 284 residents of Muncie and its immediate surrounding area (Delaware County) was selected by a random-digit-dialing technique in the fall of 1982. In addition to the factors already described for the first study of Moral Majority support, the second study measured: (1) cultural ethnocentrism with two Likert items that stated, "There are a number of groups and people in America today that are trying to destroy traditional ways of life" and "It is difficult to trust people who do not hold the same beliefs as I do," and (2) authoritarianism with two Likert items that stated, "Every person should have complete faith in some supernatural power whose decisions are obeyed without question", and "Obedience and respect for authority are the most important virtues children should learn."

The results of the second study indicated that only 14 percent of the total sample had heard of the Moral Majority and supported it. The results of the statistical analyses are seen in Figure 8.1.

Christian Right orientation and cultural ethnocentrism were directly and independently related to Moral Majority support, but religious television viewing and status quo orientation were no longer directly related. Religious television viewing, however, was reciprocally related to a Christian Right orientation (i.e., people who watch religious television tend to be Christian Rightist and vice versa) and thus this factor was indirectly related to Moral Majority support (this was also the case in the first study). (For further discussion of the relationship between religious television and Moral Majority support see Tamney and Johnson [1984].)

As in our first study, a status quo orientation was neither directly nor indirectly related to Moral Majority

FIGURE 8.1
Factors Contributing to Moral Majority Support

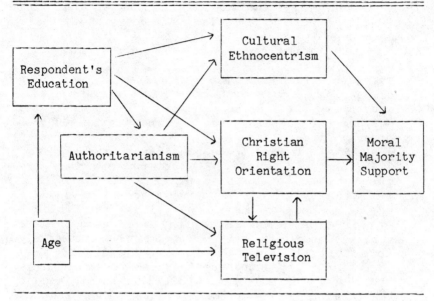

support and thus was eliminated from our model. However, we proposed that a status quo orientation was a measure of a more basic orientation called cultural fundamentalism in our first study (1981) and that the antichange component of cultural fundamentalism was measured by our cultural ethnocentrism measure; thus this more basic factor still played a role in Moral Majority support. Authoritarianism was found to relate not only to cultural ethnocentrism, but also to a Christian Right orientation (authoritarians were more likely to have this social psychological orientation) and to religious television viewing (authoritarians viewed more). Finally, older and especially less educated people tended to have those characteristics (like a Christian Right orientation and religious television viewing) that directly related to Moral Majority support.

The reasons for the direct relationships between a Christian Right orientation and Moral Majority support and between cultural ethnocentrism and Moral Majority support have been already presented. The other major finding of this study was that authoritarianism was found to relate directly and independently to both of these two factors and to a third factor that related indirectly to Moral Majority support, i.e., religious television viewing. We interpreted the latter finding as supporting the idea that authoritarianism is a <u>personality basis</u> for the appeal of the religious political Right movement in the United States today. As we went on to state:

> The authoritarians of America then seem to be a group of people who readily attend to right-wing, religious causes and serve as a foundation of support for the purposes of these causes. The need for a feeling of order in their lives and their tendency to condemn what they consider to be non-conformists (Adorno, 1950; Cherry & Byrne, 1977) make authoritarians more susceptible to the preachings that there is a threatening group of liberal secularists who are trying to destroy their conventional, traditional way of life. The authoritarians' need to have authorities direct their lives makes them more likely to accept the authoritarian structure of many Christian Right churches, in which the minister <u>is</u> the church (Hill & Owen, 1982:131), and to accept the ideological view of many Christian Right churches that God is the only sovereign or real authority over all persons and nations (Conway & Siegelman, 1982:72). Further, according to our data, authoritarians would be more attracted to the preachers and other advocates on religious television who frequently promote these ideas (Johnson and Tamney, 1984).

The third and final study of Moral Majority support (1983) brought into our model the possible social structural influence of having one's minister (or other church or synagogue leader) advocate (or condemn) the Moral Majority (Johnson and Tamney, 1985a). This influence is proposed by such students of the New Christian Right as Liebman (1983) and Latus (1983). Liebman, for instance, contends that the mobilization of the Moral Majority was mainly due to the activation by Jerry Falwell and others of an already existing national network of conservative, fundamentalist clergy. These were mainly Baptist preachers in a number of rather large churches throughout the United States, and in the latter 1970s these preachers began to advocate to their congregations the virtues of the emerging religious/political organization that was attempting to attack "secular humanists" and return the nation to traditional religious ideals, i.e., the Moral Majority.

Three hundred and ninety-three residents of Muncie were again interviewed over the telephone in the fall of 1983. In addition to all those factors assessed in the two previous studies, the interview list contained questions measuring: (1) the extent of confidence in the presidency vs. the Supreme Court (This measure was obtained because the occupant of the presidency in 1983 [Ronald Reagan] has supported the issue positions of the Moral Majority such as school prayer and antiabortion proposals, whereas historically recent decisions by the U.S. Supreme Court concerning these issues have been severely criticized by the Moral Majority); (2) the extent to which we are spending too much (or too little) money on military defense; and (3) the extent to which the respondent perceived that his pastor or other church or synagogue leader speaks out in favor of (or against) the Moral Majority (In subsequent discussions this measure will be called "church support").

Findings of this third study indicated that 19 percent of the sample had heard of the Moral Majority and supported it. The statistical analyses of the factors that influenced Moral Majority support indicated that a Christian Right orientation, religious television viewing, and church support all had a direct and independent influence on Moral Majority support but that cultural ethnocentrism did not. Further analysis indicated that another, fourth factor did directly influence Moral Majority support independent of those just named. This was what we called political "conservatism." It consisted of three measures: confidence in the presidency vs. the Supreme Court, support for military spending, and identification of oneself as a political conservative. Also, authoritarianism was directly related to a Christian Right orientation and political conservativism (for the latter, the more authoritarian, the more politically conservative).

The results confirmed the hypothesis that advocacy of the virtues of the Moral Majority by the leaders of one's own church is another social structural influence, in addition to exposure to conservative religious television, that has mobilized support for the Moral Majority. We also found: (1) the "return" of religious television viewing as a direct influence on Moral Majority support; (2) the continued influence of a Christian Right orientation; (3) the continued influence of authoritarianism as a personality basis for Moral Majority support; and (4) the influence of a new, more political factor--political conservatism.

We described the latter finding as follows:

> A new finding from this study conducted in the fall of 1983, which was not found in the two previous studies of the Moral Majority in Middletown conducted in 1982 and 1981, is that general political conservativism is a new ideological perspective predisposing individuals toward the Moral Majority movement. This non-religious basis of support (unlike the other three factors directly related to Moral Majority support in this study) could have materialized due to the fact that President Reagan, the darling of political conservatives, has throughout his term in office supported the traditional religious aims of the Moral Majority, such as school prayer and anti-abortion programs, through his speeches and legislative initiatives. It could be that political conservatives have become more aware of this support as of late. The downing of the Korean airliner by the Russians in September of 1983 also particularly incensed political conservatives and the well-publicized condemnation of this incident by Jerry Falwell and the Moral Majority may have increased support for this group on the part of political conservatives in the fall of 1983. (We also found in our study that MM supporters found the U.S. response to this incident to be too weak.) This change is further consistent with Johnston's (1982) conclusion that the New Christian Right, including the Moral Majority, has changed from a "redemption crusade storming the existing political order from without" to an interest group with a particular political platform which works within the political order and which expounds norms and goals that "are predominantly specific and instrumental, rather than diffuse and consummatory" (Johnston, 1982:193).

1984 PRESIDENTIAL ELECTION

The 1984 election study again assessed the impact of the Christian Right on the election of Ronald Reagan (Johnson and Tamney, 1985b). A random sample of 351 Munsonians was obtained as in the previous studies. Four new, important factors were measured in 1984 that had not been assessed in 1980. These were (1) membership in a conservative Protestant, versus a liberal Protestant, denomination; (2) conservative religious television viewing; (3) attitude toward separation of church and state; and (4) support for the Moral Majority.

The percentage vote for Reagan and Mondale in Middletown was again close to that nationwide, with 57 percent for Reagan and 43 percent for Mondale (it was 59 percent for Reagan and 43 percent for Mondale, nationally).

As for the impact of the Christian Right, our 1981, 1982, and 1983 studies indicated that there was increased support for Reagan from 1981 to 1983 among Christian Rightists and Moral Majority supporters. Thus, we hypothesized that Christian Rightists would have a greater, but still not a major, impact in 1984 than in 1980.

This is exactly what we found. Two nonreligious factors had by far the greatest impact on the election, and they were political party preference and evaluation of the economy. Specifically, as is usually the case in all elections, Republicans voted for the Republican candidate (Reagan), and Democrats voted for the Democratic candidate (Mondale), and those who thought the state of the economy was "good" voted overwhelmingly for Reagan and those who thought the economy was "bad" voted overwhelmingly for Mondale.

Unlike 1980, however, political/religious factors did play a role. First, we did not find that our Christian Right orientation scale had a linear relationship with votes, i.e., high Christian Rightists were not more likely to vote for Reagan than low Christian Rightists. However, we did find a curvilinear relationship, i.e., those with a moderate Christian Right orientation voted more for Reagan than those with either low or high Christian Right orientations. Moreover, supporters of the Moral Majority were significantly more likely to vote for Reagan than nonsupporters (here we did find a linear relationship). But, and this is important, a further examination of the linear relationship between Moral Majority support and vote indicated that there were more people who were against the Moral Majority and voted for Mondale than there were people who were for the Moral Majority and voted for Reagan. Thus, the Moral Majority had an impact on vote for Reagan, but, overall, a negative one.

Both moderate Christian rightism and Moral Majority support also related to vote independent of political party preference and evaluation of the economy. Stating the latter findings another way, Reagan's main support came from Republicans and from those who thought the economy was doing well, and he obtained some additional support from those who were moderate Christian Rightists. But the Reagan vote was somewhat diminished by the presence of the Moral Majority.

Further analyses indicated that those with a moderate Christian Right perspective were really not Christian Rightists, but relatively young, change-oriented members of liberal Protestant denominations who did not want to see religion getting involved in politics. These people might be more modern, enlightened Christians who possibly saw Christianity as an important basis for an American way of life, but were somewhat put off by the dogmatic, past-oriented rhetoric of many Christian Right leaders. The appeal of Reagan to this type of Christian possibly came from Reagan's image as a basically good, Christian man who has demonstrated leadership in changing the United States. This stands in contrast to Mondale's image and association with the "old" politics of unions and Jimmy Carter.

The impact of the Moral Majority in the election possibly indicated that this specific religious/political activist group, rather than the more general Christian Right movement, has been somewhat successful in publicizing its conservative religious causes and Reagan's potential contribution to bringing about a more conservative Christian-oriented country. However, given that economic factors still played the greatest role in electing Ronald Reagan president in 1984 and that there were more anti-Moral Majority people who voted for Mondale, it is unlikely that the Moral Majority will have any positive impact on presidential politics in the near future.

CONCLUSIONS

In reviewing our studies, one might first consider support for the Moral Majority as coming from two external, social structural sources and two internal, social psychological sources. Figure 8.2 depicts these two basic sources.

It probably comes as no surprise that the two major sources of information and opinions concerning religious matters that come from people's social environment or relationships with others, come from church services and,

more recently, from religious television. Church leaders
have always played an important role in formulating
opinions on most religious events and issues, and thus
it would seem reasonable that many ministers, priests,
or rabbis would speak out and mold the attitudes of their
congregations concerning such a politically active and
visible group as the Moral Majority. We have found that
about 42 percent of a sample of ministers from Middletown
spoke to their congregations about the Moral Majority (see
Chapter 2 of this book). There is also the new, additional
influence of religious television, especially for those,
like the elderly, who have difficulty attending church
services (Tamney and Johnson, 1984). Most of the
televangelists are conservative fundamentalist preachers,
like the Reverend Falwell himself, who strongly advocate
the conservative, tradition-oriented values and policy
positions of the Moral Majority. The televangelists are,
further, even more likely than one's minister to take
stands on political issues, and most of those stands are
very conservative.

A second source comes from the social psychological
dispositions a person brings into this religious/political
environment. People who generally believe that
Christianity should be infused in all aspects of life and
feel particularly incensed by what they see as a
destruction of traditional values by today's politicians,
i.e., Christian Rightists, would naturally be attracted
to a political group mentioned in church and/or on
religious television, whose purpose is to restore
Christian, traditional values and practices to the
country. Our data also indicate that cultural
fundamentalists would find the advocacy of conservative
ministers and/or televangelists appealing. The importance
of traditional lifestyles, like traditional male/female
sex roles and praying in school, and the moderate anxiety
and threat that a change in these customs generates in
cultural fundamentalists would logically make them
susceptible to the claims of the Moral Majority that it
is capable of restoring such traditions. We support this
conclusion with our findings that two measures of cultural
fundamentalism--a status quo orientation in our first study
and cultural ethnocentrism in our second study--related
directly to Moral Majority support.

Figure 8.2 indicates that a major foundation for the
development of both a Christian Right orientation and
cultural fundamentalism is authoritarianism. An

FIGURE 8.2
Sources of Moral Majority Support

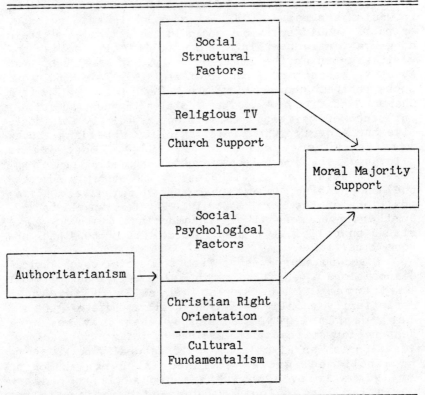

authoritarian personality is developed first during childhood. Therefore, we contend that the more recently encountered Christian Right idea of restoring the authority of Christianity in all aspects of U.S. life appeals to authoritarians and that traditionalism would also appeal to the rigid, conventional nature of authoritarians.

As for the political impact of the Christian Right and the Moral Majority, our data indicated that the latter, which is a specific political action group, did have some impact in 1984, but the more general Christian Right movement had little political impact at the presidential level in 1980 and in 1984. Furthermore, even though the mobilization efforts of the Moral Majority through direct mail and religious television brought some votes over to

Reagan in 1984, the nature of these mobilization efforts at this point seem to have been more negative than positive, because there were more anti-Moral Majority who voted for Mondale than pro-Moral Majority voting for Reagan.

Therefore, even though the Moral Majority has had some impact through religious television, the sermons of conservative fundamentalist preachers, and the appeal of its rhetoric calling for a return to Christian, traditional values, it is at best merely an emerging political force. Only future political and religious events in the country will tell if the Christian Right movement will grow in its impact on politics or die like many other religious/ political movements throughout our history.

REFERENCES

Adorno, T. W., et al. The Authoritarian Personality. New York: Harper and Row, 1950.

Bellah, Robert N. Civil Religion in America. In Donald R. Cutler (ed.), The Religious Situation: 1968, pp. 331-356. Boston: Beacon Press, 1968.

Cherry, F., and D. Byrne. Authoritarianism. In T. Bloss (ed.), Personality Variables in Social Behavior, pp. 109-133. Hillsdale, N.J.: Erlbaum, 1977.

Conway, F., and Jim Siegelman. Holy Terror. Garden City, N.Y.: Doubleday, 1982.

Gusfield, J. Symbolic Crusade. Urbana, Ill.: University of Illinois Press, 1966.

Hill, S., and D. E. Owen. The New Religious Political Right in America. Nashville, Tenn.: Abingdon, 1982.

Johnson, Stephen, and Joseph Tamney. The Christian Right and the 1980 Presidential Election. Journal for the Scientific Study of Religion. Vol. 21, pp. 123-131, 1982.

_____. Support for the Moral Majority: A Test of a Model. Journal for the Scientific Study of Religion, Vol. 23, pp. 183-196, 1984.

_____. Mobilizing Support for the Moral Majority. Psychological Reports, Vol. 56, pp. 987-994, 1985a.

_____. The Christian Right and the 1984 Presidential Election. Review of Religious Research, Vol. 27, pp. 124-133, 1985b.

Johnston, M. The "New Christian Right" in American Politics. Political Quarterly. Vol. 53, pp. 181-199, 1982.

Latus, M. Ideology PAC's and Political Action. In Robert Liebman and Robert Wuthnow (eds.), The New Christian Right: Mobilization and Legitimation, pp. 75-99. New York: Aldine, 1983.

Liebman, Robert. Mobilizing the Moral Majority. In Robert Liebman and Robert Wuthnow (eds.), The New Christian Right: Mobilization and Legitimation, pp. 50-73. New York: Aldine, 1983.

Lipset, Seymour Martin. Religion and Politics in American History. In Earl Raab (ed.), Religious Conflict in America. Garden City, N.Y.: Doubleday., 1964.

Lynd, Robert, and Helen Lynd Middletown. New York: Harcourt, Brace, and World, 1929.
_____. Middletown in Transition. New York: Harcourt, Brace, and World, 1937.

Maslow, A. Motivation and Personality. New York: Harper and Row, 1954.

Newsweek. How the Bible Made America. December 29, pp. 44-51, 1982.

Shupe, A., and W. Stacey. The Moral Majority Constituency. Manuscript sent to author, 1981.

Tamney, Joseph, and Stephen Johnson. The Moral Majority in Middletown. Journal for the Scientific Study of Religion, Vol. 22, pp. 145-157, 1983.
_____. Religious Television in Middletown. Review of Religious Research, Vol. 25, pp. 303-313, 1984.

Viguerie, Richard. The New Right: We're Ready to Lead. Fall River, Va.: Viguerie, 1981.

9

Jews, Blacks, and the Democrats: 1984

John D. Cranor

The Democratic party is a coalition. According to Walter Dean Burnham, one of the most astute students of U.S. voting behavior, white Southerners, labor unionists, blacks, Jews, and the electorally active poor have been the major groups within the party (1970, esp. p. 59). This historical coalition may be disintegrating (Burnham, 1970; Petrocik, 1981). Indeed, one of the most fascinating questions occupying scholars and politicians in recent years turns on the "realignment" of the U.S. electorate.

This chapter examines the 1984 elections in terms of coalition politics in the Democratic party. It shall do so by paying particular attention to the issues surrounding a black-Jewish confrontation within the Democratic party. As such, it will consider Jewish attachments to the Democratic party in the context of a realigning electorate.

Since 1932 the Democratic party has had the greatest number of individuals claiming allegiance to it compared to the other parties. The coalition of Democratic voters was forged by Franklin D. Roosevelt out of the social and economic chaos of the depression by attributing the national crisis to the Republicans and Herbert Hoover. Although more and more individuals are rejecting partisan identification and claiming to be independents, the fundamental division has been maintained. Its meaning, however, has been diluted through the years.

Republicans have been successful in winning the presidency in 1952 and 1956 (Eisenhower); 1968 and 1972 (Nixon); 1980 and 1984 (Reagan). Although these elections are characterized as "deviating", there may have been a fundamental change in the way U.S. citizens identify politically and participate electorally. Converts from Democrats and independents may account for a developing

Republican party. Moreover, a surge of new voters who favor the Republican party may result in a realignment of the U.S. electorate. To explain general election outcomes, analysts have long recognized that people's votes are based on personality and issues as well as partisanship. Indeed, partisan identification and loyalty may be waning across the face of the electorate.

The tensions surrounding the 1984 primary season underscore the possibility that the New Deal coalition may be in the process of disintegration. Presidential primaries, viewed as an intraparty process of winnowing out potential candidates cause issues to be aired and personalities to be revealed. In doing so, primaries often exacerbate cleavages within the party. The 1984 primaries did just that with respect to blacks and Jews.

Blacks have been regarded as solidly Democratic in their voting behavior since the New Deal. The Jewish commitment to the coalition also developed during the New Deal; it was firmed by the defeat of Nazism in Europe and the more liberal leanings of the Democratic party (Fuchs, 1956, pp. 74-78). Given the peculiarities of the presidential primary elections and the Electoral College system, demography is particularly important. New York City has the highest concentration of Jews of any metropolis in the United States. Blacks are also urban dwellers. Both of these groups are important when one is considering the mechanics of nomination and ultimate election to the presidency.

Although the two groups are crucial to the Democratic coalition, similarities between Jews and blacks can be pushed only so far. Issues dividing the Democratic party along black-Jewish lines examined in this paper will touch the charge of black anti-Semitism; differing perspectives on the U.S. role in foreign affairs; and, to a lesser extent, the issue of affirmative action. Because primaries are devoid of the partisanship that characterizes general elections, these issues cannot be ignored. Their importance was magnified when articulated by the Reverend Jesse Jackson, the first significant black candidate for president of the United States.

THE JEWS AND SUPPORT FOR THE DEMOCRATIC PARTY

In some ways the presence of the Jewish citizen in the Democratic party may appear to be an anomaly. Lawrence

Fuchs (1956, p. 74) has observed that Jews as a group have prospered to a greater extent than have other groups of the Democratic coalition and that they are atypical Democrats in terms of occupational prestige, income, and education. Fuchs (p. 113) accounts for the Jewish affinity with the Democractic Party in terms of Jews' liberalism and internationalism. This affinity, as Table 9.1 indicates, is reflected in their support for Democratic presidential candidates. The special case of 1980 will be discussed later.

Additional evidence can be marshalled to demonstrate the commitment of the Jewish voter to the Democratic party. Donner cited a poll conducted by Professor Steven Cohen of Queens College and Brandeis University for the American Jewish Committee in 1981. The poll indicated that 66 percent of U.S. Jews preferred the Democratic party (1984, p. 328). These data are confirmed by surveys conducted by the Gallup organization and the New York Times/CBS News poll in terms of Jewish voting behavior. The National Journal, drawing on these data, reported that the average vote for Democratic presidential candidates among Jews in the elections from 1968 to 1980 was 64 percent; the figure for Republican presidential candidates was 32 percent (1984, p. 2111).

Despite these lopsided margins, the issue of Jewish attachment to the Democratic party has come under close scrutiny in recent years. The partisan loyalty of the Jewish voter has been viewed as in process of realignment (Himmelfarb, 1981; Kristol, 1984). Following the defeat of Jimmy Carter in the 1980 presidential election, Milton Himmelfarb examined the question of a Jewish drift toward the Republican party. His analysis underscored Jewish dissatisfaction with Democrats. Himmelfarb noted that the 1980 three-way contest was the first election since 1928 in which most Jews did not vote for the Democratic presidential candidate.

Himmelfarb's reasoning must be understood in the context of the 1980 presidential election, that is, one should ascertain the difference between voting Democratic or Republican versus voting for or against an incumbent president. Although President Carter was instrumental in negotiating the Camp David accords, initiating a normalization of relations between Israel and Egypt, that action did not influence the Jewish electorate so much as emerging Palestine Liberation Organization (PLO) contacts with blacks within the Democratic party.

TABLE 9.1
Jewish Voting Behavior in Presidential Elections: 1964-1980

Election Year	Percent of the Jewish Vote for		
	Democrat	Republican	Independent
1964	91		
1968	83		
1972	66	35	
1976	75		
1980	45	39	15

Sources: Data for Jewish voting behavior are hard to compile. The 1980 figures are from the New York Times/CBS News poll reported on November 8, 1984, p. A19; 1976, 1972, and 1964 data are from the New York Times, October 18, 1984, p. D26; and Levy and Kramer (1972) presents 1968 data.

UN Ambassador Andrew Young's meeting with PLO officials in July 1979 against the wishes of the Carter administration ultimately led to Young's resignation (New York Times, 1979a, 1979b). In August 1979, at a meeting of national black leaders convened by the National Association for the Advancement of Colored People (NAACP) to discuss the resignation of Young, discussions broadened to encompass a series of black grievances against Jews including Jews' opposition to affirmative action (New York Times, 1979c). The PLO issue, however, was the more public point of conflict between blacks and Jews. Within the Democratic party, endorsement of PLO legitimacy and reassessment of U.S. foreign policy relative to the entire Arab world are items associated with blacks. Furthermore, these potential revisions of party positions were highlighted by Jesse Jackson's meeting with PLO leader Yasser Arafat in 1979. Jewish apprehension about Jackson could be traced to his participation in the NAACP meeting following Young's resignation, and Jackson's rise in leadership status among blacks contributed to their concerns.

Both issues settled poorly with the Jewish electorate. Indeed, Himmelfarb neatly captured the ambivalence of the Jewish voter following the 1980 presidential election: "When Carter conceded defeat on television that evening, there, right behind him, stood Jesse Jackson, the PLO's friend. Whether Gentile or

Jewish, much of the vote for Carter was not pro-Carter but anti-Reagan. For some Jews, seeing Jackson there must have tempered disappointment over the victory of the man they had voted against" (p. 30). Consequently, both Young's role in Carter's administration and Jackson's prominence in the Democratic party since have raised the specter of abandonment of Israel in the scheme of U.S. foreign policy. Jackson's pronouncements during the 1984 primary season did little to dispel the image.

A more recent controversy surrounding the logic of the adherence of the Jews to the Democratic party was sparked by Irving Kristol in 1984. Under the label of neoconservatism, Kristol argued there were ample reasons for Jewish voters to abandon traditional Democratic ties and support the Republican party. Traced by some to Jewish disillusionment with the Democratic party during the sixties and early seventies, the neoconservative movement is viewed as an alternative for those uncomfortable with the party's and administrations' weak position with respect to international communism and especially the Soviet Union (Nuechterlein, 1984; Donner, 1984).

Kristol's major arguments were advanced in the light of Jesse Jackson's political leadership of black America. His leadership raised the issue of anti-Semitism in general, and he endorsed a pro-PLO, pro-Arab U.S. foreign policy. Kristol also downplayed Jewish concern about the emergence of the religious Right in U.S. politics, and especially the Moral Majority, because the latter espoused a strong Israel (Kristol, 1984). Although the thesis advanced by Kristol prompted a vigorous debate in Commentary (October 1984), the charge was important in the context of the 1984 elections, especially for the New York Jewish community (e.g., Stern, 1984; New York Times, 1984c).

THE TURMOIL OF THE 1984 DEMOCRATIC PRIMARIES

The three issues separating the black and the Jewish electorate in the 1984 Democratic primaries were religion, internationalism, and affirmative action. These issues were crystallized by Jesse Jackson's unsuccessful quest for the Democratic presidential nomination. They were issues that Mondale had to address in order to maintain the black and Jewish components of the Democratic coalition needed to defeat a popular, incumbent Republican president.

Farrakhan and The Nation of Islam

One of the most vexing issues for Jesse Jackson was the presence of fundamentalist Black Muslim leader Louis Farrakhan. The 1984 primary season was infamous for the invective of Farrakhan, berating the Jewish religion and Israel. The issue was complex, but the major events can be traced.

In an informal news conference called at Washington's National Airport on January 25, 1984, Jackson in a moment of unguarded conversation, referred to Jews as "Hymies" and New York City as "Hymietown." Made to black newsman Milton Coleman, the comments were included in a story written by his colleague. The comments exacerbated tensions between Jews and Jackson and fueled Jewish militancy from Jews Against Jackson, an offshoot of the radical Jewish Defense League (which had been disavowed by many moderate Jewish organizations). The issue was further clouded by Farrakhan's threats against Coleman (Time, 1984b); his subsequent attacks on Jews and their religion (Newsweek, 1984d); and a warning to whites who might "lock Jackson out" of the national convention (Newsweek, 1984e).

Tension between Jackson and Jews Against Jackson were worsened by additional events. Three members of Jews Against Jackson had been arrested during Jackson's presidential announcement in November 1983; his Boston headquarters had been picketed; Jackson requested Secret Service protection, which replaced his reliance on bodyguards provided by Farrakhan; Jackson's life had been threatened; and violence against Jackson's campaign headquarters in both Manchester, New Hampshire, and in Garden Grove, California, contributed to the drama of the primaries (Time, 1984a; Newsweek, 1984a).

Subsequent developments were characterized by continued anti-Semitic statements uttered by Farrakhan and Jackson's reluctance to disavow him. Although Jackson apologized for his own anti-Jewish remarks prior to the New Hampshire primary, Farrakhan's presence and pronouncements continued to haunt him. The dilemma was obvious: To repudiate Farrakan's support would alienate segments of the black community which had no history in electoral participation. For example, Time indicated that an estimated 270,000 blacks cast ballots in the New York primary, a figure easily double the number cast in the 1980 Carter-Kennedy contest in the state (1984c, p. 15). Charles Rangel, Representative from Harlem and

Mondale's deputy state campaign chairman noted that "'If they [New York blacks] weren't voting for Jesse, they wouldn't vote'" (Newsweek, 1984b). Newsweek estimated that Jackson won 87 percent of the black vote in the New York primary (1984f, p.44) and noted Jackson believed Farrakhan's example to register and vote was instrumental in his strong showing (1984e).

Thus, regardless of the outcome of the primaries, Mondale was ultimately caught in a double bind. Mondale could not risk alienating blacks by denouncing Jackson or criticizing his association with Farrakhan. In refusing to do so, however, he incurred the suspicion and possibly the wrath of the Jewish community. Prior to the convention, Henry Siegman, executive director of the American Jewish Congress, made the point bluntly: "The real issue is whether Walter Mondale will finally screw up enough courage to publicly break with Jesse Jackson unless Jackson repudiates, clearly and unequivocally, the political support of his racist and anti-Semitic friend [Farrakhan]" (Time, 1984e, p. 9).

It is perhaps noteworthy that Mondale finally did "get tough" with Jackson on the Farrakhan issue following the release of the New York Times/CBS News poll on July 10 that showed that most blacks preferred Mondale as their presidential candidate, despite having overwhelmingly supported Jackson during the primaries (1984b).

The Desertion of a Pro-Israeli Position

The foreign relations dimension of the 1984 Democratic Primary campaign is characterized by a series of issues pregnant with Jewish concerns. Mention has been made of the PLO-Jackson meetings in 1979. Others questioned Jackson's candidacy because of revisionist values embodied in his pronouncements. His rethinking traditional U.S.-PLO relations was at the expense of support for Israel (Puddington, 1984). Nevertheless, Jackson's candidacy had a center-stage international quality to it. At its base was a critical reassessment of U.S. foreign policy.

For example, Jackson was successful in securing the release of Lt. Robert O. Goodman, Jr., a black naval aviator shot down over Syria in a military exercise associated with the U.S. presence in Beirut. Jackson's major foreign relations coup--taking the credit for Goodman's release--was dubbed the "Syria Primary." Farrakhan was in the party of religious leaders accompanying Jackson to Damascus (Newsweek, 1984c, p. 17) and

may have been instrumental in arranging Goodman's release
(Newsweek, 1984e). In addition, Farrakhan travelled
to Libya in late spring to meet with Muammar Gadaffi
(Time, 1984d). This meeting certainly reinforced the
impression among Jews that Jackson was pro-Arab.

The New York Times/CBS News poll of June 10
indicated that Jackson's Middle East position was
compatible with the position of the general electorate:
Fifty-three percent of whites and 47 percent of the blacks
polled agreed that the United States should "'pay more
attention to the Arab nations, even if this makes Israel
angry.' Among Democrats, 50 percent of the whites and 48
percent of the blacks agreed" (New York Times, 1984b).

Finally, the issue of relocating the U.S. embassy
in Israel from Tel Aviv to Jerusalem came to the fore
during the April presidential primary in New York. In
their efforts to improve their standing with the Jewish
community, both Gary Hart and Mondale promised to support
the move. Jackson remained uncommitted, and Reagan let
the issue pass. Although Hart was reversing an earlier
position opposing the relocation of the embassy, his
indecisiveness cost him support among the Jews. Thus,
Jackson maximized his vote among the black population in
New York while Mondale and Hart slugged it out for the
Jewish vote. Overcoming his upset in the New Hampshire
primary, Mondale defeated Hart convincingly in New York
and thereby increased his dependency on Jewish backing.
Thus, black-Jewish issues, which had continually plagued
Mondale, were crystallized in New York presidential primary
voting.

For Jackson to disavow Farrakhan would have demeaned
his stature among blacks and given the appearance of bowing
to white--even Jewish--pressure. Mondale was dependent
on Jewish backing and interested in maintaining both
elements of the coalition. In short, Mondale had the
poorer of two undesirable worlds. First, he was locked
in by intense preferences held by black and Jewish
leaders. Second, these leaders were to the left and the
right of the broader middle ground encompassing the general
election voters.

The Question of Affirmative Action

This final issue separating blacks and Jews emerged
later in the primary season. Highlighted by a 1984 Supreme
Court decision, the issue of affirmative action resurfaced
as a point of contention between blacks and Jews. This
decision invalidated two lower federal court orders

requiring that affirmative action efforts take precedence over seniority in firing decisions made by municipal employers (New York Times, 1984a). The announced opinion could not have come at a more inopportune time for the Democrats, who were about to convene their national party convention.

As candidates having completed the primary season with a cadre of supporters attending the national convention, both Jackson and Hart remained potential stumbling blocks in the mandatory exercise of uniting the factions of the party for the upcoming general election. One concession demanded by Jackson was a plank in the Democratic platform concerning affirmative action, a point that especially offended Jews when it was presented in terms of "quotas" (e.g., Kristol, p. 214). Although the language of Jackson's demand on this issue was moderate, the process underscored consensus building in platform writing and demonstrated that the tensions between blacks and Jews continued.

Finally, the issue of comparable worth (e.g., Levin, 1984) also emerged as an issue in the primary season. In an effort to placate women, Mondale agreed to the concept in principle and it was included in the Democratic Party platform. The addition of this principle diluted Jackson's position, but at the expense of Jewish support.

The Net Effect

The issues of a changing emphasis in U.S. foreign policy and affirmative action were articulated by Rabbi Arthur Hertzberg, a past president of the American Jewish Congress. In a Newsweek editorial, Hertzberg presented Jewish reservations about Jackson:

> Our fear is that we will wake up during the Democratic convention in July and find he is not working toward a bigger piece of the political pie, but that he is trying to radicalize the Democratic Party. Our fear is that he will try to move it away from its traditional role as a coalition of moderate reformers and turn it into a party with a pro-PLO political orientation and a party where affirmative action does not even mean an unequal advantage in training and jobs, but a quota mechanically applied that is equal to a spoils system (1984, p. 13).

With regard to these fears, the New York Times/CBS News poll of July 10 is instructive. Among black Jackson supporters, 20 percent believed that Jews had hurt blacks and 12 percent indicated they had helped blacks. Among black Mondale supporters, however, only 7 percent indicated that Jews had hurt blacks, while 33 percent said they had helped blacks (1984b). Jackson and Mondale, therefore, were appealing to different segments of the black constituency.

On a different plane, the Republican convention of 1984 revealed another set of considerations touching on the Jewish vote. The prominent role given the Moral Majority during the Republican convention at Dallas led to Jews' fearing the abridgment of the doctrine of church-state separation. Such apprehension overshadowed concerns about Jackson's unfavorable image among Jews. All this increased the likelihood that Mondale would carry the Jewish vote in the general election (Germond and Witcover, 1984).

Thus, it appears that support for Israel by the Moral Majority (Stern, 1984) did not allay historic suspicions Jews had toward the religious Right, Kristol's opinion notwithstanding (1984). The tension between Jews and blacks had seemed more important than the "Christianization of the Republican Party" (Cohen, 1984, p. 2021) during the primary phase of the 1984 presidential campaign. The presence of the Moral Majority and other fundamentalist Christian groupings within the Republican party probably did as much to keep Jews within the Democratic party during the general election as the Jackson-Farrakhan issue had contributed to Jewish-black estrangement during the primaries.

ELECTORAL OUTCOMES: THE JEWISH VOTE

What have we learned from the 1984 presidential elections? Are Jews deserting their traditional Democratic loyalties and flocking to the Republican party? Indeed, is the nation realigning? What is happening in New York State? Preliminary answers to these questions are possible, although additional data must be obtained before they can be conclusively addressed. Evidence concerning the realignment of U.S. Jews, however, has not materialized.

According to the New York Times/CBS News exit poll of November 6, 1984, there was no evidence to support a switch among Jews to the ranks of the Republican party.

As the data in Table 9.2 demonstrate, Jewish participation in the 1984 election apparently recouped defections suffered in the 1980 election. A tentative explanation of the "dip" of Jewish support in 1980 for President Carter is best accounted for by his unpopular stands on the international questions discussed earlier. If a realignment occurred in 1984, Jews should not be counted among the defectors. Among Jews, Reagan ran better in 1980 against Carter than he did in 1984 against Mondale. Born-again Christians, white Protestants, and Catholics were more supportive of President Reagan in 1984 than in 1980. The separation of church and state and the abortion issue are two considerations that might account for these splits.

In a follow-up analysis of its exit polling, the New York Times reported that only 8 percent of the voting white Catholics mentioned abortion as a factor influencing their vote; for white born-again Protestants the comparable figure was 18 percent. Moreover, the New York Times argued that the association of Moral Majority leader Jerry Falwell with the Republican party did not aid its efforts to obtain the Jewish vote. Although the Republicans had hoped to capitalize among Jews on Mondale's vacillation on the Jackson-Farrakhan connection, Jews were ultimately more skeptical of the Republican-Falwell connection (1984e).

Despite the poor showing by the Mondale/Ferraro team in the 1984 general election, Jews, in general, were loyal to the Democrats. Religious support of the Reagan candidacy must be accounted for elsewhere. Voting among Catholics, white Protestants, and born-again Christians was all noticeably pro-Reagan; the data reflect Republican gains over 1980 figures. Of major interest, especially, is the strong Reagan orientation of the born-again Christian. This religious component may constitute the seeds of realignment in presidential politics.

There are other nuances. Democrats were more likely to cross over and vote for Reagan in both 1980 and 1984 than were Republicans likely to vote for Democrat candidates. Slippage among independents, labor union households, and Hart primary supporters also aided the electoral fortunes of President Reagan in 1984. Thus, breakdowns in traditional patterns of partisan voting behavior may represent the first test of a realignment thesis. But first-time voters who overwhelmingly identified with the president may present a more plausible

TABLE 9.2
Presidential Elections: 1980 and 1984, Exit Polling

| | The Vote in '80 | | | The Vote in '84 | | Percent of '84 |
	Reagan	Carter	Anderson	Reagan	Mondale	Voters
Total	51	41	7	59	41	
White						
Protestant	63	31	6	73	26	51
Catholic	49	42	7	55	44	26
Jewish	39	45	15	32	66	3
White						
born-again						
Christian	63	33	3	80	20	15
Whites	55	36	7	66	34	86
Blacks	11	85	3	9	90	10
Union house-						
hold	43	48	6	45	53	26
Republican	86	9	4	92	7	35
Democrat	26	67	6	26	73	38
Independent	55	30	12	63	35	26
Liberal	25	60	11	29	70	17
Moderate	48	42	8	54	46	44
Conservative	72	23	4	81	18	35
Reagan '80				88	11	50
Carter '80				19	80	31
Anderson'80				29	67	5
Democratic primary supporters of:						
Mondale				4	96	15
Hart				34	65	11
Jackson				6	93	3
First-time voter				60	39	8

Source: New York Times/CBS News Poll. Data for 1984 based on interviews with 8,696 voters leaving 176 randomly selected polling places on election day. Data for 1980 based on interviews with 15,201 voters leaving polling places around the U.S. New York Times, 1984d.

explanation for realignment. First-time voters are not necessarily young. A second test of realignment will be the degree to which first-time voters will permanently swell the size of the electorate. It remains to be seen whether they will acquire the voting habit. For all these changes, however, attachments must transcend the president and remain with the Republican party. This will be the ultimate test of a realignment thesis.

No evidence from exit polling has been offered that points to the realignment of the Jewish voter. Although realignment may be underway among other sectors of the population, 1984 seemingly marked a return of 1980 Jewish defections even though an extremely popular Republican president was reelected. Since more Jews live within New York State than in any other U.S. state, confirmation of these survey findings can be pursued by examining election returns in congressional districts there.

NEW YORK: A CONGRESSIONAL DISTRICT FOCUS

Additional evidence can be presented that substantiates the interpretation downplaying Jewish realignment by comparing voting patterns for different offices in the same electoral district. Ideally, the unit of analysis would be small enough to identify "Jewish" districts and then compare the presidential vote--which is more susceptible to the forces of personality and issues--with less visible races. Congressional races in New York offer a second perspective on the stability of the Jewish vote.

The willingness of the U.S. voter to separate presidential politics from other offices may be a growing trend. We know House districts are becoming safer for incumbents (Mayhew, 1974b). As members of an institution numbering 435, and each heading more or less permanent campaign organizations, individual representatives may have had more than a casual hand in this redirection of voting behavior. If so, this trend may be linked to with what Mayhew has called "electorally useful activities" pursued by legislators such as "credit claiming," "position taking," and "advertising" (1974a).

Incumbency Advantage: Safe Districts

In New York, there are thirty-four congressional districts, each containing slightly over half a million

people. In the 1984 New York congressional races, there
were only three changes made in the delegation. In the
Ninth Congressional District, Democrat Thomas Manton was
elected with 52.7% of the two-party vote to replace
Geraldine Ferraro, who ran as the Democratic vice
presidential nominee. In the Thirtieth Congressional
District, former ambassador to Fiji and Republican Fred
Eckert was elected with 54.8% of the two-party vote to
replace the retiring Barber Conable, also a Republican.
Only in the Twentieth Congressional District did the
Republican party convert a district. Joseph DioGuardi
won the election with 51.6% of the two-party vote in the
district vacated by the retiring Democratic representative
Richard Ottinger.

In 1984, Ronald Reagan carried New York State with
53.9 percent of the two-party vote. His national
percentage was 59.1 percent. At the congressional district
level, thirteen of fifteen New York Republicans elected
in 1984 improved on Reagan's state-wide 53.9 percent margin
of the two-party vote. Of these thirteen Republicans,
ten performed better than Reagan's national margin of 59.1
percent of the two-party vote. The story among the winning
Democrats, however, is likewise impressive. Sixteen of
the nineteen Democrats in the New York delegation won by
a wider margin in their districts than did Reagan in his
state-wide showing. Moreover, fourteen of these nineteen
Democratic representatives exceeded Reagan's national
average of 59.1 percent.

Collectively, this evidence attests to the growing
stability of congressional seats independent of presidential outcomes. Although the test of the argument would
rest in a district-by-district comparison of Reagan's vote
with that of individual members of the New York delegation,
votes in the 1984 presidential contest broken out by
congressional districts were not available as we went to
press. Hence, a comparison of Reagan's congressional
district performance during 1980 compared with the
representatives' performances in 1984 will serve as the
next best measure of district safeness (see Table 9.3).

By any standard, a comparison of Reagan's performance
in New York congressional districts in 1980 with the
performance of individual representatives in 1984 confirms
the general safeness of most districts. Using the two-way
contest between Reagan and Carter as a base, the average
improvement over Reagan among Republican representatives
in 1984 was 8.3 percent. The comparable figure for

TABLE 9.3
Spread between New York Representative's Percentage in
1984 and Reagan's Percentage in 1980 in Congressional
Districts (Reagan Leading)

Democrats			Republicans		
Reagan's Percent Based On:			Reagan's Percent Based On:		
Represen-tative and District	Reagan Carter Race	Reagan Carter Anderson Race	Represen-tative and District	Reagan Carter Race	Reagan Carter Anderson Race
Downey 2	(9.5)	(5.2)	Carey 1	(10.0)	(4.8)
Marazek 3	(10.3)	(5.0)	Lent 4	7.5	12.3
Addabbo 6	46.4	48.4	McGrath 2	3.4	7.6
Ackerman 7	21.8	24.8	Molinari 14	9.1	12.8
Scheuer 8	11.7	15.0	Green 15	15.4	19.8
Manton 9	(4.4)	(1.3)	DioGuardi 20	(6.9)	(1.9)
Schumer 10	25.4	27.8	Fish 21	13.6	19.4
Towns 11	60.1	61.0	Gilman 22	9.6	14.9
Owens 12	53.5	55.2	Solomon 24	11.8	17.2
Solarz 13	19.2	21.6	Boehlert 25	15.5	20.3
Rangel 16	81.9	83.1	Martin 26	15.9	19.8
Weiss 17	52.0	54.4	Wortley 27	(1.7)	4.0
Garcia 18	66.7	67.5	Horton 29	18.1	23.0
Biaggi 19	54.3	56.4	Eckert 30	5.0	9.5
Stratton 23	32.8	37.3	Kemp 31	19.0	23.5
McHugh 28	1.1	7.4			
LaFalce 32	17.6	21.6			
Nowak 33	45.1	47.0			
Lundine 34	(3.3)	1.4			

Source: Computed from Alan Ehrenhalt, ed. Politics
in America: Members of Congress in Washington and at
Home. Washington, D.C.: Congressional Quarterly. 1983;
"Returns for Governor, Senate and House," Congressional
Quarterly Weekly Report (November 10, 1984), 2923-2930.

improvement among Democratic representatives in 1984 was
29.6 percent. Taking into consideration the presence in
1980 of John Anderson as an independent presidential
candidate, the average improvement among Republican
representatives in 1984 increased to 13.2 percent; for
Democratic representatives it was a whopping 32.5 percent.

District Types: Although high Democratic margins are related to high concentrations of blacks (Sixth, Eleventh, Twelfth, Sixteenth, and Eighteenth Congressional Districts) who vote solidly Democratic, the situation in districts with Jewish representatives (Seventh, Eighth, Tenth, Thirteenth, Fifteenth, Seventeenth, and Twenty-second) may be different. Table 9.4 considers these possibilities. First, the data confirm that exceedingly high margins within these black districts account for the high average figures. Nevertheless, a control for these districts still leaves impressive margins.

The data appearing in Table 9.4 demonstrate the stability of the Democratic vote in Jewish congressional districts compared to other nonblack congressional districts in New York. Jewish Democratic representatives won in 1984 by an average margin of 70.4 percent; the comparable figure for non-Jewish Democratic representatives was 64.3 percent, a difference of 6.1 percent. The average improvement over Reagan's performance in 1980 (computed on the basis of a three-way presidential race) by these same representatives in 1984 was 28.7 percent. For non-Jewish Democratic representatives from nonblack districts, the average improvement in 1984 over Reagan's 1980 performance was only 15.5 percent. This difference (13.2 percent) suggests that voters in Jewish congressional districts are more likely to stay with the party in both races than are voters represented by white non-Jews. Using a two-way race as a basis for considering Reagan's performance in 1980 increases this difference (14.7 percent).

These data indicate there is a difference between campaigning for the presidency and conducting a reelection bid for the House of Representatives. Moreover, these data show a higher level of partisan loyalty among voters in congressional districts with Jewish representatives compared to those with other (nonblack) Democratic representatives in the New York delegation. This suggests partisan loyalty among Jewish voters.

If we are discussing safe districts in a partisan sense, then a Presidential candidate can expect a solid base of voters. Within certain New York congressional districts, this base for the Democrats obviously is to be found in the black districts. Jewish districts also constitutes part of such a base. This has been demonstrated by comparing Democratic Jewish districts with other Democratic districts.

TABLE 9.4
New York Congressional Districts: Jewish, Black, Other

| Category and Subcategory | N | Average Winning Percent 1984 | Average Improvement over Reagan's 1980 Margin in District | |
| | | | 2-way | 3-way |
			(Percent)	
All	34	70.1	20.1	23.9
Jewish				
Districts*	7	68.5	22.2	25.5
Democrats	5	70.4	26.0	28.7
Republicans	2	63.7	12.5	17.3
Black				
Districts**	5	90.3	61.7	63.0
Democrats	5	90.3	61.7	63.0
Other				
Districts	22	66.0	10.0	14.5
Democrats	10	64.3	11.3	15.5
Republicans	12	67.4	8.9	13.7

*Districts with Jewish representatives.
**Districts with high concentrations of black voters.
Source: Computed from Alan Ehrenhalt, ed. Politics in America: Members of Congress in Washington and at Home. Washington, D.C.: Congressional Quarterly. 1983; "Returns for Governor, Senate and House," Congressional Quarterly Weekly Report (November 10, 1984), 2923-2930.

If, on the other hand, safe districts refer to incumbency advantage, then the issues of realignment and decomposition may have relevance to congressional elections as well. This interpretation is probably becoming more appropriate. An indication of its plausibility is available when incumbent representatives retire, thereby leaving an open seat.

For example, after a bitter Democratic primary, the Republican DioGuardi was able to capture the seat previously occupied by Democrat Richard Ottinger, who retired in 1984. In 1984, DioGuardi was a first-time

candidate and lagged behind Reagan's 1980 percentage in
the Twentieth Congressional District. Will DioGuardi be
able to convert the seat to a safe Republican one? If
so, there are a number of electorally useful activities
he is likely to pursue on his own behalf. They undoubtedly
will be aimed at swaying traditional Democratic support,
some of which previously went to Ottinger, a Jew.

SUMMARY

Although the religious issue figured predominately
in the black-Jewish schism within the confines of the 1984
presidential primaries, it was submerged during the general
election campaign. Both Jews and blacks supported the
Democratic nominee for president of the United States in
a lopsided losing effort. Given the historic attachment
of Jews and blacks to the Democratic party, coupled with
the alliance of the religious Right with Reagan and the
Republican party, where else could they go? The only
alternative they had electorally was to stay at home and
not vote. Without the evidence necessary to draw a
conclusion, if Jewish realignment is underway, it is at
a slower pace than that of other segments of the voting
population, except for blacks.

The cutting edge of realignment in presidential
politics will not be found among Jews. If there is a
religious component to it, realignment is likely to be
found among born-again Christians and slippage from the
Democratic party among Catholics. As interesting as the
issues surrounding religion are, there are other dimensions
of importance.

The labor sector of the Democratic party may be
drifting away from its traditional moorings, and the
explanation may be economic in nature. First-time voters--
not all of whom are young--may be another segment of the
society with a potential for lining up with the Republican
party. A regional assessment shows that the South is
apparently in a slow but inexorable drift into the
Republican fold. The recent trend for states in the Old
South to elect Republicans as both senators and
representatives is another convincing point.

The stability of congressional districts outside the
South in the face of a Reagan Republican landslide is a
feature that may force the reinterpretation of the
realignment argument. In presidential politics, people

are more willing to vote Republican than they are to become Republican. Democrats who may be willing to desert their party in presidential contests appear to be holding the line congressionally. But is this due to allegiance to members of Congress who are Democrats (or Republicans) or to allegiance to members of Congress because they are incumbents? If presidents and representatives are becoming more adept at building electoral coalitions that transcend party lines, what meaning does party have?

REFERENCES

Burnham, Walter Dean. Critical Elections and the Mainsprings of American Politics. New York: W. W. Norton, 1970.

Cohen, Richard E. "Battle for the Northeast." National Journal (October 10), No. 43:2018-2021, 1984.

Commentary. "Jewish Voters & the 'Politics of Compassion': Irving Kristol & Critics," (letters from readers) (October)78:4-17, 1984.

Congressional Quarterly Weekly Report. "Returns for Governor, State and House" (November 10), 2923-2930, 1984.

Donner, Frank. "Courting Disaster," Nation. (October 6), 239:323-329, 1984.

Ehrenhalt, Alan (ed). Politics in America: Members of Congress in Washington and at Home. Washington, D.C.: Congressional Quarterly, 1983.

Fuchs, Lawrence H. The Political Behavior of American Jews. Glencoe, Ill.: Free Press, 1956.

Germond, Jack W., and Jules Witcover. "Inside Politics," National Journal. (October 6), no. 40:1890, 1984.

Hertzberg, Arthur. "The Plight of the Jewish Voter." Newsweek. (June 18), 12-13, 1984.

Himmelfarb, Milton. "Are Jews Becoming Republican?" Commentary 72:27-31, August 1981.

Kirschten, Dick. "Falwell and Farrakhan." National Journal. (November 3), no. 44:2094, 1984.

Kristol, Irving. "The Political Dilemma of American Jews." Commentary 78:23-29, July 1984.

Levin, Michael. "Comparable Worth: The Feminist Road to Socialism." Commentary 78:13-19, September 1984.

Levy, Mark R. and Michael S. Kramer. The Ethnic Factor: How America's Minorities Decide Elections. New York: Simon and Schuster, 1972.

218

Mayhew, David R. Congress: The Electoral Connection. New Haven: Yale University Press, 1974a.
_____. "Congressional Elections: The Case of the Vanishing Marginals." Polity 6:295-317, 1974b.

National Journal. "Who Voted for Whom for President." (November 3), no. 44:2111, 1984.

New York Times. "Leaders Try to Halt a Black-Jewish Rift." (August 19), I:1, 12, 1979a.
_____. "Young Asserts State Department Learned of the P.L.O. Meeting Within Days." (August 19), I:1, 10, 1979b.
_____. "Black Leaders Air Grievances on Jews." (August 23), 12, 1979c.
_____. "Seniority is Held to Outweigh Race as a Layoff Guide." (June 13), 1, B12, 1984a.
_____. "Black Democrats in a Poll Prefer Mondale to Jackson as Nominee." (July 10), 1, 16, 1984b.
_____. "Church-State Issue May Hurt Reagan's Effort to Attract Jews." (October 18), 14, 1984c.
_____. "Portrait of the Electorate." (November 8), 11, 1984d.
_____. "Religion and Politics Mix Poorly for Democrats." (November 25), II:2, 1984e.

Newsweek. "Jesse Jackson and the Jews." (March 5), 26, 1984a.
_____. "The New York Inferno." (April 2), 31, 1984b.
_____. "The Black Muslims: A Divided Flock." (April 9), 15-16, 1984c.
_____. "What Farrakhan Said." (April 23), 32, 1984d.
_____. "The Farrakhan Factor." (May 7), 43, 1984e.
_____. "What Jesse Jackson Wants." (May 7), 40-44, 1984f.

Nuechterlein, James. "Neoconservatism and Irving Kristol." Commentary 78:43-52, August 1984.

Petrocik, John R. Party Coalitions: Realignments and the Decline of the New Deal Party System. Chicago: University of Chicago Press, 1981.

Puddington, Arch. "Jesse Jackson, the Blacks and American Foreign Policy." Commentary 77:19-27, April 1984.

Stern, Sol. "The Neo-Conning of the Jews," Village Voice (August 28), 29:1ff, 1984.

Time. "Belatedly, Jackson Comes Clean." (March 12), 27, 1984a.
_____. "'Punish the Traitor'." (April 16), 16, 1984b.

_____. "What Does Jesse Really Want?" (April 16), 15-16, 1984c.

_____. "Farrakhan Fulminations." (July 2), 16, 1984d.

_____. "Stirring Up New Storms." (July 9), 8-10, 1984e.

Religion and Liberal Issues

Introduction

The chapters in this section relate to what are considered liberal issues--social justice, the Latin American foreign policy of the United States, nuclear disarmament, civil rights, and the Equal Rights Amendment. As the editor of the National Catholic Reporter recently said: "Under the Reagan Administration, there has been a coalition of issues. One is budget cuts and the harm they are doing to the poor. Another is Central America and the harm our nation's policies are doing those poor countries. Third is the arms build-up and the harm to ourselves and the entire planet" (quoted in Kenneth P. Briggs, "From the Pulpits to the Barricades," New York Times, 10 February 1985:6E). The focus of Part Three is on the segments of institutionalized religion identified with these causes, i.e., liberal Protestantism, the Catholic church, the black church, and feminist theologians.

Readers might be surprised by the inclusion of the Catholic church in the ranks of liberal Christianity. As discussed in Chapter 7, on the abortion issue the Catholic church sides with the religious conservatives. However, when one considers the major contemporary positions espoused by the religious liberals, one finds that the U.S. Catholic church is the most effective political force advocating the liberal agenda.

It must be acknowledged that support for liberal social policies is not limited to adherents of liberal Christianity. An evangelical Christian conference produced a statement entitled, "An Evangelical Commitment to Simple Lifestyle," which included the following comments:

One quarter of the world's population enjoys unparalleled prosperity, while another quarter endures

223

grinding poverty. This gross disparity is an
intolerable injustice; we refuse to acquiesce in it.
The call for a New International Economic Order
expresses the justified frustration of the Third
World.

Poverty and excessive wealth, militarism and
the arms industry, and the unjust distribution of
capital, land, and resources are issues of power and
powerlessness. Without a shift of power through
structural change these problems cannot be solved.

Some evangelicals go beyond simply espousing such
views and engage in public protests against current
national policies (Ann Monroe, "Devout Dissidents," Wall
Street Journal, 24 May 1985:1,10). However, it is true
that for the most part support for liberal causes comes
from outside conservative Protestantism.

"The Princeton Declaration," which is included in
Part Three (Chapter 10), was the statement accepted
unanimously in 1979 by delegates to the Third Assembly
of the World Conference on Religion and Peace. Delegates
came from forty-seven countries and represented all world
religions. Christian delegates came from a variety of
churches including the Methodist and Southern Baptist
churches. The statement affirms that a world community
must be based on the values of love, freedom, justice,
and truth, and addresses the issues of a just international
economic order, nuclear disarmament, human rights, and
the environment. Although brief, the document offers a
perspective that, if followed, would radically change the
world.

After the publication of "The Princeton Declaration,"
the World Conference on Religion and Peace met in 1984
and issued "The Nairobi Declaration," which addressed the
issues of disarmament, social development, and human
rights. The Nairobi text is evidence that the commitment
to social concerns expressed some five years before in
"The Princeton Declaration" has continued among leaders
of the world religions.

Yet, such declarations have not produced significant
structural changes. In fact, local Christian churches
have done little in relation to economic conditions.
Moreover, religious involvement does not seem to foster
compassionate concern among Christian laity for others
in need. In Chapter 11, "Captive Congregations: Why Local
Churches Don't Pursue Equality", James D. Davidson explains

why religious organizations have been ineffective as agents
of social change. He concludes with recommendations as
to how to increase social activism by local Christian
churches.

The next two chapters center on the Roman Catholic
church. Ronald T. Libby (Chapter 12, "Listen to the
Bishops") describes the situation in Latin America and
how it affects religion and politics in the United States.
Ties between the Catholic church in the United States and
Latin America are close, in part, because of the number
of U.S. priests and nuns who are serving or have served
in El Salvador and other neighboring countries. As a
result, U.S. bishops have supported moderate efforts for
change in Latin America and have been critical of U.S.
foreign policy toward that part of the hemisphere.

Although the situation in Latin America has changed
somewhat since Libby wrote his article (most notably, there
was an election in El Salvador), the basic parameters
remain unchanged. In that region, the Catholic church
had been aligned with the elite but is shifting in the
direction of becoming a "Church of the Poor." This shift
is affecting the relation between religion and politics
not only in Latin America but in the United States as
well. The tie between Latin American developments and
religiously motivated political action in the United States
is quite evident as we learn about U.S. citizens imprisoned
for giving sanctuary to Salvadorians in Texas and read
statements like those given by a bishop testifying before
a congressional committee in 1985 that providing military
aid to the contras is "illegal and in our judgement
immoral."

Chapter 13, "The Churches and Nuclear Deterrence,"
concerns the historic Pastoral Letter on War and Peace
issued by U.S. bishops (May 1983). L. Bruce Van Voorst
puts the letter in perspective, comparing it with previous
statements of a related nature by various religious
groups. Van Voorst helps us to understand the uniqueness
of this pastoral letter and its implications for national
policy.

The last two chapters in Part Three concern the
political role of two forms of Christianity usually
associated with support for liberal issues. Stephen D.
Johnson (Chapter 14, "The Role of the Black Church in Black
Civil Rights Movements") shows us that religious commitment
among U.S. blacks has both worked against civil rights
activism (especially among sect members) and motivated

226

other blacks to be activists. The latter phenomenon can
be seen in the important role of black churches as a base
for black political organization. Johnson explains this
seeming contradiction. Julia B. Mitchell (Chapter 15,
"Feminist Theologians and Liberal Political Issues"),
examining the political role of feminist theologians, found
surprisingly that they did not relate their theological
views to liberal struggles such as ERA. No doubt blacks
and feminists are important political forces, but religious
leaders among these groups have not given consistent
guidelines in the case of blacks or clear guidelines in
the case of women as to the political meaning of their
distinctive religious worldviews.

10

The Princeton Declaration
(World Conference on
Religion and Peace)

PREAMBLE

The Third Assembly of the World Conference on Religion
and Peace (WCRP III), meeting at Princeton in 1979, is
the continuation of an important heritage. The first World
Conference on Religion and Peace at Kyoto in 1970, and
the second at Louvain in 1974, revealed on the
international level a basic unity of purpose and goal amid
diversities of religious belief, and widened the pathway
of interreligious cooperation for peace. In spite of the
scars of religious strife in some parts of the world, we
perceive with joy a growing ferment of mutual understanding
and respect among the followers of the great religions.
We learned in the first two assemblies of WCRP that, while
maintaining our commitment to our respective faiths and
traditions, we may respect and understand the devotion
of others to their faiths and religious practices.
We pledge ourselves to continue to grow in our mutual
understanding and our work for peace, justice, and human
dignity. The Assembly is aware that we are approaching
not only the turn of the century, but also a turning point
in human history, with the survival of world civilization
at stake. Therefore, we chose as our theme: Religion
in the Struggle for World Community.
We rejoice in the sign of world community which this
conference represents in gathering 354 participants of

Reprinted with permission from the World Conference on
Religion and Peace, 1980.
Adopted by general agreement and without dissent at the
final plenary meeting.

Buddhist, Christian, Confucianist, Hindu, Jain, Jewish, Muslim, Shinto, Sikh, Zoroastrian, and other religions from 47 countries around this common theme. We know that forces which negate human dignity are strong and all around us. We see the menace of deadly nuclear weapons and desperate national insecurity. Technological and economic power often exploits and excludes the poor of the world. Political power often represses dissidents and denies human rights. Human greed also destroys the natural environment on which we all depend. We realize that our religious insights and actions were only one contribution to the struggle against these forces. We therefore meet with humility but with urgency to face, with the resources of our traditions and beliefs, the danger before us and the world.

PEACE IS POSSIBLE: OUR CONVICTION

World community, built on love, freedom, justice, and truth, is another name for peace. It is the goal of all our striving. It is not a utopian dream. Despite the temptation to despair as competition for dwindling resources grows more fierce, as centers of economic power intensify their exploitation, and as stockpiles of nuclear weapons grow, we have come together in a spirit of hope. In our various religions, we know that we are members of one human family. Sustained and motivated by the spiritual power by which we all live, we believe that there is an alternative to violence. We believe that peace is possible.

This is the hope we would share, not only among ourselves, as followers of our various religions, but with the whole world. We dedicate ourselves to the task of becoming more effective agents of building community. We call upon believers and all human beings to share this hope and to join in a commitment to work for its realization.

We believe that, as religious people, we have a special responsibility for building a peaceful world community and a special contribution to make.

On the one hand, we realize that far too often the names of our various religions have been used in warfare and community strife and that we must work harder against this. We cannot deny that:

1. the practices of our religious communities are sometimes a divisive force in the world;

2. too often we conform to the powers of the world, even when they do wrong, rather than confronting those powers with the word of the teachings of our religions;

3. we have not done enough as servants and advocates of suffering and exploited human beings; and

4. we have done too little to build interreligious understanding and community among ourselves on the local level where prejudices run strong.

On the other hand, we have been brought to a new awareness, in this assembly, of the deep resources we share for making peace, not only among ourselves, but in the world.

Adhering to different religions, we may differ in our objects of faith and worship. Nevertheless, in the way we practice our faith, we all confess that the God or the truth in which we believe transcends the powers and divisions of this world. We are not masters, but servants and witnesses, always being changed and disciplined in worship, meditation, and practice by the truth which we confess.

We all acknowledge restraint and self-discipline in a community of giving and forgiving love as basic to human life and the form of true blessedness.

We are all commanded by our faiths to seek justice in the world in a community of free and equal persons. In this search, conscience is given to every person as a moral guide to the ways of truth among us all.

We believe that peace in world community is not only possible, but is the way of life for human beings on earth, as we learn it in our prayers or meditations and by our faiths.

These convictions we share. Therefore we can go further and share a common confidence about the fruits of religious witness in the world. We trust that:

1. the power of active love, uniting men and women in the search for righteousness, will liberate the world from all injustice, hatred, and wrong;

2. common suffering may be the means of making us realize that we are brothers and sisters, called to overcome the sources of that suffering;

3. modern civilization may someday be changed so that neighborly goodwill and helpful partnership may be fostered; and

4. all religions will increasingly cooperate in creating a responsible world community.

In this confidence, we turn to particular areas where peace and world community are at stake.

MOBILIZATION FOR PEACE: OUR STRUGGLE

A. A Just International Economic Order

It is an affront to our conscience that 800 million
people in the developing world still live in poverty, that
hundreds of millions more are destitute because they are
physically unable to work, and that 40 percent of the
world's population cannot read or write. The gap of
economic disparity between the developed and the developing
countries has widened during the current decade. In view
of the stress laid by all the great religions on social
and economic justice and the right of all men and women
to have a share in the earth's bounty, we call on religious
people throughout the world to work for a just and
equitable economic order where dignity and humanity in
harmony with nature will not be denied to any person.

Such a new international economic order of growing
justice and equity would stimulate all nations to achieve
viable and self-reliant national economies, capable of
participating in international trade on a basis of equality
rather than dependence. In order to establish this new
vision, there must be the political and social will to
promote balanced economic growth worldwide and to allocate
its benefits to the abolition of poverty, the meeting of
all basic human needs, and the creation of equitable trade
relations between the industrial and the developing
countries. We call upon religious people to work for the
elimination of the structures of economic and social
injustice in their respective countries and to mobilize
governmental public opinion in favor of anti-poverty
programs. We call on religious institutions with economic
resources at their command to work for social amelioration,
prevention of destitution, and succor of the poor.

Our sense of religious responsibility impels us to
reaffirm that social justice and democratic participation
in decision-making are essential to true development.
We are of the view that suitable measures should be taken
at the national and international levels to ensure that
the transnational corporations and enterprises of all
economic systems do not wield undue economic, political,
and social power in the host country.

All the wealth of the universe is a common heritage
held in trusteeship for all. We advocate the rights of
yet-to-be-born generations to planetary resources that
have been wisely developed rather than wastefully
exhausted.

B. Nuclear and Conventional Disarmament

We believe that a major concern for the human family on earth today is the looming danger of nuclear annihilation, either by design or accident. We acknowledge that, in spite of SALT I and II, nuclear arsenals are continuing to grow, imparting a sense of urgency to the need of a worldwide movement to outlaw war and all weapons of mass destruction.

We regard the SALT II treaty between the U.S.A. and the U.S.S.R. as an encouraging development for nuclear disarmament and hope that it will be ratified so that SALT III negotiations may soon begin. It is the duty of organized religion to oppose the proliferation of nuclear weaponry, the arms competition between the U.S.A. and the U.S.S.R., and the expansion of the conventional arms race throughout the world. Nuclear powers must not use or threaten to use nuclear weapons against nuclear or non-nuclear States.

A global moral and religious campaign which will say NO to ANY KIND OF WAR BETWEEN NATIONS OR PEOPLES is our call to governments, religious groups, and all men and women of conscience and faith. This movement must work towards disarmament and non-violent means of maintaining security. As a prerequisite, it is essential to create an atmosphere of trust and foster a spirit of conciliation between peoples.

In pursuance of these objectives, we propose that the following steps be immediately taken:

1. a cessation of all testing, research, manufacture, spread, and deployment of nuclear weapons and other instruments of mass destruction;

2. a comprehensive nuclear test ban treaty;

3. effective methods of verification to ensure the implementation of these measures; and

4. a United Nations convention against the use of all weapons of mass destruction, declaring that such use is a crime against humanity.

In order to reduce reliance on arms, we propose that the mechanisms of international security through the United Nations be strengthened, that all nations implement unconditionally all the resolutions of the Security Council, and that the present concept of balance of power be replaced by a system of collective security in accordance with the United Nations Charter.

We express our profound concern over the massive increase in military spending, which has rocketed to $400

billion a year. It seems a cruel irony that, while
millions sleep with hungry stomachs, nations and their
governments devote a great part of their resources to
armaments, ignoring the demands of social justice. We
therefore appeal to the members and leaders of our
respective communities to use every political and moral
influence to urge a substantial reduction in the current
military expenditures of their own nations and the
utilization of the funds thus saved for development around
the world.

C. Human Rights

We reaffirm our commitment, made at Kyoto and Louvain,
to the U.N. Declaration of Human Rights, and we deplore
the denial of human rights to any individual or community.
We pledge our support to all societies, organizations,
and groups sincerely struggling for human rights and
opposing their violation. We condemn religious
discrimination in any form, and urge the United Nations
to adopt a Declaration and Covenant for the Elimination
of Intolerance and Discrimination Based on Religion or
Belief. We uphold the right of citizens to conscientious
objection to military service. We urge religious bodies
to press their governments to ratify and enforce all the
U.N. declarations, conventions, and covenants for the
protection and promotion of human rights. All the
religions to which we owe allegiance enjoin us to protect
the weak against the strong, to side with the oppressed
against the oppressor, and to respect human life, freedom
of conscience and expression, and the dignity of all
people. We support the U.N. declaration and convention
against racism and racial discrimination and urge all
governments to adhere to them. The actions of the United
Nations against apartheid should be implemented by all
States, organizations, and individuals.

Noting that WCRP III coincides with the United
Nations-sponsored International Year of the Child, we
reaffirm our belief in the United Nations General
Assembly's 1959 declaration that humanity "owes the child
the best it has to give" and that the child should be
brought up "in a spirit of understanding, tolerance,
friendship among peoples, peace, and universal
brotherhood." We appeal to religious people throughout
the world to help promote and work for the adoption of
social, economic, and population policies in every country

so as to assure a better and a brighter future for every child. It is profoundly important that youth be actively involved in the movement of religion for peace, and interreligious gatherings of youth should be encouraged.

We affirm that all human beings are born free and for freedom, that they are equal in dignity and rights, and that any discrimination on grounds of sex is incompatible with human dignity. We are convinced that practices, prejudices, or laws that prevent the full participation of women along with men in the political, social, economic, cultural, and religious life of their countries are morally indefensible and should be eliminated.

D. Environment and Energy Crisis

The earth is threatened increasingly by human misuse of the environment in quest of material prosperity. We are endangering future generations by our depletion of non-renewable natural resources, our pollution of air and water with chemical and radioactive wastes, and our over-exploitation of the soil in many parts of the world. An energy crisis stares us in the face. With diminishing supplies of oil, nations and individuals will have to make sacrifices, develop alternative--if possible renewable--sources of energy, and even change their lifestyles. The resources of all religions are needed to cultivate respect for the natural world in which we live, conservation of its resources, and a style of human life that is in harmony with all of nature. The children of the earth must conserve our planet's limited resources so that the bounty of the earth may not be wasted.

E. Education for Peace

The world's religious bodies must undertake major educational programs to increase mutual appreciation of all peoples and cultures, and foster a commitment to the values of peace. Our efforts so far have not been sufficient. We therefore rededicate ourselves to the education of children, youth, and adults, to the training of our religious leaders, and to the promotion of values of peace and understanding in our conduct in personal and public life.

Ultimately, peace and justice move toward the salvation and wholeness of all humanity, and flow from them as well. We, as followers of great religions, should be the channels through which spiritual power can flow for the healing of the world. We confess that we have not been worthy of this high calling, but we pledge ourselves here anew to be its faithful servants and witnesses. World peace in world community, with justice for all, is possible. We believe that the faith and hope which brought us together in this Assembly have been nurtured and strengthened during our time together. If this faith and hope were to be shared in the same way through the whole life of the religions to which we belong, then, at last, a new force would be brought to bear in human affairs and a new era would begin in the world. We shall pray or meditate, as well as work, that this new era may be realized.

Religion and
International Economic Justice
Commission I

PREAMBLE

The attainment of peace and world community greatly depends on the establishment of economic justice. Therefore, we delegates at the Third Assembly of the World Conference on Religion and Peace (WCRP III) declare our solidarity with both people who suffer and those who strive to establish justice.

We place ourselves firmly on the side of the search for an economic order where dignity and humanity in harmony with nature will not be denied to any person.

We are in anguish when, looking within ourselves, we recognize the part that we and our religious organizations play in creating, and even perpetuating, the current situation. That situation is not order but chaos which, through structural injustice, brings tragic consequences for hundreds of millions of suffering people. We are compelled by our respective religions to work to rectify that oppression and to seek the material liberation of the poor and the moral liberation of the rich.

Human dignity is a major theme in the teachings of all religions. But gross injustices deny dignity, and even the right of survival, to many. That situation forces us to cry out for justice and to work in behalf of those who suffer.

The new order which we seek places the person at the center. No one can be fully human while being the victim

---

Rev. John G. Gatu was moderator of this commission with Shri K. Krishnan Nair as rapporteur and Rev. Robert Smylie as staff associate. Consultant-experts included Rev. Robert McClean, Dr. Howard Schomer, and Dr. Erika Wolf.

236

of oppressive power. All people and nations must be free
to grow and share in decision-making in the interrelated
process of social justice, economic growth, and
self-reliance. People's participation is necessary in
the achievement of a just, viable, and sustainable order
leading to peace.

PRIMARY ECONOMIC CHARACTERISTICS OF A JUST INTERNATIONAL SOCIAL ORDER

A just international social order, in an increasingly
interdependent world, aims at the dynamic, integral
development of the human person and community, both in
the present situation and for future generations.

In order to establish this new vision, there must
be the political will to promote balanced economic growth
worldwide and to allocate its benefits to the abolition
of poverty and the creation of equitable trade relations
between industrialized and developing countries.

The following are some of the primary economic
characteristics that would distinguish the new order as
a just one:

1. All the people affected by economic decisions
and plans would participate in their design.

2. The prevailing social ethos would stimulate the
people to demand to share the power and responsibility
of their own economic development in all the schemes of
national governments, intergovernmental agencies, trade
unions, or transnational enterprises.

3. Public opinion would press all such institutions
to promote the balance of countervailing forces over all
forms of dominating power.

4. World opinion would encourage each society to
pursue its own vision of human development, assisting it
with access to research, technology, natural resources,
and the benefits of economic growth.

5. National and international development plans would
maintain a balance between the agricultural and the
industrial sectors, mindful that 70 percent of the global
population is engaged in agriculture.

6. Planetary production would be oriented toward
the meeting of the basic human needs of a population
projected to grow to seven billion persons by the end of
the 20th century, avoiding the stimulation of artificial
lifestyles and wants, the destructive use of natural
resources, and unnecessary consumption.

7. Every person would have the right to engage in productive work, receiving--as a matter of justice rather than charity--a fair share of the value that such work has created. Society would recognize the duty to produce the opportunity for such employment. Likewise, those unable to work would, in a spirit of solidarity, be supported through the labor of the gainfully employed.

8. Under-utilized natural resources would, as a matter of social justice, be mobilized for the self-reliance and self-development of all peoples.

Such a new international economic order of growing justice and equity would stimulate all nations to achieve viable and self-reliant national economies, capable of participating in international trade on a basis of equality rather than dependence. This would reduce to a minimum reliance on arms for the defense of national interests and would thereby minimize the arms trade. It would encourage sensitive ecological balance in the mobilization of planetary resources in the service of the whole human family.

WHAT CAN RELIGION DO TO PROMOTE THEIR ACHIEVEMENT?

In the pursuit of these characteristics of a just international social order, our primary concern is to be effective as religious people.

Through our religions, we can deepen consciousness of the basic unity of humanity through an individual and national change of heart. We can demonstrate, in our multi-religious, shared life, that world community is actually possible. We can issue timely denunciations of every violation of the fundamental unity of humankind, such as all forms of discrimination: classism, racism, sexism, and any other ideas that divide the human family into hostile camps.

We can teach and witness for ethical standards in economic relations: assisting the powerless in the struggle for empowerment, joining in the drive for economic and cultural decolonization, calling on our governments to curb the abuses of many national and transnational enterprises, accelerating the economic development of the poor, while supporting international agreements which promote more equitable trade relations.

We can study any investments which our various agencies and foundations may hold in the stock of corporate business, investigating how the firms in which these agencies are shareholders actually operate at home and abroad in respect to human rights and welfare, urging that they use their leverage to stockholders to press these enterprises to follow principles and practices that promote genuine human development. We can use our other economic assets--land, buildings, and income--to help people attain a better quality of life, for example, through agricultural research and training, and more productive land usage. We can make urban properties serve urban needs and utilize income in ways that foster economic self-sufficiency.

We can advocate the rights of yet-to-be-born generations to planetary resources that have been wisely developed rather than wrongfully exhausted.

The universe--its wealth, beauty, and promise--is the common heritage of us all. All religions cherish the universe and strive to live in harmony with it.

11

Captive Congregations: Why Local Churches Don't Pursue Equality

James D. Davidson

The Judeo-Christian heritage includes the concept of building a more just and equal world (Sider, 1977; Santa Ana, 1979). The faithful are expected to identify with the poor; sacrifice some of what they have for those who have less; challenge policies and practices that foster injustice and inequality; and as Sider (1977:87) put it, "develop communities based on an entirely new set of personal, social, and economic relationships." These new relationships are symbolized by biblical practices such as a jubilee year every fiftieth year, at which time all land was to be returned to its original owners; a sabbatical year every seventh year, during which the fields would lie fallow and replenish themselves, slaves could gain their freedom, and all debts would be cancelled; a practice of setting aside 10 percent of all crops every year and every three years distributing the accumulated crops among the poor; a practice of leaving some crops in the fields for the poor to glean; setting aside a Sabbath day so all workers could rest; no charging of interest on loans; and common ownership of all goods. Sider (1977:95) says Christians are challenged "to discover the underlying principles" of these practices and "search for contemporary strategies to give flesh to these basic principles."

— Some contemporary equivalents of these practices might be for congregations to assign a portion of staff time to working with or on behalf of the poor; provide sabbaticals for staff members to work with the poor; have parish committees examine public-policy issues related to equality, and formulate resolutions based on religious principles; create and sponsor parish programs related to equality; cultivate volunteers for these programs;

allocate a significant percentage of the church budget to these programs; and donate surplus funds to the poor.

However, evidence gathered over the past twenty years indicates that very few congregations engage in such activities (Winter, 1961; Hadden, 1969; Hoge, 1976; Birch and Rasmussen, 1978; Wood, 1981; Davidson and Roberts, 1984; Davidson, 1985). Local congregations do not sponsor many charitable programs aimed at helping the poor or many justice-oriented programs aimed at reducing inequality. Moreover, church members attach relatively little importance to such matters, preferring that their congregations focus on matters of personal faith and morality (Hoge and Faue, 1973; Hoge, 1976; Davidson and Knudsen, 1977; Dixon and Hoge, 1978; Davidson, 1985).

The question is why? Why don't local congregations do more to help low-income people and to build a society that reflects the biblical principles of justice and equality? Why do church members attach so little importance to these social concerns?

Gibson Winter (1961) has suggested that churches are captives of historical and present-day forces that limit their involvement in social concerns. According to Winter, these forces foster a pattern of noninvolvement that is contrary to biblical imperatives but that churches and churchgoers assume is "normal."

Winter's (1961) analysis focused on Protestant churches in the suburbs. But Protestant churches are not the only ones in captivity; Catholic congregations are also. Nor are suburban churches the only ones in captivity; so are rural and inner-city congregations. Thus, Winter's analysis should be extended to include Catholic, as well as Protestant, congregations in rural and inner-city, as well as suburban, locations.

First, I will describe two societal forces that limit local congregations' involvement in issues related to inequality. Then, I will discuss five conditions within the sphere of religion that have the same effect. Finally, I will conclude with a brief discussion of the implications this analysis has for religious leaders who wish to increase local churches' efforts in building a more just and equal world.

SOCIETAL FORCES

Two societal forces that have curtailed local churches' involvement in social concerns are (1) the fact that elites with the most social, economic, and political resources have a special interest in maintaining the current structure of social inequality, and (2) the fact that many nonelites with considerably fewer resources also derive some benefits from the existing structure of inequality.

Elite Interests

U.S. society has always consisted of racial, ethnic, religious, gender, economic, and political groups that pursue their own interests. Whites have competed against nonwhite minorities (who also have competed with each other); Anglo-Saxons have competed against the Irish, Italians, Germans, Poles, and other ethnic groups (who also have competed with one another); men have competed against women (who also have competed with one another); people with more money have competed against people who have less (who also have competed with one another); and people with more power have competed against people with less (who also have competed with each other).

In the course of all this competition, some groups have gained the upper hand over others. Whites, Anglo-Saxons, Protestants, males, the rich, and the powerful achieved dominance early in U.S. history (Domhoff, 1970; Feagin, 1984). Nonwhites, non-Anglo-Saxons, non-Protestants, women, the poor, and the powerless became subordinate.

From their dominant position, the elite groups have been able to construct a society that reflects their interests more than it reflects the interests of other groups. Elites have been able to base the nation's family values, educational processes, economic policies, and political structures on principles reflecting their racial, ethnic, religious, gender, economic, and political interests (Feagin, 1984). That is why whites, Anglo-Saxons, Protestants, men, the rich, and the powerful have benefited the most from the prevailing system (Burkey, 1978; Roof, 1979). That also is why nonwhites, non-Anglo-Saxons, non-Protestants, women, the poor, and the powerless are still in subordinate positions (Vanfossen, 1979; Feagin, 1984; Richards and Davidson, 1985).

The nation's elites have found it is particularly important to control society's economic and political institutions. They have concentrated on these two kinds of institutions because they contain the largest share

of the nation's wealth and power (Vanfossen, 1979). Elites
have succeeded in creating a situation whereby the policies
and practices in these two spheres tend to overlap.
Policies and practices in the economic sphere (e.g., free
enterprise) are compatible with policies and practices
in the political sphere (e.g., limited government
intervention in the private sector). Policies and
practices in the political sphere (e.g., the tendency to
define crime in terms of "street crime") also are
compatible with the policies and practices of the economic
sphere (e.g., opposition to investigation of "white collar
crime").

Through their control of the nation's economic and
political institutions, elites have assumed control over
many social welfare activities. The economic sphere has
taken more and more responsibility for social services
through benefits to employees and leadership in efforts
such as United Way (in many communities, run by people
"donated" by the business sector). And the government's
involvement in the area of social welfare is well known
(Feagin, 1975).

Another way elites have extended their influence has
been to encourage other spheres to support the status
quo and limit their involvement in activities which might
promote change. This is evident in education: Public
schools have stressed the legitimacy of competition,
individual achievement, free enterprise, and nationalism
(to mention just a few processes that reinforce the status
quo) and have tended to soft-pedal theories and ideas that
are critical of the status quo or might suggest alternative
values and norms (Howe, 1981; Sider, 1977; Graham, 1970).

Elites also have tried to promote their interests
through churches (Howe, 1981; Sider, 1977; Graham, 1970).
Elites have been overrepresented on church councils,
boards, and commissions. In these capacities, elites have
promoted the importance of church programs fostering
personal growth and salvation; encouraged parishioners
to attach highest priority to functions such as religious
education for young people and pastoral counseling for
adults; stressed the importance of "vertical" beliefs about
the supernatural; and cultivated a norm that religious
groups should "stick to religion" and not "interfere" in
social, economic, and political matters. They have
discouraged "justice-oriented" parish programs; promoted
the idea that such programs are not a legitimate focus
of congregational life; created a gap between churchgoers'

"vertical" beliefs and their "horizontal" beliefs about loving one's neighbors and doing good for others; and contributed to the fact that highly involved churchgoers are as likely to support injustice and inequality as they are to believe in justice and equality (Davidson, 1985).

Nonelite Interests

Elites may have the most influence on the actual functioning of the nation's social institutions, but nonelites also have some stake in the structure of social inequality. Gans (1972) has described how elites and nonelites alike benefit from the persistence of poverty. Among the benefits most of us derive from poverty are the following:

The existence of poverty makes sure that "dirty work" is done. Every economy has such work: physically dirty or dangerous, temporary, dead-end and underpaid, undignified, and menial jobs. . . . In America, poverty functions to provide a low-wage labor pool that is willing--or, rather, unable to be unwilling--to perform dirty work at low cost.

The poor subsidize, directly and indirectly, many activities that benefit the affluent. For one thing, they have long supported both the consumption and investment activities of the private economy by virtue of the low wages which they receive, e.g., domestics subsidize the upper middle and upper classes, making life easier for their employees and freeing affluent women for a variety of professional, cultural, civic and social activities.

Poverty creates jobs for a number of occupations and professions which serve the poor, or shield the rest of the population from them, e.g., the numbers game, the sale of heroin and cheap wine and liquors, pentecostal ministers, faith healers, prostitutes, and the peacetime army, which recruits its enlisted men mainly from among the poor.

The poor buy goods which others do not want and thus prolong their economic usefulness, such as day-old bread, fruit and vegetables which would otherwise have been thrown out, second-hand clothes, and deteriorating automobiles and buildings.

The poor can be identified and punished as alleged or real deviants in order to uphold the

legitimacy of dominant norms. . . . The defenders
of the desirability of hard work, thrift, and honesty,
and monogamy need people who can be accused of being
lazy, spendthrift, dishonest, and promiscuous to
justify these norms; . . . the norms themselves are
best legitimated by discovering violations.

Another group of poor, described as deserving
because they are disabled or suffering from bad luck,
provide the rest of the population with different
emotional satisfactions; they evoke compassion, pity,
and charity, thus allowing those who help them to
feel that they are altruistic, moral, and practicing
the Judeo-Christian ethic. The deserving poor also
enable others to feel fortunate for being spared the
deprivations that come with poverty.

The poor also assist in the upward mobility of
the nonpoor. . . . By being denied educational
opportunities or being stereotyped as stupid or
unteachable, the poor thus enable others to obtain
the better jobs.

The poor serve as symbolic constituencies and
opponents for several political groups. For example,
parts of the Left could not exist without the poor; .
. . Conversely, political groups of conservative bent
need "welfare chislers" and others who "live off the
taxpayer's hard-earned money" in order to justify
their demands for reduction in welfare payments and
tax relief.

The poor, being powerless, can be made to absorb
the economic and political costs of change and growth
in American society. During the 19th century, they
did the backbreaking work that built the cities;
today, they are pushed out of neighborhoods to make
room for progress (Gans, 1972:278-283).

Thus, in addition to elites who stand to gain the
most, many working- and middle-class people also derive
benefits from the structure of social inequality. Wood
(1981) has shown that these benefits foster negative
attitudes about churches being involved in issues related
to the causes and consequences of social inequality.

RELIGIOUS FACTORS

Several conditions within the religious sphere also
have contributed to the lack of local church involvement

in issues related to equality. These include: (1) historical-theological traditions stressing the importance of personal faith and salvation; (2) the voluntary nature of U.S. churches; (3) myths justifying the prevailing pattern of noninvolvement; (4) the fact that religious leaders are not trained to lead in the area of social justice and equality; and (5) the systemic nature of noninvolvement.

Historical-Theological Traditions

The present pattern of noninvolvement is at least partly a product of historical forces within the religious sphere. Since the nineteenth century, both Protestantism and Catholicism have contained two theological traditions. One of these traditions has stressed the importance of personal faith, assuming that salvation will foster personal morality and a more just world. The other tradition has stressed the importance of creating a just world in which personal salvation is possible.

Two generalizations can be made about the history of the relationship between these two traditions. First, the two traditions have been in a continuous struggle with one another (Earle, Knudsen, and Shriver, 1976). Followers of each tradition, as if in an armed camp, worry about attacks from the other camp and are always prepared for battle. The prejudices on both sides remain and, in my estimation, frequently exceed the hostilities that have divided Protestants and Catholics, and blacks and whites. Second, the tradition stressing personal faith and salvation has been the dominant force in both Protestantism and Catholicism. It has prevailed over the social reform tradition in both the number of years the former has held sway and the depth of its influence. The social reform tradition has gained momentum from time to time but has never been able to establish itself as an equal force. Its history has been more variable, while the dominance of the personal faith and salvation tradition has been more constant.

Protestants. "Private Protestantism" gained the upper hand during the nineteenth century and has retained its position as the dominant force ever since (Marty, 1970). As Hoge (1976:25) has observed: "The program of individual Protestantism has been the majority view from the beginning. It has appealed better to middle-class America partly because it accepted the existing social order and legitimated the possessions of wealth as being proper and deserved. It has been seen as a sort of 'common core' view." This dominance of private Protestantism can be attributed, at least in part, to its compatibility with individualistic and competitive values of the larger society (Feagin, 1975; Williams, 1960).

The intellectual liberalism and social upheaval of the 1880s and 1890s fostered the social gospel movement, which lasted well into the first two decades of the twentieth century (Hoge, 1976:21-26; Wilson, 1978:218). The social gospel movement actually "stood for reforms which would preserve the basic mechanism of the free enterprise system--private property, wage-labor, and the market" (Wilson, 1978:218-219). But because it also stressed the importance of structural reform in the nation's economic and political institutions, this movement was viewed as "radical" by most churchgoers.

The social gospel movement triggered an even more powerful movement intent on returning to the five so-called fundamentals of the Christian faith: "inerrancy of Scripture, the virgin birth, the satisfaction theory of the atonement, the resurrection of the body, and the miracles of Jesus" (Hoge, 1976:26). With the rise of fundamentalism, corporate interests expanded, government interest in poor relief declined, and achievements of the social gospel movement "were constantly in danger of being rolled back" (Feagin, 1975:39).

The depression gave new life to Protestant social concerns, as "modernists" (such as Reinhold Neibuhr) tried to interpret and respond to the social and economic crises of the 1930s. Several of the reforms proposed during the social gospel movement were incorporated into the New Deal. But, "like the Social Gospel reforms, the New Deal reforms obtained the support of only a minority of church people" (Wilson, 1978:222).

Private Protestantism reasserted its dominance as Protestant churches experienced the so-called religious revival of the 1950s and early 1960s (the era in which Winter wrote The Suburban Captivity of the Churches).

At the national level at least, Protestant churches became more heavily involved in the social concerns of the 1960s: civil rights, poverty, and the war in Vietnam. But as the social turmoil of the 1960s ended and many mainline churches began to experience membership decreases, private Protestantism reestablished its dominance. Conservative churches were growing (Kelley, 1972), and liberal churches were turning their attentions inward.

Catholics. The history of U.S. Catholicism also has been characterized by the struggle between the two traditions and the dominance of the personal faith tradition. The Catholic emphasis on faith historically was buttressed by Catholic immigrants' efforts to establish their church on U.S. soil and to protect their faith from a culture that was not always friendly. Early efforts in the area of social concern were largely directed inward, as Catholics tried to care for the social, economic, and political needs of their lower- and working-class members (Abell, 1963:27,35). According to Lally (1962:48), "for the most part American Catholics as a group, at least up until New Deal times, could not be considered socially progressive. The labor movement, in which they were heavily involved, is an obvious and notable exception to this statement." McBrien (1980:644-645) argues that the Catholic church during this early period tended to "repudiate modernity."

According to Lally (1962:48), "It was not until the Depression years that we can speak in realistic terms of a widespread Catholic social consciousness and with it a willingness not simply to adapt to the community life but also to work to transform it." Positions that bishops had taken earlier on issues such as social insurance, child labor laws, labor's right to organize, and progressive taxes were increasingly supported by Catholic lay people and adopted "in whole or in part" by the New Deal (Abell, 1963:234). Other developments included: the issuance of the papal encyclical "Quadragesimo Anno" in 1931 in which Pope Pius XI "recommended . . . co-partnerships be introduced so that wage earners might become 'sharers in some sort in the ownership or the management of the profits'" (Abell, 1960:81); Dorothy Day's Catholic Worker Movement, which attempted to educate the poor about their plight while serving their social and nutritional needs; and Michael O'Shaughnessy's small but influential Catholic League for Social Justice, which called for the rich to practice self-restraint and lead in the redistribution of wealth.

However, the emphasis on faith and personal morality returned in the 1940s and 1950s. Fichter's (1951) description of Catholic "orthodoxy" during this period stressed worship, devotional activities, and personal morality--not social reform. According to McBrien (1980:647-648), the emphasis during this period was liturgical, biblical, and theological. The limited amount of "social action was primarily concerned with the problem

of establishing satisfactory relationships with the
powerful labor unionism which emerged under the New Deal
during the Depression and World War II" (Abell, 1963:264).

The 1960s witnessed an increase in Catholic attention
to issues related to social inequality. The Catholic
church actively supported the grape and lettuce boycotts
as well as the United Farmworkers Organization of Cesar
Chavez. In 1969, the church created the Campaign for Human
Development (Evans, 1979) which dispenses several million
dollars annually to "organized groups of white and minority
poor to develop economic strength and political power in
their own communities" (National Catholic News Service,
1971). Finally, Catholics developed a national network
of social activists known as the Catholic Committee on
Urban Ministry (CCUM) (Egan, Roach, and Murnion, 1979).
In 1976, CCUM played a significant role in the Call to
Action, a national assembly of Catholics that resulted
in proposals to further "the rights of minorities in church
and society, parish responsibility for neighborhood
community action, a stronger moral position on war and
disarmament, criminal justice reform, and education for
justice" (Egan, Roach, and Murnion, 1979:288).

However, even during this period of increased social
consciousness, the focus of attention was on the liturgical
reforms of Vatican II and the controversies associated
with personal morality issues such as birth control,
abortion, and divorce. As the social upheavals of the
1960s faded and the economic insecurity of the 1970s
increased, the interest in social reform waned and more
attention has been given to solidifying the church after
two decades of internal conflict and change.

This history of theological competition and of the
dominance of the private faith tradition over the social
gospel tradition helps explain the behavior of Protestant
and Catholic churches today. It helps explain why church
leaders stress issues of faith over issues related to
justice and equality; why churchgoers assume faith
questions are more important than issues related to justice
and equality; and why faith oriented activities are at
the core of most church programs while "outreach"
activities are on the periphery.

Voluntary Nature of U.S. Churches

One reason for the historic emphasis on personal faith
and morality is the voluntary nature of U.S. church life

(Davidson, 1970; Scherer, 1972). People are free to choose whether they will belong to any church, which congregation they will attend, and the conditions under which they will stay or leave. In the interest of maximizing church membership and attendance, church leaders have been inclined toward messages members will accept. "Ministers behave very much like entrepreneurs developing and 'marketing' their product in an intense competition for souls. Their message is tuned to whatever the market will bear and unattractive messages are 'dropped'" (Wilson, 1978:217).

In middle- and upper-class churches, this means a tendency for church leaders to focus on messages that (implicitly or explicitly) accept the status quo and urge affluent members to grow in their personal faith and live up to their God-given potential as individual human beings (Roof, 1977). Leaders shy away from aspects of religious social teachings that might require their more privileged members to question social policies and practices that have served their interests, or at least have limited the social and economic well-being of others. Thus, it is no surprise that people from the middle to the upper class are most inclined to join and be active in churches (Roberts, 1984; Hoge and Roozen, 1979).

Christian social teachings are more consistent with the social and economic interests of the poor and powerless (Sider, 1977; Santa Ana, 1979; Birch and Rasmussen, 1978). Thus, all other things being equal, one might expect these teachings to be less problematic in churches with poorer members. But, all other things are not equal. Lower- and working-class people tend to be fatalistic about the possibility of social reform and/or tend to blame themselves for the lack of success in the secular world (Feagin, 1975). Thus, religious leaders know there is not much likelihood that a message stressing structural reform will attract larger numbers of working- and lower-class members.

They also know they can successfully market the idea that one's lot in this life is not so important as one's fate in the hereafter--a message that deemphasizes the hardships of the present and emphasizes the glories of the future. Though one might not be able to determine one's social and economic well-being, one can determine one's fate in the hereafter by "turning against sin and coming to Jesus." The implications of this message for church growth are obvious. Churches stressing such a

250

message among lower- and working-class people tend to grow
in periods of economic hardship (e.g., the depression of
the 1930s and the inflation of the 1970s) when the
legitimacy of the prevailing social order is most uncertain
and the certainty of God's love is most appealing (Gaustad,
1968; Wilson, 1978).

Myths

Several myths have justified churches' tendency not
to pursue equality (Hudnut, 1971).

The Role of the Government. One myth is that
churches do not need to be active in social issues "because
the federal government is taking care of that." The
federal government's involvement in social welfare programs
did increase between the depression of the 1930s and Lyndon
Johnson's Great Society program of the 1960s (Miller,
1968; James, 1972; Huber and Chalfant, 1974; Roby, 1974;
Feagin, 1975; Schiller, 1976).

But political leaders have always felt there are
limits to the federal government's involvement in issues
such as welfare. They have felt that the political sector,
because it is based on competition among economic and
political interest groups, could not provide a consistent
moral basis for caring for the nation's poor. Thus, even
though the government is actively involved in social
welfare, the churches always have a role to play in
articulating the moral basis for caring for low-income
and powerless people.

Moreover, liberals and conservatives alike have
claimed that federal programs have not always been
effective. Liberals often have expressed their concern
that federal programs are nothing more than Band-Aids for
the individual symptoms of poverty, not meaningful efforts
to attack poverty's real causes. Some of these critics
feel that churches could always play a more prophetic role
in the area of social concerns, challenging society to
understand the causes of poverty and demanding that
government programs address these causes more
forthrightly. Conservatives have tended to stress the
abuse and fraud in federal programs. These critics have
argued that there would be less abuse and fraud if the
programs were conducted "closer to home" at the local level
where there would be more public accountability and control
over the funds. Some of these critics also feel that

churches and private charities could conduct similar
programs more effectively and at less cost.

Also, government programs have not reached all of
the people who need help. Evidence consistently has
indicted that federal welfare programs reach only about
half of the people who qualify for and need economic
assistance (Miller, 1968; James, 1972; Huber and Chalfant,
1974; Roby, 1974; Feagin, 1975; Schiller, 1976). Thus,
churches could play a role in reaching many people that
government programs--for one reason or another--are unable
to reach.

Finally, Ronald Reagan's election in 1980 and
reelection in 1984 have proved that government involvement
in social welfare is more negotiable than inevitable, more
variable than constant, more volatile than permanent.
Those who argued that the churches need not be involved
"because the government will take care of it" have found
that the government may not take care of it--or at least
may take care of it much better at some times than others.

Social Concerns: Divisive and Costly. A second
myth is that involvement in social concerns is divisive
and costly. Proponents of this myth argue that church
involvement in social concerns promotes a decline in church
membership.

Given my earlier analysis of elite and nonelite
interests, I assume there is some incompatibility between
the worldly interests of some church members and the
prophetic dimensions of the Judeo-Christian heritage.
Researchers such as Hadden (1969) and Quinley (1974) have
reported cases in which church members have withdrawn their
membership and financial support when clergy have become
personally involved in "radical" social action or preached
on controversial social issues.

But there are several problems with this myth. First,
the myth is based on an assumption that social concern
tends to be radical. But radical social action is not
the only form of social concern. Social concern also can
take a number of forms that are quite acceptable to large
numbers of church members (Hoge and Faue, 1973; Hoge,
1976). These forms include charitable efforts to share
the resources of the affluent with the poor and to assist
low-income people in a variety of ways. Churches can be
involved in these efforts without risking support of their
members, especially as a step in the direction of greater
overall involvement.

Second, the correlation between national church involvement in social concerns and the decline in membership among mainline denominations probably is spurious; much of it can be explained by factors such as the birthrate. The post-World War II baby boom produced much of the religious revival in the 1950s, as parents joined churches when they felt their six-, seven-, and eight-year-old children should be exposed to religion (Nash and Berger, 1962; Glock, Ringer, and Babbie, 1967; Johnstone, 1983). The boom is over, and those children--who are now in their twenties, thirties, and early forties--are not having so many babies and are not joining churches at the same rate as their parents did. Thus, mainline denominations, which (unlike sects) rely on present members for the cultivation of future members, have experienced a decline that tends to be blamed on their involvement in social concerns during the 1960s.

Third, although some church members have withdrawn their memberships and financial support from churches that have pursued equality, many others have increased their support for the same reason. Quinley (1969:17-18) found that clergy who become involved in social concerns can "rally parishioner support behind their position and may attract some new members and financial contributions to their church." Evans (1979) presented very convincing evidence of increased giving as Catholics learned more about their church's efforts to be more involved in social reform through the Campaign for Human Development. Clearly, many church members want their churches to be involved in a variety of social concerns (Hamilton, 1972; Amerson and Carroll, 1979; Vanfossen, 1979; Davidson and Roberts 1984).

Fourth, many people are among the "unchurched" because they do not see churches doing anything of real value (Perry et al., 1980). They wish churches were more involved in the social concerns of their communities, especially the concerns of people who are poor and powerless (Hoge and Roozen, 1979). They have some interest in changing social policies and practices fostering inequality and in responding to the needs of low-income people. If churches increased their involvement in social concerns, many of these people would think more highly of them and be more inclined to join. And, congregations that have acted according to this assumption provide some convincing evidence supporting this view (Hadden and Longino, 1974; Dudley, 1979). They have increased their memberships and are growing.

Dudley (1979:10) has concluded that "there is no clear statistical basis to support the claim that church involvement in social concern has been the primary reason for the decline in membership among mainline denominations; there is no exodus of members, no clear coincidence of social encounter and church membership decline." Hoge (1976:114) agrees, concluding there is "no support" for the idea that church "membership . . . declined as a result of a general opposition to the cumulative total of many social actions by the national leadership of the churches during the 1960s." He also found that, after the United Presbyterian church's controversial decision to support black activist Angela Davis, " many more persons reported increases in church giving than decreases." Overall, Hoge (1976:113) concluded, "There are no notable connections between level of giving and opinions about proper specific church actions . . . overall giving by individuals increases or decreases along with changes in overall commitment and interest in the church, not with specific social actions by the church."

Attitudes and Behavior. Another myth is that church members' attitudes must change before they will support programs calling for social involvement. Although the cultivation of compassionate attitudes is important--nobody will deny that--the myth overstates the importance of individual attitudes and results in an overemphasis on educational programs.

Research clearly shows that behavioral change probably affects attitude change more than vice versa. As Pettigrew (1971; 1975:124) has observed, "Behavior change typically precedes, rather than follows from, attitude change." Myers (1980:17) says that "the 'attitude follows behavior' principle has become an accepted fact in contemporary social psychology."

> If social psychology has taught us anything during the last 20 years, it is that . . . we are as likely to act ourselves into a way of thinking as to think ourselves into a line of actions. . . . Individuals are as likely to believe in what they have stood up for as to stand to up for what they believe (Myers, 1980:16-17).

Thus, for example, people who are raised in a church where there are no social concerns programs are likely to attach

low priority to such programs and may find it difficult
to link their vertical and horizontal beliefs. But if
they leave their hometown, get married, and join another
church that does have social concerns programs (behavior
change), the chances are that over time, they might come
to see social concerns as a normal part of church life,
attach more importance to them, and find it easier to link
their vertical and horizontal beliefs (attitude change).

Research also shows that educational campaigns have
very limited effects. People who "need" educational
programs are least likely to participate (Cooper and
Jahoda, 1947; McIver, 1957; Knupfer, 1947; Vander Zanden,
1972; Amerson and Carroll, 1979). Thus, in Myers'
(1980:16) words, "It is therefore not surprising that
attempts to change people's behavior by changing their
attitudes often produce only modest results." However,
educational programs dominate church calendars. Action
programs that are more likely to foster compassionate
attitudes are rare.

Clergy Not Trained in Social Concerns

Seminaries tend to emphasize pastoral skills more
than prophetic skills. They do relatively good jobs
preparing young clergy to preach and care for the spiritual
needs of their parishioners, but they do less well in
preparing them to deal with the church's role in society
and to devise ways of incorporating that role into the
lives of local congregations they will serve (Graham,
1970:163, 168-169).

Working in conjunction with Carl Dudley at McCormick
Theological Seminary in Chicago, Vicky Curtiss recently
examined the curricula at seven Presbyterian seminaries:
Princeton, San Francisco, Pittsburgh, Dubuque, Johnson
C. Smith, Louisville, and McCormick. She found a
consistently higher percentage of courses that dealt with
the classical studies (Bible, theology, philosophy,
history) than with the ministries (pastoral care,
preaching, education, administration, mission). Within
the ministries field, "how-to" courses on preaching,
teaching, counseling, and administration are offered with
much more frequency than strategy courses on evangelism,
stewardship, social service, and social justice.

Thus, most local congregations are headed by pastors
with considerable training in theological and pastoral
skills, but little or no training in skills pertaining

to ways of incorporating social concerns into the life
of the local church. The pulpits of most churches are
filled with "priests," not "prophets."

Systemic Nature of Noninvolvement

A final condition that fosters noninvolvement is the
systemic nature of church programs, and the priorities,
beliefs, and attitudes of lay people. They are a system
because they are interrelated and reinforce one another.
The lack of church programs dealing with equality fosters
a set of priorities in which social concerns rank low.
It also fosters the separation of vertical and horizontal
beliefs. And together these conditions allow churchgoers
to maintain attitudes that are not especially compassionate
toward the poor and the powerless. Moreover, once churches
contain substantial numbers of people whose attitudes and
activities are not consistent with Christian social
teachings, whose vertical and horizontal beliefs have been
separated, and who attach low priority to social concerns,
neither the people nor the clergy are likely to encourage
the development of programs oriented toward justice and
equality (Hadden, 1969; Quinley, 1974; Earle, Knudsen,
and Shriver, 1976). Thus, the vicious circle is complete,
spinning with a momentum of its own, making it difficult
for anyone to break the cycle.

CONCLUSIONS

I began with the assumption that the Judeo-Christian
heritage includes the goal of building a more just and
equal world. I then reviewed the literature indicating
that most local congregations do not actively pursue this
goal. In an effort to explain this discontinuity, I called
on Winter's (1961) notion that churches are in captivity.
A number of societal and religious forces limit their
pursuit of equality. These forces include: elites'
success in persuading churches to focus on personal
salvation and not to interfere with public policies related
to inequality; the fact that nonelites (including many
church members) also benefit from inequality and thus do
not want their churches to act in ways that might be
contrary to the nonelites' social and economic interests;
historical-theological traditions stressing the importance
of personal faith and salvation; the voluntary nature of

U.S. churches (that has caused church leaders to stress ideas that members and potential recruits will find acceptable); myths that justify noninvolvement in social issues; the fact that clergy have little or no training in matters related to justice and equality; and the tendency for church policies and parishioners' attitudes to form a vicious circle of noninvolvement that is hard to break.

These are substantial constraints, relating to the very structure of our society and well-institutionalized policies and practices within the religious sphere. So long as these constraints remain in effect, local churches are not likely to be very involved in the pursuit of equality.

Releasing congregations from their captivity would not be easy. But doing so could increase local churches' role in building a more just and equal world. To release churches from their captivity, religious leaders would have to address each of the constraints we have discussed. For one thing, they could recognize the incompatibility between elite interests in perpetuating inequality and the biblical imperative to build a more just and equal world. In this context, religious leaders could limit elites' participation in church decisionmaking and/or use religious principles to counteract elite efforts to limit local churches' involvement in issues related to the causes and consequences of inequality (Wood, 1981).

Religious leaders also could assert that local church policies will be based on religious, not secular, principles. Thus the benefits elites and nonelites derive from the prevailing structure of social inequality would not be involved in church decisionmaking. More emphasis would be placed on self-sacrifice, and less on self-interest, in the formulation of church policies and programs.

Third, religious leaders could oppose the historical-theological divisions between personal faith and salvation, on the one hand, and social reform, on the other. Instead of being victimized by these historical divisions, religious leaders could forge new theological visions integrating the vertical-personal dimensions of faith with its horizontal-social dimensions.

The voluntary nature of U.S. religion has resulted in a tendency for church leaders to promote policies that attract a large following and to be willing to deemphasize those which might offend members and potential recruits.

Although voluntarism tends to have this consequence, it does not necessarily have to. Religious leaders could promote a more balanced approach, urging church members and potential recruits to consider faith and action as the criteria for membership. Some of the evidence reported above indicates that there is considerable support for such an approach.

Next, religious leaders could tackle the myths surrounding the pursuit of equality. Tackling the myths might mean recognizing their distortions, replacing them with beliefs that justify social involvement, and acting on these beliefs. It might mean rejecting the myth that churches do not have to be involved because government will take care of the needy and assuming instead that churches have a commitment to the poor and powerless that transcends government's limited actions. It might mean rejecting the idea that social action is necessarily divisive and costly and assuming instead that it often is unifying and rewarding. It might mean rejecting the assumption that attitudes necessarily precede behavior and realizing that behavior often shapes people's attitudes. If churches promote behavior based on justice and equality, they can promote attitudes that are compatible with these experiences.

Religious leaders also might question the assumptions underlying seminary education, asking what concept of ministry (priesthood) is being promoted and what types of training are being offered. If the concept of ministry does not include service to the poor and powerless, and if seminary education does not include courses and/or experiences related to building a more just and equal world, then some reordering of priorities might be called for. Those seminaries that have offered students experiences in social ministry have produced graduates who are better prepared to handle that aspect of their professional responsibilities.

Finally, religious leaders must assume that it is possible to break into the vicious circle of noninvolvement. Much evidence (e.g., Wood, 1981; Davidson, 1985) suggests the most effective way to do so is to call upon biblical imperatives and church teaching to legitimate innovative programs that are likely to produce successful experiences in the area of social concern. These experiences are likely to result in a greater willingness to embrace other outreach programs. The ultimate effect might be a congregation actively engaged in the process of building a more just and equal world.

REFERENCES

Abell, Aaron I. "The Catholic Factor in the Social Justice Movement" in Thomas T. McAvoy (ed.) Roman Catholicism and the American Way of Life. Notre Dame, Ind.: University of Notre Dame Press, 1960.
_____. American Catholicism and Social Action. Notre Dame, Ind.: University of Notre Dame Press, 1963.

Amerson, Philip A., and Jackson W. Carroll. "The Suburban Church and Racism: Is Change Possible?" Review of Religious Research 20(Summer): 335-349, 1979.

Birch, Bruce C., and Larry L. Rasmussen. The Predicament of the Prosperous. Philadelphia: Westminster Press, 1978.

Burkey, Richard M. Ethnic and Racial Groups. Menlo Park, Calif.: Cummings Publishing Company, 1978.

Cooper, Eunice, and Marie Jahoda. "The Evasion of Propaganda: How Prejudiced People Respond to Antiprejudice Propaganda," Journal of Psychology 23(January): 15-25, 1947.

Davidson, James D. "Protestant Churches as Voluntary Associations," Indiana Academy of Social Science, Proceedings 1969, 110-123, 1970.
_____. Mobilizing Social Movement Organizations: The Formation, Institutionalization, and Effectiveness of Ecumenical Urban Ministries. Storrs, Conn.: Society for the Scientific Study of Religion, 1985.

Davidson, James D., and Dean D. Knudsen. "A New Approach to Religious Commitment," Sociological Focus 10(April): 151-173, 1977.

Davidson, James D., and Michael K. Roberts. "Pursuing Equality," presented at annual meeting of the Society for the Scientific Study of Religion, Chicago, Ill., October, 1984.

Dixon, Robert, and Dean R. Hoge. "Models and Priorities of the Catholic Church as Held by Suburban Laity," Review of Religious Research 20(Spring): 150-167, 1978.

Domhoff, G. William. The Higher Circles. New York: Random House, 1970.

Dudley, Carl S. Where Have All Our People Gone? New York: Pilgrim Press, 1979.

Earle, John, Dean D. Knudsen, and Donald Shriver. Spindles and Spires. Atlanta: John Knox Press, 1976.

Egan, John J., Peggy Roach, and Philip J. Murnion. "Catholic Committee on Urban Ministry: Ministry to the Ministers," Review of Religious Research 20(Summer): 279-290, 1979.

Evans, Bernard F. "Campaign for Human Development: Church Involvement in Social Change," Review of Religious Research 20(Summer): 264-279, 1979.

Feagin, Joe. Subordinating the Poor. Englewood Cliffs, N. J.: Prentice-Hall, 1975.

_____. Racial and Ethnic Relations. Englewood Cliffs, N. J.: Prentice-Hall, 1984.

Fichter, Joseph. Southern Parish. Chicago: University of Chicago Press, 1951.

Gans, Herbert J. "The Positive Functions of Poverty," American Journal of Sociology 78(September): 275-289, 1972.

Gaustad, Edwin. "America's Institutions of Faith," in William McLoughlin and Robert Bellah (eds.), Religion in America, Boston: Beacon Press, 1968.

Glock, Charles Y., Benjamin Ringer, and Earl Babbie. To Comfort and To Challenge. Berkeley: University of California Press, 1967.

Graham, James. The Enemies of the Poor. New York: Vintage, 1970.

Hadden, Jeffrey K. The Gathering Storm in the Churches. New York: Doubleday, 1969.

Hadden, Jeffrey, and Charles Longino Jr. Gideon's Gang. New York: Pilgrim Press, 1974.

Hamilton, Robert. Class and Politics in the United States. New York: Wiley, 1972.

Hoge, Dean R. Division in the Protestant House. Philadelphia: Westminster Press, 1976.

Hoge, Dean R. and Jeffrey Faue. "Sources of Conflict Over Priorities of the Protestant Church," Social Forces 52(December): 178-194, 1973.

Hoge, Dean R., and David A. Roozen. Understanding Church and Decline, 1950-1978. New York: Pilgrim Press, 1979.

Howe, Gary Nigel. "The Political Economy of American Religion: An Essay in Cultural History," pp. 110-137 in Scott G. McNall (ed.), Political Economy, Dallas, Tex.: Scott, Foresman, 1981.

Huber, Joan, and H. Paul Chalfant. The Sociology of American Poverty. Cambridge, Mass.: Schenkman, 1974.

Hudnut, Robert K. The Sleeping Giant. New York: Harper and Row, 1971.

260

James, Dorothy B. *Poverty, Politics, and Change.* Englewood Cliffs, N. J.: Prentice-Hall, 1972.

Johnstone, Ronald L. *Religion and Society in Interaction.* Englewood Cliffs, N. J.: Prentice-Hall, 1983.

Kelley, Dean. *Why Conservative Churches are Growing.* New York: Harper and Row, 1972.

Knupfer, Genevieve. "Portrait of the Underdog," *Public Opinion Quarterly* 11(Spring): 103-116, 1947.

Lally, Francis. *The Catholic Church in a Changing America.* Boston: Little, Brown, 1962.

McBrien, Richard P. *Catholicism.* Vol. 2. Oak Grove, Minn.: Winston Press, 1980.

McIver, Robert M. *The More Perfect Union.* New York: MacMillan, 1957.

Marty, Martin. *The Righteous Empire.* New York: Dial Press, 1970.

Miller, Herman P. *Poverty: American Style.* Belmont, Calif.: Wadsworth, 1968.

Myers, David G. "Faith and Action: A Seamless Tapestry," *Christianity Today* 34 (November): 16-19, 1980.

Nash, Denison, and Peter Berger. "The Child, the Family, and The 'Religious Revival in Suburbia,'" *Journal for the Scientific Study of Religion* 1(Fall): 85-93, 1962.

National Catholic News Service. "Origins" (October): 4-7, 1971.

Perry, Everett L., James H. Davis, Ruth T. Doyle, and John E. Dyble. "Toward a Typology of Unchurched Americans," *Review of Religious Research* 21 (Supplement): 388-404, 1980.

Pettigrew, Thomas R. *Racially Separate or Together?* New York: McGraw-Hill, 1971.

_____. "Black and White Attitudes Toward Race and Housing," in Pettigrew (ed.), *Racial Discrimination in the United States.* New York: Harper and Row, 1975.

Quinley, Harold E. "Hawks and Doves Among the Clergy," *Ministry Studies* 3(October): 5-23, 1969.

_____. *The Prophetic Clergy.* New York: John Wiley, 1974.

Richards, Robert K., and James D. Davidson. "Racial and Ethnic Groups in Indiana: A Socio-Historical Approach." Monograph, Purdue University, Department of Sociology and Anthropology, 1985.

Roberts, Keith A. *Religion in Sociological Perspective.* Homewood, Ill.: Dorsey Press, 1984.

261

Roby, Pamela (ed.). The Poverty Establishment. Englewood Cliffs, N. J.: Prentice-Hall, 1974.

Roof, Wade Clark. Community and Commitment. New York: Elsevier, 1977.

_____. "Socio-economic Differentials Among White Socio-religious Groups in the United States," Social Forces 58:280-289, 1979.

Santa Ana, Julio de. Good News to the Poor. Maryknoll, N. Y.: Orbis, 1979.

Scherer, Ross. "The Church as a Formal Voluntary Organization," in David Horton Smith et al. (eds), Voluntary Action Research: 1972. Lexington, Mass.: Lexington Books, 1972.

_____. American Denominational Organization. Pasadena, Calif.: William Crey Library, 1980.

Schiller, Bradley R. The Economics of Poverty and Discrimination. Englewood Cliffs, N. J.: Prentice-Hall, 1976.

Sider, Ronald J. Rich Christians in an Age of Hunger. Downers Grove, Ill.: Intervarsity Press, 1977.

Vander Zanden, James. American Minority Relations. New York: Ronald, 1972.

Vanfossen, Beth E. The Structure of Social Inequality. Boston: Little, Brown, 1979.

Williams, Robin M. American Society. New York: Alfred A. Knopf, 1960.

Wilson, John. Religion in American Society. Englewood Cliffs, N. J.: Prentice-Hall, 1978.

Winter, Gibson. The Suburban Captivity of the Churches. Garden City, N. Y.: Doubleday, 1961.

Winter, J. Alan. Continuities in the Sociology of Religion. New York: Harper and Row, 1977.

Wood, James R. Leadership in Voluntary Organizations. New Brunswick, N. J.: Rutgers University Press, 1981.

12

Listen to the Bishops

Ronald T. Libby

Since its decision to "draw the line" against communism in Central America, the Reagan administration has faced an unexpected opponent at least as powerful as the region's leftwing insurgents--the Roman Catholic church. Throughout Central and South America, growing numbers of church leaders are siding with the efforts of popular majorities to wrest greater political and economic freedom from ruling elites. In El Salvador, for example, the church's view that the extreme right is primarily responsible for the civil war in that country has led it to oppose U.S. military aid to the Salvadoran government. In the United States, bishops have sharply criticized the Reagan administration's Central America policy as "profoundly mistaken."

The church's foreign policy activity in both the United States and Central America has greatly intensified in recent years. At the same time, both the new activism and the opposition to current U.S. policy are products of developments and pressures of the past twenty years that have moved many Catholic clergy to plunge into worldly affairs, as well as products of far-reaching but little-known connections between U.S. and Central American clerics. They all but assure heavy church involvement in the Central American crisis and other foreign-policy issues for the foreseeable future.

An alliance between the Catholic church and Latin America's ruling classes has existed since the Spanish conquest of the New World in the sixteenth century. So

closely did the missionaries identify first with the royal
viceroys and colonial landholders and then with the
oligarchs who ruled Latin American republics after
independence that they often refused to ordain Indians
as priests.

The church's traditional refusal to ordain Indians
insured that the regional church would face a chronic
shortage of native clergy. Some of the gap has always
been filled by foreign clergy. Indeed, about one-half
of the clerics in Latin America today are foreign, with
the figure rising to more than 80 percent in countries
such as Panama and Honduras. Meanwhile, Latin America's
traditionally low priest-population ratios continue to
decline. In Brazil, the hemisphere's largest Catholic
country, the ratio dropped from 1:7,081 in 1970 to 1:8,528
in 1975. And the number of priests and nuns in Latin
America fell at annual rates of .6 and 1 percent,
respectively, during that period.

Moreover, the flight of 70 percent of Cuba's clergy
after Premier Fidel Castro came to power jolted many of
Latin America's roughly 650 bishops out of their
complacency toward the revolutionary change threatening
to break out throughout the region. Many clerics began
to recognize that the church would have to attack social
injustice to survive the cataclysm that seemed to be
approaching. To arrest the decline in Catholic religious
vocations in Latin America and to revitalize the church,
progressive bishops developed a new ideological orientation
now commonly known as the "Church of the Poor."

WORKING FOR JUSTICE

Internationally, the Latin American church has taken
up the call of the Second Vatican Council, held from 1962
to 1965, which urged Christians to address contemporary
social concerns and to shape their teachings according
to the signs of the times. In conferences at Medellín,
Colombia, in 1968 and at Puebla, Mexico, in 1979, the
bishops of Latin America resolved to work for social and
political justice while avoiding direct political and
electoral activities.

On the local level, progressive bishops supported
the formation of new organizations called Christian Base
Communities (CEBs) to help turn their "Church of the Poor"
orientation into concrete actions. The CEBs are most
heavily concentrated in Brazil, where they originated in

the 1960s, with about 50,000 communities and 1.2 million members today, but they have rapidly spread throughout Latin America. From 100,000 to 150,000 CEBs are now operating throughout the continent, with an estimated 1,000 in Chile, several hundred in Paraguay, and an indeterminate number scattered throughout most of Central America.

With the establishment of CEBs, the clergy's traditional paternalism and the church's traditional aloofness toward the immediate concerns of poor parishes began to break down. Lay members began to assume leadership roles in the church to compensate for the shortage of clergy, and in the process a form of democratic participation emerged in local Christian communities. CEB leaders began to address concrete problems, such as shortages of potable water, inadequate transportation, natural disasters, and increasingly, the political policies--the eviction of peasants from their land and the reflexive use of the military--on which authoritarian regimes had traditionally relied to enrich the wealthy and suppress the destitute.

The expansion of CEB activity from the religious into the social and political spheres results largely from the concurrent or subsequent formation of local civic action groups that enlist the CEBs' help in improving local conditions. Thus CEB activity places the church behind the efforts of villagers and slum dwellers to trigger sweeping social and political change. Although CEB involvement, strictly speaking, neither involves the church in party policies nor confers an official church endorsement on specific political programs, it does bring church activists perilously close to the kind of direct clerical political activity Pope John Paul II has proscribed at Puebla and elsewhere.

Even more controversial has been the role taken up by what is called the iglesia popular (people's church), largely organized in the CEBs and composed of clergy who have made a total commitment to the CEBs and the effort of the poor to liberate themselves from the government's military oppression. In El Salvador this commitment has led directly to outright clerical support for the insurgents, namely, the Democratic Revolutionary Front (FDR) and its military wing, the Farrabundo Martí National Liberation Front (FMLN).

In Nicaragua the iglesia popular's prominent involvement in the Sandinista movement since the mid-1970s provoked angry papal criticism of the people's church as "absurd and dangerous." In his June 29, 1982, letter to

Nicaragua's bishops, the pope charged that the iglesia popular pretended to the role of a "parallel church," which by definition challenged the authority of the Nicaraguan hierarchy and of Rome itself. And during his March 1983 visit to Nicaragua, his criticism of five priests who hold high-ranking positions in the Sandinista regime sharply polarized the country's clerics. Yet in the kinds of revolutionary situations that have prevailed in El Salvador and in Nicaragua, it is virtually impossible to isolate the clergy from partisan politics, as the crisis in Poland also clearly shows.

Although circumstances vary from country to country, the pursuit of a social ministry has put many of Central America's clergy on a collision course with U.S.-backed regimes and forces. In El Salvador, Guatemala, and Honduras the role of the CEBs and the iglesia popular is perceived by both the wealthy and the military to be subversive. The challenges posed by bishops, priests, nuns, and lay workers to the economic and political institutions that oppress and impoverish peasants and slum dwellers have therefore been met by increasing harrassment, intimidation, and violence.

The church's position has been most ambiguous in Nicaragua, where in 1979 leftist forces grew powerful enough to overthrow the dictatorship of Anastasio Somoza Debayle. Archbishop Miguel Obando y Bravo finally broke with the regime near the end of its rule, and the aforementioned priests continue to serve in the new Sandinista government. Moreover, the CEBs and clergy in the iglesia popular played an important role in mobilizing peasant and trade union opposition to Somoza. With opposition political parties banned by the regime, the parish church served as the organizational base for establishing a network of resistance to Somoza's main instrument of repression, the National Guard. CEBs, which were initially formed in the Nicaraguan countryside in 1968-1970, fused with the Sandinista National Liberation Front in 1978 to support the revolt against Somoza. Yet Obando y Bravo and the rest of Nicaragua's Catholic hierarchy continue to refuse to pledge their support to the Sandinista regime.

DAVID AND GOLIATH

The clash between the Catholic church's goals and the Reagan administration's objectives has been most serious in El Salvador, where both Archbishop Oscar Arnulfo Romero, who was assassinated on March 24, 1980, and his successor, Archbishop Arturo Rivera y Damas, have outspokenly supported the CEBs and "the option of the poor." El Salvador's clerics are not monolithically opposed to U.S. support for the embattled government or even to the oligarchs of the far right in El Salvador and their allies in the military. Indeed, four of the country's six bishops and the papal nuncio have been critical of the church's new direction. The Salvadoran bishops had specifically attacked Romero for placing the Salvadoran church in the position of supporting "Marxist priests" who were indoctrinating the people in "Maoist ideology." Bishop Marco René Revelo has openly criticized church support for campesino (peasant) organizations such as the Christian Federation of Salvadoran Peasants. And the support given to the army and the government by bishops such as José Eduardo Alvarez, the military vicar, has enabled the Salvadoran Right to claim church endorsement for its policies.

On the left, Salvador's iglesia popular is headed by a small group of about fifteen priests, plus an undetermined number of seminarians and nuns who in 1980 formed the Bishop Oscar Arnulfo Romero National Conference of the People's Church (CONIP). This organization commemorates the assassination of the widely respected Salvadoran prelate, who cast his lot squarely with the country's impoverished majority and who the month before his death asked then-President Jimmy Carter not to provide military aid to the Salvadoran junta.

While CONIP formally remains within the larger church and maintains its communications with the hierarchy, its clergy interpret the conflict in El Salvador as a modern-day version of the biblical duel between David and Goliath and plan their actions accordingly. In their view, today's Goliath is North American imperialism, supported by the Salvadoran bourgeoisie, which seeks to retain its power through a mixture of token reforms and repression. David is represented by the country's suffering majority, who have finally organized themselves to create a new society with a revolutionary democratic government.

In CONIP's view those elements of the church hierarchy who do not oppose Goliath and who have not chosen the "option of the poor" are by definition allied to the oligarchy and the U.S. government. The depth of these clerics' commitment was dramatically demonstrated at Romero's funeral. A group of priests, nuns, and lay

workers in the grass-roots church began a fast to protest
the killing and hung a large banner over the entrance to
the cathedral in San Salvador announcing that the papal
nuncio, the four conservative bishops, and the U.S.
ambassador were not welcome. Significantly, the only one
of El Salvador's six bishops who was welcomed at the
funeral mass was Romero's eventual successor, Rivera y
Damas.

Dissension within the church approached the boiling
point during the last years of Romero's tenure. Today,
however, all major factions within the church appear united
under Rivera y Damas's leadership. The authority he enjoys
over the restive clerics of the left and right flows
largely from his position as head of the country's largest
diocese, San Salvador, an appointment that, after a three-
year wait, was formally approved by the Vatican scant days
before the pope's March 1983 visit. But it also stems
from Rivera y Damas's great personal popularity. In fact,
he, not Romero, was the preferred choice of the San
Salvador archdiocese to succeed the aging Archbishop Luis
Chávez y González upon his retirement in 1977. Recently,
Rivera y Damas's standing was strengthened by the
retirement of conservative Bishop Pedro Arnoldo Aparicio
and by the pope's elevation of an additional auxiliary
bishop, Gregorio Rosa Chávez, handpicked by Rivera y Damas
from the San Salvador archdiocese. Consequently, only
Rivera y Damas, his designated spokesmen, and official
statements from the Salvadoran Conference of Bishops and
its officers reflect the Salvadoran church's official
position.

The church's position on the question of U.S. military
aid to the Salvadoran government is based upon its judgment
that domestic social and economic ills, not foreign
agitation, lie at the heart of the conflict in El
Salvador. The danger posed by continuing U.S. military
aid, therefore, is that it will encourage the extreme Right
and elements of the army to believe they can defeat the
guerrilla forces and restore order without implementing
the social and economic reforms needed to bring genuine,
lasting peace.

By the extreme Right the church means groups that
are associated with El Salvador's landowning elite, the
so-called fourteen families. The Salvadoran oligarchy
cemented its privileged status in 1932 when it formed an
alliance with the military that remains in force today.
For decades the oligarchy--according to one recent count,

it now numbers 244 families--has monopolized the production
of coffee, sugar, and cotton, which together represent
the bulk of the country's exports. Although consisting
of only a few thousand people in a country of five million
people, the families own approximately 60 percent of the
best farmland and control 50 percent of total national
income. The oligarchy's power has largely survived modest
changes in the country's landownership pattern encouraged
by the U.S. Agency for International Development (AID).
About two-thirds of the peasant population--one-third of
the total population--remains landless or owns plots so
small that they barely provide marginal subsistence.

In January 1983 a report by the consulting firm
Checchi & Company, which was commissioned by AID, claimed
land reform had created at least 67,000 new landowners.
The report, however, also points out that El Salvador's
large landholders retain control of the storage and
processing facilities on which the new peasant landowners
must rely. Further, many military and security units force
the peasants to make regular security payments, and the
guerrillas have imposed a "war tax" in areas where they
are active.

The extreme Right exercises its coercive power through
the National Guard, the Treasury Police, the National
Police, and other right-wing paramilitary groups, such
as the infamous but now-defunct ORDEN (Democratic
Nationalist Organization), the National Democratic Front,
White Warriors, White Hand, Falange, and others financed
by the large landowners. These security forces are largely
responsible for the so-called deathsquad killings of local
political and peasant leaders, priests, and trade
unionists. The forces have been involved in campaigns
of terror and massacre designed to intimidate and destroy
popular opposition to the Salvadoran oligarchy. Moreover,
Major Roberto d'Aubuisson, a former National Guard colonel
who now heads ARENA (National Republican Alliance) and
who was elected president of El Salvador's Constituent
Assembly, has been implicated by former U.S. Ambassador
to El Salvador Robert White in masterminding Romero's
assassination.

From the standpoint of the Salvadoran church, both
the isolation and the dismantling of the extreme Right
are essential for a resolution of the conflict. The
October 1979 military coup that ousted General Carlos
Humberto Romero, the last traditional military ruler of
El Salvador, raised church hopes of a major rupture in

the oligarchy's alliance with the miltiary. The coup was
led by junior officers who shared the church's view that
the oligarchy was the principal barrier to social justice
in El Salvador.

Despite efforts to carry out a program of social and
economic reform, the junta failed largely because the
violence of the left and of the right--especially of the
right--virtually destroyed the moderate reformist center
of Salvadoran politics. In January 1980 a new junta was
formed with the addition of several civilian Christian
Democrats as members. Rivera y Damas hoped that the
Christian Democrats could enlist the army to combat the
paramilitary death squads of the extreme right. But the
second junta was no more successful in controlling these
forces than its predecessor.

THE CHURCH AS INTERMEDIARY

The church's opposition to the extreme Right, however,
must not be mistaken for support of leftist guerrillas.
To be sure, Archbishop Romero refused to issue a blanket
condemnation of Marxism, characterizing it as a scientific
analysis of economics and society and therefore a valid
critique of society. Only metaphysical, materialistic
Marxism, he held, was incompatible with Christianity.
In addition, the priests in the people's church have made
a public commitment to the FDR and the FMLN. But Rivera
y Damas has accused the people's church of misrepresenting
the position of the Salvadoran church in other countries
and of producing a schism within the church of El Salvador.
Moreover, both Archbishops Romero and Rivera y Damas
have opposed the Left's recourse to violence. Uncritical
supporters of the FDR and the FMLN have tended to invoke
the image of the martyred Romero to justify a violent
insurrection against the government. As evidence that
Romero flirted with endorsing violent insurrection when
all other options were closed, the left has frequently
referred to the case of Father Ernesto Barrera, who was
reported by the government to have been killed in a
shoot-out between the Popular Liberation Forces (FPL) and
security forces in 1978. The FPL claimed the priest was
a revolutionary combatant who died with his weapons in
his hands. Romero's refusal to disclaim Barrera and his
personal participation in the funeral was read by some
as an expression of support for the Left's resort to

violence. But Romero himself noted that he did not accept the FPL account of Barrera's activities and specifically pointed to his obligation as archbishop to preside over the funeral of a faithful and devoted priest who followed his bishop's pastoral directions.

Changing circumstances have forced Rivera y Damas into developing a position on the Left's moral right to revolt that is clearer than that of Archbishop Romero. After all, just before Romero's assassination, the embryonic armed insurgency could not yet seriously threaten the governemnt, and the government consequently had no compelling need to seek popular support. This imbalance made it impossible for the church to assume a neutral role in the conflict. The insurgents, however, are now strong enough to challenge vigorously the Salvadoran government's control of large areas of the country, and the church now considers it more appropriate to serve as an intermediary between the two warring forces.

In January 1981 during a major guerrilla offensive, Rivera y Damas formally outlined the church's position on the moral justification for violent insurrection against the government. The archbishop argued that a popular insurrection is justified only if:

- those with political power seriously abuse their power;
- all peaceful alternatives to eliminating the abuse have failed;
- the ills accompanying an insurrection are not greater than the present ills; and
- the people believe that the insurrection will succeed.

Rivera y Damas concluded that only the first requirement had been fulfilled and that as a result the church could not condone leftist appeals for a popular insurrection.

Rivera y Damas's position is also based on very specific, publicly articulated views on the motivation and objectives of the leftist guerrillas. The archbishop has argued that the insurgents' difficulty in sparking a broad public uprising stems largely from their leftist and Communist political leanings and from the Salvadoran people's uncertainty that a socialist regime would be preferable to the existing one. Further, he has emphasized his belief that the majority of Salvadorans do not wish to replace "U.S. imperialism" (the rationale used by the

Left to justify an insurrection) with the "domination of the Communist superpower." However, the church's principal objection to the popular movements in El Salvador is the same as its principle objection to the extreme Right-- that their violent solution to the political conflict results in widespread killing, destruction, and human deprivation while primarily serving the selfish interests of the revolutionary leaders. The April 1983 murder of the FPL's second in command, "Anna Maria," in Managua, lends weight to these charges.

THE BISHOPS TAKE A STANCE

In November 1981 the hierarchy of the U.S. National Conference of Catholic Bishops (NCCB) issued a statement attacking the Reagan administration's Central American policy. The bishops rejected President Ronald Reagan's focus on external military threats to the region and his alleged neglect of the social and economic roots of conflict, and they outlined an alternative U.S. policy toward El Salvador, Guatemala, and Nicaragua, the three regional countries suffering major civil strife.

While the U.S. bishops have previously lobbied on foreign policy issues such as apartheid and the Panama Canal treaties, their statement--as well as their strong criticism of the administration's strategic nuclear weapons doctrine--was unprecedented in at least three respects. First, the bishops finally capitalized on the opportunity presented by reforms in the church's global hierarchy to address contemporary social, economic, and foreign policy issues as a group. Prior to the development of this collegiality, clerical declarations on public-policy issues were typically random statements made by the archbishop of the diocese that encompasses the country's capital, Washington, D.C. Now the U.S. bishops seek outside professional advice on issues of public concern and reach a consensus before issuing public statements.

Second, the bishops' declarations showed them to be ready to take controversial political stances whether the Catholic laity, or base church, follows or not. And third, the bishops have expertly used the news media to spread the word and sway public opinion.

In preparing their declaration on Central America, the U.S. bishops relied heavily on information from the Central American church itself. They accepted the

Salvadoran church's assessment that the civil war stems primarily from unjust social structures and formulated a position incorporating three broad themes. First, they endorsed the two Salvadoran archbishops' opposition to U.S. military assistance to the Salvadoran government, as well as to the introduction of arms into the country from any source. Second, they urged the United States to abandon the search for a military solution to the conflict and to start encouraging a negotiated settlement involving all major belligerents. This diplomatic shift they want accompanied by shipments of badly needed economic aid, health services, and food supplies to help create a climate of conciliation. Third, the bishops called on the United States to stop deporting Salvadoran refugees as long as conflict and violence in their homeland continue.

The U.S. bishops endorsed the Nicaraguan bishops' criticism of the Sandinistas' proliferating restrictions on human rights, such as free association and free expression, as well as their increasing interference in the country's Catholic schools. However, their determination to contain the adverse consequences of U.S. foreign policy toward another country ostensibly led U.S. church leaders to oppose the Reagan policy of isolating Nicaragua by cutting off U.S. aid. They have also recently expressed opposition to any direct or indirect U.S. military intervention against the Sandinista government. Instead, the bishops characterized a "mature, cooperative diplomatic relationship" between the United States and Nicaragua as the best hope for promoting human rights and stability in the region, with the important proviso that U.S. assistance be linked to the Sandinistas' compliance with internationally recognized human rights standards.

In the case of Guatemala, the U.S. bishops cited statements by that country's church leaders deploring the escalating violence inspired by a government-sponsored propaganda campaign, which was designed to discredit the church. Taking their cues from the Guatemalan bishops, the U.S. clerics declared their opposition to continued U.S. military assistance to the government and proposed a shift in U.S. priorities from military to economic aid to help meet the human needs of the Guatemalan people.

Bishops in the United States first began to speak out against U.S. policy toward Central America in February 1980 when they supported Archbishop Romero's request that the Carter administration not resume military aid to El

Salvador. A shocking wave of antichurch violence sustained
their efforts. Romero's assassination in March was
followed in December by the murder of four American women
missionaries. Since May 1980 an estimated 8 foreign
missionaries and indigenous clergy have been killed in
El Salvador and an estimated 13 in Guatemala. And while
no reliable figures exist, the roughly 100,000 killed and
300,000 left homeless by conflict in Central America
undoubtedly included a large number of lay church workers
from the CEBs. Yet the U.S. bishops' position reflects
far more than anguish over the human toll of war in Central
America. It is also a product of close, decades-old
organizational and human ties between the U.S. and Central
American churches.

Central America's large contingent of foreign clerics
and lay missionaries has long included many Americans.
The Maryknoll order has been active in the region since
1942. In 1982 the United States Catholic Mission
Association estimated the total number of American
missionaries in Central America at 650. An American,
Nicholas D'Antonio, who served for many years as the bishop
of Olancho, Honduras, is now the vicar general of the New
Orleans archdiocese. At the same time, many Central
American clerics have come to the United States. Marcos
McGrath, the son of an American tugboat captain and now
archbishop of Panama, is a trustee of the University of
Notre Dame and a frequent visitor to the United States.
Further, the organizational changes in Catholicism's global
hierarchy approved by Vatican II greatly strengthened the
U.S. church's ability to influence U.S. policy toward this
region its clergy knows so well.

The conference modified the church's traditional
commitment to a pyramidal, monarchical governing structure
and introduced the concept of a community of responsible
members. By sanctioning the creation of national
conferences of bishops, Vatican II gave national bishops
an unprecedented degree of autonomy from Rome in formulating national church policy. In response to this new
mandate, U.S. bishops reorganized the Catholic hierarchy
in the United States in 1967. They established the NCCB
under the aegis of Vatican II's constitution and an
administrative agency called the United States Catholic
Conference (USCC) to carry out policy decisions made by
the NCCB at its annual meetings. Like their Latin American
counterparts, U.S. bishops also heeded Vatican II's call
to moderate the traditional emphasis in their works on

papal encyclicals and philosophical and legal argumentation
in favor of emphasizing a more prophetic style of teaching
explicitly addressing contemporary social concerns.

The delegation of national policymaking authority
to national bishops' conferences has created the basis
for policy coordination between the Catholic hierarchy
in different countries. While national bishops' conferences retain a measure of autonomy on any policy issue
of significance affecting their countries, clergy, lay
workers, information, funds, and other resources flow among
them continuously. The interchange between the NCCB and
the Central American hierarchy is particularly heavy.

This interchange and the resultant policy coordination
between the Catholic hierarchies of the United States and
Central America have been spurred also by the impact of
U.S.-supported governments and policies on the regional
church. The U.S. bishops' statement opposing U.S. policy
toward Central America justified the decision to speak
out in precisely these terms, and the alternatives they
recommended were intended to mitigate the effects of U.S.
policies on the church.

Finally, and perhaps most important, the policy
coordination has been requested by Central American
bishops. In the case of El Salvador, for example, both
Archbishops Romero and Rivera y Damas specifically sought
the moral backing of the NCCB and other national church
groups for their opposition to U.S. and Salvadoran
governmental policy and actions. The Salvadoran church's
internal divisions and the Vatican's criticism of
Salvadoran clergy who meddle in "partisan and sectarian
politics" made U.S. clerical support particularly important
to the Salvadoran prelates.

In contrast, the Nicaraguan church hierarchy has been
generally united in its policy of nonsupport for the
Sandinista government and in its critical attitudes toward
the iglesia popular. These positions have the
Vatican's complete approval. Moreover, the Reagan administration has openly backed the Nicaraguan hierarchy's
criticism of Managua, and thus presents no threat to the
Nicaraguan church hierarchy. Nevertheless, the U.S.
bishops have spoken out against the Reagan administration's
economic and military harassment of Nicaragua independently
of the Nicaraguan bishops.

The bishops' stance has stimulated a meagerly funded
but substantial and effective Catholic grass-roots lobbying
campaign determined to galvanize congressional support

for changing the course of U.S. Central American policy. The Religious Task Force on Central America, for example, is a Catholic organization independent of the NCCB that acts as the national clearinghouse for a network of more than 300 local groups, such as the Dallas Inter-Religious Task Force on Central America and the Michigan Interchurch Committee on Central America. Through the Religious Task Force on Central America, which is based in Washington, D.C., the local organizations are informed of current developments in Central America and U.S. policy toward the region, including pending congressional legislation. They also orchestrate and publicize efforts to mobilize Catholic opinion against current administration policy toward Central America through letter-writing campaigns, phone calls and visits to congressmen, and peace demonstrations.

The USCC has also generated a large and continuing volume of mail from U.S. Catholics to Congress and the administration running, according to some reports, as high as 10:1 against existing Central America policy. And prominent Catholics from both the clergy and the laity have visited congressional representatives to press their case against administration goals and methods.

Clearly, their relations with the Central American church and direct knowledge of the region have enhanced the credibility of the U.S. bishops' words and deeds. The Reagan administration, for example, originally reacted to the December 1980 murder in El Salvador of four Catholic women with former Secretary of State Alexander Haig, Jr.'s, suggestion that they brought on their own deaths by running a roadblock and exchanging fire with Salvadoran security forces. But this position was indignantly challenged by the missionaries' archbishop, James Hickey, former bishop of Cleveland, and by Archbishop John Roach, president of NCCB-USCC. Many representatives have ostensibly based their opposition to further aid to El Salvador on the Salvadoran government's failure to prosecute the accused killers. And Secretary of State George Shultz now holds that the killings are very significant and very troublesome and agrees that the Salvadoran government's response has been unsatisfactory. Indeed, while church groups have not succeeded in ending U.S. military aid to El Salvador, they have helped persuade Congress to link future aid to biannual presidential certification of significant improvements in the Salvadoran government's human rights and socioeconomic policies.

FACILITATING NEGOTIATIONS

The church's position on the Salvadoran conflict, as expressed by Rivera y Damas and backed by the U.S. bishops and the Vatican, is that the conflict is a "fratricidal war," with the line drawn between those who regard armed struggle as a necessary means to create a new social order and those who invoke the doctrine of national security to rationalize repression. The archbishop has positioned the church between these extreme positions and strongly favors "dialogue" between the two sides.

This stance, however, places the church in opposition to both the Salvadoran government and its principal backer, the Reagan administration. The FDR and FMLN have agreed to unconditional dialogue with the government to grant them a share of political power before they participate in the elections that the Reagan administration had pressed the Salvadoran government to hold in December 1983. The FDR and FMLN contend that in the existing climate of violence and repression they cannot rely upon the rhetoric of Salvadoran politicians to protect them if they lay down their arms and begin politicking openly and peacefully. Provisional President Alvaro Alfredo Magana has adamantly refused to negotiate with the FDR-FMLN over "power sharing." Likewise, Defense Minister General Carlos Eugenio Vides Casanova, like his predecessor José Guillermo Garcia, has rejected any suggestion that an international peacekeeping force be organized to supervise free elections in El Salvador.

Yet Rivera y Damas has recently endorsed as a promising initiative the government's proposed amnesty plan guaranteeing the exiled opposition forces reentry into Salvadoran society with pardons for the guerrillas and political prisoners and economic assistance to obtain houses, seed, food, clothing, education, and medical assistance. Under Rivera y Damas's leadership the church has assumed the strategic role of intermediary to the parties in the Salvadoran conflict. For example, the archbishop and Revelo, who was recently appointed to the government's peace commission to make unofficial contacts with the guerrillas, delivered the FDR-FMLN's negotiating position to the government in October 1982 and also transmitted its call for a truce during the papal visit in March 1983.

The chief obstacle to a political solution to the conflict remains the oligarchy and its instruments of

repression--security forces and elements of the military--
who are unwilling to surrender voluntarily their class
prerogatives. In this regard, the Reagan administration's
emphasis upon military support for the Salvadoran
government only serves to encourage the extreme Right to
believe that it can maintain its privileged position in
the face of growing armed insurgency.

A proposed solution to the problem of El Salvador
is beyond the scope of this article. But whatever course
the United States follows, one point is clear: Any U.S.
policy that overlooks the profound transformation of the
role of the Catholic church in international affairs will
encounter grave difficulty not only in Central America
but also among the people of the United States. As a
result of the Medellín and Puebla conferences, a historic
change has taken place that few U.S. policymakers have
understood. That lack of understanding has already led
to unnecessary tension between Washington and an aroused
Catholic clergy. U.S. policy toward Central America will
be more solidly based when both the legislative and the
executive branches realize that the U.S. Catholic church,
because of its deep involvement in the life of the average
citizen in Central America, now has a vital contribution
to make to the formulation of U.S. policy toward the area.

13

The Churches and Nuclear Deterrence

L. Bruce van Voorst

> Because the nuclear issue is not simply political,
> but also a profoundly moral and religious question,
> the Church must be a participant in the process of
> protecting the world and its people from the specter
> of nuclear destruction.
>
> --Joseph Cardinal Bernardin

On any single Sunday, almost as many Americans attend
church services as go to all the major sporting events
held in this country during an entire year. From its very
origins, the United States has claimed a belief in a unique
ethical foundation, a nation, as G. K. Chesterton said,
"with the soul of a Church." Waves of immigrants
assimilated the conviction that there exists a peculiarly
American covenant with God and that the destiny and
guidance of this nation, both in personal and national
affairs, derives from that special compact. What was true
in peace was assumed in war as well. The persuasion runs
deep that America carries a moral banner into battle.

President Ronald Reagan expressed this conviction
in a 1983 speech to the UN Special Session on Disarmament:

> The record of history is clear: citizens of the
> United States resort to force reluctantly, and only
> when they must. We struggled to defend freedom and
> democracy. We were never the aggressors. America's
> strength and, yes, her military power have been a
> force for peace, not conquest: for democracy, not
> despotism, for freedom, not tyranny.

Reprinted with permission from Foreign Affairs, Vol. 61,
pp. 827-852, 1983.

For the most part, these ethical assumptions have been accepted and are propagated by the nation's churches. Whether the historical record shows America living up to them is of course another question. Religious leaders have often been in the forefront of opposition to particular wars, notably the Vietnam War, usually on the grounds that the practical effect, if not the stated purpose, of these wars did not meet the very criteria stated [later] by President Reagan.

But with the exception only of the Quakers and other small historic "peace" churches, all congregations in America--Catholic, Protestant and Jewish--historically have supported the nation's readiness to engage in war. They have proudly sent their children into military service--and their chaplains to minister to them. And, with the same limited exception, no religious groups have ever challenged either the need for adequate defense or the basic defense policies of the nation or government.

This support continued right into the nuclear era; almost all of the running debate on atomic weapons since 1945 has been conducted on practical issues, with much of it confined, as James Woolsey has pointed out, to a nuclear "priesthood" whose task it was to serve as "intermediaries between ordinary people and the gods." J. Robert Oppenheimer lamented, as late as 1960, "I find myself profoundly anguished over the fact that no ethical discourse of any nobility or weight has been addressed to the problem of atomic weapons."

Thus it comes as something of a surprise to see the nation's churches now edging toward a direct confrontation with the administration over nuclear weapons and deterrence policy. A special commission appointed by the National Conference of Catholic Bishops has drafted a proposed pastoral letter sharply redefining traditional Catholic teaching on nuclear issues. This draft pastoral, already twice debated by the full conference of bishops, is now being revised for submission to another bishops' conclave in Chicago in May. Similar movements, also gathering wide support, are developing in the Protestant churches and to some extent the Jewish community as well. Given this breadth of support, no government in Washington can afford not to pay attention; no statesman can be indifferent to the debate. For in effect the churches are challenging the cornerstone of America's strategic doctrine with enormous ramifications not just for U.S.-Soviet relations, but for America's relations to its European allies as well.

Why has this great church-led moral concern erupted at this time? In strictly technical terms, there is precious little "new." Back in 1950 the Department of Defense published The Effects of Nuclear Weapons (edited by Samuel Glasstone and Philip Dolan), which accurately described the general destructiveness of nuclear weapons. The considerable technical advances since then, in miniaturization and nature of yields, as well as the enormous increase in the numbers of weapons and in the sophistication of delivery systems, have not added significantly to the awesome picture described by Glasstone and Dolan. Within the debate, knowledgeable experts have long argued that 100 or so nuclear weapons are enough to destroy society as we know it.

Historically, two factors account for the timing of the contemporary debate. First is the growing awareness of the end of American strategic superiority. The oft-asked question whether America would have dropped a bomb on Hiroshima if the Japanese could have threatened San Francisco with nuclear devastation suddenly becomes germane. The reality of America's nuclear vulnerability--now publicly confirmed by presidents from Richard Nixon to Ronald Reagan--has become a steadily growing part of the public consciousness.

Another factor explaining the current nuclear activism, of course, has been the rather incautious approach to strategic nuclear issues on the part of the Reagan administration, particularly with respect to the notion of "prevailing" in a nuclear conflict and the merit of civil defense. Whether National Security Decision Directive (NSDD) 13 of November 1981 actually goes much beyond the old Presidential Directive (PD) 59 of the Carter administration in projecting a "winnable" war can be known only to those privy to the documents, but certainly the cavalier attitude of many senior Reagan administration officials toward nuclear issues has contributed significantly to the widespread fears outside government.

Whatever the explanation, however, any contemporary pronouncements by the clergy suggest a newly widespread determination among the churches to challenge public policy on nuclear issues. As one priest has observed, compared with the nuclear issues, the other controversies within the church "look like a child's sparkler on the Fourth of July." The history of American church involvement in politics, moreover, suggests that any administration in Washington will ultimately be coerced into paying heed.

Abolition was a product of the churches' moral ire; Prohibition came and went as a Protestant (particularly Methodist) campaign; Protestant church historian Martin Marty calls the ill-fated Kellogg-Briand Treaty "virtually a Protestant document." Subsequently, in issues from civil rights to Vietnam, the churches have shown themselves to be a powerful, and to some extent irresistible, force in American affairs. In this context, then, the current course of the Catholic church and many of the Protestant denominations, if continued, may result in the most direct intervention in strategic and foreign policies in this nation's history. One can suggest more; because of their enormous memberships, organization, and dedication, the role of the churches will become critical in determining the political impact and outcome of the "nuclear movement" in the United States.

War has never been an easy matter for the churches. The Bible is replete with apparent contradictions about whether to turn the other cheek or to fight aggressors. Early Christians were pacifists for almost four centuries until a fundamental justification for Christian war took shape under Emperor Constantine. Gradually, through St. Augustine and St. Thomas Aquinas, a Christian rationale for going to war (jus ad bellum) emerged, as well as guidelines for conducting war (jus in bello). The extremes to which doctrine can be twisted were demonstrated in the early Christian injunction against using the newly developed crossbow against Christians. Crossbows, according to doctrine, were to be used only against infidels. Similar intellectual rationalizations served throughout most of subsequent history to enable Christians (and Jews) to serve God while simultaneously keeping a firm grip on the sword. Even two major world wars in this century have failed to provoke an enduring public debate.

America was no exception. Professor Robert W. Tucker has pointed out that Americans traditionally asked few questions about "just" war and indeed formulated a "just war" doctrine characterized by such simplicity that it readily lends itself to "caricature." American use of saturation bombing of civilian populations during World War II and of the atomic bomb has posed many ethical questions. Nonetheless, America's normal posture of going to war only in self-defense or in pursuit of legitimate goals comes close to conforming to the jus ad bellum requirements. Now, however, church activism is raising serious concern about the ethics of conducting--or even threatening--any sort of nuclear war and is challenging the assumptions of a national strategy in which weapons conceived for deterrence become possible instruments for devastation of the world.

II

In this context, the Catholic bishops' draft pastoral letter represents by far the most radical effort by any American church to define moral standards for the nuclear era. It is the logical successor to a number of far more modest efforts by the Catholic church, the most direct of which was Vatican II's declaration that Catholics are forced by the nuclear era "to undertake a completely fresh reappraisal of war." The current document was commissioned at the annual bishops' meeting in November 1981, after an overpowering display of support for the plea by liberal Bishop Thomas Gumbleton of Detroit. He asked for an initiative in defining American Catholic responsibilities in the light of the Reagan administration's program of massive arms buildup and talk of winnable, limited nuclear war.

The ad hoc five-member bishops' commission named by Conference President Archbishop John Roach of Minneapolis to produce a draft on nuclear war issues was what political observers would call "balanced," and included Bishop Gumbleton, an acknowledged pacifist, and Bishop John O'Connor of New York, the auxiliary of the military vicar (Terence Cardinal Cooke) and, as such, particularly identified with the welfare of the nation's military. Archbishop--now Cardinal--Joseph Bernardin of Chicago was named chairman, an acknowledgment both of his intellectual capabilities and his well-known administrative skill in running committees. Charged with presenting a draft for consideration of the bishops at a meeting set for June 1982, the commission (sitting with representatives of the conference of major superiors of men's religious orders and the leadership conference of women's religious orders) took testimony from thirty-five experts in and outside of government, met fourteen times, prayed (by their own account) often, and produced a document on schedule. Aware of the enormity of their task, the bishops at the June meeting considered this to be a first draft and set to work on a second version. Again the bishops received comments (over 1,000 pages) from hierarchy and lay persons

(Catholic and, in some cases, non-Catholic) throughout the nation and abroad.

The second draft, submitted to the 285 bishops meeting on November 1982 in the ballroom of a Washington hotel, begins with a powerful assertion, drawn in part from Vatican II documents such as "Gaudium et Spes" and from recent papal encyclicals--principal among them the 1963 "Pacem in Terris"--that the nuclear issues under discussion are in fact new to mankind. This in itself reflects a considerable evolution in the hierarchy's thinking. Well into the 1950s Pope Pius XII had argued that though the nuclear threat was quantitatively new, it was not qualitatively so. He also denied the faithful any discretion in these matters related to the state. As though to emphasize the great change, the authors of the draft pastoral cite extensively Pope John Paul II's comments during his February 1981 visit to Hiroshima:

> In the past, it was possible to destroy a village, a town, a region, even a country. Now it is the whole planet that has come under threat. This fact should fully compel everyone to face a basic moral consideration: from now on, it is only through a conscious choice and then deliberate policy that humanity can survive.

Having emphasized that there is a new magnitude to the challenge, the draft pastoral offers a thorough review and interpretation of traditional church teaching on war. This exegesis points out clearly that Catholic teaching has been characterized by two essentially contradictory forces: pacifism and "just war" theory. The pastoral as it now stands in many respects reflects a tug-of-war between these two schools of thought.

On the former, the document notes that "From the earliest days of the Church we have evidence of Christians moved by the example of Christ, His life and teaching, committing themselves to a nonviolent lifestyle" (p. 311). Many similar passages reflect a strong stream of pacifist sentiment among contemporary Catholic clergy; among the hierarchy, Bishop Gumbleton, Bishop Leroy Matthiesen, Archbishop Raymond Hunthausen, and fifty-seven other bishops are members of the Catholic peace organization, Pax Christi, and these key individuals argued successfully for the strengthening of the pacifist passages. (Indeed, sources close to the commission suggest that without these passages the document as a whole would never have been accepted by the Pax Christi element, or many others.)

In describing the "just war" position, the authors are careful to point out that its limited justification of war does not conflict with the pacifist position that the taking of life is essentially wrong. But, drawing deeply on St. Augustine's teachings, they conclude that in the sinful world that unfortunately still exists the restraint of evil and the protection of good might under certain circumstances justify the resort to arms. Although the presumption remains against the use of force, for those rare instances, meticulously circumscribed, the parameters of allowable Christian participation in a "just war" are outlined.

The document reaffirms four central criteria: A just war must be declared by "competent authority," must involve a "just cause," with the "right intention" (i.e., pursuit of peace and reconciliation), and must be a "last resort" after all peacemaking efforts have failed. These criteria remain widely valid and essentially unaltered by the onset of the nuclear era.

Three other central elements of traditional "just war" theory, however, appear to be directly challenged by the nuclear age: probability of success, proportionality (the requirement that resort to arms be proportional to the threat), and discrimination (a flat prohibition on actions aimed at civilians or noncombatants). The draft pastoral takes a clear stance on each of these elements and concludes that they raise serious questions not only about the conduct of nuclear war but about whether the use of nuclear weapons is morally permissible at all.

In line with this approach, the arguments presented by the bishops at their Washington meeting in November indicated a preponderance of opinion rejecting outright pacifism in favor of "just war" properly understood, but with considerable uneasiness over whether "probability of success" can be meaningful in a nuclear exchange, or whether nuclear war can in any fashion be squeezed into the framework of the requirements for both proportionality or discrimination. Few observers on either side of the argument denied that nuclear war as currently conceived would immeasurably violate both these principles. The exceptions might be Archbishop Phillip Hannan of New Orleans, who is particularly vocal on the dangers of the Soviet system as a fate worse than death, and a few isolated spokesmen who suggested that for the Christian the real issue is not life but salvation.

The draft pastoral particularly singles out the traditional principle of discrimination, prohibiting military actions aimed at civilians. The injunction is not qualified, and the authors put it in italics for emphasis: "Under no circumstances may nuclear weapons or other instruments of mass slaughter be used for the purpose of destroying population centers or other predominantly civilian targets" (p. 314).

Although this portion of the text was not debated at length at the Washington meeting, its implications for strategic nuclear doctrine could be very significant. For at least a decade there has raged within the nuclear "priesthood" an intense controversy as to whether the deterrent posture of U.S. strategic nuclear forces should continue to be based on "mutual assured destruction," which envisages the threat of attack on population centers and in effect, in the words of two of its own supporters, "holds the entire civilian populations of both [the United States and U.S.S.R.] as hostages."

This doctrine--which for a long period dominated U.S. strategic thinking--has been defended on the ground that its sheer horror makes nuclear war far less likely. On the other hand, it has been vigorously attacked, in part on moral grounds, by advocates of "counterforce" doctrines that would put primary emphasis on military-related targets and thus "retain the use of nuclear weapons on the battlefield or even in controlled strategic war scenarios, while sparing the general civilian population from the devastating consequences of nuclear war." The advocates of "mutual assured destruction" counter that such war-fighting scenarios are unrealistic in practice, would involve vast civilian casualties in any event, and above all tend to increase the possibility that nuclear weapons may in fact be used.

It is not clear whether the authors of the draft pastoral intended to take a position on this issue. They face something of a dilemma. While their rejection of attacks on civilian populations--with which the administration concurs--clearly rules out many attacks usually associated with "mutual assured destruction," they are ambivalent on defining the appropriate use of the nuclear arsenal. Other portions of the draft denounce "hard kill" weapons as "inadmissible," noting that the MX missile "might" fit in this category, and declare it immoral to pursue a nuclear war-fighting capability. The cumulative effect of these strictures is surely to make it extremely difficult for any U.S. administration to frame a practical doctrine of strategic nuclear deterrence.

Even more controversial is the draft pastoral's flat prohibition on the initiation of nuclear war. Again, the

authors add italics for emphasis: "We do not perceive
any situation in which the deliberate initiation of nuclear
warfare, on however restricted a scale, can be morally
justified. Non-nuclear attacks by another state must be
resisted by other than nuclear means" (p. 314). This
proscription, of course, intrudes even more directly on
contemporary nuclear strategic debate. It appears to align
the bishops with those who have challenged the threat or
use of nuclear weapons in response to conventional attack
against NATO and who have urged moving toward a doctrine
of "no first use" in such circumstances. The issue goes
to the heart of longstanding NATO deterrence doctrine and
lies at the core of U.S. relations with its European
allies, which along with the Reagan administration have
continued to reject the idea of a no first use pledge.

The proscription on "first use" leads to a third issue
in the current debate--that of "limited nuclear war."
Would these injunctions still leave open the possibility
of using nuclear weapons in a "limited exchange"? Barely
so, the draft pastoral concludes after considering a wide
range of scenarios, questioning whether the senior leadership would have the necessary information, whether field
commanders could retain their cool, and whether the
casualties even in a "limited" nuclear war would not run
into the millions. The draft concludes, "This cluster
of questions makes us skeptical about the real meaning
of limited" (p. 315).

Thus, the draft pastoral argues that the "no" to
nuclear war "must in the end be definitive and decisive"
(p. 313). But how to act in a sinful world, in which
nations are threatened, and in which adversaries possess
nuclear weapons? The draft pastoral is extremely sensitive
to this issue, in effect the moral justification of nuclear
deterrence itself.

The political paradox of deterrence has strained our
moral conception. May a nation threaten what it may
never do? May is possess what it may never use?
Who is involved in the threat each superpower makes:
Government officials? Or military personnel? Or
the citizenry in whose "defense" the threat is made
(p. 313)?

The notion of deterrence, the draft pastoral notes,
existed as well in the prenuclear age and previously was
not widely challenged as doctrine. But by its very nature,
nuclear deterrence envisions the likelihood of

disproportionate retaliation. The problem is not nuclear deterrence as such, therefore, but the manner in which deterrence is supposed to function. The comments on this point are so central that they deserve full citation:

The moral questions about deterence focus on five issues:

1) the possession of weapons of mass destruction, 2) the accompanying threat and/or intention to use them, 3) the declared, or at least not repudiated, willingness to use such weapons on civilians, 4) the moral significance of the prevention of use of nuclear weapons through a strategy which could not morally be implemented, and 5) the continued escalation of the nuclear arms race with its diversion of resources from other needs (p. 316).

From the very start of the commission's deliberations in 1981, a satisfactory definition of the legitimate role of nuclear deterrence proved extraordinarily difficult. Its initial draft spoke of a "marginally justifiable deterrent policy," and elsewhere of a need to "tolerate" nuclear deterrence--terms which satisfied neither flank (and raised additional theological problems, given the specific doctrinal ramifications of the term "tolerate"). But then in June 1982, in his address to the second UN Special Session on Disarmament, Pope John Paul II provided a breakthrough formulation:

In current conditions "deterrence" based on balance, certainly not as an end in itself but as a step on the way toward a progressive disarmament, may still be judged morally acceptable. Nonetheless in order to ensure peace, it is indispensable not to be satisfied with this minimum which is always susceptible to the real danger of explosion.

Here was the solution. The "Bishop O'Connors" of the episcopate stressed that the pope had endorsed nuclear deterrence as "morally acceptable"; to the "Thomas Gumbletons" the formulation came through, as the draft pastoral now says, as a "strictly conditioned" acceptance. Having reluctantly accepted even this somewhat limited definition of deterrence, the "peace" bishops then forged ahead to include in the second draft of the pastoral a series of quite specific prohibitions and requirements,

all directed to defining those adequate measures toward
"progressive disarmament" that would make deterrence
acceptable.

Thus, the draft, in addition to its strictures against
vulnerable "hard kill" weapons and pursuit of a nuclear
war-fighting capability, now argues that weapons "blurring
the difference between nuclear and conventional weapons"
(perhaps neutron bombs) are objectionable. The draft
insists on the need to maintain a psychological barrier
between conventional and nuclear war. On arms control
it urges "bilateral deep cuts" in arsenals, which coincides
with the Reagan administration's position, and also both
a comprehensive test ban treaty and the removal of weapons
from border areas, positions the administration has
opposed. Further, the draft pastoral, while explicitly
rejecting unilateral disarmament, supports "immediate
bilateral verifiable agreements to halt the testing,
production and deployment of new strategic systems" in
language virtually identical to that of the national freeze
resolution.

Finally, while attempting to avoid any suggestion
of condoning conventional war, the bishops do concede that
"some strengthening of conventional defense" might be
justified if it reduced the nuclear threat. As to whether
the use of nuclear weapons might conceivably be justified
in response to their use by adversaries, the second draft
of the pastoral is silent--declining to comment directly
on when and under what circumstances the use of nuclear
weapons might meet acceptable moral standards. A positive
discussion of the theoretically moral uses of nuclear
weapons was dropped from the earlier draft because the
bishops found it somewhat awkward to be prescribing the
proper use of nuclear weapons. However, the presumption
is heavily weighted against use. "Today the possibilities
for placing political and moral limits on nuclear war are
so infinitesimal that the moral task, like the medical,
is prevention: As a people we must refuse to legitimate
the idea of nuclear war" (p. 313).

In presenting this document to the world, the bishops
made unusual efforts to cast the pastoral in quite
unconventional terms. Rather than the didactic preaching
common in past similar documents, the authors emphasize
repeatedly that this is a study document, an effort to
work through with believers the enormously complex issues
under discussion. "The document is an invitation to
debate," said one participant, "not an effort to close

it off." They also note that although it is primarily
meant for Catholics, it is intended for non-Catholics as
well and as a "contribution to the public debate about
the morality of war" (p. 308).

At the same time, there is an emphasis in the entire
document on "guidance" to believers. Just how "binding"
this might be is not clear, and the point was immediately
raised in the bishops' Washington parley. In fact, the
positions being fleshed out in this document could pose
an enormous problem for a church with millions employed
in defense industry or serving in the military (Catholics
are about 30 percent of U.S. military personnel) or even,
for that matter, for individual Catholics in the highest
echelons of government. So central is this consideration
that in the third draft the bishops have reportedly made
a much more careful explication of the difference between
general, universally binding moral principles and specific
applications about which reasonable people may differ.

Concern over the binding nature of the pastoral
reflects the widespread conviction that this pastoral will
inevitably exert enormous pressures on Washington. What
may be the practical ramifications of such a reluctant
acceptance of deterrence? And if the justification for
deterrence presumes progress on arms control, what happens
in the absence of progress?

III

Although it is the Catholic episcopate's initiative
which attracts most attention at the moment, the nuclear
issue has in fact been debated relatively longer and more
intensely within the Protestant denominations. In this
historical context, the Catholics are just now "catching
up." Indeed, while the Catholic bishops were meeting in
Washington, the Council of Bishops of the second largest
Protestant denomination, the 9.5 million-member United
Methodist church, wired a vote of confidence. "We thank
God for your courageous witness on behalf of peace with
justice." But as one might suspect given the structure
of the churches, the historical Protestant treatment of
the nuclear issues differs considerably from the current
Catholic initiative.

Predictably, the Protestant response to nuclear issues
has been fragmented and disparate. But it began early.
In 1946, the Federal Council of Churches (later to become
the National Council) sponsored a prestigious commission

headed by Robert I. Calhoun. While its report did not get deeply into theological issues, the moral tone was strong, as reflected in one of its opening passages:

> We would begin with an act of contrition. As American Christians, we are deeply penitent for the irresponsible use already of the atomic bomb. We are agreed that, whatever be one's judgment of the ethics of war in principle, the surprise bombings of Hiroshima and Nagasaki are morally indefensible. . . . We have sinned greivously against the laws of God and the people of Japan. Without seeking to apportion blame among individuals, we are compelled to judge our chosen course inexcusable.

Another effort, the so-called Dun Commission report, was published in 1950. It was widely criticized for failing to condemn first use of nuclear weapons, and its findings were gradually forgotten. As "just war" theorist Dr. Paul Ramsey mused in frustration at the document, "It must be said, however, that the Dun Report is very confused and confusing throughout . . . if Protestants must use terms imprecisely, they should really not use them to discredit the quite precise notions in the moral doctrine of war."

The international World Council of Churches (with which some American Protestant groups have had their differences) went somewhat further. In 1953 it commissioned a five-year study by an impressive roster of scholars and statesmen. This resulted in a provisional document, which proved to be the first in a series. Although the intellectual development was, again, fragmented, the positions argued were quite revolutionary. The initial document, for instance, argued that "A first requirement is for a discipline which is capable of possessing nuclear weapons and the means of their delivery, but of never using them in all out warfare." It suggested that in case of all-out war, "Christians should urge a ceasefire, if necessary on the enemy's terms." Moreover, in light of the contemporary resurgence of pacifism in Catholic thought, it is noteworthy that some members of the commission rejected any use of H-bombs as "an atrocity not to be justified in a belligerent even if the enemy is guilty of it."

The historic American pacifist churches, of course, were pathfinders in the peace field, laboring diligently and long with little tangible success. The Religious

Society of Friends (Quakers) announced in 1948, not for the first time:

> We feel bound explicitly to avow our unshaken persuasion that all war is utterly incompatible with plain precepts of our Divine Lord and Lawgiver, and the whole of His Gospel, and that no plea of necessity or policy, however urgent or peculiar, can avail to release either individuals or nations from the paramount allegiance they owe to Him who said, "Love your enemies."

Although the Friends have no "national" church as such, various Friends organizations have repeatedly called for a gamut of arms control measures. For the Church of the Brethren, the answer has consistently remained, as they repeated at a recent conference, a flat declaration that "All war is sin. We therefore cannot encourage, engage in, or willingly profit from armed conflict at home or abroad." There is, then, within the non-Catholic churches an articulate pacifist element quite similar to the movement reflected so clearly in current Catholic debate.

The positions taken by the more conventional Protestant denominations, however, reflect both a greater divergence of opinion and the weaker moral authority of the church arising from its diffuse structure. Despite the strong denunciations of nuclear war, there is almost no wrestling with the ambiguities of deterrence or the issue of justified use of nuclear weapons.

Such ambivalences are certainly a part of Protestant history. One need only note Reinhold Niebuhr's dualism regarding "moral man and immoral society." As a one-time pacifist, his later Christian realism argument that "to serve peace, we must threaten war without blinking the fact that the threat may be a factor in precipitating war" suggests the ambiguities in the Protestant position. Niebuhr was confident that what he called the "balance of terror" would prevent nuclear war and never addressed the full consequences of a breakdown in deterrence. Even without reflecting on the possibility of a nuclear exchange, Niebuhr appeared to accept implicitly that the United States would emerge the victor, however morally tainted. "Niebuhr was clearly ambivalent on deterrence," says his longtime associate, John C. Bennett. "While he came to think that the use of nuclear weapons would be immoral, he did not feel that their possession or the threat of their use would be immoral."

Throughout the early postwar debate, and then again
in the 1970s when the Protestants again began to speak
up, most of the statements mirrored rather than dealt with
the paradoxes of nuclear deterrence. If mentioned at all,
deterrence was seen as a guarantor of peace; there was
virtually no reflection on the conflict inherent in
threatening evil to achieve moral goals and very little
consideration of what happens if the system breaks down.
One exception has been Professor Roger L. Shinn, Reinhold
Niebuhr Professor of Social Ethics at Union Theological
Seminary, who as early as 1963 argued imaginatively that
the world would be more stable when the Soviet Union
achieved nuclear parity with the United States. For the
most part, other proclamations dealt with "easy" issues,
such as a prohibition on attacking population centers,
which the World Council of Churches in 1961 said "is in
no circumstances reconcilable with the demands of the
Christian Gospel."

Of the major Protestant denominations in America,
most have by now issued, in one form or another,
declarations condemning nuclear war. (The conspicuous
exceptions are the fundamentalist denominations, which
remain remarkably "hawkish." Indeed, a fundamentalist
leader, the Reverend Jerry Falwell, recently published
a full-page advertisement opposing a nuclear freeze and
posing questions clearly weighted in support of current
"U.S. strategic programs aimed at restoring nuclear parity
with the Soviet Union.") Even the politically conservative
Southern Baptist Convention, with over 13.8 million
members, balances concern for nuclear developments with
its reaffirmation of support for defense. The House of
Bishops of the Episcopal Church in the United States in
1981 issued a pastoral letter denouncing "massive nuclear
overkill." Parallel to this, the Regional Executive
Ministers of the 1.6 million-member American Baptist
churches (who are the chief executive officers of the
church's thirty-seven regional divisions) endorsed a
resolution that called the existence of nuclear weapons
and a presumed readiness to use them "a direct affront
to our Christian beliefs and commitments." Both the large
American Lutheran church and the Lutheran Church in America
independently passed resolutions urging the elimination
of nuclear weapons. Among the most forthright statements
was that by the General Assembly of the United Presbyterian
church in 1982, which not only backed a nuclear freeze
but added the exhortation "that we will never again be
the first nation to use nuclear weaponry." During the

debate, State Clerk William P. Thompson went further, rejecting deterrence as incompatible with a Christian striving for peace.

By comparison with the current Catholic draft pastoral, the Protestant declarations have been earlier and occasionally even more sweeping, but at the same time--with few exceptions--superficial and inadequately defined doctrinally. It is hard to find studies in the official Protestant literature comparable to the depth and the intellectural detail of the Catholic draft pastoral. Indeed, Robert F. Smylie, associate for peace and justice of the Presbyterian church, concedes that "in the statements of the General Assembly one does not find an elaborate system of doctrine worked out to provide the theological presuppositions for the authoritative witness of the Church in response to issues of war and peace." There is in Protestant statements only slight systematic grappling with the paradox of deterrence; nowhere is there an extended application of "just war" doctrine, particularly with respect to proportionality and discrimination.

There are signs, however, of a significant stirring in the National Council of Churches of Christ in America (NCCC). The organization backed SALT II and the freeze and has now called for a nationwide "Peace With Justice" week in the spring. In the past five years, the NCCC and most of the principal Protestant denominations have established "peace" offices. Privately, though, many leading Protestant figures are chagrined at the failure to posit a more formidable position on nuclear weapons. "I've been against nuclear weapons since the 6th of August 1945," church historian Martin Marty says in self-criticism. "And I've written thousands of lines since then. But I'd be hard pressed to find three or four coherent sentences on the ethics of nuclear deterrence."

IV

Perhaps the most curious anomaly in the current awakening of concern for nuclear issues by the American churches has been the relative lack of participation of the Jewish communities. As individuals, American Jews have certainly been outspoken critics of unrestrained nuclear development. Albert Einstein repeatedly warned of the consequences of nuclear war and even argued that the only way to prevent it would be the formation of a world government. He also proposed that the American nuclear arsenal be turned over to an international body. Physicist I. I. Rabi warned as early as 1949 that the use of such a weapon cannot be justified on any ethical ground. And Hannah Arendt observed some years later that when war can threaten the continued existence of mankind on earth, the alternative between liberty and death loses its plausibility. Individual Jews to this day continue to speak out, but the community as a whole, which has gained such a reputation for involvement in moral and social issues from civil rights to the environment and Vietnam, remains conspicuously aloof.

There have been some notable exceptions, especially from within the Union of American Hebrew Congregations (UAHC), whose president, Rabbi Alexander Schindler, has spoken out vigorously in support of the antinuclear movement. At its general assembly in December 1981, the Reform UAHC, which represents about one-third of American Jews, unanimously accepted a resolution appealing to all nuclear powers "to mutually agree upon a freeze on the testing" of systems, and went a step further by supporting a verifiable 50 percent across-the-board cut in nuclear stockpiles, as proposed also by George Kennan. But like so many of its Protestant counterparts, the resolution was hortatory and superficial, failed to deal either with first use or deterrence, and excluded any reference to specific weapons systems because the sponsors thought it too sensitive.

On a local level, some Reform Jewish leaders have attempted to promote concern for nuclear affairs. In New York, Rabbi Balfour Brickner sponsored a widely acclaimed symposium on "Nuclear Arms, Judaism and the Jewish Community," while Rabbi Leonard Beerman of Leo Baeck Temple in Los Angeles opened a similar conference with the biblical reminder of Deuteronomy, "I have set before thee life and death, the blessing and the curse; therefore choose life." But despite considerable enthusiasm at these symposia, a basic theme was lamentation at the failure of Jewish congregations to grapple with the moral and theological issues of nuclear warfare.

It is worth asking why Jews, whose entire history has been marked by war, have been comparatively reluctant to participate in efforts to achieve some form of nuclear arms control. There is no consistent answer to this. Some Jews reply that the absence of a coherent, unified

"Jewish" reaction to nuclear issues reflects the independence and fragmentation of the Jewish community. Yet this structural problem has not hindered Jews from becoming deeply involved in any number of social issues where they have played a role all out of proportion to the size of the community.

Other observers suggest that this reluctance to join the nuclear barricades reflects a fundamental Jewish theological ambivalence toward war. Jews have no strong pacifist tradition; and there is certainly a strong call to arms in the tradition of an obligatory (defensive) war, "Milchemet Mitzvah," as well as the discretionary (offensive) war in the "Milchemet Reshut." Jews, it is argued, are torn by the contradictory admonitions of the Bible. In Micah 4:1-4, for instance, there is the charge to beat swords into plowshares, while in Joel 3:9-11 it is precisely reversed ("Beat your plowshares into swords"). The twentieth chapter of Deuteronomy amounts to what has been called "Israel's own manual of war," though others see in the qualifications on going to war a sort of Israeli Geneva Convention. There is in any case only slight theological direction regarding preventive war (striking first), and even less on deterrence as a strategic concept.

Theological reflections aside, many Jewish observers concede that the reluctance to become deeply involved in the nuclear movement stems from concern over how this might affect Israel's security. This concern is on two levels. There is the fear that any weakening of the American strategic deterrent could endanger Israel, that America's role as Israel's "guarantor" might somehow be undercut. Jews as a community remain particularly suspicious of the Soviet Union, both because of its policy on emigration and its role in supporting the Arab threat to Israel's security. Then there is as well the softly articulated assumption that Israel itself has a nuclear capability and that any moral pronouncements inhibiting the use of nuclear forces might in some way weaken the deterrent value of these weapons.

The reluctance of Jews to participate, for whatever reason, in the nationwide groundswell of concern is widely regretted in the Jewish community, and many senior Jewish officials sense this is already changing. The Union of Orthodox Jewish Congregations has just adopted a strong endorsement of the SALT and START process, and this organization, which represents roughly another third of religious American Jews, is described by officials as "determined to get involved." The Rabbinical Assembly of America, the rabbis of the Conservative Jewish congregations, probably the largest of the three religious groups, endorsed the nuclear freeze in April 1982. Probably the most important, the Synagogue Council of America, a loose umbrella group for all branches of Judaism, on February 25 (1983) endorsed a resolution urging President Reagan and Soviet General Secretary Yuri Andropov "to implement a bilateral mutual cessation of the production and deployment of nuclear weapons." "I'm dismayed at our lack of Jewish participation in what must be just about 'the' issue of our times," says Rabbi Walter Wurzburger, a leading Orthodox rabbi and president of the council. "We have been totally neglectful in analyzing the ramifications of the nuclear race."

Several of these groups have plans for the immediate future. The UAHC has just published a basic manual for synagogues and community organs on how to participate in the nuclear debate. Several congregations are calling for a major meeting to bring together scholars and rabbis from all the Jewish denominations, not to seek resolutions but to explore the meaning of the nuclear age for Halachah, Jewish law. Samuel Pisar, an internationally known lawyer and survivor of Auschwitz, has already suggested a fundamental theme for such a conference. Pisar, during a convocation in Israel of survivors of the Holocaust, recently asked before the Knesset, "From where, if not from us, will come the warning that a new combination of technology and brutality can transform the planet into a crematorium?"

V

Given the church activism, as well as the freeze movement, the administration evidently felt impelled to react. In the spring and summer of 1982, it began to track development of the Catholic pastoral. During preparations for the first draft, several administration witnesses, including Defense Secretary Caspar Weinberger, Under Secretary of State Lawrence Eagleburger, and arms control negotiator Edward Rowny, testified as expert witnesses before the Bishops' Commission, emphasizing that the government was pursuing an energetic and comprehensive arms control policy. As work on the second draft progressed, the administration sought to exert further pressures. In July, national security adviser William

Clark wrote, in a letter subsequently forwarded to
Apostolic Delegate Pio Laghi, "I am troubled in reading
the draft pastoral letter to find none of these serious
efforts [of the Administration] at arms control described
or even noted in the text, even though they so clearly
conform with many of the most basic concerns and hopes
of the letter's drafters." Apparently uneasy with the
thought of a confrontation with the bishops, Clark, in
an obvious misreading of the pastoral, concluded, "On the
subject of overall nuclear deterence strategy, then, I
find that the position recommended by the Pastoral letter
is remarkably consistent with current U.S. policy, with
one notable exception--the issue of no nuclear first use."

Weinberger, in September, wrote a curious letter to
Archbishop Bernardin that also attempted to embrace the
first draft while at the same time interpreting it for
the archbishop. "I am particularly pleased," wrote
Weinberger, "that the draft directly recognizes and
supports the right of legitimate self-defense and the
'responsibility to preserve and pursue justice.' But,"
he continued, "I am concerned that the draft pastoral
letter fails to do justice to the efforts by the United
States and its Allies to maintain the peace through
deterrence and negotiation."

As the November Washington Bishops' Conference
approached, administration officials, clearly responding
to the election day success of freeze resolutions in eight
of nine states, and evidently fearful that the bishops'
action would further coalesce the peace movement, launched
a determined public drive to influence the drafters. On
the opening day of the conference, Navy Secretary John
Lehman, Jr., a Catholic, penned an appeal in the Wall
Street Journal arguing that the bishops were neither
informed nor logical, and "what is worse, if adopted, such
recommendations could lead directly to immoral
consequences." On the eve of the Washington meeting, White
House representatives suggested that the drafting
commission meet with the president, or, alternatively,
that Secreatary of State George Shultz address the
conference. Both the appeals for a further hearing and
suggestions that they were ignoring the administration's
serious peace efforts were rejected for the time being
by the bishops.

An evidently frustrated administration then took the
unusual step of having Clark, a Catholic, write to the
commission on behalf of the president and the cabinet.

In his letter, released to the media before it reached
the bishops, who were already in deliberation, Clark
contended that the draft Pastoral

> continues to reflect a fundamental misreading of
> American policies and continues essentially to ignore
> the far-reaching American proposals that are currently
> being negotiated with the Soviet Union on achieving
> steep reductions in nuclear arsenals, on reducing
> conventional forces, and through a variety of
> verification and confidence-building measures, on
> further reducing the risks of war.

The bishops appeared more irritated with the tactics than
impressed with the arguments. At the same time, a group
of twenty-four distinguished academics and former
government officials, ranging from ex-CIA Director William
Colby to one-time SALT negotiator Gerald Smith, wrote an
open letter supporting the bishops' justification for
taking a stand on the nuclear issue, and concluding that
"there is increasing evidence that we cannot rely on
governments to act in this matter in a timely fashion."
For their part, the bishops let it be known that they were
prepared to meet further with administration figures after
the meeting.

Meanwhile, the White House, recognizing the church
as an international institution, was hoping to stimulate
pressure on the bishops, either from the European hierarchy
or the pope. A number of German and French bishops had
responded with commentaries critical of the initial draft
of the pastoral, but the American bishops seemed to give
them no particular credence. As one observer suggested,
"neither the French nor the German Bishops have
distinguished themselves in articulating the issues."
Key American bishops met in January 1983 in the Vatican
with the European bishops to hear their views. The outcome
was inconclusive.

More curious was the apparent assumption on the part
of the administration that somehow Pope John Paul II might
intervene against the American bishops. Some Washington
sources have suggested that Ambassador Vernon Walters,
who met with the pope in November before the bishops'
meeting, had asked the pontiff to move against the supposed
"nuclear heresy." If so, none of the pope's statements
would appear to give encouragement to the hope of his
intervention against the bishops. On the contrary, the

course of the debate has suggested that the American
bishops' position is not inconsistent with that of John
Paul II. The pope has clearly made "peace" a central
elemenmt in his papacy. Although invited to comment on
the original draft, the pope asked for no changes; instead,
two senior aides delivered basically complimentary
commentaries. And, as we have noted, the pope's UN speech,
with its emphasis on conditional acceptance of deterrence,
provided the breakthrough for consensus within the drafting
commission. Finally, at the Washington meeting, the pope's
own delegate in Washington, Pio Laghi, commended the
bishops for "playing a leadership role" and added that
it "coincides remarkably well with Pope John Paul II's
commitment to peace in the world and to authentic doctrines
of the Church."

Indeed, John Paul II in 1982 asked his prestigious
Pontifical Academy of Science to prepare a detailed study
on the effects of nuclear war--a report then hand-carried
by his emissaries to Leonid Brezhnev and Ronald Reagan.
It is also noteworthy that the pope, in his 1983 New Year's
homily in St. Peter's Basilica, reaffirmed the dedication
to arms control which has become a hallmark of his papacy,
without expressing the slightest hint of discord with the
American bishops. In February, Archbishop Bernardin was
the only American elevated to cardinal, hardly a sign of
papal dissatisfaction with the bishops' initiative.

VI

It appears evident from the debate at the November
bishops' meeting that a majority of the bishops are
determined to bring the pastoral to a vote when they
convene for further discussion in May in Chicago. There
is certain to be intense debate, and the third draft
reportedly does reflect some changes. There is stronger
criticism of the Soviet Union's role in the arms race;
there is further clarification of the legitimate use of
nuclear weapons as well as discussion of the degree to
which the pastoral is binding on Catholic conscience.
But these modifications do not detract from the fact that
the bishops are preparing a ground-breaking condemnation
of key elements of America's nuclear strategy and that
they enjoy the broad support of wide segments of Protestant
opinion. A process has been set in motion, and a new level
of debate unleashed, regardless of what text is finally
accepted.

Thus, the Catholic church, and, to a somewhat lesser extent, the nation's Protestant denominations as well, appear to have embarked on a course which will have enormous repercussions in three areas: (1) the potential for tension within the Catholic church; (2) relations between Catholic and Protestant churches, in particular with respect to church-state relations; and (3) most fundamental of all, on America's national security policy in the nuclear age.

Within the Catholic church there is already a considerable debate on the wisdom of the bishops' initiative. The initial challenge has been to the bishops' competence--theological and strategic. Critics question the authority and ability of the bishops to attempt to describe doctrine on a secular issue of this nature. "As a Catholic, I don't exercise much independence in matters of faith like the infallibility of the Pope," observes Professor Robert Spaeth, of St. John's University in Minnesota (author of a forthcoming book on ethics and deterrence), "but if a Bishop tells me the MX missile is bad, that's politics--that's my field." Added archconservative Phyllis Schlafly, criticizing the bishops for failing to recognize the dimensions of the Soviet threat, "The Bishops are over their heads in a subject they don't understand."

The bishops' response is that few persons actually have true technical competence and that they have in fact become "experts" through intense study and briefings. To challenge their competence is as irrelevant, they add, as complaints that priests cannot make judgments on married life. "For that matter," adds one bishop, "what particular competence does President Reagan have on nuclear strategy issues?"

"People who raise this issue," says Bishop Daniel Reilly of Norwich, one of the five members of the drafting commission, "are begging the point, for we aren't claiming this is Almighty God handing down the truth from the mountain as with Moses. It's simply the Bishops of the United States trying to bring to bear analysis on issues never before faced by the human family."

But even supporters of the general tenor of the bishops' draft pastoral are sensitive to the inherent implications for the unity of the Catholic church. The bishops, some observers charge, are far more liberal than their congregations. Bishop Francis Schulte of Philadelphia cautioned that "we have already witnessed movement toward polarization within the Church on this

issue." To a large degree, of course, the extent of any
divisiveness will depend in the final judgment on just
how binding the pastoral might ultimately be. Although
this is still somewhat unclear, if the pastoral is passed
by a two-thirds majority, the statutes of the National
Catholic Conference of Bishops state that it "should be
observed by all members as an expression of collegial
responsibility and in a spirit of unity and charity."
On the other hand, some earlier pastorals were pretty much
ignored. Several members of the drafting commission are
confident that the current draft is "close to mainstream
Catholicism." Other bishops, on and off the commission,
doubt this.

Nevertheless, participants in this debate are
constantly reminded by critics to be alert to the
possibility of serious fissures among the believers on
this issue. No one wants to repeat the experience of the
encyclical "Humanae Vitae," which contained papal teachings
on sexual matters that have been disregarded by large
numbers of the faithful. Similarly, there is a reluctance
to take any action which would further exacerbate the
church's current internal problems, such as the declining
number of priest candidates and an alarming disaffection
among various women's orders.

But some would argue that the potential for division
is posed already by the draft pastoral. If the bishops
side with the pacifists, they alienate perhaps the majority
of the church; but to adopt a stance more conservative
than the current draft brings with it the risk of
disaffecting some of the church's most pious supporters,
for example the Pax Christi wing to which fifty-seven
bishops belong. "To force believers into making a choice,"
say Thomas Fox, editor of the liberal National Catholic
Reporter, "creates the potential for the greatest
religous-political clash in U.S. history."

There are already rumblings of just that sort of
revolt. Largely as a response to the bishops' original
draft, an American Catholic Committee was set up,
organizationally modeled after its Jewish counterpart,
with the intention of mounting an aggressive nationwide
political campaign to blunt the bishops' efforts.
Prominent among the members is Michael Novak, a formidable
publicist, who is circulating a "counter-pastoral" and
urging it as an alternative to the bishops' efforts.

Another active voice in opposition to the tenor of
the bishops' pastoral is the Ethics and Public Policy
Center in Washington, whose president, Ernest Lefever,

has sponsored symposia and published useful studies
offering conservative commentaries on traditional Catholic
war doctrine. The Catholic Center for Renewal in
Washington has also become a catalyst for determined
criticism of the bishops.

If the new nuclear doctrine represents a threat to
the internal unity of the Catholic church, it also raises
issues of considerable moment for the Protestants. Neither
Protestants (nor, even less so, Jews) will be torn
internally over the posture of their respective churches
in the same fashion as Catholics. For Protestants, the
various statements and declarations represent at most moral
guidance, as they do for the Jews. Also, because the
Protestant statements have until now been less theological
and more hortatory, they place fewer restraints on
Protestants than the rather precise Catholic draft
pastoral. But if the antinuclear initiatives create no
particular threat to Protestant denominations, there is
detectable a widespread caution within the Protestant
churches over the new Catholic activism. This country
has a history of interdenominational quarrels, often
bloody, and not so many years ago. Many of the same
Protestants who welcome Catholics to the nuclear arena
take great exception to Catholic political activism on
issues such as abortion and tax relief for parochial
schools.

For all the warm words of greeting from liberal
Protestants to the Catholics on this issue, many reflect
as well concern over demonstrated Catholic aggressiveness
in the political arena. Not a few Protestants at the
moment echo the hope that the Catholics will take a "stand,
not a side." After all, Catholics, as the largest single
denomination and a political force, if united, of enormous
potential, stir some Protestant concern. How this will
be resolved cannot be predicted. Properly handled, of
course, the nuclear issue itself could be a great binding
force between the two groups.

VII

Apart from theological issues, the ultimate political
question raised by the debate is how this religious
involvement, Catholic, Protestant and Jewish, will
influence American strategic nuclear doctrine. Conflict
with the Reagan administration, or with any administration
in Washington, now seems inevitable, regardless of the

particular drafting changes in Chicago. It is clear that
nuclear policy and the general atmosphere in Washington
have already been affected. Although impossible to measure
quantitatively, it is evident that to some extent the loss
of support for military spending stems from public
awareness of the current nuclear debate; the rejection
of the MX dense-pack basing mode by Congress in December
1982 would have been quite unthinkable without the
intervention of an uncommonly aroused public. The entire
spectrum of defense and strategic deterrence is being
placed under public scrutiny with a fervor seldom before
experienced.

Opponents of the bishops' initiative, and for that
matter many supporters, emphasize, of course, that the
force of Western public opinion is creating an unbalanced
situation, because pressures that might be brought to bear
in Washington are not similarly possible in Moscow.
One-time Kissinger adviser Helmut Sonnenfeldt has
emphasized "the asymmetrical effect from the pronouncements
of clergymen in free societies: What they say may indeed
affect the public policies of the United States and its
allies, but would have no impact whatsoever on the Soviet
Union." Some observers worry particularly how this
asymmetrical facet will affect America's relations with
its European allies.

Yet another level of criticism is that the bishops
really have not taken account of the true alternatives
to nuclear deterrence. Paul Ramsey said recently, "to
judge the morality of deterrence, one must judge as well
the morality of the alternatives." This was the theme
of a critical letter to Bernardin drafted by twenty-four
Roman Catholic members of Congress, who wrote that "Our
real threat comes from an ideology which challenges our
fundamental faith in human dignity. . . . The crisis we
face today does not involve two morally equal forces, but
the contention of human freedom against totalitarianism."

What may in time become increasingly clear is the
bishops' profoundly human inability to square the circle.
Nuclear weapons cannot be wished away. Many observers
have suggested that ultimately the paradox of deterrence,
the readiness to commit an evil in hopes of preventing
an even worse evil, cannot be resolved. Canon G. R.
Dunstan, in a remarkable new volume, argues that "there
is no 'Christian' solution to it. There is only a choice
among evils; and there is everlasting mercy for those who,
in good faith, are driven to choose."

There remain, however, the qualifications placed on deterrence policy in the pope's own commentary, where deterrence in itself is judged wrong unless accompanied by progress toward arms control. Cardinal John Krol of Philadelphia raised the same point in his historic testimony (on behalf of SALT II) before the Senate Foreign Relations Committee on September 9, 1979:

> The moral judgment of this statement is that not only the use of strategic weapons, but also the declared intent to use them involved in our deterrence is wrong. . . . [However] . . . as long as there is hope of [negotiations] occurring, Catholic moral teaching is willing, while negotiations proceed, to tolerate the possession of nuclear weapons for deterrence as the lesser of two evils. If that hope were to disappear, the moral attitude of the Catholic Church would almost certainly have to shift to one of uncompromising condemnation of both use and possession of such weapons.

What may this mean in practice? Will there be a point at which an absence of progress in arms control forces a harsher condemnation of deterrence by the bishops? Absent progress, can the bishops opt for rejection of the only policy the nation has thus far found to prevent nuclear war?

The central lesson in this whole experience may be that, along with the technical and political complexities of deterrence, a tangle of ambiguities awaits those who would try to sort out the moral quotient. Archbishop John Roach suggested as much at the close of the bishops' meeting. "Ambiguity," said Roach, "is a legitimate and treasured part of our moral tradition. Perhaps," he concluded, "the consensus will be on ambiguity."

14

The Role of the Black Church in Black Civil Rights Movements

Stephen D. Johnson

Rich Allen believed he had found a place at the St. George's Methodist Episcopal Church on Fourth Street in Philadelphia. The former slave had been invited in 1786 to preach to the mainly white church because of his spellbinding powers as an orator. But his success created a problem. Allen's eloquence attracted an ever-increasing number of black worshipers to St. George's, and the white church elders felt a need to assign these blacks segregated seats along the walls. Finding this intolerable, Allen and several of his close followers protested by going boldly to the gallery reserved for whites. The white men of the church descended on the Allen group and wrenched them from their knees as they prayed. Allen's response was to walk out of St. George's, never to return, and eventually, with one of his companions named Absalom Jones, to set up a church of their own in a blacksmith shop—calling it the Free African Society. Later, in 1816 Allen founded the African Methodist Episcopal Church, which today is one of the largest black churches in the United States (Brink and Harris, 1964).

Thus the founding of one of the major black church movements in the United States was itself a protest, and Allen and his followers continued to demonstrate for black rights. As Wilmore stated, "The subject of continuous concern among them was how to organize and employ the extremely limited resources of their churches to fight for freedom" (Wilmore, 1972). With the continued oppression of blacks throughout the nineteenth century, the black church continued to fill a great vacuum in their lives. It was the one place blacks could have some independence from the "white world." It was one of the places they could be "somebody," and a place they could organize and plan at least some resistance to white domination (Brink and Harris, 1963; Rose, 1964; and Wilmore, 1972).

The black church has further been considered the major repository of black heritage as best represented by the "Negro spiritual" (Brink and Harris, 1964). As E. Franklin Frazier stated: "The most important cultural institution is, of course, the Negro church. It embodies . . . the cultural traditions of Negroes to a far greater extent than any other institution" (Frazier, 1963).

But others present a contrasting point of view of the historical influence of the black church on black protest (as Frazier does himself, as we shall see later). For instance, there were slaveholders who controlled the services of black churches. As Stampp stated:

> Through religious instruction, the bondsmen learned that slavery had divine sanction, that insolence was as much an offense against God as against the temporal master. They received the biblical command that servants should obey their masters, and they heard of the punishments awaiting the disobedient slave in the hereafter. They heard, too, that eternal salvation would be their reward for faithful service. (Stampp, 1956).

But probably a more important inhibitor of protest was the "refuge" the black church provided (Frazier, 1963). The reality of being denied most of the opportunities in U.S. life led many black preachers to give up and try to provide solace to their congregations by sermonizing on such "otherworldly" ideas as the virtue in suffering and the need to prepare for the "life after." They preached that one's reward will not be here on this oppressive earth but in the glorious life after death. The inhibiting effect these religious experiences have had on black protest has been called the "opiate effect" by Gary Marx (1969).

THREE BASIC POSITIONS

This brief historical assessment reflects the present debate over the influence of the black church on the civil rights movement of the 1960s and up to the present. Many writers have examined this influence and have drawn different conclusions about the role of the black church.

These various positions can be summarized by Nelsen and Nelsen's (1975) classification. According to these authors, there are three basic positions: (1) an opiate view as probably best represented by E. Franklin Frazier (1963), (2) an intermediate view as found in Gunnar Myrdal's (1944) work, and (3) an inspirational view as seen in Gayraud Wilmore's (1972) writing.

E. Franklin Frazier was one of the leading U.S. black sociologists of the 1950s and 1960s, and his book The Negro Church in America (Frazier, 1963) has been one of the most influential statements on the black church. Frazier stated that as blacks became more drawn into the secular life of especially urban areas in the 1950s and 1960s, the Negro church lost much of its influence as an agency of social control. The church, which had been the chief source of economic aid to many blacks, no longer was, as the government took over more of this function and as urban blacks pursued more individual and secular business activities. The new urban life of many blacks also led to a breakdown of the social control the black churches had over the marital and family life of blacks. Fewer family activities took place in the church and the biblical sanctions on sex and other family behavior seemed less important. With this increase of secular influences on blacks also came the decrease in influence of the black church on the political and civil rights activities of blacks. As Frazier stated: "The church is no longer the main arena for political activities which was the case when Negroes were disfranchised in the South. Negro political leaders have to compete with the white political leaders in the 'machine' politics of the cities" (Frazier, 1963, p. 72).

Another point Frazier made concerns the patterns of control and organization in the black church and their effect on the progress of blacks. Historically, most black churches were headed by authoritarian leaders, i.e., by strong men who dominated their congregations. And because Frazier considered the black church to be the most important black institution, this pattern was copied by other black organizations. Frazier stated that:

As a consequence, Negroes have had little education in democratic processes. Moreover, the Negro church and Negro religion have cast a shadow over the entire intellectual life of Negroes and have been responsible for the so-called backwardness of American Negroes. .

. . It is only as a few Negro individuals have been able to escape from the stifling domination of the church that they have been able to develop intellectually and in the field of art. This development is only being achieved on a broader scale to the extent that Negroes are being integrated into the institutions of the American community and as the social organization of the Negro community, in which the church is the dominant element, crumbles as the walls of segregation come tumbling down (Frazier, 1963, p. 86).

Gunnar Myrdal is a Swedish economist who conducted a classic study of race relations in the South during the 1930s and 1940s and published his findings in a book called An American Dilemma (Myrdal, 1944). Myrdal saw the black church as having both stimulating and inhibiting influences on black activism. He depicted the church, on the one hand, as a place where blacks over the years have gathered together to pursue common causes--it was frequently the only community center blacks had. It was a place where blacks were away from the presence of whites and where blacks could feel a sense of freedom. It was a place where black leaders, many of whom were black ministers, could reach large numbers of blacks and, in the long run, build up a spirit of protest among blacks.

Myrdal stated, on the other hand, that the black church in general has been conservative and accommodating and that poverty prevented black churches from paying salaries that could attract ambitious young black men. He further stated that the otherworldly outlook preached in many black churches was itself an expression of political fatalism.

These inconsistent characteristics of the black church may have also contributed to changes in the black church that Myrdal talked about in a concluding statement:

When the Negro community changes, the church also will change. The Negro church is part of the circular process that is moving the American Negroes onward in their struggle against caste. The increasing education of the Negro masses is either making them demand something more of their church or causing them to stand aloof from the institutionalized form of religion. With some lag, the Negro clergymen, too, are acquiring a better education, which is reflected in their work. The movement to the North and to the Southern cities also tends to free the Negro preacher from white pressure. These trends are making the Negro church a more efficient instrument for betterment of the Negro's position at the same time as they are reducing the relative importance of the church in the Negro community (Rose, 1964).

Gayraud Wilmore is one of the leading liberal black theologians in the country today. He was heavily involved in providing theological justification for the civil rights crusade of Martin Luther King, Jr., and especially for the activities of the "Black Power" advocates of the latter 1960s.

Wilmore has pointed out that the experience of slavery and the generations of struggle against second-class citizenship for blacks has forced the black church to become the major advocate of black rights. Black ministers have been required to take problack stands on public issues, and as a result, have become the most trusted interpreters of public affairs for blacks (Newsweek, 1984).

Wilmore noted that not only were the major leaders of the civil rights movement in the 1960s religious leaders, such as Martin Luther King, Jr., and Malcolm X, but that the only true black religion is one that embodies the struggle for black rights. He said about black protest, or what he calls black radicalism: "For most of its existence it has been an adjunct of Black Christianity because it was precisely through the Biblical story, the Negro Spiritual, and the event of Christian worship that black people knew the existence of being bound together in the persecuted family of a righteous God who destined them someday to break the bonds of oppression" (Wilmore, 1972, p. 230). He further stated in a recent article in Newsweek (1984, p. 31) that "black church people have been taught that political struggle is a permanent characteristic of human life."

Wilmore wrote that white churches and white religion have been a corrupting influence on black people and their religion (Wilmore, 1974). Integration of black with white churches, he said, will destroy blacks' pride in themselves and their culture. The only way the black church can successfully participate in the black struggle is to devoid itself of all dehumanizing elements of white Christianity, such as a white Jesus. Black churches need to accept

312

such black power ideology as a <u>black</u> Jesus, the African roots of blacks, and the idea <u>that</u> blacks should have complete control over all aspects of their religious life.

THE MARX STUDY

Frazier claimed that the black church has had a "stifling" influence on black advancement and the only way blacks could succeed in the secular world was to leave the black church behind. Myrdal saw the black church as a conservative institution, but one that was changing. And Wilmore saw the major force behind the black struggle coming from the truly black church. Which position is correct? To help answer this question, we turn to more systematic, and possibly more objective, research on the matter.

Probably the first study that directly examined this question was one by Gary Marx (1969). Marx's study was a survey of 1,101 blacks from various major urban areas, both north and south, throughout the country in 1964. Marx first measured the extent of civil rights activism among his nationwide sample of blacks by asking them several questions such as the extent to which they were impatient over the speed of integration, supported civil rights demonstrations, and expressed a willingness to take part in a demonstration. He then divided his sample into <u>militants</u> (those who strongly supported civil rights activities), <u>moderates</u> (those who somewhat supported civil rights activities), and <u>conservatives</u> (those who did not support civil rights activities).

Having studied the denominational membership of blacks, Marx surmised that those who were members of sects such as Jehovah Witnesses and Holiness groups would be little interested in movements for secular political change such as the black civil rights movement. As Marx stated, the sects "with their otherworldly orientation and their promise that the last shall be first in the great beyond, are said to solace the individual for his lowly status in his world and to divert concern away from efforts at collective social change which might be brought about by man" (Marx, 1969).

Table 14.1 indicates that Marx indeed found that sects were less likely to be "militants" than those from the mainline denominations studied.

Marx next turned to a consideration of what type of social psychological religious orientation might make

TABLE 14.1
Black Militants by Religious Denomination

Denomination	Number in Sample	% Militant
Episcopalian	24	46
United Church of Christ	112	42
Presbyterian	25	40
Catholic	109	40
Methodist	142	34
Baptist	658	32
Sects and cults	106	20

Source: Gary Marx. Religion: Opiate or Inspiration of Civil Rights Militancy Among Negroes? American Sociological Review 32, pp. 64-72, 1969.

mainline church blacks more (or less) likely to participate in secular political activities. In this regard, Marx developed a measure of religiosity. This consisted of asking the sample of blacks several questions about the orthodoxy of their religious beliefs such as the extent to which they had no doubt about the existence of God and the devil, one question about how important religion was to them, and one question about how frequently they attended worship services. Scores on these measures were combined to form a measure of overall religiosity. The black respondents were then classified into four levels of religiosity: (1) very religious, (2) somewhat religious, (3) not very religious, and (4) not at all religious. At the extremes, "very religious" were people who attended church at least once a week, felt that religion was extremely important to them, and had no doubts at all about the existence of God and the devil; whereas, "not at all religious" were people who attended church rarely if ever, did not consider religion personally important, and had many doubts about the existence of God and the devil. With people who were members of sects excluded, Table 14.2 indicates that as religiosity increases, the percent of militants decreases. So it seems the more religiously involved a black is, the less likely he is to favor civil rights activities.

Marx found that religiosity and militancy were also both related to the age, sex, education, religious TABLE denomination of the respondent, and the region of the country where he/she lived. Specifically, blacks who were

14.2
Black Militants by Religiosity

Religiosity	Very Religious	Somewhat Religious	Not Very Religious	Not at All Religious
Percent militant	26	30	45	70
Number of people in category	230	523	195	36

Source: Gary Marx. Religion: Opiate or Inspiration of Civil Rights Militancy Among Negroes? American Sociological Review 32, pp. 64-72, 1969.

older, less educated, women, southerners, and members of black denominations (as contrasted to blacks who were members of mainly white denominations) were more likely to be religiously involved and not to be militant. Thus it was possible that the relationship observed between religiosity and militancy resulted from the fact that both are caused by one or more of these third factors. For example, it could be that the reason religiosity and militancy are related is that less-educated blacks are very religiously involved and not at all militant, and blacks of higher education are not religiously involved and very militant. However, as can be seen from Table 14.3, even when each of these factors is held constant, the higher the religiosity of a black, the less militant he/she is. That is, no matter what education level, how old, what region, what sex, or whether or not in a predominantly black denomination (e.g., Baptist, Methodist), blacks who were religiously involved were less likely to be militant.

Therefore in general, Marx found that religiosity was inversely related to militancy among blacks. However, further analyses by Marx discovered an important qualification. Examining the percentage of those at the four levels of religiosity for the three levels of militancy, Marx discovered that, although there were lower percentages of "very religious" and "somewhat religious" for militants than for moderates and conservatives (66 percent vs. 81 percent and 83 percent, respectively), still most militants were at least somewhat religiously involved (18 percent were "very religious" and 48 percent were "somewhat religious"). Marx concluded from this that religiosity can be a stimulant, rather than an opiate for some religious people.

TABLE 14.3
Black Militants by Religiosity for Education, Age, Region,
Sex, and Denomination

	Very Religious		Somewhat Religious		Not Very Religious		Not at All Religious	
	%	No.	%	No.	%	No.	%	No.
Education								
Grammar school	17	108	22	201	31	42	50	2
High school	34	96	32	270	45	119	58	19
College	38	26	48	61	59	34	87	15
Age								
18-29	33	30	37	126	44	62	62	13
30-44	30	53	34	180	48	83	74	19
45-59	25	79	27	131	45	33	50	2
60+	22	76	18	95	33	15	100	2
Region								
Non-South	30	123	34	331	47	159	70	33
South	22	107	23	202	33	36	66	3
Sex								
Men	28	83	33	220	44	123	72	29
Women	26	147	28	313	46	72	57	7
Denomination								
Episcopalian, Presbyterian, United Church of Christ	20	15	27	26	33	15	60	5
Catholic	13	15	39	56	36	25	77	13
Methodist	46	24	22	83	50	32	100	2
Baptist	25	172	29	354	45	117	53	15

Source: Gary Marx. Religion: Opiate or Inspiration
of Civil Rights Militancy Among Negroes? American
Sociological Review 32, pp. 64-72, 1969.

But what factor might determine whether religion is
related to an active concern with racial matters or has
an opiating effect? Marx hypothesized from additional
comments made by the blacks who were interviewed in his
study that a belief in a highly deterministic God could
inhibit race protest, i.e., that those who believed God
controlled the affairs of humans were less likely to be

activists. Marx's problem, however, was that he did not
have a direct measure of this type of religious ideology.
Instead, he used two measures that assessed this indirectly
by measuring acceptance of one's lot and glorification
of the afterlife as opposed to a concern with the
realization of Judeo-Christian values in the current life.
Marx also pointed out that Martin Luther King, Jr., and
his followers clearly represented this latter social gospel
orientation. As King stated, "Any religion that professes
to be concerned with the souls of men and is not concerned
with the slums that damn them, the economic conditions
that strangle them, and the social conditions that cripple
them is a dry-as-dust religion" (King, 1958, p. 28-29).

Those black respondents who held this social gospel
view were classified as having a temporal orientation;
whereas those with the afterlife view were classified as
having an otherworldly orientation.

Table 14.4 indicates how these two orientations relate
to militancy for the religiously involved. It shows that
a temporal orientation indeed increases race protest among
the religiously involved.

Taking into account that from Table 14.2 one would
compute that 49 percent of the marginally to not religiously involved are militant (combining data for "Not
Very Religious" and "Not at All Religious"), along with
the results in Table 14.4 and the fact that only 33 percent
of the total black sample were militants, one might first
conclude that blacks who have little religious commitment
are the most active in demonstrating for black rights.
Obviously, there are other factors besides religion that
stimulate their activism, such as more education and/or
greater self confidence. Table 14.4, however, indicates
that there is another religious factor that stimulates
activism: a temporal religious orientation. Table 14.4
further indicates that the type of religion that inhibits
civil rights activism is an otherworldly orientation.

OTHER BLACK CHURCH/CIVIL RIGHTS STUDIES

Two other studies expanded on Marx's work. The first
attempted to replicate Marx's study in a different
setting. This study was conducted by Nelsen and Nelsen
(1975). These researchers sampled 405 black adults during
1970-1971 from Bowling Green, Kentucky (population:
36,253). They first point out (taking Gallup poll data

TABLE 14.4
Religiously Involved Black Militants by Temporal vs.
Otherworldly Concern

Concern	Very or Somewhat Religious (Combined)	
	Number	Percent
Temporal	440	38
Otherworldly	336	16

Source: Gary Marx. Religion: Opiate or
Inspiration of Civil Rights Militancy Among
Negroes? American Sociological Review 32,
pp. 64-72, 1969.

from the late 1950s through the 1960s) that blacks were
more likely than whites to desire civil rights protest
on the part of their ministers and churches. This
indicated that there could be one or more components of
black religion, not present in the average white church,
that stimulates civil rights activism. Analyzing their
Bowling Green data, Nelsen and Nelsen obtained results
basically supporting Marx's final conclusions. Specifically, they found that two out of three of Marx's
measures of religiosity were significantly and negatively
related to militancy among blacks even when income,
northern or southern birth, education, and sex were all
controlled at the same time. (Marx controlled
for them one at a time.) That is, the more important
religion was and the more orthodoxy of belief, the less
militant; church attendance was not related to militancy.
Nelsen and Nelsen further found that a measure of
sectarianism, which was similar to Marx's otherworldly
measure, related negatively to militancy (the more
sectarian, the less militant) even when education and sex
were controlled. According to Nelsen and Nelsen's measure
of sectarianism, a sectarian is a person who generally
places a lot of importance on the life after death,
believes God determines worldly events, says most of his
close friends are members of his local congregation, and
says religion is very important in his life.
    The second study that was stimulated by Marx's work
was a reanalysis of Marx's 1964 data conducted by Hunt
and Hunt (1977). They found that when they controlled

for urban or rural background, northern or southern birth,
sex, and age, at the same time for the blacks in
Marx's study, the relationship between a two-item measure
of religiosity and militancy disappeared. They concluded
from this that four secular factors really accounted for
the lesser militancy among the religious, i.e., religious
involvement does not make these blacks less militant, it
is the fact that the less militant tend to be rural, from
the South, female, and old.

The problem with Hart and Hart's reanalysis, however,
is that for some reason they dropped one of Marx's measures
of religiosity. Specifically, they included church
attendance and orthodoxy but dropped religious importance.
If this third measure had been included, there might still
have been a relationship. Further, if you control enough
third variables, the relationship between any two variables
will always disappear because there will be no variation
left in the two variables (and without variation, there
can be no relationship). For instance, a possible reason
for the lack of relationship between religiosity and
militancy for older black women from the rural South is
that they are all either mostly religiously involved
or non-militant (a lack of variation in either characteristic will prevent a relationship). Or the reason we find
no relationship for young black men from the urban North
is that they are all either mostly nonreligious or
militant. If the reader is unable to follow this
statistical reasoning, let it just be said that Hunt and
Hunt's study does not disprove the conclusion that one's
level of religiosity affects one's level of militancy.

Another finding from Hunt and Hunt (1977) supports
Marx's final conclusion. They found that a measure of
sectarian beliefs relates to Marx's measure of militancy
even when urban or rural background, northern or southern
birth, sex, and age were all controlled at the same time.

Three other studies relate to Marx's conclusions.
Johnstone (1969) interviewed fifty-nine black clergymen
who were randomly selected from the black churches of
Detroit in the latter 1960s. Johnstone found that about
20 percent of these ministers were members of the inner
core of blacks who planned and executed civil rights
actions--these ministers were labeled militants.
Fifty-three percent of the black ministers were called
traditionalists, since most of them were actively trying
to stay out of politics and just preach the gospel (a third
group, called moderates, was halfway in between these two

groups). The black militant ministers were found to be much younger and more educated, and (in support of Marx's conclusions) were much less orthodox, or fundamentalist, were more likely to be members of mainline Protestant denominations (rather than sect-type religious groups), and much more likely to support the view that in their role as ministers they should be advocates for their people in the social, political, and economic realms. They were also much more likely to allow political candidates to address their congregations and to suggest that their congregants vote for a particular candidate.

A second study relating to Marx's work was Benton Johnson's (1967) study of mainly white Methodist and Baptist pastors in Oregon in 1962. After classifying these ministers as religiously liberal or conservative based on their own self-identification, Johnson's analysis of their positions on six social issues (e.g., capital punishment and foreign aid) led him to conclude that the conservative ministers were much more concerned than the liberal ministers with preparing the individual soul for life-hereafter, and these same ministers were also much less concerned with social issues and with creating a good society in the present world. Assuming that a life-hereafter orientation has the same impact on social activism for black ministers as for the mainly white ministers in Johnson's study, this study supports Marx's conclusions.

The final study considered here that indirectly relates to Marx's conclusions is Tygart's (1977) analysis of a nationwide sample of Protestant ministers in 1972. Like Johnson's (1967) study, the sample was mainly white (97 percent). Tygart found essentially that even when the level of authoritarianism, dogmatism, efficacy (belief in individual effectiveness in making societal changes), and moral autonomy (self-direction in making moral decisions) were controlled, the fundamentalist ministers (or what Marx would call those ministers high on orthodoxy) were still much less likely to be civil rights activists.

THE BLACK CHURCH AND CIVIL RIGHTS IN THE 1980S

This chapter so far has dealt with the role of the black church as a stimulant or opiate for civil rights activism mainly during the great civil rights movement of the 1960s. But what has been happening more recently?

There is some evidence that the role of the black church in civil rights activism is at least as great today.

With the increasing educational levels of blacks today in the 1980s (Vander Zanden, 1983), one could surmise that fewer blacks accept the otherworldly religious ideology that tends to diminish activism. This is based on the frequently found phenomenon that educated people are less likely to be religiously fundamentalistic in their thinking (Johnson and Tamney, 1984; Tamney and Johnson, 1983).

During the 1970s and 1980s, the number of black elected officials in the United States has increased significantly. One source (Time, 1983) classified black elected officials into those at the federal, state, and local levels, those elected to judicial or law enforcement offices, and those elected to school-related offices. In 1970, approximately 1,500 blacks were in these offices in the United States, and in 1982, approximately 5,100 blacks were elected to these positions. Furthermore, throughout the 1970s and early 1980s, several blacks have been elected as mayors of major U.S. cities, e.g., Kenneth Gibson of Newark, Tom Bradley of Los Angeles, Coleman Young of Detroit, Maynard Jackson and Andrew Young of Atlanta, Ernest N. Morial of New Orleans, Harold Washington of Chicago, and W. Wilson Goode of Philadelphia. One might surmise from this political success and the traditional political role of many black churches that black churches are as politically involved as ever. There is indeed some evidence that the black church played a major role in the election of both Harold Washington in Chicago and W. Wilson Goode in Philadelphia in 1983 (Ebony, 1984a). But probably the clearest and best documented event demonstrating the importance of the black church in black civil rights/political action in the 1980s is the major role black churches played in the 1984 presidential campaign of the Reverend Jesse Jackson. In the early stages of Jackson's campaign, Time (1983) reported that 125 ministers met in East St. Louis in July 1983 to form a Draft Jesse Jackson Committee. They vowed to raise $250 from each of the 40,000 black congregations in hopes of raising a substantial war chest of $10 million for Jackson's campaign. Throughout the campaign itself, black churches were the main way stations for Jackson's quest for the presidency, as well as the financial and organizational base for his campaign (Cohen, 1984; Newsweek, 1984). He received the official endorsement of the 4 million strong National Baptist Convention, which is the largest black church in the nation (Cohen, 1984). In the end, black churches contributed $1 million to Jackson's campaign (Jet, 1984). As African Methodist Episcopal Bishop H. H. Brookins of Los Angeles stated, "No black politician of note can say he or she has been elected without the black church" (Newsweek, 1984).

Another source of evidence concerning the role of the black church in recent black political and civil rights activity comes from a 1984 Ebony (1984b) survey. This important black magazine sampled well-known black preachers, seminary educators, and laypersons in various parts of the United States and asked them who they thought were the greatest black preachers. Fifteen black ministers were chosen from throughout the country. Most were ministers of large urban congregations. A content analysis of their brief biographies by this author indicated that twelve of the fifteen ministers were significantly involved in civil rights activities, from writing books on black social problems (e.g., Dr. Charles G. Adam's book Equality Under the Law and Dr. William A. Jones' book God in the Ghetto) to active civil rights participation (e.g., two of the ministers were Dr. Joseph E. Lowery--head of the Southern Christian Leadership Council since 1977--and the Reverend Jesse Jackson). This informal content analysis thus supports the idea that the most respected black religious leaders are also quite involved in civil rights activities, and this implies that many blacks today believe the black church should be involved in civil rights activities.

The most systematic assessment of the role of the black church in the 1980s comes from a study by C. Eric Lincoln and Lawrence H. Mamiya (Mamiya, 1983). These researchers interviewed a sample of black clergy representing 2,150 churches (1,531 urban and 619 rural) throughout the United States in the early 1980s. These clergy also represented six mainline black churches (e.g., the National Baptist Convention) and one sect-like denomination--the Church of God in Christ (a Pentecostal church). Four of Lincoln and Mamiya's questions measure civil rights activism or militancy as we have defined it in this paper. These questions were (1) "Is it important to have Black figures in your Sunday School literature?"; (2) "Do your sermons reflect any of the changes in Black consciousness (Black pride, Black is beautiful, Black power, etc.) since the Civil Rights Movement?"; (3) a Gallup question asking about support for churches'

322

expressing their views on day-to-day social and political issues; and (4) a question measuring support for participation in protest marches on civil rights issues. Their data indicated that on (1) 69 percent, (2) 64 percent, (3) 92 percent, and (4) 91 percent of all of the black ministers gave affirmative answers to the questions. Further, the researchers found that black ministers from the sect-like denomination (Church of God in Christ) were significantly less likely to feel it was important to have black figures in Sunday School literature, to give sermons reflecting new black consciousness, and to support protest marches on civil rights issues. Moreover, although it was not statistically significant, Church of God in Christ ministers were less likely to support churches' expressing their views on social and political matters. Therefore, the Lincoln and Mamiya study supports the conclusion that black ministers strongly support civil rights activism, but that the "otherworldly" influence of sect-like denominations continues to inhibit civil rights activism.

SUMMARY

The review of literature presented here supports the view that although blacks with no religious commitment are possibly the most active in fighting for black civil rights, another important source of black activism comes from ministers and members of mainline (rather than sect-like) black churches with a social gospel orientation. This state of affairs existed during the 1960s civil rights movement and continues to be the case in the 1980s.

REFERENCES

Brink, William, and Louis Harris. The Negro Revolution In America. New York: Simon and Schuster, 1964.
Cohen, Sharon. Black Churches Comparable to AFL-CIO for Jackson. Associated Press story in the Indianapolis Star, February 26, 1984, 1984.
Ebony. The Black Church: Precinct of the Black Soul. August, pp. 156-158, 1984a.

_____. America's 15 Greatest Black Preachers. September, pp. 27-33, 1984b.

Frazier, E. Franklin. The Negro Church in America. New York: Schocken Books, 1963.

Hunt, Larry, and Janet Hunt. Black Religion as BOTH Opiate and Inspiration of Civil Rights Militance: Putting Marx's Data to the Test. Social Forces 56, pp. 1-14, 1977.

Jet. Black Churches Raise $1 Million for Jackson. July 23, p. 22, 1984.

Johnson, Benton. Theology and the Position of Pastors on Public Issues. American Sociological Review 32, pp. 433-442, 1967.

Johnson, Stephen, and Joseph Tamney. Support for the Moral Majority: A Test of a Model. Journal for the Scientific Study of Religion 23, pp. 183-196, 1984.

Johnstone, Ronald. Negro Preachers Take Sides. Review of Religious Research 11, pp. 81-89, 1969.

King, Martin Luther, Jr. Stride Toward Freedom. New York: Ballantine Books, 1958.

Mamiya, Lawrence. The Black Church and Justice. Paper presented at the annual meetings of the Society for the Scientific Study of Religion, Knoxville, Tenn., Fall 1983.

Marx, Gary. Religion: Opiate or Inspiration of Civil Rights Militancy Among Negroes? American Sociological Review 32, pp. 64-72, 1969.

Myrdal, Gunnar. An American Dilemma: The Negro Problem and Modern Democracy. New York: Harper and Row, 1944.

Nelsen, Hart, and Anne Kusener Nelsen. Black Church in the Sixties. Lexington, Ky.: The University Press of Kentucky, 1975.

Newsweek. Politics and the Pulput. September 17, pp. 24-32, 1984.

Rose, Arnold. The Negro in America: The Condensed Version of Gunnar Myrdal's An American Dilemma. New York: Harper and Row, 1964.

Stampp, Kenneth. The Peculiar Institution. New York: Alfred A. Knopf, 1956.

Tamney, Joseph, and Stephen Johnson. The Moral Majority in Middletown. Journal for the Scientific Study of Religion 22, pp. 145-157, 1983.

324

<u>Time</u>. Seeking Votes and Clout: Jesse Jackson Spearheads
     a New Black Drive for Political Power, August 22,
     pp. 20-31, 1983.

Tygart, Clarence. The Role of Theology Among Other
     "Belief" Variables for Clergy Civil Rights Activism.
     <u>Review of Religious Research</u> 18, pp. 271-278, 1977.

Vander Zanden, James. <u>American Minority Relations</u>.
     New York: Alfred A. Knopf, 1983.

Wilmore, Gayraud. <u>Black Religion and Black Radicalism</u>.
     Garden City, N.Y.: Doubleday, 1972.

_____. The Case for a New Black Church Style.
     In <u>The Black Experience in Religion</u>, C. Eric Lincoln
     (ed.), pp. 34-44, Garden City, N.Y.: Archor Press,
     1974.

15

Feminist Theologians and Liberal Political Issues

Julia Benton Mitchell

Feminist thought in the discipline of religious studies is developing a new model for describing the relationship between religion and other aspects of life, including politics. A "model," as used herein, is an intellectual construct against which reality can be measured. Historically, the dominant model might be characterized as "What has God to do with Caesar, or Caesar with God?" The new model being developed in the current literature strongly indicates that (at least in theory) God and Caesar definitely do have to do with each other, that religion and politics are very closely linked indeed. But do the writings of feminist theologians bear out this theoretically espoused linkage? An investigation of three contemporary political issues--the struggle for passage of the Equal Rights Amendment, interest in the development of more ecologically sound lifestyles, and concern over the threat of a nuclear holocaust--provides a concrete case study of how well practice embodies theory. How responsive is the church--this time in the writings of its best known feminist spokespersons--to these widely recognized "liberal issues"?

THE MODELS

Historically, spirituality and overt participation in the political process have usually been thought to be antagonistic to one another. Political activism has been, and in some instances continues to be, regarded as a "worldly" distraction that impedes genuine spirituality, and spirituality has been accused of being an "other-worldly" pursuit that siphons energy away from the real

326

task of sociopolitical change. Christianity, especially
in its more traditional forms, distinguishes sharply
between Creator and creation and hence between the things
of God and of this world, with the preference given to
godly pursuits. On the other hand, secular humanists often
regard spiritual pursuits as less effective than political
action and hence as a waste of time.

It has been pointed out that this gulf between the
spiritual and the political is encouraged and perpetuated
because it helps support the patriarchal political power
structure to do so. Feminist scholars who think along
these lines believe that this separation is a divide-and-
conquer strategy on the part of the patriarchy, a way of
attenuating women's power by keeping women divided from
one another by interests defined as "opposing."

As feminist scholarship has developed, methodological
approaches that integrate the religious and the political
have become predominant. The details of how this integration is understood to take place vary, but in any case
a shift in models has clearly occurred, from the older
view that religion and politics are antagonistic toward
(or at best, have nothing to do with) each other, to a
model that brings the two together.

Two examples from current scholarship will help to
make this clear. Charlene Spretnak, whose primary interest
is in feminist spirituality and women's political power,
wrote: "Spirituality is a sustaining force in our politics
not only because it helps us channel energy--the power
within us that we were conditioned not to acknowledge--
toward political goals. We consider it absolutely
essential to birth the new way of being in our hearts and
minds, as we actively oppose the present system" (Spretnak,
1982: 426).

Dorothy Riddle, cofounder of and partner in
Alternatives for Women, a feminist counseling and
consulting service, wrote:

Politics has to do with the "what" of the process
of change. Spirituality, on the other hand, is the
process component, the "how" of the process of
change. Our spirituality has to do with our sense
of who we are and the ethics of how we use our power
for change. Thus, every process of change has both
a political and a spiritual dimension.

Traditionally, we have tended to focus either
on spirituality or on politics, either on process

or on product; but they are interrelated. Spirituality focuses from society to the individual, emphasizing uniqueness and individuality. Politics focuses from the individual to society, emphasizing our membership in a group. At the same time, spirituality focuses on our interconnectedness and sense of oneness, while politics focuses on our differences which result in our experience of separateness (Riddle, 1982: 374).

By and large, feminists who call for the integration of the two dimensions do so for the following reasons: It allows tapping the power of religious conviction in the service of political action. It prevents the division of the "whole" person into conflicting spheres of outer and inner, action and reflection, material and spiritual. This in turn reflects the underlying view of these scholars that such separations are not indicative of how things really are. Rather, they result from false dichotomies of thought.

Since the balance of current feminist thought holds that the political and the religious are, in one way or another, closely related, feminist theologians would be expected to comment upon the political scene. This hypothesis was first investigated with reference to the passage of the Equal Rights Amendment, then with reference to ecology and peace issues.

THE SAMPLE

Women have taken two points of view as distinctively feminist theologians have emerged. The "reformist" view begins with the affirmation that there is a changeless, eternal core of truth revealed in the Judeo-Christian religions that has been distorted and falsified by centuries of patriarchal interpretation. Scholars who hold this view undertake to free this core of truth from its distorted interpretations, believing that, when this is done, Judaism and Christianity offer ample support for feminist theology. This view allows women who are feminists to continue to participate in Judaism or Christianity if they so choose, without feeling that they have compromised their feminism. This view permits these "reformist scholars" to remain loyal to church and synagogue, working from within to reform them.

The second view, "revolution," is chosen by women who find the Judeo-Christian traditions hopelessly corrupt. Rather than trying to reform their inherited religions, these women leave church and synagogue to seek other avenues by which to fulfill their spiritual needs (Collins, 1974: 40-43)./1/ Contemporary witchcraft, neoPaganism and a variety of other goddess-centered religions are among the religious choices being made by women who choose to leave the Judeo-Christian religions. Others simply stop being religious in any ordinary sense of the term and turn to humanism to fulfill their "spiritual" needs.

Scholars who take the reformist and those who take the revolutionary approaches are included in the sample of feminist theologians upon which this essay is based. The reformers include Sheila D. Collins (Protestant), Judith Plaskow (Jewish), Rosemary Radford Ruether (Roman Catholic) and Letty M. Russell (Protestant). The revolutionaries are represented by Mary Daly and Naomi Goldenberg. The initial list of six names was developed from the author's experience and knowledge of the following factors: books and articles published by the scholars, and the scholars' participation in professional conferences. More written scholarship has come from the reformist theologians than from the revolutionaries, and thus there is greater representation of reformers in the sample. Formal criteria for the inclusion of specific scholars, once the initial list was compiled, included the number of published books by the scholar, reviews of these books in significant journals, the number of articles published both in professional journals and in the popular press, inclusion of the scholar's work in representative anthologies and bibliographic essays, and the scholar's participation in the American Academy of Religion, the major professional organization in religious studies.

This information was obtained through an exhaustive computer search utilizing three databases: Religion Index, which indexes over 200 professional journals and over 300 multiauthor works (collected essays, proceedings, irregular series, and the like), and also includes book reviews; Magazine Index, which covers over 435 popular U.S. and Canadian periodicals and includes all periodicals indexed in the Reader's Guide to Periodical Literature and book reviews. The information about published books was obtained through the OCLC (On-line Computer Library Center) database, which catalogues Library of Congress acquisitions along with those of many cooperating research libraries. Information on American Academy of Religion participation was obtained by manual search of the organization's national meeting programs. This search yielded the following total number of entries for each author: Collins, 13; Daly, 36; Goldenberg, 13; Plaskow, 9; Ruether, 152; and Russell, 55.

Of course, this is not an exhaustive list of feminist theologians. It is, however, a representative list of those whom the majority of scholars in the field would consider most significant./2/

The initial search covered all the authors' known publications. The first issue considered was the struggle for the passage of the Equal Rights Amendment. The output was screened to narrow the data to the decade between the submission of the ERA proposal to Congress in 1970 and the end of the extension of the ratification period in 1980. Within this narrowed field, the computer output was searched manually to eliminate listings pertaining to unwanted materials such as sound recordings, books of poetry and children's church/synagogue education materials. The remaining listings were assessed in the following way:

1. Books
    A. Read through table of contents for section and chapter titles and subtitles that might be relevant.
    B. Read through index for references such as ERA, Equal Rights Amendments, equal rights, politics, employment.
    C. Check the references from A and B carefully.
    D. Skim remainder of book for anything missed.
2. Reviews of books by selected scholars--read in their entirety.
3. Essays by the selected scholars, appearing in collected works--read in their entirety.
4. Professional journal articles--read wholly.
5. Articles by selected authors in the popular press--read in their entirety.

Despite the strong theoretical linkage between religion and politics, this linkage was found not to be reflected in the writing of feminist theologians of either reformist or revolutionary persuasions. Among the almost 300 entries analyzed, no references to the passage of the

ERA were found. This specific political struggle seems to have remained as an isolated political issue. Feminist theologians did not address questions such as: "What are the religious reasons for passing or not passing the Equal Rights Amendment?" "What resources does religion offer those engaged in pro- or anti-ERA action?" "What are the religious implications of equal rights for women?" "What do the teachings of the Jewish and Christian faiths have to say about women's rights as this applies specifically to the ERA?" Questions such as these would seem to be obvious, if not inevitable, for feminist theologians to raise in the decade of the 1970s. Given the consistency with which models integrating both points of view have appeared in the literature, it is surprising that a significant specific issue such as the ERA did not receive the type of attention those models would lead one to suspect.

The issues of ecology and nuclear peace were then investigated. The original output was screened to include data from 1960 to 1985. This longer time period is appropriate for these issues, because concern about them began earlier than 1970 and has extended to the present. An assessment procedure parallel to that used for the Equal Rights Amendment question was then followed. For this twenty-five-year time period, there was a very limited number of references to either ecology or peace issues. For all six authors inclusively, the total number of citations was less than ten. If ecology and peace issues are taken as representative, two conclusions seem obvious. Feminist theologians are beginning to address liberal sociopolitical issues but to only a limited extent. Again, given the integrative models that dominate the theory, this lack of attention to specific, significant issues is startling.

Although it may not be possible to give a definitive explanation for these startling findings, there are several suggestions that can be made. The separation-based model has a very long history, and old models give way to new ones slowly. Most feminist scholars currently writing, and all involved in the sample, have been trained in academic institutions dominated by the old style of thinking. To begin to operate with the new model involves an "unlearning" of the old as well as an internalization of the new. Feminist theology is relatively a very young discipline. Scholars are still defining what feminist theology is and what its basic issues are, distinguishing

it not only from traditional patriarchal theology but also
from allied yet not identical work such as liberation
theology. It is still developing its own distinctive
methodology. Because it has developed so recently, much
attention is being given to the theory of method itself,
sometimes at the expense of less attention given to
content. As the emerging theories suggest, this will be
a method that substitutes integration for separation, but
it has yet to develop fully and be taken up into practical
usage.

Further, the religious dimension of sociopolitical
change, because long discredited by customary (male-
dominated) power structures, has been underdeveloped even
within the women's movement. (See the quotation from
Riddle, above.) Thus, in the early years of the movement,
the emphasis has been on "rediscovering and strengthening
women's 'spiritual' powers and knowledge" as a way of
redressing the balance (Inglehart, 1978: 13). Women have
concentrated, for example, on rediscovering or creating
rituals that will enable them to get in touch with this
long-neglected dimension of their lives./3/ For many
women whose sense of their own power has been suppressed
by male domination, such rediscovery must come first in
order for the necessary integration to be possible.

A further factor, for the reformist theologians, is
that the Bible--the foundation of Judeo-Christian faith--
does not deal directly with the problem of women's rights
and how to make them operative in a twentieth-century
society. Suggestions are there, certainly, but not
specifics. By contrast, the relationship between human
beings and the natural world, on the one hand, and the
imperative for peace, on the other, are more directly
biblical. In Genesis, for example, humans are told that
they are in charge of the other animals and are to subdue
the earth (1:26,28) but also care for it (2:15). The
coming Messiah foretold in Isaiah's prophecy is referred
to as the "Prince of Peace" (Isaiah 9:6), and a coming
era of peace is described metaphorically as a time when
animals we think of as natural enemies will no longer be
at odds with each other (Isaiah 65:25). Of particular
interest to Christians, in the well-known Beatitudes
(Matthew 5:9), Jesus blessed those who make peace.

Historically, there has been something of a division
in religious studies between the theoretical and the
practical dimensions of religion. Systematic theologians
(or simply, theologians) concentrate on the theoretical,

while the practical theologians deal with application. Sociopolitical issues such as the ERA, ecology, and peace are regarded as practical applications of the more basic theology. Thus, even though some specifically feminist theorizing currently emphasizes integration, this interest has yet to make a significant impact on writers whose focus is more theoretical than practical. Fully developed and rigorously applied, feminist methodology calls into question this division of theology into theoretical and practical realms, much as it questions the division of life into spiritual and political spheres.

An additional factor that helps to explain why well-known feminist theologians have not written more about current sociopolitical issues is a characteristic of theology generally, feminist as well as traditional. Particular theologians specialize in one issue or set of issues and often write little about others. In part, this is encouraged by traditional doctoral programs, which frequently emphasize depth at the expense of breadth. The demands of publication also encourage a scholar to become identified with a particular area of expertise. A survey of the scholarship of the six women included in this sample bears this out. After an early overview of the issues in feminist scholarship in religion,/4/ Collins's efforts have been focused on missions and the Third World. Daly is identified with a radical critique of patriarchy from a philosophical standpoint. Goldenberg's interest is in the relation between feminist thought and the psychologies of Freud and Jung. Plaskow's area of interest is harder to identify because many of her contributions are edited volumes. She writes on specifically Jewish topics and also on the distance between traditional theology and women's experience. Russell has written primarily on the basic issues and agenda of theology from a feminist viewpoint and also on both feminist biblical interpretation and Christian education. Ruether, easily the most published member of the group, writes on sexism and liberation, sexism and religion from a theoretical perspective, Roman Catholicism, and documentation of the historical role of women in religion.

This lack of integration left those who espouse a feminist stance in religion without an effective written voice on the question of whether or not the United States should have an Equal Rights Amendment. It continues to leave feminists in religion without a clear voice on ecology and peace issues, although as we have seen, the situation

here is improving. This has meant that the field has been
left primarily to two groups with sharply opposing points
of view: mainline Christianity and Protestant Christian
conservatism.

Due to a sharp difference in overall style, compounded
by an equally sharp disparity in funding, the disagreement
between these two groups takes on an even more problematic
aspect. The New Christian Right is very well funded and
extraordinarily vocal (one might say, without fear of
overstatement, "vociferous"). The mainline, on the other
hand, operates with a style that is both much lower key
and less public, as well as less well supported finan-
cially. The strong impulse to convert others to its point
of view is notably lacking, whereas the urge to sway others
is a mainstay of the New Christian Right. What this adds
up to is that the voice of the New Christian Right is
present in the media to a much greater extent than that
of the more moderate mainline and is heard in opposition
to liberal sociopolitical issues more than its numerical
strength warrants./5/

CONCLUSIONS

We have seen that feminist theologians, although having
developed a theoretical model that mandates integration
of theological and sociopolitical concerns, have been slow
to put that model into practice where three specific issues
--the ERA, ecology, and peace--are concerned. It was
hypothesized that factors having to do with the relative
newness of feminist theology, as well as other factors,
played a role in this situation.

It can be predicted, then, that we will see an
increasing flow, or at least a steady flow, of writing on
sociopolitical issues from a feminist theological viewpoint. In addition to the six scholars who constitute the
sample, Charlene Spretnak and Grace Jantzen, scholars whose
work did not warrant inclusion in the original list, have
written on ecological issues./6/ Mary Daly's most recent
book, Pure Lust, is a work on metaphilosophy and is not
directed toward concrete sociopolitical issues. However,
she notes in the Preface:

This book is being published in the 1980s--a period
of extreme danger for women and for our sister the
earth and her other creatures, all of whom are targeted

by the maniacal fathers, sons, and holy ghosts for
extinction by nuclear holocaust, or, failing that,
by chemical contamination, by escalated ordinary
violence, by man-made hunger and disease that proli-
ferate in a climate of deception and mind-rot./7/

The entrance to the field of younger scholars, trained
in doctoral programs gradually influenced by feminist
methodologies, should foster integrative approaches. And
as the discipline matures and less attention needs to be
given to defining the area and its fundamental questions,
that energy can be directed toward commentary on current
issues.

NOTES
1. Collins relies on sociologist of religion Peter
L. Berger's work for the distinction between "reformist"
and "revolutionary" postures. See Berger, The Sacred
Canopy (Garden City, N. Y.: Doubleday, 1967). The
distinction has been widely used in analyses of feminist
theology. See, for example, Carol P. Christ, "The New
Feminist Theology: A Review of the Literature," in
Religious Studies Review 3:4 (October 1977), 203-212.
2. It should be noted here that this study is limited
to theologians per se and does not include scholars in
the fields of church history, biblical studies, history
of religions, sociology, or psychology, for example. This
was done because it is in the field of theology that the
questions relevant to this issue should be addressed. It
does not, therefore, represent a premature limitation of
the sample. Another factor that contributed to the small
sample size is that feminist thought is a relatively recent
development within theology. Therefore, there are not many
scholars who have attained the stature delineated in the
sample.
3. See, for example, the following books in which
women's rituals and their uses are discussed: The Spiral
Dance: A Rebirth of the Ancient Religion of the Great
Goddess (New York: Harper and Row, 1979) and Dreaming
the Dark: Magic, Sex, and Politics (Boston: Beacon Press,
1982), both by Starhawk (Miriam Simos), as well as Hallie
Inglehart's Womanspirit: A Guide to Women's Wisdom (New
York: Harper and Row, 1983)
4. See Sheila Collins, A Different Heaven and Earth
(Valley Forge, Pa.: Judson Press, 1974).

5. For documentation on the "media presence" of the New Christian Right and their use of direct mail to get their message out, see the following: Flo Conway and James Siegelman, Holy Terror: The Fundamentalist War On America's Freedoms in Religion, Politics and Our Private Lives (Garden City, N. Y.: Doubleday, 1982); Jeffrey K. Hadden and Charles E. Swann, Prime Time Preachers: The Rising Power of Televangelism (Reading, Mass.: Addison-Wesley, 1981) Samuel S. Hill and Dennis Owen, The New Religious Political Right in America (Nashville: Abingdon Press, 1982); Peter G. Horsfield, Religious Television: The American Experience (New York: Longman, 1984); John L. Kater, Jr., Christians on the Right: The Moral Majority in Perspective (New York: The Seabury Press, 1982); and Robert C. Liebman and Robert Wuthnow, The New Christian Right: Mobilization and Legitimation (New York: Aldine, 1983).

6. See Charlene Spretnak and Fritjof Capra, "Green Politics: The Global Promise," Sojourners 13 (September 1984), pp. 36-38, and Grace Jantzen, God's World, God's Body (Westminster Press, 1985).

7. See Mary Daly, Pure Lust: Elemental Feminist Philosophy (Boston: Beacon Press, 1984).

REFERENCES

Alder, Margot. Drawing Down the Moon. New York: Viking Press, 1979.

Collins, Sheila. A Different Heaven and Earth. Valley Forge, Pa.: Judson Press, 1974.

Conway, Flo, and James Siegelman. Holy Terror: The Fundamentalist War on America's Freedoms in Religion, and Politics and Our Private Lives. Garden City, N. Y.: Doubleday, 1982.

Davis, Judy, and Juanita Weaver. "Dimensions of Spirituality." Quest 1:2-6, 1975.

Hadden, Jeffrey K., and Charles E. Swann. Prime Time Preachers: The Rising Power of Televangelism. Reading, Mass.: Addison-Wesley, 1981.

Hill, Samuel S., and Dennis E. Owen. The New Religious Political Right in America. Nashville: Abingdon Press, 1982.

Himmelstein, Jerome L. "The New Right." Pp. 13-30 in Robert C. Liebman and Robert Wuthnow (eds.). The New Christian Right: Mobilization and Legitimation. New York: Aldine, 1983.

336

Horsfield, Peter G. Religious Television: The American
    Experience. New York: Longman, 1984.
Inglehart, Hallie. "Unnatural Divorce of Spirituality and
    Politics." Quest 4:12-24, 1978.
Kater, John L., Jr. Christians on the Right: The Moral
    Majority in Perspective. New York: Seabury Press,
    1982.
Liebman, Robert C., and Robert Wuthnow. The New Christian
    Right: Mobilization and Legitimation. New York:
    Aldine, 1983.
National Council of Churches of Christ. "Resolution on
    the Equal Rights Amendment." New York: National
    Council of Churches of Christ, 1983.
Riddle, Dorothy I. "New Visions of Spiritual Power."
    Quest, 1:7-16, 1975.
_____. "Politics, Spirituality, and Models of
    Change." Pp. 373-381 in Charlene Spretnak (ed.) The
    Politics of Women's Spirituality. Garden City,
    N.Y.: Anchor Press/Doubleday, 1982.
Spretnak, Charlene. The Politics of Women's
    Spirituality. Garden City, N. Y.: Anchor
    Press/Doubleday, 1982.

Conclusions: The Future Political Role of Religion in the United States

In our general introductory statement we said that modern conditions make it difficult for churches and for religious values to influence peoples' lives. Nothing in the contributions in this book requires changing this conclusion. Several chapters documented the importance of secular or nonreligious ideologies. In the chapter on the policy positions of the Middletown clergy, it was shown that a humanist perspective and a laissez-faire philosophy are more important determinants of social attitudes than religious rationale even among ministers. Most of the chapters on the Christian Right referred to the importance of cultural fundamentalism as a motivating force. Abortion attitudes seem to reflect several perspectives including the self-realization ethos. The United States is a cultural battleground, a field of competing ideologies, and the religious worldview is only one of the players.

THE CHRISTIAN RIGHT

The studies presented in this book indicate that the Christian Right has had great difficulty in reversing the secular trends in our society.

Two of the chapters in the section on the Christian Right provided the best support for the proposal that conservative fundamentalists could have influence in the future. From Merle Strege's chapter we found that a strong belief in the jeremiad should lead many conservative fundamentalists to continue to fight against "sinful" liberal issues. This is so since, according to their interpretation of the jeremiad, the United States must

repent to avert the disaster that the wrath of God most
assuredly will bring if the country continues with its
secular, liberal ways. From Michael Johnston's chapter
we learned that the Christian Right has gone from an
uncompromising religious movement trying to Christianize
all America and save the nation from secular humanists
to a less rigid "political interest-group" movement working
within the political order to achieve more specific goals.
This could mean that the Christian Right might be more
politically effective in future years.

If the past record of the Christian Right can be used
to predict the future, however, this movement will have
little impact on political events. The remaining four
chapters presented in the Christian Right section indicated
that this movement is having a fading and/or even negative
impact on U.S. politics. Stephen Johnson reported that,
although the traditional themes of the Moral Majority have
appealed to some people, the Christian Right had no
influence on Reagan's election in 1980 and its major
political arm, the Moral Majority, had a negative influence
in 1984, i.e., the presence of the Moral Majority in the
1984 campaign brought more votes over to Mondale than to
Reagan. This is further supported by John Cranor's
conclusion that Reagan's association with Christian Right
leaders and issues during the 1984 campaign drew many Jews
away from their recent support of the Republican party
and back to their traditional support of the Democratic
party. Joseph Tamney went on to point out that even if
the Christian Right's antiabortion position gains greater
favor on the part of the U.S. public, people who are
against abortion base their position on a number of
different ideologies. This would mean that it would be
difficult for the Christian Right to unite with other
antiabortion factions in advocating a common antiabortion
policy. Finally, Donald Tomaskovic-Devey contended that
conservative economic elites used the Christian Right
by associating their conservative economic cause with the
more appealing, profamily causes of the Christian Right.
But now that Reagan and his free enterprise economic
policies have become more accepted by the general public,
the Christian Right may no longer be needed.

One might conclude by agreeing with Harvey Cox (1984)
that conservative fundamentalists oscillate between
withdrawal and political combat. Due to the events just
described, the Christian Right seems to have not had too
much impact on politics and will probably be "withdrawing"
shortly. But conservative religious fundamentalists may

have learned enough during this round of political combat
to be a more effective political force when they reemerge
in the future.

LIBERAL CHRISTIANITY

    Although statements such as The Princeton
Declaration receive little or no attention from the mass
media, these manifestos bear witness to the emergence of
a worldwide liberal religious movement. The General
Introduction pointed out that U.S. Catholic activism is
probably related to Catholicism's position in the world.
The same can be said of liberal Christians in general.
Much of the liberal religious agenda is a program for
citizens of the world. The global orientation of
Catholicism is explicit. As the bishop who chairs the
committee responsible for a forthcoming economic pastoral
letter said, "We have to think in international, global
terms. The Church is already a multinational moral force
and so it is already in place to examine and speak about
the moral implications of economic issues" (quoted in:
Kennedy, 1984:30).
    Central liberal issues are the world economy,
disarmament and peace, as well as democracy and human
rights. In the United States the first two issues are
paramount, and it is the Catholic church that is the
leading religious actor, with other liberal religious
groups in support. The pastoral letter on disarmament
was a milestone, and as Van Voorst noted, was supported
by liberal churches. The bishops have released a draft
pastoral letter on economic issues, the final version of
which will be determined in 1986. One of the major liberal
themes of this letter is a call for greater governmental
assistance to the poor. "American bishops have spoken
out on economic issues before this statement, but never
in a pastoral letter that analyzed the roots of the
economic system and called for action" (Sciolino,
1984b:16). This document will probably be the source of
more discussion and controversy than the pastoral letter
on the nuclear issues. Even before the publication of
the final version of the bishops' letter on the economy
it has become a rallying point for liberal Christians.
Thirty-six Protestant and Jewish leaders in a statement
to members of Congress cited the draft pastoral letter
and called for an end to poverty in the United States,
urging a specific program of economic changes (UPI, 1985).

The chapter by Stephen Johnson also pointed out that the black church continues to be an organizational base and a source of spiritual guidance for black civil rights activities. Although the sect-like black churches tend to discourage civil rights activities, it seems as though the more mainline black churches will always be a willing base of support for programs and politicians who fight for black rights.

But the chapter by James Davidson reminded us that liberal challenges to the system failed to achieve much real social change. Julia Mitchell also pointed out that liberal Christianity has not contributed much to the advancement of women's rights since few liberal Christian writers have spoken out on this issue.

Further, the lack of internal unity, especially in the Catholic church, limits how successful liberal Christianity can become. The pastoral letters have evoked challenging criticisms from within the ranks of Catholicism. L. Bruce Van Voorst discussed Catholic critics of the peace pastoral, and the letter on the economy has its own critics. Anticipating the draft letter on economics, twenty-seven conservative Catholic business and professional leaders formed the Lay Commission on Catholic Social Teaching and the U.S. Economy. Included in the memberships were William E. Simon, former secretary of the treasury and Alexander M. Haig, Jr., former secretary of state (Briggs, 1984a). The commission has published its own statement that "is a strong celebration of the capitalist system and the individual entrepreneur, not the government, as the true benefactors of the poor and jobless" (Silk, 1984:21).

The Catholic Church is deeply divided. "American bishops, more vocal, perhaps, than ever this year in promoting the teachings of the church, are finding it ever more difficult to command obedience from either the clergy or the laity" (Sciolino, 1984a:40). Over the past twenty years or so Catholics have remained critical of the church's official stand on birth control, sexual behavior, and abortion. U.S. Catholics are now well educated and independent, and many no longer simply accept all church pronouncements. A planned future pastoral letter on women's role will no doubt add to the tensions within Catholicism. Catholic deviants are numerous. "And their independence of conscience is accepted--or at least tolerated--by growing numbers of parish priests and nuns who feel their primary pastoral mission is to meet the everyday needs of the faithful" (Sciolino, 1984a:40).

The Catholic church is a divided institution, and although its leaders speak forcefully on public issues, local priests, because of their desire to maintain the community, will tolerate much divergence of opinion from official stances.

The self-image of the liberal churches as community builders affects their political actions. Whereas the Christian Right tends to see itself as a vanguard, liberal churches have sought to be mediators. This can be seen in the actions of Catholic leaders. Poland and Latin America are important areas where Catholicism is being challenged and is trying to find its place in the modern world. In both instances, bishops are trying to play a mediating role. For instance, in El Salvador the church offers neutral ground where the government and rebels have met for discussion. In Poland, the church protects Solidarity leaders and bargains with the government (New Statesman, 1984). In a similar vein, it was announced that the next version of the pastoral letter on the economy would be more sympathetic to the middle class (Buursma, 1985). Liberal churches, or perhaps it would be more accurate to say nonfundamentalist churches, have continually recognized and emphasized their role as community builders, as sources of cohesion and agents of reconciliation and peace. Such a self-image dampens the ardor with which change is pursued and generates further internal division by alienating those committed to significant change. The alienated include those in the popular church in Latin America--priests, nuns, and lay people who are dissatisfied with the degree of change sought by church leaders.

What then is the future political role of liberal religion in the United States? Given the internal divisions and the relatively small numbers as in the case of black churches, the liberal churches are unlikely to sway vast numbers of people. Yet they have the will and the resources to make many people rethink their attitudes on critical issues and perhaps even to change the nature of public discourse on national policy. Religious values have become, and will increasingly become, politically relevant.

THE PRIVATIZATION THESIS

It has been suggested by a number of scholars that in a modern society religious values would have an impact

only in the private realm. Although this may have been
true in the recent past, privatization seems outdated as
a description of contemporary religion. Modern people
are in search of the good life. This is defined in as
many ways as there are ideologies available. Basic,
however, is the tendency to interpret the social condition
in relation to wants, not just needs; ideals, not just
necessities. It is no surprise that in such an atmosphere
there would be more pressure for religious ideals to become
more relevant to behavior. The Christian Right and liberal
Christianity are benefiting from this reflection about
a more ideal life.

If, in the future, religious beliefs and values do
not influence politics, it will not be because churches
have not expended considerable resources seeking political
clout. These efforts are bound to produce some success.
But success will probably take the form not of laws exactly
as desired by religious leaders, but will be reflected
in a greater awareness of the nation's moral traditions
and of a stronger role for those values championed by the
churches in the inevitable compromises made by political
leaders.

REFERENCES

Briggs, Kenneth A. "Catholic Group Extols Capitalism as
    Bishops Ready Economic Study." New York Times (7
    November):1, 21, 1984a.
Buursma, Bruce. "Bishops Discussing Pastoral Letter."
    Indianapolis Star (17 June):24, 1985.
Cox, Harvey. Religion in the Secular City. New York:
    Simon and Schuster, 1984.
Kennedy, Eugene. "America's Activist Bishops." New York
    Times Magazine (12 August):14-18, 24-30, 1984.
New Statesman. "Church Gaining the Initiative." 108
    (9 November):23-24, 1984.
Sciolino, Elaine. "A Time for Challenge." New York
    Times Magazine (4 November): 40, 70, 74-75, 84-85,
    93, and 100-101, 1984a.
_____. "Applying a Tradition." New York Times
    (13 November):16, 1984b.
Silk, Leonard. "In Celebration of Creative Capitalism
    in Society." New York Times (7 November):21, 1984.
UPI. "Religious Leader's Statement Asks Action Against
    Poverty." New York Times (17 February):14, 1985.

Index

Christian Churches and
Churches of Christ,
25(table)
Christian civilization,
108, 110
Christian Democrats, 270
Christian Federation of
Salvadoran Peasants, 267
Christianity, 24, 72, 239–
240. See also Born-again
Christians; Evangelical
Christianity; Fundamen-
talism; individual
denominations
Christianity Today (publi-
cation), 87, 93(n8)
Christian Life Commission
(Baptist General Con-
vention of Texas), 91
Christian Life Commission
(Southern Baptist
Convention), 91
"Call for Racial
Reconciliation" re-
port, 78
Christian Ministries of
Delaware County, 48
Christian Right, 5, 67,
184(table), 190
abortion, 165–166
defined, 4, 6, 182–183
Moral Majority, 185, 186,
191
1984 election, 192–194
political power, 337–
339
See also New Christian
Right
Christian Voice, 23, 90,
129
Churches of Christ,
25(table)
Church of Christ, 177(n5)
Church of God in Christ,
321, 322
Church of Jesus Christ of
Latter Day Saints

(Mormon), 25(table),
176(n5)
Church of the Brethren, 68(n2),
292
Church of the Poor, 264
Citizens for Religious Freedom, 84–85
Civil disobedience, 68(n1)
Civil rights, 80, 83, 86
black activism, 312, 314–
316, 320–322
black churches, 308–312,
316–318
and religion, 99, 307–308
Civil Rights Act of 1968, 85
Civil War, 109
Clark, William, 298–299
Clean Up America campaign,
112–113
Clergy
in Latin America, 264, 265,
266, 274
liberal versus conservative,
48, 53, 55, 56(table)
Middletown study, 49–50,
51(table), 53, 55–59,
68(n4)
personal morality, 47, 48,
66–67
political activism, 69(n9),
84–85, 321
political views, 48,
60(table), 61–65
sermons, 55–59
social issues, 46–47, 48,
51(table), 252, 254–255,
256
theology, 59–60(table), 61–
62, 104–105, 108
Coalition politics, 199
Coe, Douglas, 88
Coleman, Milton, 204
Collins, Sheila D., 328, 329,
332
Colson, Charles, 88
Committee for Survival of a
Free Congress, 26

Common decency. See Porno-
graphy
Commonweal (journal), 168
Communism, 65, 76-77, 121,
267
anti-, 7, 8, 80, 82, 267,
270, 271-272
Conable, Barber, 212
Conference of Bishops. See
National Conference of
Catholic Bishops
CONIP. See Bishop Oscar
Arnulfo Romero National
Conference of the
People's Church
Conlan, John B., 89
Connally, John, 129
Conservatism, 47, 67,
68(nn2,4), 73, 129, 151,
154, 210(table), 250
and evangelical Chris-
tianity, 71, 73
Moral Majority, 185, 192
political activism, 74,
75, 80, 82-83, 86, 112
political views, 52,
54(table), 56(table),
57, 58(tables), 59,
64, 69(n9), 74, 89, 90
public issues, 48, 56
and religion, 7, 50, 52,
191
versus liberalism, 47,
48, 52(table), 55, 65-
66, 90
Conservative Caucus, 149
Coughlin (father), 127
Covenant, 105-106, 107, 108,
109, 110, 114, 115-122,
279. See also Evangel-
ical Christianity; Fun-
damentalism; Jeremiad
Crane, Philip, 129
Cuba, 264
Cultural fundamentalism,
166, 167, 170, 187,
189, 195-196. See also

Fundamentalism
Curtis, Carl T., 85

Dallas Inter-Religious Task
Force on Central America,
276
Daly, Mary, 328, 329, 332
Danbury Baptists, 18
D'Antonio, Nicholas, 274
Darwinism, 110
d'Aubuisson, Roberto, 269
Davis, Angela, 253
Day, Dorothy, 247
Death penalty, 133
Defense spending, 90, 121, 191.
See also Israel; Nuclear
issues; War
Dellenback, John, 85
Democratic Nationalist Organi-
zation (ORDEN; El Salva-
dor), 269
Democratic party, 199, 202
Jews and, 200-203
1984 election, 203, 205-206,
207, 208, 209, 212-213,
216-217
See also Democrats; Liberalism
Democratic Revolutionary Front
(FDR; El Salvador), 265,
270, 277
Democrats, 209, 210(table), 213,
214. See also Democratic
party
Department of Defense, 281
Desegregation issues, 83
Deuteronomic doctrine, 105,
106, 108
Dignity of human life. See
Abortion; Euthanasia
DioGuardi, Joseph, 212, 215-216
Disciples of Christ church,
25(table), 68(n2)
Dispensational premillenialism,
See Millenialism
Docherty, George M., 82
Dogma, 6, 188. See also
Religious ideology

1960 election, 84–85
political activitism, 24–
  25, 71, 73–74, 75, 76–
  81, 86, 91, 112, 122,
  181, 182
political power, 24, 85,
  88, 89, 91
political views, 87, 89,
  92
varieties, 72–73, 132–
  133
See also Born-again
  Christians; Fundamen-
  talism; Moral Majority,
  New Christian Right
Evangelicals for Social
  Action, 177(n8)
Evangelism. See Evangelical
  Christianity
Evangelists for McGovern.,
  87
Everson v. Board of Education of Ewing Township, 20
Evolution, 74, 90, 120
Excessive entanglement, 29
  administrative involve-
    ment, 29–32, 39
  cases, 30, 31–32
  political divisiveness,
    32–38
  See also First Amendment

Facism, 81
Falange, 269
Falwell, Jerry, 1, 5, 115,
  119, 121, 134, 166
  on abortion, 170, 176(n4)
  criticism of, 133, 139
  electronic media, 111,
    128, 129
  on the family, 116–117
  jeremiad, 106, 110–111,
    114, 122
  millenialism, 114–115
  Moral Majority, 100, 103–
    104, 113–114, 130
  1984 election, 103, 209

political activism, 112–113,
  122–123, 135, 181
political rights, 138, 139
pornography, 117–118
Puritan beliefs, 107–108,
  109, 122
school prayer, 119–120
work ethic, 118–119
See also Moral Majority
Family, 160
  Moral Majority, 113–114,
    116–117, 166
  and New Christian Right, 5,
    6, 150–151, 152
Family planning, 166
Farabundo Martí National
  Liberation Front (FMLN;
  El Salvador), 265, 270,
  277
Farrakhan, Louis, 204–205, 206
Far Right, The, 86
Faubus, Orval, 77
FCC. See Federal Communica-
  tions Commission
FDR. See Democratic Revolu-
  tionary Front
Federal Communications Commis-
  sion (FCC), 129
Federal Council of Churches,
  290–291. See also National
  Council of Churches
Federalist Papers, The, 26–27,
  28, 35, 36–37
"Fellowship, the." See Inter-
  national Christian Leader-
  ship
"Fellowship House," 79
Feminism, 152, 165, 173
  religion and politics, 325,
    326–327
  scholarship, 328–330, 332,
    333–334
  See also Feminist theologians
Feminist theologians, 328, 329,
  330–332, 333, 334(n2). See
  also Feminism
Ferraro, Geraldine, 212

First Amendment, 17, 18, 108
  excessive entanglement,
    30, 33, 35
  religious establishment
    clause, 18, 21, 29-30,
    36, 40(n8)
  violations, 16, 31
FMLN. See Farabundo Martí
  National Liberation
  Front
Ford, Gerald, 89-90, 128
Foreign policy
  in Latin America, 263,
    266-267, 269, 272, 273,
    275, 278
  See also El Salvador; Is-
    rael; Nicaragua; Pale-
    stine Liberation Organ-
    ization; Roman Catholic
    Church
Fourteenth Amendment, 29,
  40(n8)
Fox, Frederick E., 81
FPL. See Popular Liberation
  Forces
Frazier, E. Franklin, 309-
  310, 312
Free African Society, 307
Freedom of choice. See Pro-
  choice movement
Freedoms Foundation, 76
Free market economy, 118-119
Freund, Paul A., 35
Friends. See Religious
  Society of Friends
Friends Committee on Na-
  tional Legislation, 91
Fundamentalism, 4-7, 76,
  293
  political activism, 74, 337
  social issues, 162, 166,
    246
  See also Born-again Chris-
    tians; Evangelical
    Christianity; Moral
    Majority; New Christian
    Right

Fundamentalist insurgency, 134,
  135, 136, 139, 142
Fundamentalists, 46, 69(n9),
  100, 109-110, 177(n7). See
  also Cultural fundamen-
  talism; Evangelical Christianity; Fundamentalism;
  Moral Majority; individual
  denominations

Gallup poll, 72, 131,
  132(table), 133, 201
Garvey, John, 171-172
General Assembly of United
  Presbyterian Church, 293
General Social Surveys (GSS),
  160, 162-163
George Washington Medal, 76
Gibson, Kenneth, 320
Goddess-centered religions, 328
Goldenberg, Naomi, 328, 329,
  332
Goldwater, Barry, 86
Goode, W. Wilson, 320
Goodman, Robert O., Jr., 205,
  206
Goodwill Industries, 79
Government, 82-83, 121, 133,
  150, 242, 250-251
Graham, Billy, 82-85, 86-87
Grant, Robert, 23
Great Society, 250
GSS. See General Social Surveys
Guatemala, 266, 272, 273, 274
Gumbelton (bishop), 284

Haig, Alexander, 26, 276, 340
Halachah, 297
Ham, Mordecai Fowler, 75
Handicapped infants regulations.
  See Baby Doe regulations
Handy, Robert T., 73
Hannan, Phillip, 285
Hargis, Billy James, 5
Harrison, Beverly Wildung, 173
Harris v. McRae, 16, 30, 39-
  40(n1)

Hart, Gary, 206, 207
Hatfield, Mark O., 85, 86,
    87–88, 89, 93(n9)
Hays, Brook, 77–78
Helms, Jesse, 89
Hertzberg, Arthur, 207
Hickey, James, 276
Higginson, Frances, 104
Holiness groups, 312
Homosexuality, 5, 90, 117,
    133, 161
  Middletown study, 49, 50,
    51(table), 53, 54(table),
    55, 56(table), 57,
    58(tables), 59, 60, 61,
    63(table), 64, 65,
    69(nn7,8)
Honduras, 264, 266, 274
House of Bishops of the
    Episcopal Church in the
    United States, 293
Hughes, Harold E., 85, 88
Humanism, 2, 48, 89, 120,
    136. See also Secular
    humanism
Human rights, 232–233, 273,
    276, 277
Hunt and Hunt study, 317–
    318
Hunthausen, Raymond, 284
Hyde, Henry, 30
Hyde Amendment, 16, 30

ICL. See International
    Christian Leadership
Iglesia popular, 265–266,
    267, 275. See also
    Christian Base
    Communities
Immigration, 80
Industrial plant closing
    laws
  Middletown study, 49, 50,
    51(table), 53,
    54(table), 55, 57,
    58(tables), 60(table),
    61(tables), 63(table),
    64

Institute for Christian
    Economics, 67
Interdenominational beliefs, 73
International Christian Leader-
    ship (ICL), 78, 79
Inter-Varsity Christian Fellow-
    ship, 73
Israel
  1984 election and, 205–206,
    208
  support for, 118, 208

Jackson, Jesse, 200, 202, 203
  1984 election, 204–205, 206,
    207–208, 320–321
Jackson, Maynard, 320
Jefferson, Thomas, 17, 18, 19,
    35
Jehovah Witnesses, 312
Jeremiad, 105, 106, 110, 337–
    338
  in colonial America, 105,
    106, 107
  Falwell, 110–111, 114, 122
  19th-century America, 108–109
Jewish Defense League, 204
Jews, 121, 129
  Democratic party and, 200–
    203, 209
  1984 election, 204, 205–206,
    207, 209, 216
  nuclear issues, 294–297, 303
  religious membership, 24,
    25(table)
  views on abortion, 162, 170,
    176(n2)
  voting patterns, 27(table),
    208, 209, 210(table), 211,
    214, 215(table)
  See also Black-Jewish con-
    frontation
Jews Against Jackson, 204. See
    also Black-Jewish confron-
    tation
John Birch Society, 150
John Paul II, 15
  nuclear deterrence, 284, 288,
    299–300

Manton, Thomas, 212
Marsh v. Chambers, 30
Martin, John A., 74
Marxism, 270
Marx study, 312-316, 318
Maryknoll order, 274
Massachusetts Bay Colony, 104
Matthiesen, Leroy, 284
Mayflower Compact, 106
Media ministers, 5, 90, 91,
    100, 111, 127, 128-129,
    134, 195. See also
    individual ministers
Membership, 24, 25(table),
    40(nn9,13), 162, 252
  black activism, 312-313
  social involvement, 251,
    252-253, 255-257
  voluntary association,
    248-250
"Memorial and Remonstrance"
    (treatise), 22-23
Mennonite Central Committee
    Peace Section, 91
Methodist church, 74, 75,
    313(table), 315(table)
Michigan Interchurch
    Committee on Central
    America, 276
Middletown study, 45-46
  justification for
    beliefs, 59-65
  methodology, 48-49,
    57, 62, 68(nn2,4,5),
    182-183, 184-185,
    188
  political orientation,
    183, 184
  results, 50-55, 68(n5),
    69(nn7,8,9)
  sermons, 55-59
  support for Moral
    Majority, 184-192
"Michelmet Mitzvah," 296
"Michelmet Reshut," 296
Millenialism, 107-108, 110,
    114-115, 119, 133

Ministers. See Clergy
Missionary activity, 76, 89,
    264, 274, 276
Mizell, Wilmer D. "Vinegar
    Bend," 77
Modernism, 110, 246
Mondale, Walter, 64, 103
  1984 election, 193, 194, 203,
    205, 206, 207, 208, 209,
    210(table)
Moral issues. See Social con-
    cerns
Moral Majority, 1, 5, 91, 114,
    139, 140, 203, 208
  abortion, 166, 176(n3)
  formation, 90, 100, 113
  importance, 129, 130, 197
  Middletown study, 181, 184-
    192
  New Christian Right, 149, 184
  1984 election, 100, 104, 192-
    194
  political activism, 122-123,
    138, 190-191, 196-197, 338
  principles, 115-122
  religious television, 186,
    190, 191-192, 195
  support for, 185, 187-189, 196
  See also Falwell, Jerry
Moral Majority, Inc. See Moral
    Majority
"Moral Majority Report" (news-
    letter), 122
Morial, Ernest, 320
Mormon church. See Church of
    Jesus Christ of Latter-Day
    Saints
Mueller v. Allen, 37-38
Muncie. See Middletown study
Myrdal, Gunnar, 310-311, 312

NAACP. See National Association
    for the Advancement of
    Colored People
NAE. See National Association
    of Evangelicals
Nairobi Declaration, 244